"Every Brok

Should Own This Book"

300 Ways to Buy, Sell or Exchange Real Estate

by Robert W. Steele

OUTSIDE THE BOX & INSIDE/OUTSIDE THE COUNTRY

STEELE 300

300

Ways to Buy, Sell or Exchange Real Estate

Volumes 1-12

"Every Broker & Investor Should Own This Book"

by Robert W. Steele

Robert@steele300.com
(760) 522-5362

ISBN: 978-09908622-9-1
IMPRINT: PIXELS GRAPHIC DESIGN

300 Series Books

by Robert W. Steele

		Page
Volume 1 Strategies 1—25	***25 Basic Creative Real Estate Strategies*** *(Initially developed by Richard R. Reno)* by Robert W. Steele, Foreword by Michael E. Stewart	17
Volume 2 Strategies 26—50	***25 Formulas & Strategies: Creative Real Estate Level 2*** by Robert W. Steele, Foreword by Chester W. Allen	51
Volume 3 Strategies 51-75	***25 Formulas & Strategies: Creative Real Estate Level 3*** by Robert W. Steele, Foreword by Arlene Wright-Correll	83
Volume4 Strategies 76—100	***25 Formulas & Strategies: Creative Real Estate Level 4*** by Robert W. Steele, Foreword by Ronald J. Robinson SEC	115
Volume 5 Strategies 101—125	25 ***Ways to Buy, Sell or Trade a House*** by Robert W. Steele, Foreword by Don DeBeau	147
Volume 6 Strategies 126—150	***Multiple Exchange Philosophies, Formulas and Strategies*** by Robert W. Steele, Foreword by Madge Davis	179
Volume 7 Strategies 151—175	***The Art and Science of Brainstorming: Obtaining Ideas not Available Through Conventional Thinking*** **by Robert W. Steele, Foreword by Nancy Steele**	211
Volume8 Strategies 176—200	***Real Estate and Business Counseling*** by Robert W. Steele, Foreword by Steven L. Cropper	243
Volume9 Strategies 201—225	***Blending Your Real Estate, Business & Life into the International World*** by Robert W. Steele, Foreword by Alexander J. Krem, BA, MBA, JD (University of California, Berkeley	275
Volume 10 Strategies 226—250	***Hal/the World is Vacancy*** by Chester W. Allen & Robert W. Steele, Foreword by Robert E. Baines	307
Volume 11 Strategies 251—275	***Combining Real Estate and Stock Strategies*** by Robert W. Steele, Foreword by Clifford L. Strand, SEC, EMS	347
Volume 12 Strategies 276—300	***Barter, Exchange and Trade Credits*** by Robert W. Steele, Foreword by Ron Moser	379

VOLUME 1
CONTENTS

Introduction
Foreword: Michael E. Stewart

Strategy .... Title
#1 .... Unpriced
#2 .... Creation of Wealth #1
#3 .... Creation of Wealth #2
#4 .... Creation of Wealth #3
#5 .... Exchange and Buy Back
#6 .... Missouri Waltz: One, Two, Cash Out
#7 .... REO Exchange (Real Estate Owned)
#8 .... The Don't-Wanter is a Key to Many Transactions
#9 .... Multiple Exchanges
#10 .... The Un-Built Building
#11 .... Share the Wealth
#12 .... How to Play a Falling Market
#13 .... Brainstorming and Individual Ideation
#14 .... People in Hell Want Ice Water
#15 .... The In-Lieu-of Formula
#16 .... Charlie the Thief
#17 .... Share the Loss Formula
#18 .... The Weasel Clause (Escape Clause)
#19 .... Front Porch
#20 .... Head 'Em West 'til Their Hat Floats
#21 .... Broker Cooperation
#22 .... Verbal Exchange Offers Don't Work
#23 .... Counseling and Control
#24 .... Being Flexible Benefits an Exchangor
#25 .... Un-Priced Exchange Meeting

VOLUME 2
CONTENTS

Introduction

Foreword: Chester W. Allen

Strategy	Title
#26	Assess Yourself vs. the Deal
#27	Are All the Legs in the Room?
#28	Blanket Mortgage
#29	Consulting Time
#30	Front Side, Back Side
#31	Front Gate, #1, 2 and 3
#32	Tail Gate
#33	Pencil Paralysis
#34	Zeckendorf Technique #1
#35	Zeckendorf Technique #2
#36	Zeckendorf - Dornbush (SEC) #3
#37	Is the Date Right?
#38	The Truth is Only Momentary
#39	We Create from the Inside Out
#40	Who or What is the Most Important in an Exchange?
#41	How to Operate at an Exchange Meeting
#42	How to Write an Exchange Offer
#43	Negotiating an Exchange Offer
#44	Benefits that Grow
#45	Know-How Item: Kick 'Em in the Kidneys
#46	Know-How Item: The Extra Value of a User
#47	Know-How Item: I'll Make You Quit in a Negotiation
#48	Know-How Item: A Zero Means Nothing
#49	Know-How Item: Monday Morning Escrow Check
#50	Trading Sardines & Currency Land

VOLUME 3
CONTENTS

Introduction
Foreword: Arlene Wright-Correll

Strategy	Title
#51	Trade Percentage of Ownership
#52	Funding with Sale of Notes plus Courage
#53	Idea Tracking
#54	Taker Tracker Form
#55	Baseball Formula
#56	Keep the Income in a Trade
#57	"I'll Pay More Than You Ask, If..."
#58	Move from Defense to Offense
#59	Gold and Silver Retirement Plan
#60	Stutter Mortgage
#61	A-Bag, B-Bag
#62	Definance
#63	Personal Notes to Balance Equity
#64	Creating a Leasehold
#65	Creating a Leasehold in an Exchange or Sale
#66	Present the Correct Package for the Market You are In
#67	Over-Trade
#68	Specialty Clients (Like Users) & Partners
#69	The Buyer is a Potential Lender
#70	The Tenant Solution
#71	Two Plus Three Equals Two
#72	Creativity—We are Going to Need It
#73	Liquidate and Diversity
#74	The Easiest 3-Way Exchange There Is
#75	Prediction Heard: "Only 27% of the Real Estate Fraternity Will Weather the Storm"

VOLUME 4
CONTENTS

Introduction

Foreword: Ronald J. Robinson SEC

Strategy	Title
#76	Crop Futures Strategy
#77	A Bunt May Be Exactly the Right Strategy
#78	The Performance Mortgage: A Wonderful Tool
#79	Performance Trust Deed & Note
#80	Performance Trust Deed & Note #2
#81	SAMPLE Performance TD Package
#82	Great Formula For Growing a Corporation
#83	Inflation
#84	Superstar Strategy
#85	The Un-Built Company Formula
#86	Broker-Brokers & Finders
#87	Bag of Silver Strategy and New Variation
#88	Gold and Silver Mortgage Insurance
#89	Note Payable In Silver (or Gold)
#90	Learn to Spend Real Money
#91	Linear vs Spatial Idea Tracking
#92	Performance Land Lease
#93	Attorney's Strategy - Sit in The Office
#94	Burn the Bridges Formula – There is No Way Back
#95	Turn Vacancies into Wellness Units
#96	Counter Trade
#97	Multiple Notes in Quantity
#98	Derivative #1
#99	Derivative #2
#100-A	Liquefying Mining Assets
#100-B	U.S. Dollar: A Derivative + Hyperinflation Tactic

VOLUME 5
Contents

Strategy	Title
	Introduction
	Foreword: Donald E. DuBeau, SEC
Strategy	**Title**
#101	Buying or Selling a House for Cash
#102	Owner Carry-Back Financing
#103	List Below Market in a Buyer's Market
#104	"Talk Story" about Buying Houses
#105	Don't Drop Your Price If ...
#106	Over-Trade: a Viable Technique for Moving Equity in a House
#107	Strategic Withdrawal (Default) on SFR Loans not Uncommon
#108	Short Sale in SFRs
#109	Use Performance Mortgages When You Can in Buying SFRs
#110	Don't Buy Houses In Your Own Name
#111	Use Gold & Silver to Offset (and Eventually Pay Off) Your Loan on an SFR
#112	If You Have a F/C House (or a long equity) Refinance It Now and Buy Gold, Silver or Other Inflation-Resistant Assets
#113	Buy 1, 2, 3 or More SFRs & Form an Assisted Living Business
#114	Sell, Trade or Donate a Percentage of Interest in Some SFRs
#115	Diversify SFRs to Maximize Returns
#116	Educate Yourself about Owning SFRs
#117	Retirement Ploy Using SFR
#118	You Have 1,000 Things (OPS) to Use as a Down Payment into SFRs
#119	Stretch Geographically to Acquire SFRs if Necessary
#120	SFR Wellness Rentals
#121	Become a Teacher & Speaker on SFR Acquisitions
#122	Motivation Is a Motivator in SFRs
#123	Sell Out the Reverse Cash Flow in Rental SFRs
#124	Hitting Singles With SFRs
#125	Foreign SFRs
#125-A BONUS.......	When to Buy Real Estate Again

VOLUME 6
CONTENTS

Introduction

Foreword: Madge Davis, SEC

Strategy	**Title**
#126	Using Multiple Exchange to Facilitate Breaking Up a Partnership
#127	When to Formalize the Multiple Exchange Avenue
#128	The Logic of Multiple Exchanges
#129	Idea Tracking
#130	Client Selecting First Leg of Multiple Exchange
#131	Multiple Exchanges Spawned By Smaller Groups
#132	Taker Tracker Form
#133	The Easiest 3-Way Exchange There Is
#134	The In-Lieu-Of Formula
#135	Double In-Lieu-Of
#136	Trading Into a Performance Mortgage
#137	Multiple Exchanging on One Property
#138	Multiple Exchange Going Up: Using Zeckhendorf – Dornbush Concepts
#139	Multiple Exchange with Broker Buy Out
#140	Missouri Waltz #1
#141	Missouri Waltz # 2
#142	Definancing via a Multiple Exchange
#143	Escrow Clockwise – Pass Deeds Counterclockwise
#144	Cowboy Auction— Recreation
#145	Cowboy Auction — Professional
#146	Credits Represent Delayed Multiple Exchanges
#147	BLM Multiple Exchange — Gov't Exchanging
#148	The Continuous Multiple Exchange
#149	Multiple Sale and/or Exchange of a Business
#150	International Multiple Exchange — the Easiest Way

VOLUME 7
CONTENTS

Introduction
Foreword: Nancy Steele

Strategy	Title
#151	The Five (5) Steps to Brainstorming
#152	Assessing the Situation
#153	Defining the Problem
#154	Brainstorming the Problem
#155	Use of the Subconscious
#156	Using Judgment
#157	Signs Following
#158	Idea Tracking
#159	Killer Thoughts
#160	Forced Relationship Technique -
#161	Best Ideas Come Last -
#162	Quantity Breeds Quality
#163	No Limitation to Creativity
#164	Deferment of Judgment
#165	Group vs. Individual Ideation
#166	The Gordon Technique
#167	Don't Drive With Your Brakes On
#168	Hitchhiking and More
#169	Reversal Brainstorm
#170	Set a Deadline When Brainstorming
#171	Association of Ideas
#172	Dr. Osborn's Rules for Brainstorming
#173	The Moveable Brainstorm
#174	Diversification in Brainstorming
#175	Brainstorming as a Way of Life

VOLUME 8
CONTENTS

Introduction

Foreword: Steven L. Cropper

Strategy	Title
#176	Counseling and Exchange: History and Evolution
#177	Becoming a Counselor Takes Time
#178	Information to Obtain Through Counseling
#179	The Client Needs to Be Eyeball to Eyeball; Property Can Be Anywhere
#180	Other Counseling Techniques
#181	Pre-Counseling Techniques
#182	Counseling Time
#183	Counseling and Control
#184	Assess Yourself vs. the Deal
#185	Setting Fees as a Consultant or Broker
#186	Are All Legs Under the Table?
#187	The Don't Wanter is a Key to Many Transactions
#188	Counseled Clients Tell You Their Truth
#189	Value, What is It? Is It in the Eye of the Beholder?
#190	Value of an Asset in an Exchange
#191	Would-Ya-Takes
#192	Counseling Is an Individual Thing
#193	People in Hell Want Ice Water
#194	Head 'em West 'Til Their Hat Floats
#195	DFTP—Don't Fight the Problem
#196	Miscellaneous Counseling Techniques
#197	Counseling May Unearth a Good User
#198	When You Have Exhausted All Possibilities, Remember This: *You Haven't*
#199	Entitlement Syndrome: Call a Spade a Spade
#200	Counseling for Escrow

VOLUME 9
CONTENTS

Introduction

Foreword: Alexander J. Krem, BA, MBA, JD

Strategy	Title
#201	Think International
#202	St. Kitts & the Chinese Market
#203	Gibraltar & the Spain Market
#204	Zimbabwe
#205	Vote with Your Feet
#206	Falling Dollar
#207	Virgin Vacancy Ploy
#208	Butterfly Effect
#209	Japanese Carry Trade
#210	Liquefying Mineral Assets
#211	Derivatives #1
#212	Derivatives #2
#213	Inflation
#214	Hyper-inflation #1
#215	Hyper-inflation #2
#216	You Can't Play Baseball in a Hurricane
#217	DMI International Wheel
#218	Soft T.D. Exchange
#219	Panama Trader Traces
#220	International Trading Opportunities
#221	Friday is International Day
#222	Wholesale Trade Credits
#223	International Cold Calling
#224	Reasons to do International Business
#225	Where Did This Dirt Come From?

VOLUME 10
CONTENTS

Introduction
Foreword: Robert E. Baines, BA, JD

Strategy	Title
#226	Turn Vacancies into Wellness Units
#227	Virgin's Vacancy Ploy
#228	The Un-Built Building
#229	Vacant Air Rights & Mineral Rights
#230	Use of Consignments Fills Commercial Vacancy
#231	Personal Notes in Vacancy Exchange
#232	Subdivide the Vacancy
#233	Give Away the Vacant Building
#234	Trade Credits
#235	Apartment House with Many Vacancies
#236	Trade Credit for Special Hotel Vacancy
#237	Create Your Own Credit Card to Fill Vacancy
#238	Open-Ended Note Tied to Insurance Policy to Soften Assisted Living Payments & Fill Vacancies
#239	Create Open End Reverse Mortgage to Fill Assisted Living Vacancies
#240	Combining Strategies to Fill Assisted Living Vacancies
#241	Trading Vacant Lots for Corporate Stock with a Put Option for Additional Trades
#242	Trade Credit to Help Fill Shopping Center Vacancies
#243	Create Low Percentage Land Lease and Exchange for Higher Yielding Asset
#244	Create Low Percentage Land Lease On Vacant Land (or Under Buildings) and Exchange for Trade Credits
#245	Resort Hotel/Motel Vacancy Problems & Seminars
#246	Vacancy Equals Equity, #1
#247	Vacancy Equals Equity #2
#248	Trade Vacancy for Equity in Business
#249	Give Vacancy to Charity
#250	Use Vacancy as Investment Security to Generate Income
#250A	Bonus: Rent or Trade Your Vacancy via Telemarketing
#250B	Bonus: Hotel Vacancy for Semi-Retired
#250C	Bonus: Trees for Vacancies, etc.
#250D	Bonus: A Vacancy in Your Mind Can Be Good
#250E	Bonus: Sandwich Vacancies for Profit

VOLUME 11
CONTENTS

Introduction

Foreword: Clifford L. Strand, SEC, EMS

Strategy	Title
#251	PUT #1 (Option) Using Real Estate
#252	PUT #2 (Option) Using Real Estate
#253	Stock Traded for Real Estate but Not Income
#254	Covered Call (Option) in Stock Vernacular
#255	Covered Call #2 (Option)
#256	The Double or Nothing Contract
#257	Variable Purchase Price of Real Estate Based on Performance
#258	Disappearing Trust Deed
#259	Real Estate Owner Keeps the Eat
#260	Stock for Installment Sale
#261	Stock for Geographical Trade (or Multiple Exchange)
#262	Mitigating the Downside
#263	Growing a Corporation Partially with Real Estate
#264	REIT — Real Estate Investment Trust
#265	Crop Futures Strategy
#266	Stock Exchange with the Option to Buy Back
#267	Developing Internal Exchanging Department within Corporation
#268	Major Trader Obtains a Seat on the Board
#269	Public Company Trades Stock for Expense Items
#270	Derivatives of Real Estate
#271	Trading Stock for Space
#272	Upsiding Currency Land
#273	Charitable Trust Alternative
#274	Funding Corporation with Real Estate
#275	Stock For Troubled Paper
#275-A	Middle Corp Escrow

VOLUME 12
CONTENTS

Introduction

Foreword: Ron Moser

Strategy	Title
#276	**Barter – The One-On-One Trade for Goods or Services**
#277	**The Birth of the Trade Credit**
#278	**Trade Credits #2 – Basic Trade Club**
#279	**Three Options: Direct Barter, Direct Trade Credit, or Trade Club Trade Credits**
#280	**Crop Futures Strategy**
#281	**Trade Credit for Hotels**
#282	**Trade Credit for Assisted Living**
#283	**Printing Your Own Money #1**
#284	**$250 Trade Credit©**
#285	**Printing Your Own Money #2**
#286	**Printing Your Own Money #3**
#287	**International Trade Clubs**
#288	**Starting & Running a Trade Club**
#289	**Breakage in Trade Credits**
#290	**Outlaw Dates on Trade Credits**
#291	**Holder in Due Course of Trade Credits**
#292	**Trade Credits Can Represent a Delayed Multiple Exchange**
#293	**International Trade Credits #2**
#294	**Trade Credits to Help Fill Shopping Center Vacancies**
#295	**Barter & Trade Credits on the Internet**
#296	**Becoming a Trade Credit & Barter Broker**
#297	**Trade Credit Trade**
#298	**Multiple Barter Trades**
#299	**Bartering Education**
#300	**300 Trade Credits for 12-Volume E-Book Set**

NOTES

300 STRATEGIES FOR MAKING
REAL ESTATE & BUSINESS DEALS

VOLUME 1

STRATEGIES
1 – 25

25 Basic Creative Real Estate Strategies

Initially Developed by Richard R. Reno

ROBERT W. STEELE

Foreword by Michael E. Stewart

OUTSIDE THE BOX & INSIDE / OUTSIDE THE COUNTRY

300 Strategies for Making Real Estate & Business Deals

Outside the Box & Inside / Outside the Country

VOLUME 1

Strategies 1 – 25

25 BASIC CREATIVE REAL ESTATE STRATEGIES *Initially developed by Richard R. Reno*

by Robert W. Steele

Foreword by Michael E. Stewart

Design, Layout & Graphics
Victoria Vinton
Coyote Press Graphic Communications
www.coyotepressgraphics.com

VOLUME 1
CONTENTS

Introduction

Foreword: Michael E. Stewart

Strategy .... Title

#1 .... Unpriced
#2 .... Creation of Wealth #1
#3 .... Creation of Wealth #2
#4 .... Creation of Wealth #3
#5 .... Exchange and Buy Back
#6 .... Missouri Waltz: One, Two, Cash Out
#7 .... REO Exchange (Real Estate Owned)
#8 .... The Don't-Wanter is a Key to Many Transactions
#9 .... Multiple Exchanges
#10 .... The Un-Built Building
#11 .... Share the Wealth
#12 .... How to Play a Falling Market
#13 .... Brainstorming and Individual Ideation
#14 .... People in Hell Want Ice Water
#15 .... The In-Lieu-of Formula
#16 .... Charlie the Thief
#17 .... Share the Loss Formula
#18 .... The Weasel Clause (Escape Clause)
#19 .... Front Porch
#20 .... Head 'Em West 'til Their Hat Floats
#21 .... Broker Cooperation
#22 .... Verbal Exchange Offers Don't Work
#23 .... Counseling and Control
#24 .... Being Flexible Benefits an Exchangor
#25 .... Un-Priced Exchange Meeting

INTRODUCTION

25 Creative Real Estate Strategies

Originally Developed by Richard R. Reno

These are the basicformulas that started the formalized marketplace of real estate exchanging which, over 50 plus years, has morphed into what is now called creative real estate and business. Today there are hundreds of variations coming from these original concepts.

Reno did several major things in his life and while this is not intended to be a biography it needs to be pointed out that he, at least for me and many who followed, took the real estate out of the discussion and redefined it as an inanimate object. He was one hundred percent politically incorrect and organized real estate really did not appreciate him. He actually believed that real estate should not be priced in many instances. Was this the mutterings of a heretic?

He believed that it was primarily the people that counted and that the real estate was just a vehicle to help people get where they wanted to go in life. He was a real estate broker. He believed it was demeaning for a broker to leave his desk to go see a client and/or under no circumstances should a broker ever show property. He would say, "The only time I look at property is if I am thinking about buying it but even then I do not see half the property I own." He didn't believe that clients had to see property either, any more than a stock holder in the NYSE had to see the company represented by the stock.

Add to that the fact that he felt any broker that worked on Saturday or Sunday, at least with clients, was a disgrace to the industry. He called what today is referred to as Excel Cap Sheets, Chinese lottery tickets. He believed that you only gave actual and factual information; no projections, which was just the opposite of the going theories. Consequently there were many who disliked him and some for multiple reasons.

Even though organized real estate really didn't like him, he continued to try and work his ideas through the California State Real Estate Association and the National Association of Realtors. When he wanted to form a national traders club, they finally agreed to let him do it under the banner of organized real estate but they insisted that he start with at least 200 members. Reno believed that the professional group that he envisioned would never exceed 100 brokers because most brokers just could not get the concept, so he refused to acquiesce and broke away from the national association and formed the National Society of Exchange Counselors, (SEC). At this writing the society is about 50 years old and can be Googled at www.secounselors.com.

Reno was the benevolent dictator of the group until his retirement so in its formative years it was strongly controlled by him. The SEC membership stayed around the 100 number that he envisioned, sometimes it went down to 80 and then swell to 120 but his concept was proven. He would only allow two guests at a meeting as he felt the SEC meetings were not a training ground but only for true practitioners.

He taught many seminars around the U.S. and today a great many of his formulas are used and taught within organized real estate. He asked a few members of the SECs to also teach seminars on various portions of the subject. I taught a seminar on formulas and concepts under his auspices for several years.

His classes grew into large crowds over the years and after he retired he asked me and one other broker to teach his class, which I did for a while. I had up to 300 students at a time and these were six day venues. It was tough work. The large numbers were due to Reno's recognition and there was only one real Richard R. Reno.

I was fortunate to do a lot of business with him. I did some exchanges with him and he absolutely did just what he taught. He never looked at any property and never left his desk unless it was to have lunch. Another SEC, Cliff Weaver and Reno and I were partners in a magazine called Creative Real Estate and we started and owned a national convention called the Real Estate Expo that was held in Las Vegas annually.

This book, the first in a series, is comprised of some of the basic formulas and what he called Know How Items that he taught in his course. I have attempted to analyze them and structure them so they retain his true consciousness. There have been hundreds of variations derived from these formulas. Someone once told me that retention was only 20% so I ended up taking Reno's class five time. I waited one year between each attendance so I could practice the lore, make mistakes and then back for more training.

One last bit of philosophy for all of us to ponder at this time, 2010. We have a down real estate market, way down and, (IMO) in my opinion, a lot farther to fall. Someday it will turn but we have never in modern history had as complex a problem to solve and one with so many parts. To come out of other down markets, while our currency was fiat (unbacked paper) it was much stronger, we had lots of equity as many homes were free and clear, banks would lend money, and the country had a stronger moral fiber. Today our problem includes a very weak dollar, much of our equity has been borrowed out in the form of dollars and spent, so the strong equity positions are gone, the banking business as a whole is suspect in many ways and all the bankers' equity in the smaller banks have eroded leaving a very weak system. All of this topped off with a moral fiber that is wont from corruption in Washington to the gangs in our cities makes for a difficult situation.

So there, Mr. and Mrs. Real Estate broker, business person and investor/entrepreneur, is your problem to solve and it also represents the biggest opportunity to ever exist in real estate and business. Properties are stuck by the thousands. Equities in Internet Exchange and Real Estate web sites must be in the quadrillions waiting to be sold or exchanged. These problems need to be solved. Herein are the Reno basic formulas. Within them is the genesis for at least some of the needed solutions. They are different but I guarantee that when properly applied they work.

Here is a plan: Read this book five times.

Michael E. Stewart

Foreword

I am honored to have been asked to write the forward for this particular set of formulas, as these are the time honored originals as taught by Richard R. Reno, Founder of the Society of Exchange Counselors. Dick taught us a new way to think about almost every part of our lives. Looking back over the last 45 years, almost all of my personal, recreational, financial, social and spiritual needs, as well as the lifelong friendships and the people I hold most dear in my life were a direct result of my involvement with the other members of The Society.

I was not a charter member, but the group was still very young when I was invited to membership at the tender age of 26, and I am reasonably sure that I still hold the record as the youngest member ever invited into the Society.

During the early years, Dick Reno, Bob Steele and Cliff Weaver were a fearless threesome that built "The Society" and its philosophies into the most effective creative real estate marketplace, for U.S. Real Estate Problem Solving, in the country. The Society represented the consummate source of creativity and imagination in the structuring of Real Estate transactions and was based on the idea that people, not property, were what made transactions go together.

"The S.E.C. Brokers" were in the people business not the property business. "You can't Dance with a Ranch" or "Take a Condo to Lunch." All of this was at another time, similar to today, when there was little money or loans in the marketplace. About 25 years ago, cash became easy and creativity took a back seat. People solved problems by going to cash rather than benefits and started playing the "greater fool game" of taking near worthless FRNs (Federal Reserve Notes) in exchange for their Good Stuff: Real Estate, and then hurry fast and find some other fool to take the worthless paper for their property.

Now the currency is worth almost nothing and everyone still thinks it is a panacea for their problems. The more savvy players are dusting off the old formulas and recognizing that benefits and commodities and other stores of value are what are important in the current economy.

Bob Steele is probably the one voice that can bring the old formulas as well as the new strategies back to life and put those of you, who have the eyes to see and the ears to hear, back on the road not only to recovery but on a path that will give you a life worth living.

If I could offer you, the reader, the greatest gift I could imagine, it would be for you to be able to have and enjoy a life and relationship like Bob and I have had for the last 45 years. We've grown up and old together, traveling and fishing all over the world.

Most of our old buddies are gone now like Dick, Cliff, Jim Farley and Kenny Johnson to name a few, but a few of us are still here. The knowledge is slowly going away. We need to build new, young, knowledgeable standard bearers who have the vision to enjoy life and share the knowledge with a new generation in need. The time for the Barter System of doing business has returned, and understanding it has become a matter of survival.

This book of formulas and those that follow serve as a very good starting point, but I also suggest that you get serious about your education and seek out the instructors that can get you up and running efficiently in this new world and economy.

Thank you for your attention and I wish you the very best of luck,

Michael E. Stewart

STRATEGY 1
Unpriced

This is probably the most important exchange formula there is and it is rarely used as people do not understand its significance, or possibly it is so unconventional that they are afraid of it. The true key to the philosophy of exchanging is within this formula. If you do not understand the importance of this, you will not really understand exchanging.

SITUATION	1. Abel has a property with a problem. He has been trying to sell or trade it. 2. For one reason or another Abel is locked to a price. 3. There is no functioning sales market. The buyers are way below the asking prices from either market manipulation or other outside forces.	Price: Loan: Equity:	$ 1,000,000 - 400,000 $ 600,000
POSSIBLE SOLUTION	1. Explain the logic of benefits vs. price. 2. List the property as un-priced if you are a broker and make the contract, if an entrepreneur, at any price agreeable to the seller (or you), as the case may be. 3. Exchange or transact for benefits.	Price: Loan: Equity:	Unpriced - 400,000 Unpriced
CONCLUSION	1. Price is in the eyes of the beholder. 2. If you are a real estate broker or an entrepreneur set a flat fee for your brokerage.		
NOTES	1. You will need a dollar number for title insurance that at least equals any mortgage on the property. 2. Weigh the benefits and negatives when making a deal, not the price.		

STRATEGY 2

Creation of Wealth #1

Probably the most highly recognized formula originated by Richard R. Reno

SITUATION	There have easily been a thousand variations on this formula. The basic formula is creating a TD or mortgage against or secured by the equity in one property and exchanging this piece of paper (TD or Mortgage) for a second property or asset.	Abel Bldg: Loan: Equity:	$ 1,000,000 - 300,000 $ 700,000
CREATION OF WEALTH	Create a $400,000 2nd TD/note on Abel's property and exchange to Baker who has a building with a $600,000 equity. Abel gives Baker a $200,000 additional 2nd TD back on his own building to balance.	Baker Bldg: Loan: Equity:	$ 800,000 - 200,000 $ 600,000
CLOSE	Abel ends up with two buildings.	Abel Bldg: Ist Loan: 2nd Loan: Equity:	$ 1,000,000 - 300,000 - 400,000 $ 300,000
		Baker Bldg. Ist Loan: 2nd Loan: Equity	$ 800,000 - 200,000 - 200,000 $ 400,000
	Baker ends up with two trust deeds and notes totaling an equity of $600,000.	2nd on Abel 2nd on Baker TOTAL	$ 800,000 - 200,000 $ 600,000

STRATEGY 3

Creation of Wealth #2

Get the other side of the exchange to be your banker which will allow you to free up part of your equity during the holding period.

SITUATION	1. You are in a market in which land is not selling. The parcel you are concerned with is well-situated and will at some time in the future become a prime development parcel. You peg the value at $1,500,000. 2. You have various options to free this equity, one of course being an exchange, or you could use an exchange and buy back, etc. But being a little concerned about some tax problems you might consider using the Creation of Wealth formula.	Land Value:	$ 1,500,000
POSSIBLE SOLUTION	1. Offer to create up to $1,000,000 (or any number you are comfortable with) first TD/note secured by this property and use it in an exchange into something acceptable to you. 2. Remember you are offering to create the note so you want to set terms that are the best for you. Don't be bashful. We have often set these at 2% interest-only for 10 or more years. Real estate brokers have the habit of thinking this rate of interest is too low but it represents approximately what the market is currently for CDs. You will get exchange offers at this rate that are often acceptable. You can always negotiate up if you wish.	Create Note/TD Secured By Land:	$ 1,000,000

STRATEGY 4

Creation of Wealth #3

This Creation of Wealth variation allows someone with a commodity to leverage their investments while hedging their profits.

SITUATION	1. In this one we were working with a broker who had a large tomato farmer as a client. We had a building in another state that my client wanted out of with a price tag of $2,000,000. There was no cash sale market. 2. The tomato farmer was interested in acquiring some property for appreciation but also for some tax shelter.
POSSIBLE SOLUTION	We offered to exchange our building for $2,000,000 worth of tomatoes delivered over five years ($400,000 per year) at a price fixed at the close of escrow.
SOLUTION	The transaction was secured by a blanket TD against both parcels of real estate.
POSSIBLE SOLUTION	In essence, the client with the building cashed out over five years. The was no guarantee where the price of tomatoes would go during that 5 years even though the quantity of tomatoes he was to receive was fixed. If the price went up he would make a profit. If it went down he would have a loss. He received no interest during the holding period. It was a true hedge.
SOLUTION	The tomato farmer spent a "Future" or a Covered Call if you wish. He acquired real estate and added to his holdings. He pre-sold some of his tomatoes at a fixed price.

STRATEGY 5

Exchange and Buy Back

There are many variations on this. It can be a pre-set buy back, a buy back triggered by something happening or some other event, it can even be just an option to buy back or just the basic REO formula.

SITUATION	1. Remember, in learning the basics about this formula, to be cognizant that in an exchange of real estate your book basis moves with you from the old property to the new property. If you do buy back your original property, you have established a new basis set by the new purchase price. 2. You can see then in your planning why in some instances you might use the Exchange and Buy Back formula, and in others you might use the Blanket Mortgage formula. They both do similar things, but the book basis is handled differently.
POSSIBLE SOLUTION	1. A builder who is holding land for future development might use this formula to exchange the land he is land-banking into something he could use now, and agree to buy back the land he is trading in at some future date. In one, two or three years perhaps, he could be contracted to do it or it could be an option. 2. If you offer a building you have into one you would like to have and they will not accept your transaction, you might consider buying back the building you are trading in on some terms that would make the deal acceptable to both sides. 3. If you are a broker in an exchange transaction and one side will not consider what is being offered, you—the broker—can consider being the one buying back the one property with the commissions earned in the deal. 4. Also you can consider using the Charlie the Thief formula for this buy back. To fully understand this formula and its multitude of options, you can look up the related formulas here-in: Blanket Mortgage, REO, Options and Charlie the Thief.

STRATEGY 6

Missouri Waltz: One, Two, Cash Out

This is the old formula that later was accentuated by two court cases, The Starker Cases, and it then became known as the 1031 Exchange. It is in fact not an exchange but a delayed sale and has nothing to do with exchanging. The Missouri Waltz on the other hand is an exchange subject to one property selling out. The 1031 exchange comes from the other direction: It starts with a sale of one property and the funds are held in an escrow and then another property is purchased to the satisfaction of the buyer but in compliance with certain rules.

SITUATION	1. The entire exercise must be recognized for what it really is. It is a man-made bureaucratic manipulation of the market. It makes sense to exploit these as long as one can, but recognize at some point in time it will be changed because it is man-made. 2. It is like the entire 1031 law which allows a tax deferred exchange and moves an artificial tax thing called a book basis from one property to another. It is all artificial. 3. People get trapped when they rely just on a government-sponsored program because I can guarantee you it will be cancelled at some point, and some people will be looking for chairs when the music stops. You can actually get to the point where you believe it is real. As of this writing (2010) thousands of brokers and clients are stuck in the 1031 exchange belief and of course the cash sale market is not functioning, so the people have been led down a trail that has dead-ended. 4. Properties are being foreclosed, clients are losing their equities and brokers are failing out because they believed entirely in one government ruling.
POSSIBLE SOLUTION	1. The simplest way to solve or resolve these transactions is to first make an exchange that makes economic and personal sense, and then come back and look at the tax consequences and structure to minimize same. 2. The transaction should stand on its own feet first without tax considerations (IMO).

STRATEGY 7

REO Exchange (Real Estate Owned)

This was originally designed to assist lenders in divesting themselves of real estate properties they had foreclosed on. Several other applications have derived from the original formula.

SITUATION	1. Foreclosed real estate assets become scheduled items for certain lenders which affects them in many ways. At some point it can cause the failure of the bank and/or a forced merger with another lending institution.
POSSIBLE SOLUTION	1. A typical example might be as follows: You own a $1,000,000 dollar parcel of land, free and clear. A lender has four houses they have foreclosed on with a value of an average of $250,000 each or a total of $1,000,000. You offer to exchange your land for the four houses subject to the lender loaning you 80% on the houses ($800,000) with favorable terms. You agree to buy back the land for $1,000,000 giving the lender $300,000 in cash down (out of your new loan proceeds) and a new loan back on the land for $700,000, so that it is based on terms that take it out of the scheduled category. The lender has $1,500,000 invested, $800,000 in legal loans on the 4 houses and $700,000 loan on the land. No items are scheduled and they are in total compliance. You now still own your land, but with a new tax basis on it, and four houses. You also have $500,000 in cash less whatever your costs were. 2. The formula also works with any company of merit that has the where-with-all to act as a lender. This formula is sometimes referred to as The Buyer is a Lender. A corporation might be vacating a building that they would like to get rid of. Say you are a developer with land that you want to build a shopping center on and are having trouble finding a loan. Offer to exchange the company the land under the shopping center for the building they want to get rid of, and you will lease back the land under the shopping center with maybe an option to repurchase it. This offer is subject to the company loaning you the money to build the shopping center. 3. In all REO transactions there is usually a lender making a loan.

STRATEGY 8

The Don't-Wanter is a Key to Many Transactions

There is a basic difference between an exchange and a sale.

SITUATION	1.	The motivations in a regular sale are hidden within the cash in the transaction. While everyone values cash in a different way, it is still a common denominator. In an exchange, where there is no cash or minimal cash, then the desires of the participants are often very visible.
	2.	There is another very significant factor in an exchange that often either visible or just below the surface. The motivation of the participants can be on either the front side of the exchange (what they are receiving) or on the back side (what they are getting out of).
	3.	When there is a high degree of motivation on the back side of the exchange, that participant is said to be a Don't-Wanter. From my experience this is the key to many exchanges. He is highly motivated and brokers will often state that this person is a number eight (on a scale of 10) Don't-Wanter.
POSSIBLE SOLUTION	1.	In counseling with people it is important to get at the key reason they are transacting business when you are considering a structured transaction and not a normal sale. If you can uncover the person's Don't-Want, why he wants out of the property, you have found the key to the transaction. Now it is a matter of finding the opposite side and putting it together and you will have a completed transaction.
	2.	Note the difference in the backside motivation between the following examples: a. A person losing his property to a foreclosure scheduled to be complete in 30 days. b. A free and clear house rented at a high rate. c. A person who has just inherited a motel a thousand miles away in a very bad section of a city and the person has no understanding of how to run same. d. A wealthy person owning an industrial building leased for 20 years to Coca Cola.
	3.	Numbers 1 & 3 are highly motivated on the backside of the exchange and would be considered as a high number Don't-Wanter, maybe a 10 on "a" and a seven on "c". They definitely want out of what they own. The higher the number the easier the deal is to get together

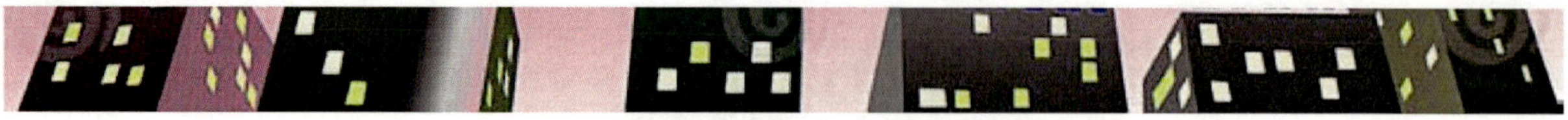

STRATEGY 9

Multiple Exchanges

Thirty to 40 years ago multiple exchanges were used more often than they are today, as new strategies and formulas have developed whereby transactions can be closed in two way deals. However, I am still of the opinion that the easiest exchange to make in real estate or business is to start with a multiple exchange, to wit:

SITUATION	1. **Property:** It is very easy to find the first leg of a multiple exchange. All you need is for one person to say, "I'll take that property in exchange for my property." It is easy to find this first step; however, you need to know that the overall exchange aspects and prognoses are improved by this move. Is it going to be easier to find a fit with this new property and the owner who is still searching? 2. **Owner or client in-lieu-of:** In this second step you have a hypothetical owner of the property that is in-lieu-of. Everything should be improved with this step or you should not be in this multiple exchange. By this I mean that the hypothetical owner of the property should be bringing more motivation, flexibility or other assets to the table and making the hoped for exchange easier. If it would make the exchange more difficult, do not enter into the first step. 3. **Other principals or brokers:** It is critical that you get the multiple exchange started with others who will carry their share of the load. If they are clients they must be well counseled.
POSSIBLE SOLUTION	**Example of a good start to a multiple exchange** a) You are a broker and your client has a nice commercial building, fully rented, but a small equity, there is a large 2nd TD coming due and the owner needs to get into a neutral position and eliminate what is causing him stress. b) Another broker with whom you have had previous dealings and you know is a good broker, has a builder client that she has done several deals for, and he has some rental houses that carry their mortgages and have a positive income. Her client can also add cash and is looking for development land in exchange for his houses. c) All of the ingredients are here for a successful multiple exchange: You write the other broker an offer that you will take the houses and your client locks down on his step. Her client accepts in-lieu-of the broker finding another property for her client. Here are the salient points: Her client has the cash to pay off the second coming due on the commercial property which makes it more acceptable into the marketplace. She is a professional and knows what she is doing and she has a long-term relationship with a client who knows what he is doing, and now he has two brokers working to find the third leg for the exchange when before there was only one broker. Everything has improved and the odds just went up that this deal will get done.
NOTE	On multiple exchanges, enter escrow clockwise and pass deeds counterclockwise for tax reasons.

STRATEGY 10

The Un-Built Building

This can work on anything where you dream the dream and then create the item

SITUATION	1. Abel is a developer and he has land to build on. Have the building designed, have it costed or bid as the case may be and then sell, exchange or lease the building as though it were completed. Even though it is in an un-built building, it can be marketed. If you are exchanging, an obvious exchange would be to exchange it for another parcel of development land. 2. Many high-rise buildings and shopping centers are developed this way but this formula can apply to almost anything: businesses, farms, ships, etc. 3. When you are in a down real estate market you can use this formula by going through a middle step. Say you are developing a small apartment complex. The credit market is difficult and you cannot get enough of a loan to build the building. Perhaps use the Un-built Building formula and exchange the equity into a crankable or borrowable building, like an SFR, where you get enough cash to complete the building by borrowing on the house. You need to handle the paperwork allowing this to happen.
CLOSE	It is suggested that the builder and future owner go over all the plans in a fine tooth manner and make any corrections and/or additions that are necessary, initial same, and then the plans go into escrow. Any further changes then require a change agreement and payment as required. Escrow closes after notice of completion is filed on the building. I learned this the hard way.

STRATEGY 11

Share the Wealth

Fresh financing in one way or another is shared by principals. Wealth in this instance is cash or sharing of the cash per as an agreement.

SITUATION	1. You have a $400,000 trust deed and note that you would like to trade back into real estate but you would also like some cash. 2. The other side has a $500,000 free and clear building you would like to own and your TD and note would be acceptable to them.	Note: Building F/C:	$ 400,000 $ 500,000
POSSIBLE SOLUTION	1. You offer your note plus $100,000 cash for the building which is accepted. 2. In escrow you borrow 70% on the building, $350,000. 3. From the proceeds of the new loan you pay the other side their $100,000.		
CLOSE	1. Your started with a note for $400,000 and you ended up with $250,000 cash from the new loan and $150,000 equity in the building. 2. The other side started with a $500,000 building and they end up with your $400,000 note and $100,000 in cash. 3. Always try to be sure, if you can, that there is enough cash available so everybody can solve their short term requirements.	Note: Cash: Total: Building: Loan: Equity: Cash: Total:	$ 400,000 + 100,000 $ 500,000 $ 500,000 - 350,000 150,000 + 250,000 $ 400,000

STRATEGY 12

How to Play a Falling Market

When fundamentals tell you that the real estate and business market is falling, don't listen to the talking heads or the press. Have a real estate broker tell you what she can sell it for in 30 days and list it 15 to 20% below that figure.

SITUATION	1. People usually list their properties a little bit above the market so they have some room to "negotiate." 2. As the market drops further they lower their price but they lower it just above the market again. 3. As the market continues to drop, they lower it again but just above the market.
POSSIBLE SOLUTION	1. Have a real estate broker tell you what she can sell it for in 30 days and list it 15 – 20% below that figure if it is land or a vacant building, and 10 – 15% if it is improved and rented or residential. 2. Recognize that you manifest from the inside out. While your mind is on the defense about this property you are not manifesting new things. You must get your mind clear. It is far more important than the money that you mistakenly think you have coming in a falling market.
CONCLUSION	1. Go on the offense. There are many ways to do this. 2. Your mind needs to stay on something positive.

Strategy 13

Brainstorming and Individual Ideation

There is no other business that I know of where participants have the opportunity to use their constituent's creative minds to help solve situations they might be working on. The advertising business is well known for its brainstorming but that is almost always within one company and for mutual benefit. In the exchange market it is a free gift by all members to each other. It is an extraordinary gift. And when one knows how and why it works it becomes extremely effective in closing transactions that could not otherwise be made.

SITUATION	Brainstorming is such an important subject that we are doing one full book about it in this series. However, it must be mentioned in this beginning book because of its importance. I have, over the years, learned a lot about this subject, and for those who are interested there is a wealth of material now available on it. I first became interested when I discovered a Dr. Parnes and a Dr. Osborn, one the student of the other, and their constituents who made a comprehensive study in the collegiate and business world. There were several approaches running from three steps to seven. Knowing the exchange marketplace, I designed what I called Idea Tracking—a five-step brainstorming system, designed specifically for exchanging, to brainstorm real estate problems—and taught this for many years as part of a three day seminar.
POSSIBLE SOLUTION	1. Knowing the techniques, anyone can develop 100 ideas or solutions on almost any subject or transaction that had not been thought of before. It is mechanical if you know how to use your mind. 2. Each of these steps are comprehensive and represent a total of about a four-hour workshop. The five steps are: a. Assess to the problem b. Define the problem c. Brainstorm – several different methods d. Subconscious time e. Selecting the best idea 3. "b" above is the major key. When I was studying the subject I did not understand the importance of this when one author said always go to a minimum of 77 different definitions of the problem before you make a selection. I just didn't get it, but I can tell you from experience and what I have seen that most of the reasons things fail is because people have defined the problem incorrectly. I would say that many great ideas are born in the wrong world because you were trying to solve the wrong problem. It is another reason why counseling is so important. 4. Once you learn how to do this effectively it changes your life in many ways. Many impossible things become possible.

STRATEGY 14

People in Hell Want Ice Water

When people want impossible things there is always an agent or broker who will waste their time trying to deliver the impossible.

SITUATION	1. There are a lot of cases of this, but today let's use someone wanting a cash sale when there is no cash market. 2. You as a broker or possibly an exchangor tell them there is no cash market, would they consider exchanging. They say, "No, we need a cash sale." 3. If you are a broker you might say, "OK, I'll do the best I can," and take the listing. Both parties waste time and money.
POSSIBLE SOLUTION	1. Between steps 2 & 3 the broker or agent or principal should try to do some counseling. Ask the client how, if there are no cash buyers in the marketplace, they going to sell for cash. 2. If something can't be done, it can't be done. From the agent's point of view it is better to use the other formula, "Head 'em West 'til Their Hat Floats" or sow a seed that will bring them back later. E.g., "Please go ahead and list your property with (name your competitor down the street) and if they are not successful in selling, come back to me and I will exchange it for you." 3. When they come back they will be more attuned to what is real and will have eliminated the impossible requirement.

STRATEGY 15

The In-Lieu-of Formula

Phrase to use in acceptance: "This offer is being accepted provided the brokers, clients or principals herein are able to re-exchange what is being offered in-lieu-of something satisfactory to the undersigned within 90 days."

SITUATION	1. There is a need here to recognize a truth: many times it is easier to make a three-way exchange than a two-way. They are many times much purer. 2. The advent of two things have made the three-way exchange a seldom used tool over recent years. a) The Starker Law cases provided that you could use cash in the middle of an exchange with a facilitator, so during the inflationary period of fiat currency and inflation, the need for using three-way exchanges diminished appreciable (#1031). b) the development of many new strategies and formulas did likewise.
EXAMPLE	1. Present a situation or a property to a group. Ask the group who will take what is being offered regardless of what they have to exchange. 2. These offers are written. First see if there is anything acceptable in a two-way exchange, bouncing the idea against various formulas. 3. If not, then take one of the items offered and see who will trade for it. Offer the things being offered to the first party and if any of them is acceptable you have a three-way exchange. 4. It is not complicated and at the first step the motivation and intensity increases as three of the four parties are ready to close; two brokers and one principal.

STRATEGY 16

Charlie the Thief

The Player Everyone Needs

SITUATION	Many times there needs to be someone in a transaction who brings cash liquidity when the cash can not be circumvented. Cash usually demands a price and one sometimes needs to be willing to sacrifice additional equity to get the liquidity. It is most helpful to have a money person, often referred to affectionately (with tongue in cheek) as Charlie the Thief—someone who will come into the deal and buy a position for the cash that is needed at a deep discount.
CHARLIE THE BROKER	There is nothing in the rule book that says that a broker cannot be Charlie the Thief. Full disclosure is always important.
CHARLIE THE HARD MONEY BROKER	The hard money broker can also play the Charlie role.
SOMETIMES THERE ARE RISKS BUT OFTEN THESE ARE MINIMAL.	Who will be Charlie? The profile is someone who can make rapid business decisions, has the cash on hand and performs in a timely manner. By definition this pretty much eliminates anyone who works with a board of directors.
NOTE	See Share the Loss Formula which often works in concert with Charlie the Thief.

STRATEGY 17

Share the Loss Formula

This often works in concert with the Charlie the Thief Formula

SITUATION	You are closing a three-way multiple exchange and there is a $300,000 loan that cannot be assumed and must be paid off in order to close the transaction, and a standard mortgage is not available based on the timing necessary to close.
ENTER CHARLIE THE THIEF	Charlie agrees to bring the $300,000 cash to the table in exchange for buying the existing note and modifying the terms and conditions. Charlie wants a $450,000 note back (modifying the original note) in exchange for his $300,000 cash, but he is willing to close in one week.
NEGOTIATE WITH ALL THREE PRINCIPALS	All three principals in the exchange agree to each take a $50,000 hit or loss of equity and the holdings are reworked to reflect this change. The transaction closes with each principal sharing in the loss of the $150,000.
THERE ARE MANY WAYS TO NEGOTIATE THIS OUT	The one who cares the most will usually end up taking the biggest share of the loss.

STRATEGY 18

The Weasel Clause (Escape Clause)

You only need one Weasel Clause - don't use too many

SITUATION	1. When you initiate an exchange offer there almost always are some sort of contingencies. These are often written at meetings that are miles from clients or properties. 2. Beside an inspection of property(s) that perhaps need to be made, you might need verification of several other things. 3. Remember that you are trying to arrive at a meeting of the minds, and a lot of the real estate requirements are secondary to trying to solve a problem that the property in some way manifests for the owner. 4. If you spend your time putting in a lot of contingency clauses, you are just taking a mind off the target of what you are trying to accomplish.
POSSIBLE SOLUTION	1. One Weasel Clause is all that you need even if in your mind there are a dozen contingencies. Don't bother to list them when one is all you need. Some of those contingencies will probably disappear without ever writing them up. 2. A simple one is "This offer is subject to site inspection and written approval by Mr. A within 30 days of this date." That Weasel Clause is all you need. Another might be, "Subject to inspection and written approval of the title policy," etc. 3. All you need is one Weasel Clause.

STRATEGY 19

FRONT PORCH

Always put something into an offer that the other side can take out without hurting what you are trying to accomplish

SITUATION	1. The concept of the "Front Porch," for example, is to state in your offer that you will take the property they want you to take if the owners will paint the front porch. You really don't care if they paint that porch. 2. This causes their minds to go over and fight you on that part of the offer and not on parts of the offer that you really don't want them to fight you on. 3. The front porch is easy to add to an offer and really can help you in negotiations.	Examples: 1. Ask the other side to pay all the costs of closing. 2. Ask the other side to charge no interest and require no payments for a year on a Junior mortgage they are to carry back. 3. Ask them to include an automobile they own that has nothing to do with the property. 4. Actually ask them to paint the front porch.
POSSIBLE SOLUTION	For instance if you are buying a house and the owners are very proud of their art work, the Front Porch concept is to ask for the art work to be included at no additional price. This is the same technique used by attorneys in law suits. It gives you a bargaining chip to work with.	
EXAMPLE	I was closing an escrow with a broker I knew quite well and he kept pestering me continually about something they wanted I did not want to give up. After we left the escrow office he laughed and said, Bob, you were jumping all over the front porch. I never did find out what it was they obtained that they didn't want me negotiating.	

Strategy 20

Head 'em West 'Til Their Hat Floats

Arbitrarily let's pick a number — 90% of the situations in real estate and business are not worth your time, so the maximum situations you have to pick from is 10%. I am not saying that if you are a retail real estate broker not to take a quantity of listings. I am saying that if you are interested in a somewhat selective life don't take on situations where the other side of the transactions is difficult to work with.

SITUATION	1.	When you are counseling someone or even in a pre-counseling mode the attitude might be one of "The quicker I decide not to get involved in this deal the quicker I can get on to doing something I want to do."	Head 'em west 'til their hat floats
	2.	There are many signs that you can pick up in counseling that are red flags that tell you not to get involved with this person or in this situation. The thought often goes through my mind: Would I rather be helping this person or going fishing?	Head 'em west...
	3.	Some of the salient things you might watch for are those that play the victim role. The world has mistreated them. Others are those that have a best friend that is great advisor. Another one is they have three other partners: Remember that each partner has a spouse and an attorney and a best friend advisor, that totals well over 10 people before a decision can be made.	Head 'em west...
POSSIBLE SOLUTION	1.	Of each degree of difficulty you might consider raising the fee or your profit structure. At some point you might consider that it is just not worth the potential anguish vs. the potential reward.	If you are closer to the east coast, head 'em east...
	2.	There is always one more deal right behind this one. The trite saying does come into play: "Some of the best deals you ever make are the ones you turn down."	

STRATEGY 21

Broker Cooperation

The most important ingredient in any brokered transaction is the other broker IMO, (In My Opinion).

SITUATION	
POSSIBLE SOLUTION	There is no other business that I know of where broker cooperation is the rule not the exception. The cooperation in exchanging can lead you to doing transactions with the same broker or client or partners over and over again. A few years ago I met a broker in Alaska at the airport in Juneau as we were headed out on one of the many fishing trips we had done together over the years. We had just gone out of title to a property we had owned jointly. He said when he saw me, "Bob, do you know that this is the first time in 30 years that you and I have not been partners in some sort of a deal?" Cooperation solves a lot of problems.

STRATEGY 22

Verbal Exchange Offers Don't Work

You are wasting your time to even try to make verbal offers. Professionals call these, "Wouldja Takes." These are sometime used in counseling, but in the field always, and I literally mean always, write down and sign what you actually would do. Not what anyone wants you to say or do but simply write down what you would close on and sign it. The act of signing means you expect the other side to do the same if there is a meeting of the minds. You do not need multiple pages of legalese to get you aimed at a meeting of the minds. There is plenty of time to "fine-tooth" the offer and get the legal work done later. These types of mini forms are available from many sources and take but a few minutes to fill out. Below is a sample.

MINI OFFER FORM

This is a non-binding preliminary proposal presented to parties in hopes that a binding agreement might be reached. It can be rejected by either party at anytime until there is a complete meeting of the minds and the signing of final documents

Check one: Purchase ☐ Sale ☐ Exchange ☐ Lease ☐ Option ☐ Other ☐

First Party:

Second party:

Identify property(ies) that is/are the subject of this offer:

What are the terms and conditions of this offer:

Attach another page if more space is needed.

Thoughts, data and ideas that are pertinent to help make this transaction go together:

Date:
Owners Name:
Agent:

Acceptance:
Date:
Owners Name:
Agent:

STRATEGY 23

COUNSELING AND CONTROL

Counseling leads automatically to control or disassociation with the opportunity to associate at some later date

SITUATION	1. Counseling is: a) Listening to what is being said and to what is being implied. b) Advising potential clients, partners, or those you are doing business with what the current market conditions permit you to make happen. c) etc. 2. Counseling is not: a) Getting picked up in the attributes of a parcel of land or a business opportunity. b) Telling the client how great you are. c) etc.
POSSIBLE SOLUTION	1. If you analyze what you are being told by the person you are talking to, and match that against what is actually happening in the marketplace, you will have an idea as to whether what needs to be done can actually be done in the current conditions. 2. At the same time you are trying to analyze whether or not this person has the capacity and the malleability it will take. 3. Early in my life as an exchangor, I paid for three or four major clients to go to Dick Reno's six day exchangor's class to get counseled. It was the complete way to get the job done. I did a lot of business with these people. I have used books to help in counseling. The more a person understands the more flexible he or she becomes.

STRATEGY 24

BEING FLEXIBLE BENEFITS AN EXCHANGOR

Your chances for success as an exchangor increase with flexibility!

FLEXIBILITY	It is pretty easy to understand. The following situations have to do with geographical limitations. We are not advocating flexibility, we are explaining it.
GEOGRAPHICAL SITUATION Area of take	1. If you have the flexibility to accept properties in exchange that are outside of your city, you have a bigger selection to choose from than someone who doesn't. 2. If you have the flexibility to accept properties in exchange that are outside of your state, you have a bigger selection to choose from than someone who doesn't. 3. If you have the flexibility to accept properties in exchange that are outside of your country, you have a bigger selection to choose from than someone who doesn't.
ACCEPTABLE PROPERTY TYPE	1. If you have the flexibility to accept two different kinds of property, say an apartment house or a commercial building, you have more chance of a successful exchange than a person who will only accept one of these. 2. If you have the flexibility to accept five different kinds of property, say an apartment house, a commercial building, a motel, a hotel or a marina you have more chance of a successful exchange than a person who will only accept two of these 3. If you have the flexibility to accept a dozen different kinds of property you have more of a chance of a successful exchange than a person who is not as flexible. 4. The same is true for every other facet.

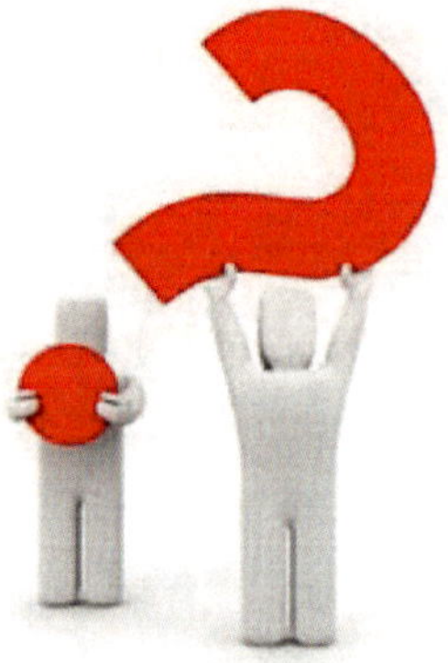

STRATEGY 25

UN-PRICED EXCHANGE MEETING

This is also referring you back to formula #1

The truest form of an exchange meeting is to have all packages be presented "un-priced." Brokers and principles have a terrible time letting go of the need for prices. Once they start dealing in benefits instead everything starts to work.

SITUATION	In a market similar to the one we are in now (2010), where the marketplace is manipulated, a false market is created. The banks, lenders and home owners are being falsely supported and the market is not allowed to fall as in a free market system. The buyers are still there but below and perhaps way below the falsely supported asking prices
POSSIBLE SOLUTION	1. Have an exchange meeting where only "un-priced" packages are permitted. This helps people start to understand the need to concentrate on benefits. 2. It changes the focus from the property to the owner and it will, and I repeat the statement, it *will* help unlock transactions that could not be made when working with a priced package. 3. There is no risk for the owner as the transaction is always made at any price agreeable to the owner, but it opens doors for people to make offers that they would have never made before—offers the seller would never see under normal circumstances—and after all, it is the owner who should have the right to say what he will accept.

NOTES

NOTES

300 STRATEGIES FOR MAKING
REAL ESTATE & BUSINESS DEALS

VOLUME 2

STRATEGIES
26 – 50

25 Formulas & Strategies
Creative Real Estate Level 2

ROBERT W. STEELE

Foreword by Chester W. Allen

OUTSIDE THE BOX & INSIDE / OUTSIDE THE COUNTRY

300 Strategies for Making Real Estate & Business Deals

Outside the Box & Inside / Outside the Country

VOLUME 2
Strategies 26 – 50

25 FORMULAS & STRATEGIES: CREATIVE REAL ESTATE LEVEL 2

Robert W. Steele

Foreword by Chester W. Allen

Design, Layout & Graphics
Victoria Vinton
Coyote Press Graphic Communication
www.coyotepressgraphics.com

VOLUME 2
CONTENTS

Introduction

Foreword: Chester W. Allen

Strategy	Title
#26	Assess Yourself vs. the Deal
#27	Are All the Legs in the Room?
#28	Blanket Mortgage
#29	Consulting Time
#30	Front Side, Back Side
#31	Front Gate, #1, 2 and 3
#32	Tail Gate
#33	Pencil Paralysis
#34	Zeckendorf Technique #1
#35	Zeckendorf Technique #2
#36	Zeckendorf - Dornbush (SEC) #3
#37	Is the Date Right?
#38	The Truth is Only Momentary
#39	We Create from the Inside Out
#40	Who or What is the Most Important in an Exchange?
#41	How to Operate at an Exchange Meeting
#42	How to Write an Exchange Offer
#43	Negotiating an Exchange Offer
#44	Benefits that Grow
#45	Know-How Item: Kick 'Em in the Kidneys
#46	Know-How Item: The Extra Value of a User
#47	Know-How Item: I'll Make You Quit in a Negotiation
#48	Know-How Item: A Zero Means Nothing
#49	Know-How Item: Monday Morning Escrow Check
#50	Trading Sardines & Currency Land

INTRODUCTION

The Truth is Only Momentary...and More

This book and its strategies and formulas represent part of the opening salvo of the creative real estate exchanging and business marketplace of the United States moving into the international marketplace. Currently, this being the beginning of 2010, there are approximately 100 creative real estate and business exchange groups in the United States meeting one to two days per month. There are two main national associations of creative thinkers that meet for marketing purposes: The Society of Exchange Counselors with approximately 100 members, that has been in business for approximately 50 years, and the National Council of Exchangors with approximately 300 members, that has been in business over 30 years. These groups meet three to six times a year, for from three days to a week, to do creative business transactions between themselves and their clients.

There is also the CCIM group, Certified Commercial Investment Member with approximately 12,000 members, that deals in sophisticated transactions under the umbrella of organized real estate but dealing primarily in the numbers business and not necessarily in the creative thinking arena.

The newest company, Deal Makers International S.A., which is designed specifically to operate in the creative international marketplace, is opened to both investors and entrepreneurs of all natures. These marketing meetings, currently scheduled for five-day tenures, will be held throughout the world in any country that is receptive to free enterprise.

Chet Allen, SEC, CCIM, EMS

Foreword

Real estate formulas are not thought up and invented just to create formulas. A formula's genesis is a creative agent running into a roadblock and a transaction that is about to fail. Nothing in the agent's experience works. In today's parlance, there are no solutions "inside the box." So a new formula gets created to solve a specific problem and ultimately, if the formula proves useful to others, it becomes one that is used throughout the creative real estate world.

No one has closed more creative transactions than Bob Steele. And he has been able to close them because he is the best "outside the box" thinker is real estate. A large portion of the formulas in this book were created by Bob, and were created because they were needed to close his transactions.

Bob is not a middle of the road thinker. He sees opportunities in places where most of us don't even look. I am not sure he knows the term "impossible." By not letting traditional belief systems inhibit him, Bob has been able to create. And his creations (his formulas) have significantly assisted the rest of us, who are in creative real estate, in closing transactions.

Bob is probably the most honored member of the creative real estate community. From being elected into the Exchangor's Hall of Fame to becoming a Society of Exchange Counselors' Legend; from his seminars to his books and articles; from co-creating the Real Estate Expo and The Real Estate News Observer to Global Wealth and Steele's Strategies; Bob has been at the forefront of change and growth.

This formulas book is just one of his many contributions to our industry.

I am honored to be able to write this forward.

Chet Allen, SEC, CCIM, EMS

STRATEGY 26

Assess Yourself vs. the Deal

If the shoe doesn't fit...

SITUATION	1. Assess what is important to you: Peace of mind, cash, cash flow, ego, stature, geography, your time, etc. 2. If it is a business deal, assess what it is going to cost you in money and time: If, as a broker, you take 10 listings a year, your overhead is $100,000 per year and you work an average of 2,000 hours a year; it means that for you to sign on a listing as a broker with a client it is going to cost you $10,000 in cash and 200 hours. Is the deal worth this investment? 3. In the above situation, who is taking the risk in this deal, you or the client?
POSSIBLE SOLUTION	1. Unless there are extenuating circumstances at least know what you are doing and don't waste your time. 2. Don't be locked to a percentage. If the listing will only generate $10,000 with a 5% fee, quote a 15% fee or something else to make it worthwhile, or don't do the deal. It is your option alone as to what you will work for.
CONCLUSION	1. You are only working on things that profit you. If you don't make a profit you won't be here tomorrow to help the next person. 2. If you can't find things that produce a profit go fishing or to the beach or go to a seminar.
NOTE	If you are entrepreneurial there are thousands of things to work on and invest your money and time on and there will be a thousand new ones tomorrow. There is never an end to opportunities.

STRATEGY 27

Are All the Legs in the Room?

If it takes two people to make a decision on a transaction, then you need four legs in the room or don't present the deal.

SITUATION	1. A serious key to deal making is making sure that everyone necessary to consummating the deal is in the room. Colloquially, you are wasting bullets and wasting your time to present to one person when it takes two people to make a decision. Wait until the two people are together. 2. Remember that if it is real estate you are discussing, that it is not just about bricks and mortar; add the people to the equation. I studied real estate in college. If I had it to do over I would study psychology. If the people have a scientific bent I would give them lots of numbers. If they are more earthy the last thing I would ever give them is a capitalization sheet and a lot of numbers.
POSSIBLE SOLUTION	1. Understand that people think differently and arrive at conclusions in different ways. You can actually have these different approaches in just two people so your presentation may have to be structured to accommodate both and they have to be in the room together for you to sense and know the nuances. 2. The last thing you need to be is Carl Jung but also you make a serious mistake if you make the presentation as though it were you on the other end. If you solve whatever it is that the other person(s) needs, you will usually get the transaction together.
CONCLUSION	If you are in a market where cash sales are almost impossible to find and that is all the client or other side will accept, then the sooner you go on down the road and do something else the better off you will be. The saying on the west coast is, "Head 'em west until their hat floats."

STRATEGY 28

Blanket Mortgage

SITUATION	1. Abel has a 10-unit apartment. He has upgraded it and it has good cash flow. 2. He would like to continue building his estate. 3. There are several formulas that he could use to accomplish this. 4. One is via using a blanket mortgage.	Price: Loan: Equity:	$ 1,000,000 - 400,000 $ 600,000
POSSIBLE SOLUTION	1. Baker's apartment: Locate another apartment that needs upgrading, perhaps it has some reverse cash flow or other problem that Abel knows how to solve.	Price: Loan: Equity:	$ 700,000 - 400,000 $ 300,000
	2. Offer $300,000 blanket mortgage secured by both apts. Both apartments are now security for the new debt.	Blkt Mtg.	$300,000
CONCLUSION	1. Baker has a total of $900,000 in security. It makes no difference whether the blanket mortgage is a 2nd TD on one building and a 3rd TD on the other. Terms of the blanket mortgage are negotiated. 2. Abel had $1,700,000 in assets and more units to upgrade, more tax shelter and leverage.	Total Value: Total Loans: Total Equity:	$ 1,700,000 - 1,100,000 $ 600,000
NOTES	1. Abel might consider building in a release clause for the first building at some point. 2. If in separate counties or states be sure recordings are made where necessary.		

STRATEGY 29

Consulting Time

SITUATION	1. Assess your thinking capacity: Little, medium or big. Same with the people you deal with. Same with all things in your life. 2. If you earn $500,000 per year you are probably in the medium category and your time is worth approximately $2,000 per day. Convert this to benefits and it means you probably can't afford to work on little deals. 3. Maybe you need to eliminate everything that brings in less that $10,000 per deal or benefits that approximate what that might mean to you.
POSSIBLE SOLUTION	1. Don't spend your time on people or things that do not make you feel fulfilled 2. If you are dealing with a person that only has a capacity to think at a certain level don't present to him/her things that are out of their stretch zone. 3. Present a $10,000,000 package at a national or international marketing session and present a $1,000,000 package at a local meeting.
CONCLUSION	Use your time wisely.

STRATEGY 30

Front Side, Back Side

It helps if you understand what is happening in your mind when you and/or a client are involved in an exchange.

Here most of the motivation is on the back side of the exchange: what's being left behind.

SITUATION	1. Abel is entertaining the exchange of property #1 which is vacant land with a loan on it and Abel can not handle the payments. 2. Baker owns 1/2 interest in a house with his ex-wife and they can't stand each other. The house is rented and has no reverse cash flow. Baker has plenty of net worth and personal cash flow and wants out out out of this situation. 3. Prince Galahad (you) are a broker for Abel and are emotionless.
POSSIBLE SOLUTION	Exchange #1 for #2
CONCLUSION	1. Abel's motivation is to get out of reverse cash flow. He is now out of reverse cash flow. The association in the half ownership interest in property #2 is less offensive than having the reverse cash flow. 2. Baker could care less about the reverse cash flow and is very happy to be out of the situation with his Ex. 3. Both had higher motivation on the back side in this transaction. The motivation on the back side solution was the key to the deal.

STRATEGY 31

Front Gate #1, #2 and #3

Change a 30-year loan to a 18-year (or 11-year). Every extra dollar you pay during the front end of a note equates to saving approximately ten dollars over the life of the loan and reduces the months remaining to pay off the loan.

SITUATION	Abel has a 30-year loan he is paying on in a face amount of $100,000. Interest at 8 ½%. Payment $768.91 per month.
POSSIBLE SOLUTION #1	Make one extra payment a year toward principal. *(This strategy was developed by Michael E. Stewart in training people who were borrowing money from his mortgage company. His company closed hundreds of millions of dollars in mortgages partly as a result of the unique training he gave his borrowers.)*
CONCLUSION	If you make one extra payment per year for 18 years, a total of $13,840.44 in excess principal payments, the loan will be paid off saving 12 years of payments, or $110,723.54.
POSSIBLE SOLUTION #2	Same situation. Pay $5,000 on principal now, one more in three years and one more in six years. You make no extra payments during the year.
CONCLUSION	Same result as in first example. Pay off loan in 18 years.
POSSIBLE SOLUTION #3	Combine and do both # 1 and # 2 above; e.g., one extra payment per year plus three $5,000 principal reductions over six years.
CONCLUSION	Loan pays off in 11 years.
NOTE	If you use a credit card at 23.99% to make the $5,000 reductions over 9 years, it costs $21,182. You still save almost $90,000.

STRATEGY 32
Tail Gate

Trade or sell the back end of the note, or maybe trade the balloon payment, or all or part of the interest, etc. This is called slicing and dicing in the stock game and then called a derivative.

SITUATION	1. Abel has a trust deed and note that is for \$100,000, payable interest only at 6% per annum, which is \$500 per month, and the principal amount is due and payable in three years. 2. Abel can use the monthly payments but he is also cognizant that inflation is really running about 15% per year and that when the balance of \$100,000 is paid off the purchasing value of the dollars received will be perhaps in the range of \$60,000. If so, he will be taking a loss of around \$40,000 in purchasing power for holding a dollar-denominated asset.
POSSIBLE SOLUTION	Exchange the back end of the note which is the balloon payment of \$100,000 for some asset that is growing.
CONCLUSION	He will continue to receive the \$500 per month but the person he exchanges with will receive the \$100,000 payment in three years.
NOTE	Analyze the assets you hold in the light of exchanging out that portion of the asset most subject to the ravages of inflation.

STRATEGY 33

Pencil Paralysis... The Death Knell for Entrepreneurs

Barter

SITUATION	1. Abel sees a business opportunity. She decides to think about it. A new idea shows itself the next day. She forgets about the first idea and decides to think about this new possibility and on infinitum. 2. She would like to increase her business but nothing seems to happen.
POSSIBLE SOLUTION	1. Write an offer when the opportunity presents itself. Not always, but usually, you can draft an offer that you would do regardless of what the other party might be seeking. 2. Deal making is the art of the positive. Don't try to analyze the other person's statements or writings. Offer what you will do. Don't waste your time saying what you won't do or saying that the other person is asking too much. 3. Write, write, write. Verbal offers, most of the time, don't work. A person must add his or her signature.
CONCLUSION	If you are not used to writing offers, keep score. Write down the offers you make and number them and see how many offers you have to make before you connect.
GUARANTEE	We guarantee that if you do write your offers down and number them, you will eventually make a connection. It might be the first one or the 50th one, but you will make a connection and make a deal. If, however, you have Pencil Paralysis and don't make offers, we guarantee you—you will not make a deal.

STRATEGY 34

Zeckendorf Technique #1

Zeckendorf was the epitome of the creative thinker in the real estate business.

SITUATION	1. Zeckendorf headquartered in the New York market but developed throughout the nation and Canada. He purchased and developed high rise buildings. 2. He said you always should be able to sell a building for three times what a real estate broker said it was worth 3. He asked, "How can I make this building worth $3,000,000?"	Price:	$ 1,000,000
POSSIBLE SOLUTION	1. The target price is $3,000,000. 2. He sold the land under the buildings and leased the land back. He developed a system in which he leased it back in 5 traunches which allowed him to maximize his sale price. (Please look up the Sandwich Lease formula elsewhere in this series of books). 3. He also sold the elevators, furnishings and so forth and leased those back. 4. They did not have the condo concept at that time or he would have used that also. 5. He then sold or often traded the leasehold building	Price:	$ 3,000,000
CONCLUSION	Dividing the real estate into pieces and creating a leasehold delivered a greater total price.		

STRATEGY 35

Zeckendorf Technique #2

Zeckendorf was the epitome of the creative thinkers in the real estate business.

SITUATION	1. Zeckendorf headquartered in the New York market but developed throughout the nation and Canada. He purchased and developed high rise buildings. 2. Creative thinkers take some chances but they often open up avenues that are successful that others never consider. 3. Zeckendorf had some innovative ideas on marketing.
POSSIBLE SOLUTION	1. He created air rights and then developed them over the Penn Central Station in New York. 2. He sold the concept to the board of Alcoa in one un-announced visit and developed the Century City Complex in Los Angeles. 3. He contracted to build the United Nations Building with one phone call. 4. The buildings he was building in Montreal were delayed and caused him to go bankrupt. He bought his business back out of bankruptcy and went back to his same chair and kept developing.
CONCLUSION	There are no ends to opportunities at any size. Zeckendorf said he could never understand why anyone would buy a duplex when they could buy a high-rise building instead.
NOTES	Zeckendorf was an extremely creative individual. The list of real estate transactions that he completed was historic. You can take almost any of the formulas he used and expand them into today's market and they create unending opportunities. For example, his air rights formula could be used in many areas of almost any city. Always be on the offense when you can.

STRATEGY 36

Zeckendorf - Dornbush (SEC) #3

Zeckendorf developed a formula he used with insurance companies in New York. Sturgis Dornbush, SEC used this same formula multiple times with industrial clients.

SITUATION	1. Zeckendorf wanted to buy a building occupied by an insurance company. They wanted a larger facility. 2. There were no buyers for their building except Zeckendorf and he didn't want to use money.
POSSIBLE SOLUTION	1. He found another larger building occupied by a larger insurance company. They also wanted a larger facility. He traded the smaller building into the larger one and continued the multi-exchange until he found another building for the second company. 2. He continued the trade process going up until his real estate commissions totaled enough to allow him to purchase the first building. 3. Sturgis Dornbush was working the same formula in the mid-west with industrial buildings and did several of these transactions.
CONCLUSION	In all multiple exchanges, at some point, there are enough commissions earned to buy out one property and close the deal if the real estate brokers are amenable to this.

STRATEGY 37

Is the Date Right?

This is an excellent philosophical strategy to understand when negotiating.

SITUATION	1. You have received an offer that is basically not acceptable. 2. However, there is always something right about most offers, even if it is only just the date on the offer.
POSSIBLE SOLUTION	1. If there is the slightest chance that it could go someplace, then try to counter offer. You can always make some offer. 2. Would you take the deal if the other side would offer an additional $1 million in cash? 3. Whoever wrote the offer was motivated for some reason. You have no idea how strong that motivation might be. Always counter offer if you can.
CONCLUSION	1. If you have a knowledgeable broker or investor on the other side of the transaction and if even a small part of an offer is acceptable, then you can get negotiations started, 2. The transactions must be of sufficient size to warrant the time it takes to negotiate. 3. If the other side is vociferous about why the transaction won't work, ask the broker or investor if the date is right. It always garners a funny look and you can explain why you said it and negotiations will usually get back on tract.
NOTES	1. Always be on the positive side when you can. 2. Some deals go together miles from where they started which would not happen if the deals were not kept alive.

STRATEGY 38

The Truth is Only Momentary

The truth can change like the wind. What I say now is the truth but something can happen in the next minute that, for me, changes that truth

SITUATION	1. The truth is only momentary. One minute its sunny and the next it's raining. 2. This is true about everything else. Everything. 3. A client (or you) might say I will only take something that I can drive to in one day. The next thing you know he/she has accepted something in another country. 4. Never believe the limitations you or a client sets. They change like the wind and if you search in just one area you will be missing opportunities.
POSSIBLE SOLUTION	1. When offered something outside your physical or mental take arena, and negotiations are bogged down, then sign off where you are and give the mind time to think about the possibilities. We will cover this in more detail later. 2. It is very important if you are representing others in a transaction that you do not impose your personal limitations on a possible deal as that client has his/her own right to make decisions and to succeed or fail. 3. Give clients a chance to become whatever it is they wish to be.
CONCLUSION	Is your connotation of the word Truth the same as it was at the top of this page? Every person in the world has a different connotation of that word.

STRATEGY 39

We Create from the Inside Out

When you ask a potential exchange client, "What will you take?", the client will usually go on a mental shopping trip. You basically can't go shopping with an equity like you can money so you are letting a client go a-field from reality.

SITUATION	1. Once they have said what they will take, which is just a mental image, you have created for them and yourself a golden calf to be revered. From the client's mind, after being asked what they would take, they said a commercial building. Then you, as a broker, go into the world trying to manifest that commercial building. If you don't ask that question, you open up the area of what they will take. A lot of other things could be acceptable, not just the commercial building. 2. A target makes sense to write into but if you lock down on the one target only you will preclude others that might write you an exchange offer if they want what you have. They will be hesitant to write if you say you will only take just the target item. 3. Again, never believe the limitations you or a client sets. They change like the wind and if you search just in one area you will be missing opportunities.
POSSIBLE SOLUTION	You can write out into certain directions but you want to leave the door open to receive offers from directions you have never considered.
CONCLUSION	This concept does not hold true for specific personalities. A developer wanting an inventory of land has a specific business target. But I have also seen where they might snap up a boat or an airplane that you had never discussed in counseling. Stay open.
NOTES	Always keep the door open.

STRATEGY 40

Who or What is the Most Important Thing in an Exchange?

The following is IMO (in my opinion).

SITUATION	As a broker in a transaction here are your choices for answers to the above question: a) your client b) your client's property c) the other client d) the other client's property e) the other broker f) financing g) geography
POSSIBLE SOLUTION	1. (IMO) It is always the other broker who is most important. 2. The property is inanimate and never hurts. 3. If the other broker is knowledgeable, many times that will circumvent other short-comings of the property, geography and/or finance. 4. I have closed up to 10 transactions with certain brokers. That weighs heavily, IMO, that the other broker is the most important thing in an exchange (as a general rule)
CONCLUSION	When a knowledgeable broker is presenting an opportunity or writing you an offer, pay close attention as the chances of success go up.
NOTES	You can mechanically improve your odds by transacting with brokers who can deliver.

STRATEGY 41

HOW TO OPERATE AT AN EXCHANGE MEETING

Everyone has a unique style but these are some of the things that can mechanically increase your odds of making a transaction at a meeting.

1. When you first walk into the room try to find a seat next to and hopefully between two brokers or investors who are known closers. Preferably ones you have closed transactions with before. **Your chances just went up.**
2. Have two sets of all the exchange packages you have put together and put them in front of these two people. During the day they will look them over. Ask each of them to show you their packages. **Your chances just went up.**
3. When someone is presenting his or her own property, don't leave the room as they have a better chance of delivering than someone else. **Your chances just went up.**
4. If the presenter says he/she has closed deals with this client before, or you know they have, don't leave the room. **Your chances just went up.**
5. If the presenter is presenting a third leg of an exchange, don't leave the room. The motivation is higher and **your chances just went up.**
6. Have a list of your properties or clients in front of you so you can bounce the idea of the presented package fitting with any of yours. Use different formulas to facilitate this. **Your chances just went up.**
7. Write a mini form offer on even the smallest hint of an idea. **Your chances just went up.**
8. Have lunch with someone who has a package you are interested in. **Your chances just went up.**
9. Do it now. If you see something that should go together and can call a client or a partner and have the property checked out while the meeting is going on so you can write a firm offer, **your chances just went up.**
10. Be the last one to leave the meeting if you can. In brainstorming we learn that the best ideas almost always come during the last part of the brainstorm when people and minds are thought out. **Your chances just went up.**

STRATEGY 42

HOW TO WRITE AN EXCHANGE OFFER

Remember the mind of the person you are writing to is more important than the property he/she owns. It is subtle but you are trying to connect to the subconscious not the conscious.

TECHNIQUE	1. Keep it very simple and use as few dollar signs as possible. The eyes go first to dollar signs so try to leave them out all together if possible. E.g., "A" will exchange his f/c land to "B" and assume B's loan of record. That transmits what is in one mind to another and there are no dollar signs used. 2. Put something in the offer they can take out without hurting your cause, this is often referred to as "the front porch," alluding to Dick Reno's ploy of asking them to fix the front porch even if it did not need fixing. Always give them something to take out. 3. All you need is one weasel clause. That will suffice and not clog up all the thinking. Due diligence answers most of these contingencies downstream and they never need to be mentioned. You can say, "subject to inspection and approval," and that can cover everything. 4. Mini-forms will usually suffice at meetings. Long forms can come into play if you definitely have a taker. Letters of intent are easy to develop when you are at your desk.

STRATEGY 43

NEGOTIATING AN EXCHANGE OFFER

Sometimes a mind can only move so far before it freezes up. Recognize when a mind is at that point. Stop negotiations, sign an agreement to what has been agreed to so far and send the offer back to the other side. After the mind rests and thinks about it, further progress can often be made.

TECHNIQUE

1. You almost always have some point from which to start. However, the transaction has to be large enough to warrant your time.
2. Always try to make the other side quit. You can always counter offer with something; "We will accept if you add $1,000,000 in cash." Keep the offer alive, you have no idea where it might go.
3. It is perfectly all right to add other properties, take properties out, bring in a partner, take a part of the transaction yourself with disclosure, etc.
4. Sometimes add counter offers to the bottom of the offer. Paste, scotch tape or staple. By doing so it dramatically shows the way the minds have been working on bringing the deal to fruition.
5. Mano y mano or eyeball to eyeball is always the best way. Nothing will ever replace personal contact for getting a deal done. If you are getting close and can get to the table, the personal contact will often close the gap and make it happen.

STRATEGY 44

BENEFITS THAT GROW

PROCESSING SMALL BENEFITS INTO LARGE ONES.

Like miners finding a small outcropping of minerals and following them to a lode, in counseling you might find a key thing or hear a significant phrase that might turn a transaction around. Exploit and magnify that item.

Dig, Dig, Dig. Learn your fundamentals better than anyone else.

EXAMPLE	1. In the late 1960 I read a short article about a new tax code #1031. The author hypothesized that it just might cause people to start exchanging. This was years before the Starker Law cases came down which allowed you to use money in the middle of an exchange. I could only find one teacher that taught true exchanging, Dick Reno. He had a five day class. Over the next five years I took his class five times (someone told me maximum retention was 20%) and I sent multiple clients to his class for counseling purposes. Benefit: I exchanged millions in real estate.	Find a key
	2. As a result of #1 above I was invited to join a group called the Society of Exchange Counselors (SEC) with none other than Dick Reno as founder and president. Within this group I met people who were willing to take calculated chances with their investments and their lives. As a result of that association I have owned or invested in a wide variety of items, dealt with clients with imagination, I have lived in several different countries, flown airplanes, fished throughout the world, hiked in some magnificent parts of the world, educated my children internationally, etc., etc.	Exploit it and become an authority
	3. At this time I am playing a role in helping to expand the exchange business into Panama, Latin America and the rest of the world. It is great fun.	Enjoy the fruits

STRATEGY 45

KNOW-HOW ITEM: KICK 'EM IN THE KIDNEYS

Or, Tip Over The Chair

SITUATION	1. Dick Reno had a saying that when those you were working with, whether associates or clients, strayed from the path, to kick them in the kidneys, meaning let them know in no uncertain terms that it was time to stay on track and get something accomplished. 2. The following are a few of these techniques I have seen used by various brokers over the years.
POSSIBLE SOLUTIONS	1. Art Hamel, a business opportunity broker, stood up in a fit of pique during negotiations, tipping his chair over backwards in the process and forcefully telling his client to stay on track. 2. Art Alwen, a real estate broker, looked another broker in the eye and, knowing that the other broker really did want the deal, said something to the effect that taking that approach had finally killed the deal. He then tore a long form real estate agreement he was presenting in half. The other broker acquiesced. 3. Chuck Chatham, a real estate consultant, had a rule that if a client was late for a meeting he would leave the office so that when the client did arrive, he was gone. Clients were seldom late the second time. 4. I had a client who owned a parcel of vacant land with high real estate taxes, around $100,000 a year, and this was one of the main reasons he wanted to exchange out of title. When he would get off track I would remind him that his taxes were costing him close to $10,000 a month or $2,000 a week, or I would ask him, "How much do those taxes cost you per hour?" The saying is "Stay focused."

STRATEGY 46

KNOW-HOW ITEM: THE EXTRA VALUE OF A USER

The person who is willing to work adds value to his/her assets.

SITUATION	1. The extra value of the user in a transaction is often overlooked. Most clients in our society today are looking for passive ownership, where they can obtain the benefits without the headaches. Things like hotels, motels, marinas, etc. require a user. Building a shopping center requires a user in the form of a developer. 2. These users are willing to roll up their sleeves and actively get involved in building their net-worth, cash flow, etc. 3. Sometimes they have the ability and the desire to tackle projects that are beyond their financial capability. This is often the case when a real estate broker finds a situation with a nice up-side potential, but requires financing or something else that is not available.
POSSIBLE SOLUTION	1. You simply build a team to do the project, whatever it might be. If you need an equity partner, design your transaction that way. If a user's client doesn't have the assets necessary to acquire a hotel he/she wants, simply go into the marketplace and find a partner, with assets to use, who wants passive ownership, and build a partnership plat-form as needed. 2. User-projects like hotels and motels are a combination of business and real estate. Whereas businesses, properly operated, have a higher financial yield than real estate, nice cash flow may be obtained along with leverage and growth.
NOTE	Covet a good user. If you have a client who acquires hotels and resorts or any other user type property—from developer to fish camp operators—they are wonderful people to work with once you know their criteria.

STRATEGY 47

KNOW-HOW ITEM: I'LL MAKE YOU QUIT IN NEGOTIATIONS

Or, No Linear Thinking.

SITUATION	1. I am making two assumptions here, and those are that the potential transaction merits the work and energy necessary, and that there are serious players involved. I learned this way back in the '70s and it has worked for me faithfully ever since. 2. If you make me an offer or I make you an offer, I will not quit in the negotiations. It will be up to you to kill the deal, not me or my client (this is assuming that there is a counseled client involved). 3. I can always counter you by asking you to add money, changing property (ies), taking on some of my debt, becoming partners, go into a 3-way deal, etc., etc., etc. I have had transactions close over a year after negotiations started and with completely different properties and assets involved.	
CONCLUSION	Transactions will close that you never thought possible if you use this technique. Peoples' minds, including yours, can only move so far at any given time. When you add the ingredients of additional time, a brainstorm and subconscious work, many things are possible that are normally by-passed.	

STRATEGY 48

KNOW-HOW ITEM: A ZERO MEANS NOTHING

A springboard to doing transactions with bigger dollar signs

SITUATION	1. Back in the '70s in the pre-Nixon era, we still had the fundamentals (not the actuality) of a gold standard and sound (er) money. Richard R. Reno, the mentor of the exchange business, often said that he thought that while the needs of the client were the primary motivator, the best size package (property) for exchanging in our marketplace was around $250,000. Remember that when this man wrote his book on exchanging and we had a solid gold backed currency, one of the examples he used was the exchange of a $6,000 house. 2. When Nixon embraced the economist Lord John Maynard Keynes (advocating going off the gold standard and government intervention in monetary policy and that a little bit of inflation was good for the economy) and we went off the gold standard, prices started to rise – slowly at first and then faster and faster until now (2010) we are looking over the horizon at possibly hyper-inflation (600% per year) and the prices are moving up fast.
POSSIBLE SOLUTION	By the late '70s I was having a problem wrapping my mind around moving from $50,000 packages to $500,000 packages and up. I came up with an idea and later wrote an article about it: "Why not just take off a zero." My mind could handle $50,000 deals but the $500,000 deals were a stretch. I just took off a zero in my mind and it all became easier. A broker friend of mine, Don DeBeau from Montana, later told me that he read the article and started to do the same thing and never again had a commission less than $50,000.
CONCLUSION	Poor Mr. Nixon was trapped but took the easy way out. He lost that battle for us and subsequently the dollar lost the war and inflation is rampant on a worldwide basis now as the dollar is the reserve currency of the world. Therefore, this simple little "Drop the Zero" formula could have a serious play in your mental future. We have moved from $500,000 packages to $5,000,000 packages (even single family homes) and the next steps will be $50 million and then $500 million. The die is cast. Use this formula if it helps and stay ahead of the curve. It, in all probability, is coming.

STRATEGY 49

KNOW-HOW ITEM: MONDAY MORNING ESCROW CHECK

Something you want to get done this week is stuck on someone else's desk. The time to get that item unstuck is Monday morning.

SITUATION	1. There is always something that we have to get done in the business world that requires action by someone else. Everyone has his own idea of what is important and those are usually the items that get done first. Procrastination and stonewalling are definitely in play. 2. In my business of real estate there are always things that have to be done, and escrow agents usually have many files they are working on. It is important that your files do not end up on the bottom of their "to do" lists.
POSSIBLE SOLUTION	1. Routinely call everyone who is doing something for you on Monday morning. Try to establish a time for the items to be completed. 2. If people lose patience with you always calling them, simply tell them that the easiest way to get the phone calls to stop is to get their job done. When they know you will religiously be calling them every Monday until it is completed, they tend to get their job done. 3. E-mails are OK but not as effective as voice communication.

STRATEGY 50

Trading Sardines & Currency Land

"Trading sardines" are usually personal properties that have little utilitarian value, and "currency land" is represented by the multi-millions of acres of desert and mountain wasteland that will probably never come into the developing arena for perhaps hundreds of years.

SITUATION	1. Just like every business, real estate has its junk dealers and there are those who say that the junk dealers in automobiles make more money than the new car dealers. Ours is not to reason why but to explain. 2. Thousands of people, for instance, own lands that are actually useless. Some say the land is there just to hold the world together. The sale market is almost non-existent for these people so it is only natural that they have found their way into the exchange market. 3. Likewise there are million of dollars worth of gem stones, etc.	Example: A section of desert land (640 acres) is on the market for exchange at $250 per acre: $160,000. There never will be any "comps" but someone highly motivated to get out of the other real estate might accept the land. For instance, everyone in foreclosure would. If the owner of this land would add $100,000 cash to the deal, hundreds of people would accept it.
POSSIBLE SOLUTION	1. These two items, Trading Sardines and Currency Land, are places where someone can hold all or part of their equity for a while to solve another problem and then comeback and re-trade it into something they can use later. 2. One I will never understand: I had a client that owned a $500,000 hard money 2nd TD/note representing money he had loaned on an apartment house in Phoenix, Ariz. All the notes on the property were in default and the 1st TD was foreclosing underneath him. I got him an offer for 2,000 acres of desert land ($250 per acre) He refused because he said no one would want desert land, and he ended up loosing all his equity.	$500,000 TD being lost. Could have had 2,000 acres of currency land at a hypothetical value of $250 per acre. There are some smart people that use currency land in concert with cash to trade for T.Ds. (often being created) in the exchange market. The client above had the ability to do that but chose instead to lose his equity.

NOTES

NOTES

300 Strategies for Making Real Estate & Business Deals

Volume 3

Strategies 51 - 75

25 Formulas & Strategies Creative Real Estate Level 3

ROBERT W. STEELE

Foreword by Arlene Wright-Correll

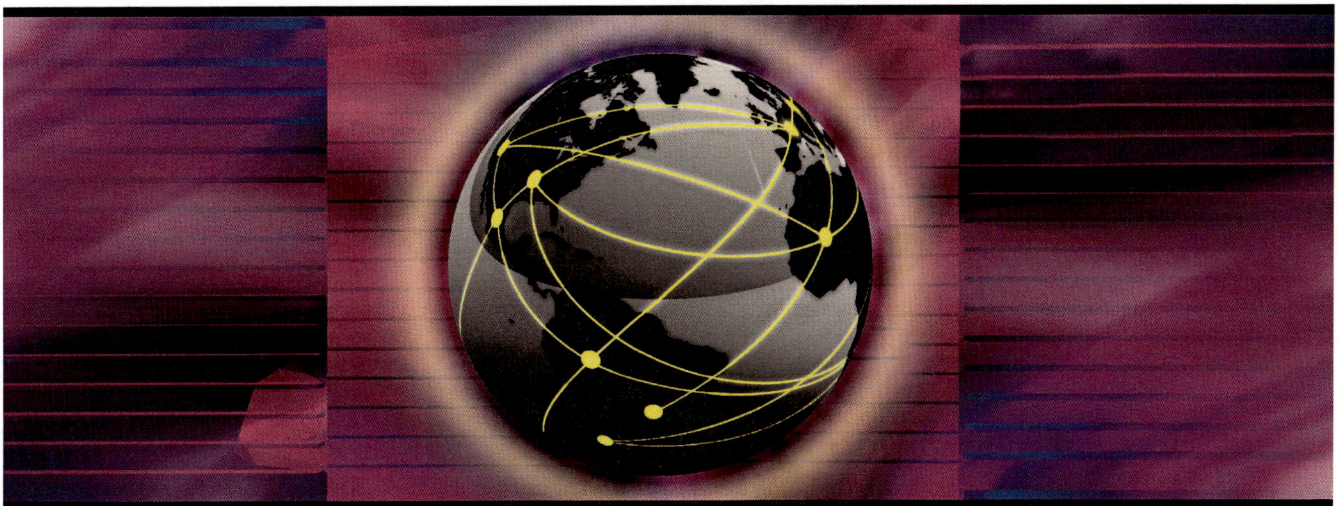

Outside the Box & Inside / Outside the Country

300 Strategies for Making Real Estate & Business Deals

Outside the Box & Inside / Outside the Country

VOLUME 3

Strategies 51 – 75

25 FORMULAS & STRATEGIES CREATIVE REAL ESTATE, LEVEL 3

by Robert W. Steele

Foreword by Arlene Wright-Correll

Design, Layout & Graphics
Victoria Vinton
Coyote Press Graphic Communications
www.coyotepressgraphics.com

VOLUME 3
CONTENTS

Introduction
Foreword: Arlene Wright-Correll

Strategy	Title
#51	Trade Percentage of Ownership
#52	Funding with Sale of Notes plus Courage
#53	Idea Tracking
#54	Taker Tracker Form
#55	Baseball Formula
#56	Keep the Income in a Trade
#57	"I'll Pay More Than You Ask, If..."
#58	Move from Defense to Offense
#59	Gold and Silver Retirement Plan
#60	Stutter Mortgage
#61	A-Bag, B-Bag
#62	Definance
#63	Personal Notes to Balance Equity
#64	Creating a Leasehold
#65	Creating a Leasehold in an Exchange or Sale
#66	Present the Correct Package for the Market You are In
#67	Over-Trade
#68	Specialty Clients (Like Users) & Partners
#69	The Buyer is a Potential Lender
#70	The Tenant Solution
#71	Two Plus Three Equals Two
#72	Creativity—We are Going to Need It
#73	Liquidate and Diversity
#74	The Easiest 3-Way Exchange There Is
#75	Prediction Heard: "Only 27% of the Real Estate Fraternity Will Weather the Storm"

INTRODUCTION

Creative Real Estate, Level 3

This volume moves us from learning how to exchange a percentage of interest in real estate through learning how to use hard assets like gold and silver to stabilize our retirement needs. It moves on to the last strategy that recites a prediction that only 27% of those in the real estate business will weather the storm that currently exists in the real estate market, and concludes with a quote from Doug Casey, researcher, that one of the main things you are going to need in order to survive and prosper is the knowledge on how to think creatively.

We, of course, modestly suggest that you read our Volume 7 in this series of books, "The Art & Science of Brainstorming, Obtaining Ideas Not Available through Conventional Thinking." This book will start you off on thinking creatively in these challenging times.

How close this prediction comes to reality is a guess at this time but we do know that the majority of residential real estate people are programmed for just selling real estate. They will suffer the most as well as the investors in that category. This being 2010 we know that the commercial market is running about three years behind the residential market so the commercial brokers will last longer.

It is so very important right now that we acknowledge that the real estate business is not just made up of Bricks and Mortar but people. The buildings are inanimate; it is the people that hurt. The sooner the brokerage fraternity and the investors realize that there are a lot of ways to move assets other than just cash, the sooner this market will start moving again.

Learning these strategies is a major step in the right direction.

Thanks and good luck,

Robert W. Steele

Arlene Wright-Correll

Foreword

Little did I know years ago when I attended a Bob Steele Seminar that I was on the way to my destiny. One of the things that his seminars taught me is that there is more to real estate than bricks and mortar. I learned that real estate itself rarely has a problem unless there is a hole in the roof or the plumbing is broken. Most real estate problems revolve around ownership and the reasons why people are buying, selling or exchanging it. The people are the point, the focus if you will, not the property. Through studying Bob's books I have learned the art of the deal and how to become a true problem solver. The advanced formulas in Volume 3 have helped me in my ability to work with clients with more complicated situations. In fact, the 300 formulas in all of the books have become my bible and have supported me in becoming one of the top exchangors in the United States

There is a delight in knowing that the formulas in these books have not only known the test of time, but have continued to be workable today regardless of what else is transpiring in the real estate field. What you have in these books are TRUE formulas that transcend time and worldly conditions. They are applicable no matter what else is transpiring in real estate.

School is never out and those of you who have the foresight to ride the winds of destiny will purchase not only this volume, but all of Bob Steele's volumes and become a leader in the field of helping people with their real estate situations.

Remember that you only have to win 51 percent of the time to become a top gun. Babe Ruth may have been surpassed as the home run king, but he was never surpassed as the strikeout king.

Reading Bob Steele's books and attending his workshops and seminars will make you a true survivor and winner in the world of real estate exchanging and creative deals. Remember, you must be a problem solver in order to succeed and Steele is the Babe Ruth of problem solvers!

Tread the earth lightly. And in the meantime ...

May your days be filled with ... Peace, Light and Love,

Arlene Wright-Correll

STRATEGY 51

Trade Percentage of Ownership

This can be used as an exit strategy or as a way to bring an entity into ownership with you to solve a problem.

SITUATION	1. Abel owns a 1/10 undivided interest in a $5,000,000 ranch that is controlled by his ex-wife's family. 2. He is being pushed around and does not receive his proper share of the revenues from the operation. 3. He does not want to start a lawsuit. 4. His position is untenable.	Price: Percent: Equity	$5,000,000 10% $ 500,000
POSSIBLE SOLUTION	1. Go on the offense. 2. List your 1/10 interest in the property with an exchange broker. Be willing to add cash or other assets as a sweetener if you can. 3. This equity is real. You do not need anyone's permission to exchange what you own as long as you are a registered title owner. 4. Exchange or transact for benefits.	Price:	$500,000
CONCLUSION	Who would take this position? Hundreds of people. You could probably get a dozen attorneys that would exchange you pre-paid attorney's fees for this position and you could exchange the attorney's fees on in a 3-way. It is not hard to find an exchange but you would have to be flexible. You can't go shopping with this. You can use this in other ways: If you owned this $5,000,000 property, you could offer to exchange 10% of this ($500,000) for a house you might want. There are no rules.		
NOTE	Always be on the offense when you can.		

STRATEGY 52

Funding with Sale of Notes (either personal or secured) plus Courage

Funding for little deals to major ones: If you can go to your bank and borrow $10,000, $100,000 or $1,000,000 and you use your personal Note with them, why can't you use these same Notes in other ways?

WANTED: BUSINESS OPPORTUNITY	Little deal: Abel, in concert with three other people, wanted to start a private money mortgage business. There were also several investors wanting to have this happen.	Start with an Idea
FUNDING WITH AIR	Abel and the three others each put a $10,000 personal Note into the corporation, formed to house the mortgage company, to buy their stock in the company.	Add Know-How and Courage
OPERATING CAPITAL	The Company sold these personal Notes to investors at a discount of 15% and received back into the corporation $8,500 cash for each of the four Notes for a total of $34,000. This cash was sufficient to incubate the new company and the company paid off the Notes for Abel, et. al., as agreed, from profits. The payoff of the Notes resulted in investors receiving dividends on their stock.	They Become Operating Capital
COULD YOU BUY ANYTHING YOU WANTED THIS WAY? WHAT PART DOES COURAGE PLAY?	Larger deal: A broker put together the acquisition of a large cattle ranch plus timber holdings in Oregon by syndicated a group of investors. Many of the investors created large TD/Notes against their real estate holdings to acquire their interest in the syndicate. The syndicate sold these TDs and Notes for cash to use as part of the purchase.	The largest real estate deal ever made in Orange County, CA, the purchase of the Irvine Company, was derived from this formula.

Strategy 53

Idea Tracking

This is a derivative of the Forced Relationship Brainstorming technique. I developed this form for my own use both at exchange meetings and for my own brainstorming. It forces me to consider the exchange possibility between two clients and then to use different formulas. There is no end to the possibilities. Thanks to Ron Bowden, a friend, for this design of the technique. On a scale of 1 to 10, this rates 9 as a functional tool that delivers deals that close.

There are over 5,000 ideas on this page

IDEA TRACKING

Client or Package

Broker	Package								Ideas/Thoughts

Formulas and Questions:

1. Would I take this?
2. Would he take mine?
3. Could two of mine take his?
4. Could I take part of his?
5. Is there a 3-way on the page?
6. Do two other brokers match in a 3-way?
7. Exchange - Buy Back
8. Leasehold
9. Share of wealth
10. Subdivide
11. Thief
12. Defianace
13. Creation of Wealth
14. Exchange and Lease-back
15. Un-Built building.
16. Refinance
17. In-lieu-of
18. Use of personal Notes
19. % of interest.

Courtesy of R.W. Steele and Richard Reno Educational Foundation

STRATEGY 54

Taker Tracker Form

Form for looking for a multiple transaction courtesy of Ron Bowden

TAKER TRACKER FORM

This is neither an offer nor acceptance - merely an idea of how we might identify a multi-leg exchange

FROM:	TO:
PHONE: FAX: EMAIL:	PHONE: FAX: EMAIL:

MY CLIENT: PROPERTY:	YOUR CLIENT: PROPERTY:

TAKER: My client may be a taker for your property. If we can't do a two-way exchange, I may be able to help deliver one of the properties listed below which have indicated that they are takers for my property. Please forward my property package and this list to anyone who has what you want, but who is not interested in your property. You may have better luck finding what you need with my property or one of the properties listed below and we'll have a multi-leg transaction.

MULTI-LEG POSSIBILITIES: I have received the following taker proposals:

	TAKER #1	TAKER #2	TAKER #3	TAKER #4
Description:	______	______	______	______
	______	______	______	______
O.V. $	______	______	______	______
Loans $	______	______	______	______
Equity $	______	______	______	______
Agent	______	______	______	______
Attached	☐	☐	☐	☐

	TAKER #5	TAKER #6	TAKER #7	TAKER #8
Description:	______	______	______	______
	______	______	______	______
O.V. $	______	______	______	______
Loans $	______	______	______	______
Equity $	______	______	______	______
Agent	______	______	______	______
Attached	☐	☐	☐	☐

NOTE: This list of takers is neither an offer nor acceptance. It is intended to stimulate discussion between us about potential multi-leg transactions. Under no circumstances shall this proposal be considered a contract or part of a contract. My property will not be withheld from the market unless our clients agree otherwise in a written and executed long form exchange agreement. If you have any questions, please ask.

STRATEGY 55

Baseball Formula

You can't get back a called strike.

BASEBALL SITUATION	When an umpire makes a really bad mistake and calls an obvious ball a strike, it is absolutely futile for the batter to argue. To date, an umpire has never reversed his call but he is a human being and often knows he makes the error, but posture precludes him from correcting it. If you, the batter, start berating the umpire, he is not only embarrassed but forced to defend his position, and he is not happy with you. The way to handle it is to say something like the following without ever looking at the umpire: "George, you really really missed one that time. You owe me one." You are not arguing for the strike that has already passed you, you are negotiating for the next close call to go in your favor.
REAL ESTATE SITUATION	If you are negotiating and you run into a deal breaker or a point that the other side is adamant about and you are going to lose the negotiated point no matter what, then move on past it—but make your point to the people on the other side that, "they owe you one," and then someplace down the line, when you have a point you really want, remind them.

Strategy 56

Keep the Income in a Trade

(Formula to mitigate the risk and/or leverage the upside using a stock formula.)

Great formula for growing a corporation. This also is a good ploy when you are taking a property some distance from your base. The lease-back makes the property management free.

SITUATION	The owner has a $500,000 office building with a $300,000 loan. The building net cash flows $25,000 per year.	
KEEP THE INCOME	The company trades him $200,000 in stock for his equity and lets him lease back for two or three years, giving the owner all the cash flow.	
LEVERAGE	If he is willing to roll the dice on a public company, his upside may be much greater than holding the building equity and at the same time the building equity is added as a plus to the corporate balance sheet.	
AUTHOR'S NOTE	Whenever you move from one field of endeavor to another, you will find there are new strategies and formulas available. The same thing is highlighted when you move assets into the international arena and each country has different laws. You can do something legally in one country that is illegal in another. All kind of avenues open up.	

STRATEGY 57

"I'll pay more than you ask if..."

Fiat currency makes a mockery of convention. Be willing to step out of the box and make proposals that are non-conventional. There are hundreds of variations of this formula.

SITUATION	1. Abel wants to buy a building that Baker has priced at $1,000,000. It has a value of $700,000 to $800,000. Assuming this is a reasonable income-producing building, Net Operating Income $6,000, would you be willing to pay Baker a price higher than he asked, perhaps $1,400,000, nothing down and $3,000 per month with no interest until paid (approx 39 years)? 2. There is a very soft sales market, almost non-existent. 3. The building is free and clear	Price: Worth: Offer:	$1,000,000 700,000 $1,400,000
POSSIBLE SOLUTION	1. Real estate people usually say this can't be done. Stock brokers believe that it can and they do it all the time with TIGRs and Strips (bonds). 2. Do whatever it takes to make the deal work. If Baker won't take the deal but is willing to go in-lieu-of, meaning 3-way, then trade the $1,400,000 paper into something else that will satisfy Baker. A lot of people will take a $1,400,000 1st TD paying $3,000 per month for 39 years. Some people live on less than that.	Go 3-way if needed	
CONCLUSION	1. Abel gets building and cash flow. Baker gets a high price. 2. Abel has inflation on her side		
NOTE	Price is just one ingredient in the deal. They can have almost any price they want if you can have your terms.		

STRATEGY 58

Move from Defense to Offense

If you are on the defense with a property where you are waiting for something positive to happen, try to find a way to go off the defense and go on the offense.

SITUATION	1. Abel has been trying to sell a building for three years. There is a loan on the building that is eating Abel's lunch. 2. Abel has managed to keep the loan payments current but he is using up his life savings to do so. 3. There does not appear to be any solution and the unfortunate thing is that for three years now, while playing defense, Abel could have been spending his time on something positive.
POSSIBLE SOLUTION	At some point Abel will run out of the ability to make these payments. So the question becomes, would you rather stop making the payments while you still have some savings or quit making the payments when you are broke? One Option: Make up a deed in-lieu-of foreclosure in favor of the lender and make a copy of it. Send the copy with a letter when you make your next payment. Tell the lender that you can no longer make the payments asked for but you can make this much smaller payment (which does not require you to use your savings). If this is not satisfactory, you will send them the deed to the property.
CONCLUSION	Go on the offense. There are many ways to do this. You mind needs to stay on something positive.

STRATEGY 59

Gold & Silver Retirement Plan

Silver Used in This Example.

PROBLEM	1. If you realize that saving dollar denominated assets is foolish if a country's fiat currency is heading into high inflation or hyper-inflation, then what should you do with capital that you want to keep liquid but you don't want to devalue? 2. This formula is for those who truly do not want to gamble. However, some are so sold on the dollar that anything else is called unsafe when actually the opposite is true. Gold and silver are money, not the dollar bill. My authority is the constitution.	The time of this writing is 2010. This strategy we have in play with several clients and some for over five years. 100% are working. No matter how you analyze this and compare it with dollars in a savings account, this is the better of the two. You are withdrawing part of the principle to live on so your corpus is diminishing. The inflation ravaging your dollars in the savings account is also taking away your purchasing power and even with withdrawal of principal, silver is ahead substantially. Simple test: Multiple ounces of silver by price and it will continually add up to more dollars than are in the savings account.
POSSIBLE SOLUTION	1. I am sure this formula has been around since the beginning of time. We initiated it when silver was in the $4.00 per oz. bracket. 2. Set your retirement plan based on how much you would require a month for living expenses. For estimate purposes, let's say you want $15,000 per month. 3. Put $200,000 of your savings or investment capital into silver. 4. That will buy you 50,000 oz. of silver. 5. Every time silver goes up 1 cent you make $500. It needs to go up .30 cents a month to make your $15,000 target.	
CONCLUSION	1. The gold and silver assets go up in value every time something bad happens in the economy. It is truly the right hedge. It is always easy, looking backwards, to see what you should have done—Monday Morning Quarterbacking. If you see a rosy future in front of you now, then this formula is not for you. If it does, however, look a little suspect, you might think about implementing this ASAP. 2. This is tax-deferred Balance Sheet asset. Not Profit & Loss.	

STRATEGY 60

Stutter Mortgage (or Note)

These Notes are designed so the payments are not standard. Design a Note anyway you want. Make the Note do the work you want done and don't be locked to convention.

TECHNIQUES	Stutter Notes originated with payments from farms, resorts and the ilk that had seasonal income. The Notes are designed for payments only during certain times of the year. We have used these Notes in a variety of other ways: 1. One or more months a year no payments are required. 2. Some months no interest is charged and the entire payment goes on principal. (See Stewart's formula in Volume 3 about paying off 30 year mortgages in 11 or 18 years called "Front Gate"). 3. Build a Note to wrap other financing and part of the Note bears one rate of interest and another part of the Note bears another. 4. This can include balloon payments on one section of the Note and not on another. 5. Part of the Note can be based on a performance of some nature (see Performance Notes or TDs) and the other on standard payments.
NOTES	1. When designing Notes on properties in the desert make no payments or low payments during summer months. 2. You can design Notes in a performance nature that during the most prosperous time of the year the Note bears a higher interest rate. That allows the beneficiary to enjoy a large return during the high season. 3. Notes can be a great tool for negotiating as there are so many options open.

STRATEGY 61

A-Bag, B-Bag

SITUATION	A-Bag — Keepers B-Bag — Sell, convert to an A, trade or let go.	
POSSIBLE SOLUTION	1. There are different philosophies as to what is an A-Bag or B-Bag item so it is your connotation that counts. 2. I use this for both assets, people and situations. If something or someone makes me feel positive, I consider it or them as part of my A-Bag. 3. If the opposite is true then it or they are in the B-Bag. 4. If I get a negative connotation when I think about it or them, they are in my B-Bag.	
CONCLUSION	1. People sometime spend years working on B-Bag items. Don't spend your time trying to save something that can't be saved. 2. Some times A-Bag items can slip back into the B-Bag so be sure to re-analyze the status of assets from time to time. 3. See Volume 2 for Currency Land and Trading Sardines. These would both fall in the B-Bag category.	

STRATEGY 62

Definance

Definance refers to moving financing against or secured by real property, but the connotation extends beyond just that usage.

SITUATION	1. Client Abel has a small apartment property which he would like to exchange with Baker. For information purposes, this 2nd TD is payable at $750 per month including interest at 6% and no due date. 2. Baker has free and clear land valued at $1M. 3. Both parties would like to make this exchange but Baker will not accept Abel's land with the 2nd TD on it.	Price Loans: 1st TD 2nd TD Equity Price	$2,000,000 1,000,000 100,000 $ 900,000 $1,000,000
POSSIBLE SOLUTION	1. Negotiate with the beneficiary of the 2nd TD to see if they will Defiance the 2nd TD and move it over on to Baker's property land, which will be owned by Abel after the ex-change. 2. There are several things that might be done to encourage the beneficiary to make such a move. It is a benefit to have Abel still making the payment, as Baker is accustomed to working with Abel. You could increase the interest rate from 6% to 8% or 10%. You could increase the payments to $1,000 per month or $1,500, you could add a 5-year due date to the Note, or you could offer to pay his Note down by $20,000, etc.		
CONCLUSION	Baker ends up with Abel's apartment with just a 1st TD on it.		
NOTE	Definance also refers to eliminating a partner from a partnership. Separating anything from an association can be referred to as definancing.		

STRATEGY 63

Personal Note(s) to Balance Equity

Personal Notes are representative of the malleable forms of paper with which we have to work. They can be designed to solve a lot of situations.

SITUATION	You can effectively change the cash flow from one property to another using two Notes with different payment schedules. An example: A client was exchanging out of a cash-flowing property into one with negative cash flow and was concerned about the reverse cash flow during the time he was remodeling the building he was going into.
POSSIBLE SOLUTIONS	We added to the exchange with each party giving the other party a $50,000 personal Note. The Note received by the party going into the negative cash flow property had payments on it of $3,000 per month including interest. The Note received by the one going into the cash-flowing property had no payments on it (interest accumulating) for two years giving the other party the time it needed to get the negatively flowing building up and producing income. The one very difficult problem was mitigated. The person going into the negative cash flow property had the cash needed to make the deal work.
CONCLUSION	There are many forms of paper to work with. If your business is real estate, you are not locked to using trust deeds or mortgages.

There are many forms of paper to work with:

- Personal Notes
- Trust Deeds
- Mortgages
- Contracts
- Bonds
- Trusts
- Options
- Sight Drafts
- Letters of Credit
- Performance Agreements
- Chattels
- Inheritances
- Subdivision Trust Agreements
- Foreign Documents of all kinds

STRATEGY 64

Creating a Leasehold

This is an excellent tool that could be used a lot more than it is. It has extensive use in areas where there is a finite amount of land in particular islands such as Hawaii or England. I have found it viable on land expected to appreciate such as waterfront or view property. It also has a lot of uses as a problem-solving tool.

Years ago when I was teaching creative real estate classes, I lived in Newport Beach, California. The Irvine Company was next door and they had thousand of acres of land that they were developing, subdividing, leasing and creating leasehold estates. I would visit their leasing department every year to find out what was new in their technique, as they had to be one of the forerunners of the technique in the U.S. They happily shared this information with me for my classes and I was able to take advantage of the knowledge for use in my own business.

SITUATION	Visualize what is happening in a leasehold: For those who have not previously separated a building from the land, you can start to understand the leasehold by thinking of a vacant lot first. This lot is leased for a period of time (10 years to 200 + years). The lessee has a leasehold interest in the land. They use their own money to build a building on the lot. They own the building and they are leasing the land. There are no loans on the building. The land-lease is primary or in first position. If the lessee does not make lease payments, the land owner has the right to evict them and they lose their building. If the lessee wants to borrow money to build the building, there are two choices: Either the land-lease is in first position or the land-lease subordinates and the mortgage is in first position. We had lenders in Newport Beach who would allow their loans to be secondary providing the first re-evaluation period on the land-lease was at least as long as the loan. If it were a 20-year loan, the lease payments could not increase for at least 20 years. I have found that you can sometimes get the lessor to allow subordination if you put up another asset as additional security during the period of subordination.

STRATEGY 65

Creating a Leasehold in an Exchange or Sale

The majority of times that you create a leasehold in an exchange situation there will already be a loan on the property. You do not have to move the loan. The land-lease just automatically is initiated in a subordinate position to the loan or loans of record. You can be trading either the building or the land, whatever suits your purpose.

SITUATION	1. You are working with a $4,000,000 building. You have a loan of $2,000,000 and the land has an estimated value of $1,000,000. You like your building but you would like to grow your estate and increase your holdings.	Total value	$4.000,000
		Loan	2,000,000
		Equity	2,000,000
	2. Offer to exchange the land that is under the building for $1,000,000 into other real estate that you would like to own. Lease the land under the building back for 100 years (if the leasehold interest exceeds 30 years it can be treated as a 1031 item for a tax deferred exchange). Whereas you will be making the payments on the land- lease, offer a land-lease payment that suits you. Let's suggest 5%.	Offer leased land for exchange	$1,000,000
CONCLUSION	1. You should have a lot of people who would like to make an exchange with you on this package as it is neutral, no management and income producing.	Equity in 1st property	$1,000,000
	2. Your equity in the original property is now $1,000,000 and you own some other property acquired in the exchange that also has a $1,000,000 equity.	Equity 2nd property	$ 1,000,000
	3. A lot of other things need to be considered such as re-evaluations on the lease, future re-development of the property, option to tie the land and building back together, abandonment of lease, etc. You will find a copy of a generic land-lease in our *Creative Forms* book and we also have for sale a full leasehold document kit with copies of everything one might need to initiate land-leases.	Total Eq.	$2,000,000

STRATEGY 66

Present the Correct Package for the Market You are In

By presenting a package or offer that can be handled by the majority of people you are dealing with, you will have a higher percentage of closed transactions.

SITUATION	1. Richard Reno use to say that he thought the best package to present at an exchange meeting was around $250,000. What he meant by that was that the majority of brokers or principals in the room could make a deal of this size. 2. Today, of course, the falling dollar and the subsequent inflation have made his standards obsolete. Just estimating that it is maybe 10 times higher today, then perhaps the easiest investment package to move is between $2,000,000 and $3,000,000.	
SOLUTIONS	1. Also it makes a difference as to where you present packages. If you are at a local exchange meeting, then the $2,000,000 to $3,000,000 package is about right. If you have a $10,000,000 package it is probably best to present it at a regional or national marketing session. 2. Now that international investment meetings are taking place, if you have a $10,000,000 or $100,000,000 package, that is the place to present it. 3. If you are working with someone else, if you present opportunities that are sized to that person's capacity or norm, you will probably have more success.	

STRATEGY 67

OVER-TRADE

The Over-Trade is usually used to accomplish something on the back side of the exchange (the property you are going out of).

I saw this formula used one time in a test in which the broker made maybe as many as ten over-trades in one ongoing exchange where he had everything as an un-priced item and kept moving through properties just taking benefits off the back side (the property he was leaving).

SITUATION	Abel has some free and clear land in California. Value $1,000,000. He would like to create some action but there is no market to sell his land at this time. It is on the market to exchange and Abel will also entertain an over trade. (It can be likened to a deferred multiple exchange – not a 1031-type because cash cannot be generated at this time—or it can be closed in a 2-way exchange and then moved on later to another property.)
OVER-TRADE #1	You offer the land into some vehicle that has less equity (less than $1 million). The main criteria for the other property is something that fits what you are trying to accomplish. Let's say we offer in and are accepted on a house in Florida priced at $1,500,000, a loan of $750,000 with $750,000 equity. You ask them to give you back a $250,000 first TD/Note to balance equity on your land on terms agreeable to both parties. The building owner has to be motivated to do this deal and Abel assumes the role of problem solver. There could be many reasons, let's just say the client wants his equity back in California.
OVER-TRADE #2	Your over-trade to this point has generated you one $250,000 piece of paper (TD/Note). You can leave the house priced or make it un-priced at this point. Offer it back into the exchange market where you will accept something else that has less equity, in other words another over-trade. You are offered a small $500,000 free and clear farm in a small town in Nebraska where the owners want to move to Florida to retire. You accept, providing they give you back a $250,000 2nd TD on the Florida house on agreeable terms to balance equity. They accept. At this point you have $500,000 in paper, two $250,000 TD/Notes & a $500,000 farm in Nebraska.
CONCLUSION	You know now how an over-trade works. You can continue or stop trading at any time.

STRATEGY 68

Specialty Clients (like users) & Partners

Specialty clients and partners add a great deal to the life of an entrepreneur. Particularly when they are users. Users are people or companies that will roll up their sleeves and add their business acumen and time to developing businesses or properties.

SITUATION	Let me start by discussing a motel owner that I worked with for several years. He had a unique system patterned after an idea garnered from Art Hamel's (an SEC) business seminar (I keep mentioning sending clients to seminars so they learn and are counseled). He wanted motels with a minimum of 40 units (no maximum but they were all below 100 units) with no restaurants but contiguous to one. The three had to be in a series of three motels, each within a four-hour drive of the others. He then used one manager and three assistant managers for the three motels and would move on and acquire three more. I don't know exactly how many were acquired but it was approximately 15. All but two were acquired by exchanging.	When you learn the system of a user or partner, it is relatively easy to spot what will work for them. Once you have closed a transaction with someone, the second one is always easier as the ice is broken. When you have confidence in someone else that she will perform, you are willing to invest more capital and time on her behalf. As mutual trust is established bigger risks and rewards are a possibility.
POSSIBLE SOLUTIONS	I am going to list here other users and partners I have dealt with in exchanging and you will start to see how repetitive this business can be. Once a partner or client is established, multiple transactions happen. The number of transactions listed are realistic estimates: Motels ... 15 House (SFR) acquirer ... 25 Apartment building acquirer ... 15 Builder - development project ... 10 Land for improved property client ... 25 Boats for a sport fishing company ... 7	
CONCLUSION	User clients and partners create an ongoing business relationship for an entrepreneur.	

STRATEGY 69

The Buyer is a Potential Lender

When someone writes you an offer in an exchange there is motivation that is causing that action. That motivation can sometimes be channeled into additional benefits.

SITUATION	1. Let's assume you are being offered $500,000 in TDs /Notes in an exchange. This is very secure paper but the payment and interest are soft. This basically will work for you or your side of the deal 2. You could get by without cash but it would be nice to have a little walking around money.	Income from Notes would be acceptable to you. Perhaps you can borrow some of that income, in advance, from the buyer.
POSSIBLE SOLUTION	1. You counter offer that you will make the deal if the other side will loan you $50,000 cash against the TDs you are taking in the deal and on favorable terms. 2. You treated the buyer as thought she were a lender. 3. There are other ways to utilize this person's motivation. For instance you can, in the course of negotiations, find out what other assets this party might have to work with.	Income from the TDs will retire the loan from the buyer.
CONCLUSION	1. Let's say she has a small $500,000 farm. You might then counter the offer for the TDs you are going to accept anyway and say that you will accept them if she will give you a pre-paid 6-month option to purchase this farm for $400,000 (a potential $100,000 profit). 2. Again you are treating the buyer like a lender asking for a pre-paid option. What else does she own that you might like to buy if the terms are right?	What else might the buyer lend you? How else can you channel her motivation?

STRATEGY 70

The Tenant Solution

Look Inside the Deal for the Solution.

SITUATION	1. Lots of transactions are made between the owner and someone who is in some way connected to the owner or the property. Before you go out into the market searching for a sale or an exchange, look within.	It is easy to deal with someone you trust. Some say the people are more important than the property or asset. Ask yourself, who do I know well enough that I would trust in making this deal? Another way to find the right person is to ask yourself, "Who would I take a personal Note from?" That just might be the right person for this deal.
POSSIBLE SOLUTION	1. This also shows the importance of the people in the deal and that it is not just bricks and mortar we are talking about. The tenant is the easy one to visualize. If you wanted to sell a building you owned, it is just logical to consider that one of the tenants might be the buyer or exchangor. Often the owner will give a better deal to someone he knows than to a stranger. 2. But there are many other subtle insider deals that people miss. Let's say you are the same building owner but you want to retire. Consider this: Separate the land from the building in a land-lease deal. You keep the land under the building and take management-free income from the land-lease payments. Sell the building for nothing down to your children or someone else you already know and trust. 3. This is another option: Again you are the same building owner. You can offer the building to your neighbor and agree to carry back a blanket mortgage secured by both properties.	
CONCLUSION	The insider options are only limited by the scope of your imagination.	

STRATEGY 71

Two Plus Three Equals Two

Use a second and third trust deed instead of just a second trust deed.

SITUATION	1. This is often used to help create cash in a cashless exchange. 2. You are going out of title to a building valued at $1,500,000. You owe $500,000. You are taking in some land valued at $500,000 and have been asked to carry back a $500,000 2nd TD to balance equities. They have offered terms of $5,000 per month and 6% interest and all due in five years.
POSSIBLE SOLUTION	1. The transaction is OK with you except you need a little cash which is not available from the other side of this deal. 2. One solution might be to counter them saying you will accept the deal if they give you back two trust deeds instead of one. The terms will be: 3. 2nd TD – Face amount of $100,000 payable at $2,000 per month at 8% and all due in three years, and a 3rd TD – Face amount of $400,000 payable at $3,000 per month including interest at 5% and all due in seven years.
CONCLUSION	Your plans are, of course, to sell the 2nd TD on the open market to generate the cash you want. By structuring the payments like you have, the borrower is making the same payment he had agreed upon but you will receive far more from selling the 2nd with these stronger terms. Depending on the market you might receive $90,000 cash for the second the way you have it vs. $60,000 to $70,000 with the softer terms.

Price	$1,500,000
Loan:	500,000
Equity	$1,000,000
Xchange Offer as down payment:	$ 500,000
TD offered to balance equity:	$ 500,000
Break this $500,000 TD into two:	
2nd TD	$ 100,000
3rd TD	$ 400,000

STRATEGY 72

Creativity – We Are Going To Need It

The last few Strategies in this volume will be a precursor to the next nine volumes in the series. These first three volumes have laid the groundwork for using creativity in the business and real estate world. Hopefully the knowledge gained so far will help in the transition to the world we are moving into, and that armed with some of these creative strategies we will be able to make profits and prosper.

SITUATION	In Vol. 4 we will be dealing with gold and silver and real estate and business strategies, with Performance Mortgages and means of combating inflation, hyper-inflation and/or deflation. Many people who are very astute when it comes to understanding social life, the science of engineering or medicine, or law and philosophy, may be totally clueless when it comes to the monetary theories of Lord Keynes or Austrian Economics. These are the forces in play in this year of 2010. It is these forces that are determining your destiny right now and why certain strategies work and others no longer do.
POSSIBLE SOLUTION	We encourage you to read Vol. 7 in our series, "Brainstorming" which will help prepare you for creating strategies as you need them. The markets of the past are gone. If they come back you will have no trouble in knowing how to live with them. If they do not come back then these creative strategies may become extremely valuable to you.
CONCLUSION	Learn to barter, learn to trade, learn to swap – these will be your defense and foundation. Monetary policy is set by our politicians and they are making decisions that cause our markets to swing wildly. This creates unlimited opportunity for someone to prosper who has the creative tools to work with. This is the area where we hope our strategies may be of help.

STRATEGY 73

Liquidate and Diversify

It is what you don't see coming that might damage you and transparency is not the norm of the day. Granted there is an expense involved when you change position in assets but it is far better to accept these expenses now than to risk the loss of the entire assets.

SITUATION	Here is the meat from just two articles this week: 1) Detroit has 33,500 empty houses and 91,000 vacant residential lots. They want to bulldoze 20% of the city and make it into farms. 2) Kansas City, Missouri elects to close 50% of their schools because of budget difficulties. What is next? How can you protect yourself and yet set up the pins so you can prosper in the future.
POSSIBLE SOLUTION	Liquidate: Get rid of any assets you have that might have been favored by the old economy. Maybe even sell your house, if you can, and rent instead. Or certainly if you keep your house, get a big mortgage at a fixed low rate that will probably be inflated out of existence. If you do neither of these two things it is obviously okay, as it is your call, but recognize your vulnerability. Put your 401K into gold and silver. If banks fail a lot of assets are going to go away.
CONCLUSION	Diversity: On the other side of the coin, acquisition is great if you use things like a Performance Mortgage and the like. Knowing how to exchange opens up not only a market that can be stuck for the lack of cash, but also opens up the entire world to trade into. There are over 200 countries and territories. Expand your thinking to include international opportunities. Please see our Volume #9, "Blending your Real Estate, Business & Life into the International World."

Strategy 74

The Easiest 3-Way Exchange There Is

This is a 3-way exchange that almost can't miss and works for everyone. It takes two things: A taker on the front end who will take the first asset and a person in-lieu-of who is reasonable for what will be acceptable to close out the exchange. Understand this strategy and you are armed to make an offer on any property that will support rental income regardless of inflation or deflation. It is an excellent tool for both the lender and the payor. There would be no foreclosures if everyone used this strategy.

SITUATION	I am going to use, in this example, the one item that is probably the most difficult item there is to exchange: An owner-occupied single family residence. The reason is that people are more emotional about their home than they are with investment property. I normally will not get involved with trading an owner-occupied residence for this reason. I am going to use a $300,000 house in Florida as the example. It is free and clear in a good residential district. The owners want to relocate to California and move this equity there and are willing to accept other things, not just a house.
POSSIBLE SOLUTION	You are willing to buy this house on your terms and rent it out as an investment. You offer them nothing down and a performance first TD back against the property for $300,000. It is a Performance Note (see Vol. 4) and will recite that it will pay the holder of the Note ½ of the net rents (after all expenses) from the property as interest for a period of 20 years at which time the Note is due and payable, plus at any time the property is sold they are to receive 1/2 of any net profit over $300,000. As rents go up their income will increase. If the house brings in $2,000 month rent and expenses are $700 month, they would receive $650 (1/2 of the net of $1300).
CONCLUSION	Normally sellers will not accept this offer as the buyer has put nothing down, but there is little or no risk that there will ever be a foreclosure because it is a Performance Mortgage and engineered for our modern world. However, the easiest thing to do is put the offered Note & TD (or mortgage) into the exchange market for something in California. You will get lots of offers for a first TD that brings in some income now & potentially share in profits of a higher price later, and one that they don't have to risk foreclosing on. This is an excellent piece of paper and much, much, much, easier to trade than is the house in Florida. It is a very simple three-way transaction. I sincerely hope the redundancy in the last sentence will be heard. This is the easiest multiple-leg transaction there is, in my opinion.

STRATEGY 75

Prediction Heard: "Only 27% of the Real Estate Fraternity Will Weather the Storm." No Prediction for Real Estate Investors.

The following is a quotation from Doug Casey, International Research Consultancy:

"Create: In the coming years, the world is likely to change as radically as it did entering the industrial revolution. This is going to be a really major change, economically, politically, technologically, demographically, socially, militarily – the whole ball of wax. This is a good time to look around and ask yourself, not, "Who will give me a job?" but, "What goods and services can I provide that people will need in the future and pay me for?" What worked during the late Long Boom won't work – in order to create, you're going to have to think creatively."

EDITORS NOTE: Consider reading our Volume #7 in this series on Brainstorming.

SITUATION	We are possibly just about to watch the biggest transference of wealth in the history of mankind. If you know your history you know the seeds were sown for this about 70 years ago.	Re: Retirement income, see our gold and silver retirement strategy.
POSSIBLE SOLUTIONS	Here are some basic strategies to first stop the bleeding and next to make a profit. 1. Establish an independent cash flow. If you are working for someone else, start your own business now running parallel to your job where you control your own destiny. Decide what is needed and stay in this arena. Try to select something that can be international in scope and that you can run from anywhere. On a computer when possible. 2. Acquire holdings using performance obligations. 3. Diversify and definitely get some holdings internationally. 4. Learn another language. Three main ones, English, Spanish & Mandarin Chinese. 5. Get out of banks or other companies that are subject to failure. 6. Solidify and then start selected acquisitions.	At some point everyone will learn that dollar bills are a debt, not money. Get into hard assets and deal in benefits rather than dollars.

NOTES

NOTES

300 STRATEGIES FOR MAKING
REAL ESTATE & BUSINESS DEALS

VOLUME 4

STRATEGIES
76 – 100

25 Formulas & Strategies
Creative Real Estate Level 4

ROBERT W. STEELE

Foreword by Ronald J. Robinson SEC

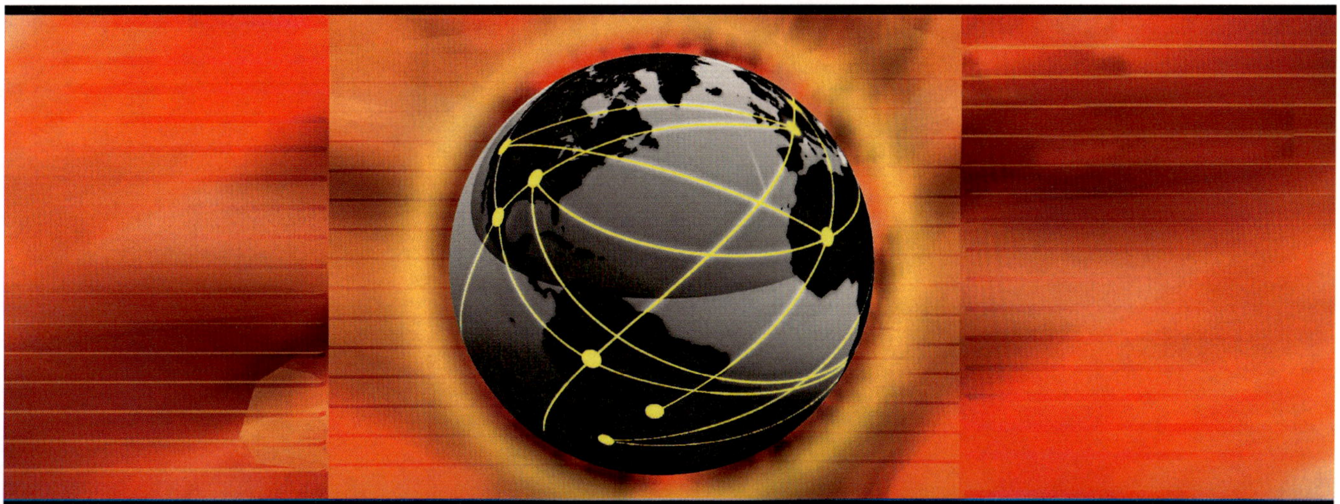

OUTSIDE THE BOX & INSIDE / OUTSIDE THE COUNTRY

300 Strategies for Making Real Estate & Business Deals

Outside the Box & Inside / Outside the Country

VOLUME 4
Strategies 76 – 100

25 FORMULAS & STRATEGIES: CREATIVE REAL ESTATE, LEVEL 4

by Robert W. Steele

Foreword by Ronald J. Robinson SEC

Design, Layout & Graphics
Victoria Vinton
Coyote Press Graphic Communications
www.coyotepressgraphics.com

VOLUME 4
CONTENTS

Introduction
Foreword: Ronald J. Robinson SEC

Strategy	Title
#76	Crop Futures Strategy
#77	A Bunt May Be Exactly the Right Strategy
#78	The Performance Mortgage: A Wonderful Tool
#79	Performance Trust Deed & Note
#80	Performance Trust Deed & Note #2
#81	SAMPLE Performance TD Package
#82	Great Formula For Growing a Corporation
#83	Inflation
#84	Superstar Strategy
#85	The Un-Built Company Formula
#86	Broker-Brokers & Finders
#87	Bag of Silver Strategy and New Variation
#88	Gold and Silver Mortgage Insurance
#89	Note Payable In Silver (or Gold)
#90	Learn to Spend Real Money
#91	Linear vs Spatial Idea Tracking
#92	Performance Land Lease
#93	Attorney's Strategy - Sit in The Office
#94	Burn the Bridges Formula – There is No Way Back
#95	Turn Vacancies into Wellness Units
#96	Counter Trade
#97	Multiple Notes in Quantity
#98	Derivative #1
#99	Derivative #2
#100-A	Liquefying Mining Assets
#100-B	U.S. Dollar: A Derivative + Hyperinflation Tactic

Introduction

25 Formulas & Strategies: Creative Real Estate, Level 4

Volume 4 is a special book for me. I am moving from what has been with out standard formulas that that have been developed over the last 30 to 40 years into a realm of strategies where some of the formulas have not had the test of time like in volumes 1 through 3. If there has ever been a time for newer concepts it is now.

In Volumes 1 through 3 we were builders. Not literally, but figuratively. We developed something that could be relied upon really for the rest of our lives. I had one client who told me that that was always his goal: To be paid every day of his life for the work he did today. Even though he also built several buildings, what he meant was figuratively building.

By the time in history that we arrive at Volume 4 things are different. If we build just the old way there is a reasonable chance that what you build might be nationalized. As of this writing GMC that was the epitomy of free enterprise is now owned 61% by the government, The air lines and many in the banking industries are partially owned by the government and still close to collapse and the city and state governments are teetering. There is a new sentiment on the street that the government should take care of us in our retirement years.

It is with this as a backdrop that we develop some of the formulas that you will find in Volume 4, For instance if you will check strategy 169 in Volume 7, our brainstorming book you will find that reverse brainstorming was the genius for the Performance Mortgage strategies in Volume 4. We had to have strategies that build around the demise of the capitalization sheets and the pro forma business plans that were no longer serving because manipulated markets and inflation make them obsolete & impotent. Now with the hint of hyperinflation to come we have so many new issues that have to be built into our strategies that is sometimes a little mind boggling.

We add to this the need to expand our businesses into to the international markets and the added brainpower that this takes makes the entrepreneur practice quite different than it was even just a few years ago. The opportunities are greater than ever because of this expansion but we are forced to stretch a little further than we use to.

Volume 4 is meant to help in this transition. You will find some of the formulas from this volume show up in our international volume that validates what we are saying here. Thanks for joining us and we hope you like this volume.

Robert W. Steele

Ronald J. Robinson SEC

Foreword

A treasure trove awaits the reader of this volume of creative thinking. Nothing in this world has ever been created such as you will find in these writings. Out of the well spring of Robert Steele's monumentally creative intelligence you find solutions to problems dealing with Real Estate such as you will find no where else. These are solutions with a foundation in total reality, not just some fantasy, but tried and proven in real life transactions.

I am honored in being able to set forth this foreword to Mr. Steele's magnificent world of creativity. Mr. Steele and I have been close friends for more years then I can count. Through his never-ending artesian well of creativity, I have been fortunate enough to have a lifestyle that most could only dream. Together and with others, we have put together millions of dollars of transactions, which have provided me with the trappings of a luxurious life.

I hasten to mention I am not possessed with any more intelligence than the average person, but by applying the formulas found in this volume and understanding fully what this volume conveys, can launch you into another world, a world of real and lasting enjoyment and the pride of being of benefit those who you will serve in the real estate business.

Focus, learn and apply.

Ronald J. Robinson SEC

STRATEGY 76

Crop Futures Strategy

If the commodities brokers can use futures so can the real estate brokers or principals. There is literally no end to how far this particular strategy can go. It is truly open-ended.

COMMODITIES MARKET	Futures can be used by those wanting to protect a buying or selling price for some time in the future. The farmer growing corn can pre-sell his crops at a price now to insure the price in the future, if she thinks the market may go down. In this instance the futures is a hedge.	Bldg. value $2,000,000. $2,000,000 in tomatoes delivered at $400,000 worth per year. In this transaction the building was at a fixed price and the tomato price floated with the market. It can be designed both ways, either fixed or floating on either side. This futures formula is a derivative of the Creation of Wealth formula, see Volume 1 plus it also moves into the stock market or commodities market, see Volume 11.
COMBINING WITH	It can also be structured so it guarantees a delivery some time in the future even though the price may change to a new market price but the delivery of product is guaranteed.	
REAL ESTATE MARKET	Actual example from our files: Client exchanged tomatoes from a farm in California for a Big Box Building (old White Front Store) in Oregon that was leased. It was for a floating quantity of tomatoes delivered to the crop buyer, selected by the farmer, at the rate of 20% of the building's value per year for the first year plus the next four years. The building price was delivered at a fixed price but the tomatoes were delivered at market value at the time that their delivery was made direct to the wholesaler on behalf of the building owner. Building owner gets fixed price on building. If price of tomatoes goes up during the coming four years, the tomato farmer makes additional profit because he delivers fewer tomatoes. He would lose if the price drops because he would have to deliver more. Tomato farmer had no interest to pay on loan by negotiations. There was actually a small $200,000 loan on the building which was paid off out of the first delivery of tomatoes.	

STRATEGY 77

A Bunt May Be Exactly the Right Strategy

Home runs are nice but many games are won with a bunt

BIG DEALS VS. SMALL DEALS	Once you truly learn how to think creatively making a deal becomes rather easy. You can work it either forward or backward. You can work one formula and become successful like Dick Reno's Missouri Waltz formula. That turned into the 1031 exchange used currently by 12,500 CCIM brokers. Or, you can find a problem that needs solving and then use any existing formula or strategy to solve it, or design a new one.	Deals are easy to make if you just want to keep the pot boiling.
RISK VS. REWARD	Likewise you can work on just big problems with potentially big rewards or losses. Or smaller, bunt-size deals where the rewards might be lesser but also smaller risks or the third option is a mixture or combination.	Stroke that ego.
TEST	I analyzed my business at the end of each year. My office consisted of myself and my secretary and everything else was outsourced. I remember once being quite surprised when I found that about 50% of my small company's business overhead (for instance, approximately 200 hours logged in a twin engine plane with pilot) and about six months of my time was spent on making one big transaction. I made the deal and it delivered about 30% of my income for the year. The risk was obviously higher also. Would I have been better off to have had several bunt-hyphen-sized deals which delivered a higher ratio of profit? Your decision.	Does thinking get in the way?

STRATEGY 78

This is an article I wrote in the SEC Real Estate News Observer in 2002 or 2003 (as the real estate bubble was forming) about the importance of knowing about and using Performance Mortgages as we head into hyperinflation. Everyone who picked up on this information weathered the collapse of the real estate market with minimal problems. Some of those who didn't may have suffered. This tool is here to stay and it is worth a reprint in this book.

The Performance Mortgage: A Wonderful Tool

by Robert W. Steele

Mortgage payments tied to the actual net income from the property. Now that makes sense!

The popularity and usage of the Performance Mortgage is rapidly making inroads into the fabric of American Real Estate. We are becoming blessed with innovative lenders designing a variety of lending instruments that make modern real estate loans really work for our citizenry.

It was just a short while back when the reverse mortgage was designed, and that has played such a wonderful role for our retirees. Through the reverse mortgages retirees can borrow on their homes and have no payments to make. The interest accumulates and is paid off when the home is later sold. The retirees, in essence, are living off part of their equity but still remaining in their homes.

An enormous number of foreclosures, that no one wanted to make, have been completely eliminated by using these mortgages, thus making the final years of many people so much happier. In real estate these are called Single Pay Notes or Balloon Notes that are secured by the real estate. In the stock market they are called Zero Coupon Bonds or Strips that are secured by corporate assets, or they are secured by the U.S. Government's Treasury Investment Growth Receipts (TIGRs).

There have been many bonds like these over the years that come due in a single payment 10, 20 or 30 years out including the war bonds many of us purchased during the war years.

Other new mortgages that have come into play are ones where a person's FICO credit score might permit them to borrow even over the actual value of their real estate. Others loans are being designed with lower payments at the beginning and increasing in time as perhaps the borrower's capacity to pay increases or rents from their property increases. Many of these, in some way, are using the potential appreciation of the real estate as a factor in determining how to structure the loans. The growth in the value of the real estate may play a prominent roll and the proper loan structure eliminates or decreases foreclosure problems. These sub-prime loans may also prove very damaging if the market reverses. Not so with Performance Mortgages.

The Performance Mortgage is innovative as it allows the net income from a parcel of real estate to dictate the payments. As the income increases so do the payments. These work very well with a property that is only partially developed, underdeveloped or one with vacancy problems. By using a standard loan the income will not cover the payments which causes reverse cash flow, other problems and often foreclosure. Again, these are foreclosures that no one wants, certainly not the lender or the borrower.

By using a Performance Mortgage another innovative thing can take place. For years the Gnomes of Zurich and other wise lenders have known and made use of the fact that the growth in the value of the real estate is a huge asset. The lender usually does not share in this growth. However, by properly structuring the loan, i.e. a Performance Mortgage, the lender can share in it. In the Performance Mortgage, a percentage of the real estate profit on sale can be directed to the lender.

Now a loan on an under-developed property can be made and the payments based on a lower than normal income from the property. As it is developed and rents increase the payments increase. When it is sold and profits are realized, the loan is retired and the lender shares in a pre-determined percentage of the net profit.

From the lender's perspective many nice thing happen. They don't have to keep looking for a place to put their capital. It not only is working but is increasing in income. Potential problems like foreclosures are eliminated or reduced. The capital loaned is not "static" or not "fixed" where it is subject to the ravages of inflation and the loss of spending power.

Nothing is ever a panacea, but the Performance Mortgage is a real step in the right direction. Hats off to the New Breed of Lenders.

STRATEGY 79

Performance Trust Deed and Note

This could be one of the best formulas available today but it is like the low interest rate notes, people just don't get the advantages the first time around. It is the same formula that has been used by the Swiss for years.

SITUATION	1. Abel wants to buy a building. We are going to use 100% leverage in this example to maximize the point. The building is $1,000,000, has an upside and is rented at marginal rates. Abel has good credit and a good statement. 2. Baker is a private lender and has the $1,000,000 to lend Abel as a first TD on the building. Baker is cognizant that the dollar is devaluating at perhaps 15% per year so when his loan is repaid the dollar will be worth much less than when he loaned it. The loan is made to Abel.	Price: Loan:	$1,000,000 $1,000,000
POSSIBLE SOLUTION	Abel gives Baker a PERFORMANCE 1st TD/Note. This can be made payable on any terms and conditions agreeable between the parties. In this instance we structured it with no interest and all due in five years. Baker is to receive 50% of the net rental income form the building during the five years (in-lieu-of interest) and upon sale Baker gets the $1,000,000 back first and 50% of any profits above that.		
CONCLUSION	1. Foreclosures are eliminated using these Trust Deeds. 2. As rents go up Baker's income goes up. 3. In this instance Baker has risk if value drops.		

STRATEGY 80

Performance Trust Deed/Note #2

This is an excellent tool for acquiring a cash-flowing asset in a 3-way transaction (in-lieu-of).

SITUATION	1. You find an owner with a $5,000,000 shopping center. Owner Abel would like out of management and would take an exchange for land. He owes $1,000,000 with a low constant so it has excellent cash flow. You offer the owner nothing down and a 2nd PERFORMANCE TD back on the shopping center payable with no interest but 50% of the net rents and all due in 10 years, plus 50% of any future profits. 2. The owner will not accept the transaction because there is no down payment.	Price: Loan: Equity: Perf. TD:	$5,000,000 1,000,000 $4,000,000 $4,000,000
POSSIBLE SOLUTION	1. Take the PERFORMANCE 2nd TD in-lieu-of and exchange it to Baker for his $4,000,000 land. Abel gives Baker the PERFORMANCE 2nd TD/note. 2. You end up with the shopping center and receive nice cash flow. 3. Abel gets $4,000,000 in land. 4. Baker gets $4,000,000 2nd PERFORMANCE TD with good security and nice cash flow.		
CONCLUSION	1. You can buy anything of any size with this formula. Seller has to stand still why you find the third leg. 2. Where originally the owner wouldn't accept the nothing down, the land owner viewed the PERFORMANCE 2ND TD through different eyes.	In-lieu-of	

STRATEGY 81

SAMPLE Performance TD Package

EQUITY PARTNER/LENDER WANTED

Loan wanted: $180,000 for rental condo in the Panama Canal Zone.
Lender shares in Equity Growth.

PANAMA is becoming a safety valve and global hub real estate market. The Canal is being widened to accommodate boats of any size (transit fees $80,000 to $300,000 each plus), the banking community is reaching global status, retirees are flooding in from all over the world and major business are locating at this new pivotal spot. Johns Hopkins Medical Center is now in and even Mr. Trump is building a tower there. Presently there are no real estate taxes for 20 years on new construction, transferable on resale.

We own or are in acquisition of several rental condos. The following is a unit we own and we are looking for a first loan. We can fill an order for rental condos as needed.

Number: PF1002	**Title: PANAMA - SAN FRANCISCO BAY TOWER** **2 -Bdr. View Condo–construction finished**	
$180,000	**Loan Wanted: $180,000**	**Location: San Francisco area of Panama City**
PRICE: $180,000 Have: 2 BDR. 2-BATH HI-RISE CONDO SAN FRANCISCO BAY TOWER Panama Canal Zone	**WANT Equity Sharing Partner/Lender.** The SAN FRANCISCO AREA is recognized as one of the nicer areas of downtown Panama City. This is a city whose coastline looks like Miami Beach with the number of high-rise condo and office complexes built, under development or planned. This condo has a marvelous view and is located on the 24th floor in the San Francisco area. The building has a nice lobby, 2 elevators, a total of 38 floors and 130 condos. There is a pool, Jacuzzi, sauna, party hall, gym, deck and open terraces. In concert with an adjacent tower there are tennis courts and an additional pool for children. Rent schedule $1,500 month. There are no real estate taxes on this property for 20 years. Want $180,000 equity sharing partner/lender. Secured by first T.D. Lender receives 50% of the net rents as interest and money back first plus 50% of profits on resale.	

STRATEGY 82

Great Formula For Growing a Corporation

This is a sneak preview into our volume using stock formulas with, or as an adjunct to, real estate strategies. This is a formula to mitigate the risk and/or to leverage the upside using a stock formula. Please see our Real Estate & Stock Strategy book for more of these types of formulas.

PUT (OPTION) SITUATION:	Owner has a $200,000 F&C parcel of land and two heavily encumbered houses, $400,000 each with $250,000 in loans on each. A public company would like to grow its balance sheet with some real estate assets. Owner trades land for stock at $1.00 per share (200,000 shares) and receives an option to exchange the SFRs free and clear for stock at the same number for 18 months.
UPSIDE / DOWNSIDE	Downside risk: $200,000, or some part thereof, if the stock depreciates or goes to zero value. Upside is huge! If the stock goes to $5.00 the owner would net $4,500,000 ($5,000,000 less the $500,000 to pay off the two houses).
NOTES	A Put Option (usually just called a "Put") is a financial contract between two parties, the writer (seller) and the buyer of the option. The buyer acquires a short position by purchasing the right to sell the underlying instrument to the seller of the option for a specified price (the strike price) during a specified period of time. If the option buyer exercises their right, the seller is obligated to buy the underlying instrument from them at the agreed upon strike price, regardless of the current market price. In exchange for having this option, the buyer pays the seller or option-writer a fee (the option premium). In the above example the consideration (fee) was the exchange of the $200,0000 in land for the stock. When in negotiations, a Put Option is an excellent "to boot" consideration that can potentially have significant value.

STRATEGY 83

Inflation

Inflation is a monetary event and not an economic one. It is one of the ingredients of the perfect storm brewing for the world economic and monetary market.

SITUATION	Inflation: Monetary policies play a major role in inflation in all countries. Pick any area you want but let's just use Europe today: 1. Cost of a single fare on the London Underground (the Tube) in 1957 was 1.5 cents. Now $7.80. Increase of 51,900 percent. 2. Cost of three course dinner at Munich RathsKeller in 1957 was 40 cents. Now $25.00. Increase 6,150 percent. 3. Cost of one night at Paris' Hotel du Pantheon in 1957 was $3.00. Now it is $219.00. Increase of 7,200 percent. 4. Cost of admission to Athens Acropolis in 1957 was 30 cents. Now it is $15.60. Increase of 5,100 percent. 5. Cost of a half-day sight-seeing tour in Rome in 1957 was $2.20. It is now $79.00. Increase of 3,491 percent.
POSSIBLE SOLUTION	Position one's assets so as to take advantage of the forces. Try not to buck the tide and know and understand the fundamentals. Is it better to owe money or be receiving it?
CONCLUSION	Know your fundaments during inflation so you will be positioned right when hyper-inflation pays a visit. AT the point where hyper-inflation arrives, it might be wise to owe a lot of money on mortgages that are static and that can be paid off with cheap (inflated) money. Take a look at your portfolio and/or the portfolio of your clients in this light.

Strategy 84

Superstar Strategy

The real estate market is just starting to learn what Hollywood, the Sports World, the Political World, and Business World have known for years: Superstar Power is worth a lot of money. Hollywood pays millions every day for this; business is miles ahead of real estate in learning to pay for this through multi-million dollar signing bonuses, stock options and perks. Real Estate is still in the Dark Ages in this arena...with a couple of exceptions.

TECHNIQUE	Everyone has an opinion of Donald Trump. Whether this is good, bad or indifferent doesn't matter. Everyone knows his name, "The Donald." Does he do a lot of real estate? Probably more than anyone reading this.	People want to do business with those they know or know about. Barriers go down if people know you. The condos in Trump Towers are usually at least $100,000 more expensive than comparable ones. His name and image result in a higher price.
	Name the top ten movie actors and everyone knows them. Just to sign them to a movie you pay them big bucks. Super Stars also deliver.	
	Name the top athlete in every sport. Tiger Woods charges 3 million to just show up at a tournament. Super Stars makes hundreds of millions in ad fees.	
	Businesses pay millions to advertise their logo and their major officer's make millions more. Any major stock person bets on management: The Super Stars.	
	Do you want to become a major player in real estate or barter? Become a Superstar. You can become a Star by learning your business and doing it better than the next person. To become a Superstar it takes something extra and public relations is often needed to move up that one step. Do your PR work. Do your PR: Give talks on your subject, teach, write articles and/or books. Become known with your clients and your peers. Write your own PR for the newspapers. Brand yourself.	

STRATEGY 85

The Un-Built Company Formula

It is the same as the Un-Built Building formula, where the developer dreams the dream of building a building and then puts all the pieces together, and when he is finished, there is a building built, or in this case a company in operation. You simply manifest the dream.

YOU WANT TO START A BUSINESS	You do a complete business plan: Outline the business operation, its need in the marketplace, the qualifications of the people involved and the people you might need. You locate where you would like the business to be, you do the necessary demographics and do the spread sheets needed to substantiate the profit potential, etc.	Satisfy all legal and accounting issues.
PREPARE A PACKAGE FOR THE MARKET-PLACE	Determine the capital you will need to initiate and run the business. Show what contributions the management is making to the endeavor and what you will require in capital contributions to make the business go. Also explain how the profits will be shared between the investors and the management and/or developers.	Show on the spread-sheet pro forma what you will need in cash over what time period plus a hefty amount for contingencies and/or incubation and projected profits.
CASH INVESTORS VS. TRADE INVESTORS	If you are working in good economic conditions, then cash investors abound. There is always more cash in these markets than there are good ideas. If, however, it is in what would be considered a down market with a cash shortage, then using a trade investor(s) becomes viable. The difference is as follows: If you need $1,000,000 cash to initiate the business, you might require $2,000,000 or $3,000,000 in trade items in order to obtain the hard cash of $1,000,000 by borrowing on the trade items.	There are a whole series of formulas that come into play when exchanging stock or company ownership for trade items to fund business operations.

STRATEGY 86

BROKER-BROKER & FINDERS

(When three brokers share two commissions)

In the world of real estate the broker-broker can play a very important role as can the finder in the business world. In real estate, when knowledgeable people are working together and they see a possible exchange match between two other brokers or principals, they usually just advise one or both of the others and move on. Sometimes there is a referral fee but often it is a just a professional courtesy. I have found one area which I use successfully and closed deals that otherwise would not have been made. Please see below. It is available at almost every exchange meeting I have gone to.

SITUATION	You see a package presented at a meeting by a relatively new exchange broker. You can see a match for it with another broker's property and that broker is not at the same meeting. You are relatively sure that the newer broker's inexperience would probably preclude the deal from going together. Example from the files: I saw a package presented at a meeting in Southern California by a new broker. It was for a doctor, his wife and eight or ten children. The doctor had wanted to move out of Southern California and had gone to Northern California and built an 8-bedroom McMansion on the coast in a very small town. After this, his wife would not move there. The house had been empty for a couple of years and the broker was trying to trade it for him. I asked him if he would do a broker-broker deal with me and he said yes. From the meeting, I phoned a very capable exchangor I knew who lived about 30 miles from the house, told him the situation and asked him if he had something or someone who would make a trade with the doctor et. al. He realized he had one client, who owned a motel, who would do the deal. I re-met with the original broker, wrote up the transaction including the three-way split on the two commissions, and the right to meet personally so I could counsel with the doctor and his wife. All was accomplished. There was no need for me to go to Northern California as the broker there was very capable and they all signed including the three-way split on the two fees. Inspections were made and the deal closed.
NOTES	Things had to be tightened up in order to make this transaction. The client had to be counseled and signatures obtained regarding the commission. You can go to exchange meetings and come out with a transaction just by manufacturing it. IMO there are more deals missed than ones that go together.

Strategy 87

Bag of Silver Strategy & New Variation

Colloquially a bag of silver denotes a bag of $1,000 face value of pre-1964 silver coins, either dimes, quarters or halves. This equates, for instance, into 10,000 - 90% silver dimes. After 1964 they no longer contain silver. These are available for purchase or sale at all coin stores. There are thousands of locations where these coins represent 24-hour cash. A bag weighs 55 lbs. and represents 715 troy ounces of silver. Every electronic device and every refrigerator has some silver in it. Thousands of commodities require silver. Silver is also money, as is gold.

SITUATION	After 1971 the U.S. was off the gold standard. We no longer backed our currency with gold or silver and our currency became fiat. The government could print paper money as they wished, in huge quantities, and this caused a disparity to occur between silver coins and the paper that was now called money. A bag of silver might cost $10,000 because the silver was worth that much, and yet the face amount of the U.S. coins still said the bag totaled $1,000.	A Bag of Silver: 10,000 silver dimes: 90% silver. 4,000 silver quarters: 90% silver.
ONE ANSWER	The ploy was then, if someone with a tax problem sold his real estate or other asset, you simply offered him 10 bags of silver for his $100,000 parcel of real estate. You were actually giving him only $10,000 as that is what the face value of the coins said. The silver in the coins, however, could be sold for $100,000. The Government now had a problem, so naturally after a period of time they created a new law to eliminate the tax loophole, which was an arbitrage of sorts.	2,000 silver halves: 90% silver 1,000 silver dollars: 71½ % silver.
SECOND ANSWER	However, the more money printed the more expensive a bag of silver becomes, as it is a true currency, not a debt such as the fiat paper. The ploy now, and it is only available in the private lending sector of our market, is to borrow on the bags of silver, using the silver as collateral, and then paying for the real estate with the cash. By holding the bags of silver you still get the growth. If you go out of title, you would have a tax consequence based on the phantom profit. The profit is only on the fiat. The truth is so very fragile sometimes.	Silver dollars also have numismatic value and there are some 50% silver coins in Kennedy halves, etc.

STRATEGY 88

Gold and Silver Mortgage Insurance

Double insure the lender while insuring yourself and – get this – hold and own the premium yourself.

SITUATION	You own a property that supports a $1,000,000 1st TD. There is ample equity but the lending market is suspect and loans are difficult to get. You would like to implement backing up your mortgage with 10% in gold and silver but loans are tough to come by right now.	$1,000,000 1st TD on your property.
POSSIBLE SOLUTION	Locate a $110,000 private secondary loan. If someone will do a reverse mortgage, great, but if not work out terms to mutual satisfaction. You need $100,000 to back up your mortgage with gold and silver. Try to obtain a five year loan minimum.	$100,000 2nd Mortgage + 10,000 costs $110,000 Total
STRATEGY #1 (See Previous Strategy)	Buy $100,000 in gold and silver to implement the 10% strategy of backing up mortgages in order to pay them off as gold and silver rise against a static dollar mortgage. Concept being that the 10% back-up will appreciate and will pay off the entire mortgage.	Buy the hard stuff or know what you are doing if you use Exchange Traded Funds (EFTs) or the like.
STRATEGY #2 (Double Insure This Lender)	If necessary, offer to add the gold and silver as additional security for the $110,000 loan. You will probably have to use a private storage facility in order to implement this new strategy.	Assuming you have good equity in the real estate, you are providing more than ample security plus liquid security of 24-hour cash.

Strategy 89

Note Payable In Silver (or Gold)

The most insidious part of the currency debacle today is that we are experiencing the demise of the fiat currencies of the world one percentage point at a time. The U.S. dollar is just one of the currencies, but the main one. The real currencies of history, being gold and silver, have been maligned by our banking and governmental systems so most people are not aware that we have not been using real money for a long time. The following note, with numbers rounded and amounts and names eliminated to protect the innocent, is a real note actually used in a transaction. The numbers below will exemplify how you may be losing wealth daily by not understanding how the game is being played.

October 1, 2008

Promissory Note: $100,000

Within one (1) year of this date, for funds received this date, ______ hereby agrees to pay _______, at _______, California, the sum of One Hundred Thousand ($100,000.00) Dollars, plus interest at Eight (8%) Percent per annum, plus or minus the equivalent value of the change in the value of silver during the loan period. The current value of silver is $12.00 per troy oz resulting in the underlying value stated herein being worth 8,333.33 oz of silver. The underlying value of this note then is 8,333.33 oz of silver and the said interest would also be payable in silver. The principle and interest may also be paid in any currency acceptable to lender.

____________________, President ________________, Inc.

Had this note been denominated in dollars at the time of pay off one year later, the beneficiary would have received $108,000 representing the principal plus 8% interest.

Based on the price of silver, however, that had moved from $12 per troy oz to $18, the payoff number would be:

8,333.33 oz X $18.00 = $150,000 + interest of 8% or $12,000 for a total of $162,000.

To be blunt, if you don't understand what real money is and/or don't believe what is happening, you may find yourself in front of a tsunami. This is not difficult to understand once the blinders are removed.

STRATEGY 90

Learn to Spend Real Money

Make offers in gold and silver. Technically this should read "Relearn to Spend Real Money."

TECHNIQUE	If we could stretch our imagination a little we could make a leap into the future to say it just might be possible that we might once again be using gold and silver as real money. The old formulas, where the use of silver coins at face value to offset tax consequences, is no longer applicable because it was made illegal to use the face value. You had to use the silver value. Example: 10,000 U.S. pre-1964 dimes have a face value of 10 cents each or $1,000 total. However, they might have a silver content value of $1.00 each or a $10,000 total. If you took the dime to the store, you could only buy 10 cents worth of something. If you took it to a coin store, you could get $1.00. This primarily reflects the devaluation of the dollar. This spread was often used to lower tax consequences in sales. Start to use gold and silver in your business. Make offers reflecting its use. If you are $100,000 apart in a negotiation, counter perhaps that you will give them 30 one oz. U.S. Gold Eagles with a market value at this writing of about $800 each or $24,000. It affects one's mind when negotiating. The next time you make an offer to buy something, make the offer in gold and/or silver and watch the reaction. It almost always leads to your favor.
NOTES	There is a transition taking place. The paper currencies are devaluating and the hard currencies are slowly moving front and center. You can speed up the transition for yourself by using the hard currencies whether in negotiations, or some other form, every day.

STRATEGY 91

Linear vs. Spatial Idea Tracking

LEFT BRAIN	**Linear:** Abel owns a vacant lot and would like a property that could be rented as an investment. He lists the vacant lot with a broker who sells his lot and he then buys a rental house with the proceeds of the sale.	Vacant lot to cash to rental house.
RIGHT BRAIN	**Spatial**: There is no sales market so Abel cannot sell his lot. This is like the sculptor who takes away all the stone except the part that leaves the figure the sculptor wants. Start taking away all the things that could stop Abel from getting the house he wants. Take away the real estate broker who does not know how to exchange. Take away all the houses or other rental properties that will not consider exchanging. Take away all of the items that are outside of Abel's geographical or price-take area and all other things that could stop Abel from getting where he wants to go. What is left is the solution to Abel's situation.	Vacant lot direct to rental house circumventing the need for cash as the medium of exchange.
CONCLUSION	Same result via two different methods.	

STRATEGY 92

Performance Land Lease

A land lease can be for any period of time: 5 years, 50 years or 200 years. You can do anything within the lease that is legal and that people will agree to. In this example it is used to mitigate all markets so it will always work and it also acts as a contract and an option. We put together a leasehold document kit which we sell on our web site along with our books.

SITUATION	1. You are negotiating to go into title on a mini warehouse. 50% or more of the value is in the land. If you have to pay on a carry-back mortgage, the property cannot handle it and deliver any kind of a net cash spendable to you. 2. Offer to acquire just the buildings, not the land, and to lease the land back at a rate of 6 – 10% of the net cash flow from the warehouses. 3. In one example, we actually did it on a 1% rate the first year as there was so much deferred maintenance that had to be repaired and it went up 2% a year until it got to 10% where it went flat. 4. You can design these so that at the end of 50 years the land goes to the building owner or the building goes to the land owner, or the building owner can remove the buildings if they want. 5. It can be designed with options to purchase out one side or both throughout the land lease or it can be designed so the land subordinates to new construction in the future. 6. There is no end to the ways they can be designed but I usually prefer the performance land lease over the percentage one.	Remember that the land lease makes an excellent path into a three way transaction. It can give people cash flow without any management responsibilities and they can still share in the growth in the value of the property because their income can increase.

STRATEGY 93

Attorney's Strategy — Sit in the Office

Not picking on attorneys but, using them as the example and recognizing that real estate has a lot of complicated parts, it means that there is often legal counsel involved in a deal. I know it's not true that attorneys are taught in Law-101 not to return phone calls, but they are busy people working around a court system that pressures them for time commitments, and sometimes you are on the back of their "to do" list.

SITUATION: THREE EXAMPLES OF UNBLOCKING REAL ESTATE SNAGS USING THIS STRATEGY	I was in an exchange escrow with the broker who wrote the forward in this book, Mr. Chet Allen. My client had been in a lawsuit, not relevant to our real estate transaction, but the attorney on the other side of that lawsuit had failed to file a paper necessary to clear the title on the property we were exchanging, and several million dollars in real estate were tied up because of it. We could not get our exchange closed. The attorney was in another city. I went to the attorney's office unannounced and waited patiently in his office for the piece of paper I needed to get recorded. At the end of the second day, he finally got tired of my presence and gave me the document I needed. The escrow closed the next day. Another broker SEC member, Cliff Strand, and I were doing an interstate exchange. We were in California and an attorney in Portland, Oregon was reluctant to do some work that had to be done before we could close. We took a plane to Portland and walked in unannounced to the attorney's office. We were prepared to stay as long as it took and we told him so. In less than a day, we had what we needed and closed the escrow. I was closing an interstate exchange and the real estate commissioner in another state was dragging his feet and had some land tied up in a bureaucratic snafu. I had worked a month trying to get it handled to no avail. I sent my secretary to the other state and told her not to come back until it was done. It took her three days of lunches, dinners, and arm twisting to finally break the log jam. She got what we needed and the escrow closed. Was the commissioner an attorney? I don't know. This is really a powerful tool when used tactfully and has a pattern of being very successful.

STRATEGY 94

Burn the Bridges Formula – There is No Way Back

This may remind you of the Attorney Strategy. It is different but contains the same level of resolve.

SITUATION:
There are two examples here. I don't believe you can be involved in real estate in a major way without confronting this situation at some time or another. Currently we are in a serious down market and there are literally thousands of cases where this formula could be implemented.

If you have to take a loss, make it as clean as you can and get your mind clear so you can move forward doing positive things.

In concert with another broker I was building houses in a small town in California. These were nice little starter 3-bedroom homes in a picturesque grove of trees.

Over time, we had four houses left that we couldn't get sold and it drug on and on. The tract reserves were gone and the reverse cash flow was not fun.

This was the first time I implemented this formula: I told my wife I was going to this little town and I would be back when the houses were gone. I would either get them moved or give them to the lender and take my loss. There was no way I was coming back without the deal being done.

I traded these for anything I could get and they all worked out. I remember one I traded for a TD on an apartment in Tacoma, Washington. I traded one for pre-paid gas at a service station in the town and I don't recall the other two deals. It took maybe 10 days,

Another time, it was about two apartment houses I had built in the wrong city and the wrong place. I left again and was gone about two weeks. I traded one for a down payment of pre-paid credits at a furniture store, and I met with the lender on the last one and worked out a deal and deeded the apartment units to them. When I went home those deals were done.

I have learned over the years that the sooner I implement this formula, usually the greater the savings. When the deal is dead, take your licking, pay the penalty and cut the property loose.

I am not exactly sure how life works but it seems that when you add an element of resolve to a situation things seem to get done.

I know how this formula works.

I have seen people fret over one real estate problem for sometimes years, whereas, if they would use this formula the problem would last about one week or a maximum of two.

If it is F/C land you can let it resolve over time. But other things can be handled with this formula.

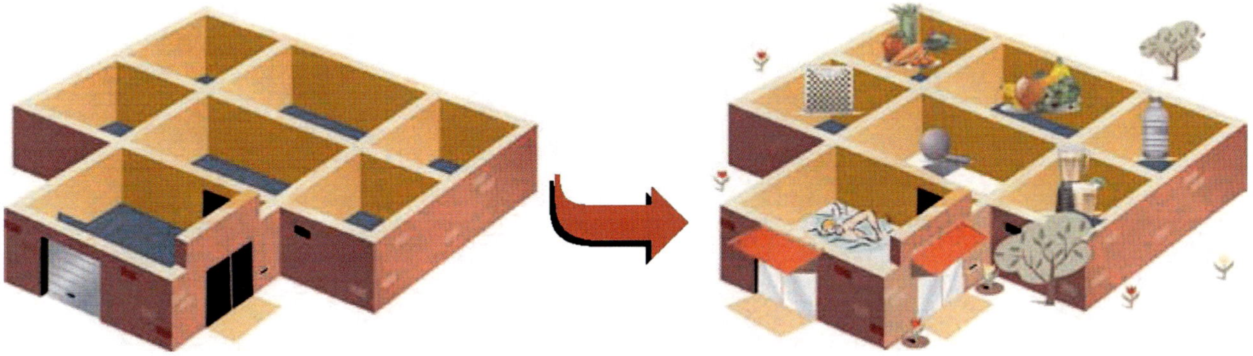

Strategy 95

Turn Vacancies into Wellness Units

Create wellness rooms in hotels, motels, resorts, assisted living facilities, trains, cruise ships, condos, apartments, office buildings, etc.

COMMENT	Macro planning is difficult but micro events are relatively easy to see coming and they can play a role even to the point where they can help fill vacancies. For instance, cultural changes are hard to plan for as they are so slow in developing: e.g. some social groups are very slow to turn. Some, even today, are stuck back in the 7th to 19th centuries. But social consciousness shift can happen over a shorter, maybe 25, 50 or 100 year span of time and can be planned for. For instance, smoking has changed in the western world and now the percentage of smokers is less and non-smoking rooms in hotels and so forth are the norm. Likewise other things are subject to consciousness change in our western societies like the acknowledgement concerning organic food that is showing up in more and more grocery stores, restaurants, etc. How can you use some of these micro changes to help fill vacancies?
SITUATION	You own a nice hotel and while you have a modest vacancy factor you would like to lower it.
POSSIBLE SOLUTION	Consider converting a few of your rooms to Wellness Units. More and more people are becoming conscious of wellness programs even to the point that occasionally you will hear of a developer considering building wellness houses. The cost of building and furnishing Wellness Units is considerable higher than the norm. But existing structures can be converted, if even on a modest scale initially. They will definitely attract clientele and some of your regular clientele will be willing to pay more for a room that is design with wellness in mind. Using certain tiles or hardwood floors, the right paint, the rights beds, having the right water, air filtration, etc. converts a room to a wellness unit.
CONCLUSION	Having wellness rooms helps your advertising, and a tasteful sign on the check-in counter, or offering these accommodations at the time of reservation, will help sell them. Another big plus is that these clients are possible buyers of wellness merchandise that can be sold from the rooms by the hotel menus on the TV screen in the rooms, or with printed information in the room.

Convert some of your vacancies to Wellness Units.

Advertise & charge extra for these rooms.

Convert existing clientele to higher rates and/or obtain new clients.

Sell merchandise from the rooms.

STRATEGY 96

Counter Trade

I first learned about this phrase "Counter Trade" years ago while I was living in England and pursuing exchanging and barter. There was a book available at the time on the subject of "Counter Trade" for the use of people within the government as a guide for negotiating international trades. I have used this technique routinely ever since.

PHILOSOPHY	These examples seem simple but the philosophy is sophisticated. Some of their examples were in the transportation field. Let's say you are representing the English government and you are having a ship or airplanes built in another country because of their capabilities. As part of your negotiations with the contractor, you require them to buy certain products from England to go in your ship or airplanes. Perhaps it is the electronics.	You don't want the "Counter Trade" philosophy to get in the way of the main purpose of the negotiation. There is hardly any negotiation, however, that cannot be enhanced some way by thinking "Counter Trade."
COUNTER ACTION	Counter trading goes even further: You may say you would like to have them also buy the electronics from you for the other ships or planes they are building, even if those ships or planes have nothing to do with the one(s) you are negotiating on. Counter trade suggests that the negotiations are not done until you have other things accomplished, often completely unrelated to the subject at hand.	
POSSIBLE SOLUTION	A simple example is prior to completion of negotiations on a real estate transaction you might say you would also like, as part of the deal, a one year option to purchase another building they owned at some agreeable figure. While you are negotiating you are also counseling the other party and you want to unearth things that you might be interested in as part of a counter trade before the negotiations close.	

STRATEGY 97

Multiple Notes in Quantity

We are referring here to TD/Notes or Personal Notes. There are a lot of uses for this formula. We are using just one example.

SITUATION	I first used this concept at an SEC meeting when negotiating with a very successful broker from Michigan. I had a small apartment building listed in Torrance, California, and there were three or four owners. The Michigan broker was only lukewarm about the deal so I asked him if he would create $100,000 worth of personal notes and not put up anything except his good credit. He liked that idea.	Unused credit is a vacancy issue. This same formula could have been designed with one TD using 10 notes. This also works. There are other issues involved and all should be analyzed. Do you have $1,000,000 in unused credit in your net worth? It is an unused asset.
POSSIBLE SOLUTIONS	We drafted an offer for him to create ten $10,000 personal notes. Interest was, I think, 6 percent and they were interest-only notes, payable monthly, with one note becoming due and payable each year. They were paid off in a total of 10 years. I, of course, took the note paying off the first year for my commission and the rest of the notes were split up by the partners who owned the building. $100,000 doesn't sound like much in an inflated economy but it was comparable to $500,000 in inflation-adjusted dollars today. Transactions are made in the business world where millions of dollars are contracted for in corporate debentures (just notes, and weak ones at that, as they are issued dependent upon being paid for out of company profits). I have no reservations about drafting a million dollars in personal notes from a worthy investor in a real estate deal.	

STRATEGY 98

DERIVATIVE #1

BENEFITS, BENEFITS, BENEFITS, BENEFITS

Derivatives, partially from the sub-prime mortgage market, play a significant role in the perfect storm raging in the U.S. and International economic and monetary markets today: 2010.

Believe it or not, the neat little pile above is $1 million dollars (100 packets of $10,000). You could stuff that into a grocery bag and walk around with it.

Fiat currency: We still think of it as real and it plays tricks on our minds. If it is worth two cents on the dollar and if you think you are a millionaire you are really worth $20,000. Real estate and other hard assets are real, we know that. Could we start to think in benefits rather than dollars?

STRATEGY 99

DERIVATIVE #2

While a measly $1 million looked a little unimpressive, $100 million is a little more respectable. It fits neatly on a standard pallet...

Now look at the number of pallets above. Ladies and gentlemen... I give you* $1 trillion dollars*... see the little man in the left hand corner? (And notice those pallets are double stacked.)

So the next time you hear someone toss around the phrase "a trillion dollars"... that's what they're talking about.

Derivatives: The total number the government reports is **ONE QUADRILLION: ONE THOUSAND ONE HUNDRED and 44 TRILLION to be exact. (1,144 of the above display)**. Approximately one-half of these are said to be Credit Default Swaps (CDS) and the ones where the notional value becomes real value when they default. Payment is then dependent on the loser's balance sheet to have the ability to pay. AIG, Bear Sterns and Lehman Bros. were losers. Internationally, I give you Iceland & England as failure examples from these CDS derivatives. Those who received bail-out money watched it go in their front door and out their back door to pay off the winners of these derivatives. Were you a real estate or business pawn somewhere in this game because you didn't see the whole picture?

APPROXIMATELY THREE TRILLION DERIVATIVES HAVE FAILED TO DATE. How many are left to fail? 500 trillion maybe?

Derivatives are just part of the perfect storm. Let's look at hyper-inflation next and then let's bring in the formulas and strategies to help ease the problems, protect our assets or generate profits on both a national and international level.

STRATEGY 100A
Liquefying Mining Assets

Proven assets are determined by geologists. They are factual. In mining, particularly in hard rock mining, it takes a long time and a lot of money to extract minerals. If the assets are real, we can create against them.

SITUATION	1. An exploration company has proven reserves of 10 million oz. of silver. The market is $15 an oz. and extraction cost is $5 an oz. They have a net asset value in this of $100 million dollars. 2. They need $5 million dollars in cash for operating expenses to see them through until they can get roads built and the infrastructure established. 3. Miners usually go to banks and hedge some of their deep storage minerals to raise capital. This presents a problem for both management and stockholders of the mining company as the banks usually want the loans paid back in either dollars or ounces of the product, whichever is the dearer. It is conceivable that the mine might have to pay back five or even 10 times the borrowed amount if the minerals appreciate rapidly. Mining is a global business. Minerals from all over the world are critical to everyday living. You can use the Creation of Wealth formula in any currency and make an exchange for assets in any other country of your choice.	Price: $150,000,000 Cost: $50,000,000 Equity: $100,000,000
POSSIBLE SOLUTION	Have an exchange broker list the right to create up to a $10 million loan against the proven assets and exchange the paper into a real estate asset where the miners can borrow the $5 million and pay it back without having to hedge some of their product.	
CONCLUSION	The mining company ends up with $5 M cash and a $5 M equity in a parcel of real estate. They have an un-hedged loan.	

STRATEGY 100-C

U.S. Dollar: A Derivative + Hyperinflation Tactic

The dollar can be considered the stock in the company, the United States of America, and/or a derivative of this company reflecting its economy and health. Any way you choose to perceive or connote it, it is difficult to look at these two charts and not wonder about the wisdom of eliminating the gold backing the dollar had when we were so prosperous.

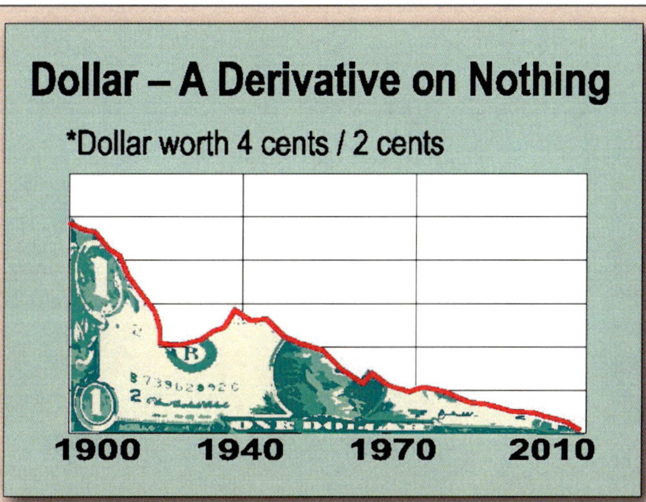

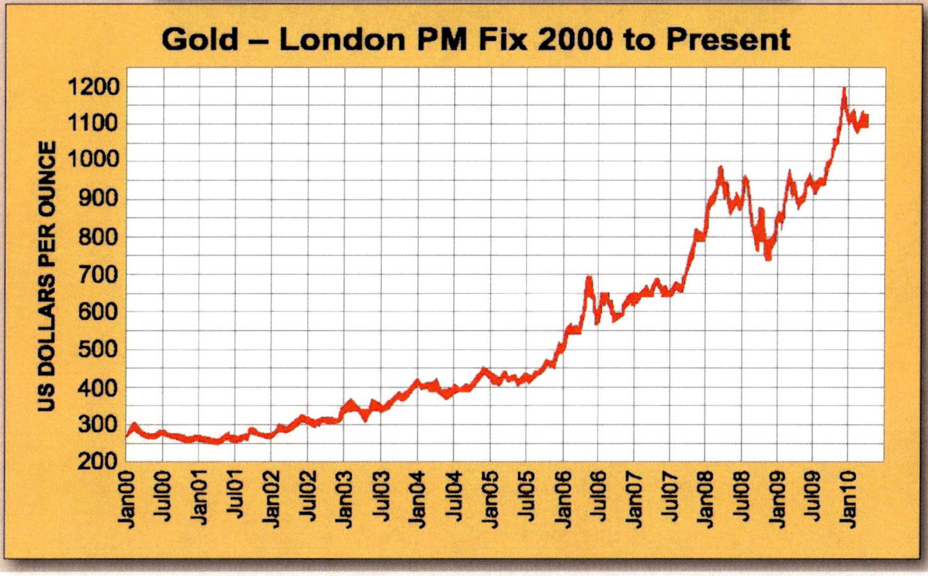

NOTES

300 STRATEGIES FOR MAKING REAL ESTATE & BUSINESS DEALS

VOLUME 5

STRATEGIES
101 – 125

25 Ways to Buy, Sell or Trade a House

ROBERT W. STEELE

Foreword by Donald E. DuBeau, SEC

OUTSIDE THE BOX & INSIDE / OUTSIDE THE COUNTRY

300 Strategies for Making Real Estate & Business Deals

Outside the Box & Inside / Outside the Country

VOLUME 5
Strategies 101 – 125

25 WAYS TO BUY, SELL OR TRADE A HOUSE

by Robert W. Steele

Foreword by Donald E. DuBeau, SEC

Design, Layout & Graphics
Victoria Vinton
Coyote Press Graphic Communications
www.coyotepressgraphics.com

VOLUME 5
CONTENTS

Introduction

Foreword: Donald E. DuBeau, SEC

Strategy	Title
#101	Buying or Selling a House for Cash
#102	Owner Carry-Back Financing
#103	List Below Market in a Buyer's Market
#104	"Talk Story" about Buying Houses
#105	Don't Drop Your Price If ...
#106	Over-Trade: a Viable Technique for Moving Equity in a House
#107	Strategic Withdrawal (Default) on SFR Loans not Uncommon
#108	Short Sale in SFRs
#109	Use Performance Mortgages When You Can in Buying SFRs
#110	Don't Buy Houses In Your Own Name
#111	Use Gold & Silver to Offset (and Eventually Pay Off) Your Loan on an SFR
#112	If You Have a F/C House (or a long equity) Refinance It Now and Buy Gold, Silver or Other Inflation-Resistant Assets
#113	Buy 1, 2, 3 or More SFRs & Form an Assisted Living Business
#114	Sell, Trade or Donate a Percentage of Interest in Some SFRs
#115	Diversify SFRs to Maximize Returns
#116	Educate Yourself about Owning SFRs
#117	Retirement Ploy Using SFR
#118	You Have 1,000 Things (OPS) to Use as a Down Payment into SFRs
#119	Stretch Geographically to Acquire SFRs if Necessary
#120	SFR Wellness Rentals
#121	Become a Teacher & Speaker on SFR Acquisitions
#122	Motivation Is a Motivator in SFRs
#123	Sell Out the Reverse Cash Flow in Rental SFRs
#124	Hitting Singles With SFRs
#125	Foreign SFRs
#125-A BONUS.......	When to Buy Real Estate Again

INTRODUCTION

25 Ways to Buy, Sell or Trade a House

I feel that this is an important book for the average person, a real estate licensee or an investor. For the average person it is often the aim of a lifetime to own his own home. I majored in real estate as I thought that a house (SFR – Single Family Residence) would be the most expensive thing I would ever buy, so why not learn about it. The study, of course, led me into a life where real estate played an important part.

For the average person this little book should also be a quick way to erase any mystique about owning SFRs. They are the simplest form of improved real estate and there are so many ways to go into and out of title that you can literally write books about it. Anyone can own a house – it is just knowing how to do it right that is important.

For the real estate licensee I seriously believe that you could not read this book without making an extra transaction per year. 40 years ago I wrote a little book about how everyone should obtaining at least one extra house as an investment so I didn't sell people just one house I sold them two or three.

Real estate licensees usually are trained to just make a sale one way. Hopefully this book will open some doors that will show you there are a lot of ways to make sales or trades that will solve clients' problems.

For the investor there is a wealth of information in this book. As I look back on the history of the SFR business, I think the biggest errors I have seen have been caused by not having good financing or simple buying your houses in poor locations, often just because you live there. This book will help you get in or out of SFRs and will also help you broaden your horizons as far as where you buy them. If you want to buy 1 or 100 houses, this book can be helpful.

Good luck,

Robert W. Steele

Donald E DuBeau, SEC

Foreword

TWELVE (12) TRILLION DOLLARS. That is the amount of loans currently on the books of the mortgage holders of single family homes in the United States alone. Mortgage amounts are equal to approximately 50% of the total value of homes in the United States alone. This gives investors in the United States an opportunity to invest in assets worth over TWENTY FOUR (24) TRILLION DOLLARS.

Over 68% of households in the United States own their own home.

The opportunity to invest in single family homes is at an all time high now.

I have had the pleasure of knowing and benefiting from Bob Steele's creative real estate transactions and the generous sharing of his experiences and knowledge for over forty years. You could search the world over and never find another creative mind like the mind of Bob Steele. Bob has been a mentor and educator to thousands of colleagues, students, partners and clients throughout the world.

I am extremely pleased to write the forward to one of the many books Bob has been so kind in sharing with the rest of the world so they too can benefit from his extensive knowledge and experiences.

For most people the largest investment they will make in their lives is the ownership of their own single family home. Many years ago at the start of my real estate career, one of the most enjoyable real estate transactions was to educate young families on how to own their own home and also own a single family home for rental purposes. In owning a second home as an investment property, we were able to demonstrate how the income and ownership advantages of the second home could assist in building an estate and cutting down on the out-of-pocket costs of the ownership of their own family home.

In this book Bob Steele will demonstrate the many ways to buy and sell or exchange single family properties by utilizing the many formulas that have been tested over the years.

Donald E. DuBeau, SEC

Whitefish, Montana

STRATEGY 101

Buying or Selling a House for Cash

This is really simple. Don't make it complicated. There is nothing very complicated about this unless it is your first time and then a great deal of the complication is that you have a learning curve to go through concerning the meaning of a lot of new words such as title policies, deeds, mortgages, credit scores, and a plethora of legal work that makes a realtor seem like a genius. On a scale of 1 to 10, buying or selling a house is a 2. It isn't difficult. Take your time – learn it. I majored in real estate and really for one reason, I thought it might be the most expensive thing I ever purchased in my life so it made sense to me to learn it. It is so simple one of my children acquired five houses during their first year of college. It just isn't hard to do.

SITUATION	1. Cash is a common denominator but it means something different to every single person alive, even if the difference may be subtle. 2. If this is your first brush with business and negotiations just remember that the people involved are every bit as important as the real estate. I think honestly that they are more important. 3. This is not rocket science. Ask or find out what the people do. Do they have wealth, are they just comfortable or are they stretching in this deal. Really find out about them.	IMO (In My Opinion) Buying or selling real estate is like playing a violin. Buying or selling a car is like beating a drum. They are just different.
POSSIBLE SOLUTIONS	1. What you are trying to do is make the deal work for the other side but be able to extract as much out of the situation as you can for yourself. 2. Remember that he who cares least wins in negotiations. If someone is anxious it shows through. 3. Don't be in a hurry. Everyone wants your commitment now but listen to your hunches. If you are unsure, sleep on it. If it is a deal that makes sense and you are not leaving too much on the table, do the deal now. The longer you stall usually, not always, the better you do.	Remember, while a house is just brick and mortar, it is the people that make it a home. It is hard to separate the house & the home They are both investments but of different kinds.

STRATEGY 102

Owner Carry-Back Financing

There isn't just one way to do this. Are there 100 different ways to carry-back equity? Maybe. Don't be locked to convention. Design this so it does what you want it to do.

SITUATION	You are selling a house in a down market. Buyers are scarce but you have one in negotiation. Price has been agreed to at $300,000. You owe $150,000. The buyer wants to put $50,000 down and asks you to carry back a loan for $100,000. What should the terms be on this paper? The design of this carry-back paper depends a lot upon what you intend to do with it. If you are going to hold it, you design it one way. If you plan to sell it, then you design it another way. If you are going to trade it you design it yet another way.	Price: Loan: Equity: Downpmt: Owner finance:	$300,000 150,000 150,000 $ 50,000 $ 100,000

POSSIBLE SOLUTION

1. Standard terms, if there is such a thing, might be 1% a month payment or $1,000 per month including interest at 6 percent and all due and payable in three years.
2. The buyer says she can't afford that and can only pay $500 per month and is concerned about the three year due date.
3. You might counter offer at $500 per month increasing to $600 the 2nd yr. & then increasing $100 per mo. per yr. and all due in 5 years w/ 8% interest. The increase to 8% is to improve the note's value if you sell or trade it.
4. You can do anything you want with this paper that both parties agree to:
   a) It can be no interest and no payments for one year.
   b) Or Interest accumulating.
   c) Or no payments during three months in the summer.
   d) Or if they don't pay it off in 3 years the note goes up $5,000 in face value.

There are absolutely no absolutes. Be as creative as you need to be.

Strategy 103

List Below Market in a Buyer's Market

When the market is falling, list to sell below the price your realtor suggest.

SITUATION

Philosophy: The realtor wants your listing. He is also battling what he thinks the market is doing but he is unsure because governments and industry manipulate the markets to make them look rosier then they are. Also, realtors often suggest that you be a little above the market so you can negotiate down to make a buyer happy, etc. The seller contributes to this dance as they always likes to think they will get top dollar. Here is what I do and suggest: Ask the realtor to give you a price that he can sell it for in 30 days and then list it for less than he says. You can get more than one opinion before you set your price. If I think the market is dropping, I get right after it. I'll list it from 5% – 15% below their price depending on what I think is happening.

CONCLUSION

Real estate is always liquid just like the stock market: If the market is truly falling and you list a little above the market, the market falls and you lower your price a little and you are still above the market and you follow the price all the way down and don't sell until you get to the bottom of the market. Real estate is liquid. There is always a cash market. The system keeps you from finding what the true market is. That is why real estate auctions work.

Get down to where the buyers are and it will sell. If you don't want to do that, then exchange.

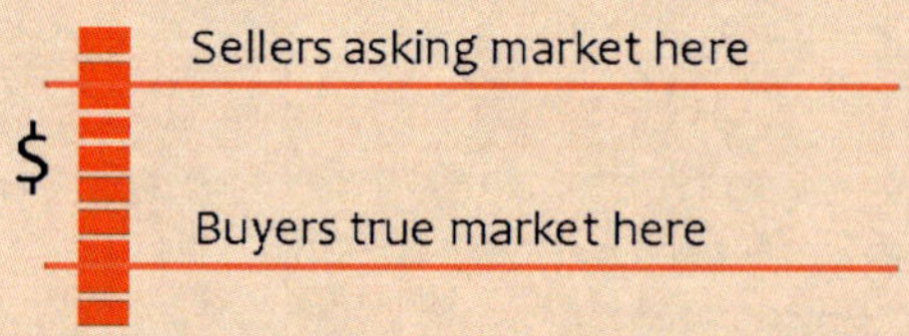

Remember that in a falling market as you are dropping your price the buyers market is also dropping out from under you.

Do not take any contingency escrows in a falling market if they tie your hands. Don't miss the market because it will be gone tomorrow.

STRATEGY 104

"Talk Story" about Buying Houses

I used to live on the island of Maui in Hawaii. Native Hawaiians get together and chat about different things and when they do, it is said colloquially, that they are "Talking Story." So let's be informal here and "Talk Story" about buying houses.

I probably qualify to sit in on this "Talk Story," as I have played a role in buying more or less a hundred houses and countless more for investors. But let's start with some simple background.

STORIES

The simple strategy of paying off one rental house and then combining the income from that one and paying off the second one and on and on is exemplified by the couple that started riding their bicycles to work. They saved all their gas money for the car, maintenance, etc. and all this saved capital was paid on the principal of the rental house they were paying off. Saving is the key.

On the other hand one of my Ex-SEC (Society of Exchange Counselors) broker friends acquired 600 houses in an REO deal (real estate owned). These were transactions from lenders who had foreclosed on them.

The three examples above typify the acquisition range that is available in SFRs (single family residences) from 1 to 600.

I discussed the merits of SFRs with a client of 30 years who had started by buying houses from me as a broker. She was a highly motivated individual who, over a period of five years, was at a point where she was buying a small rental house from me about every 90 days. We bundled these all up at one time and exchanged them into a larger investment property. Then together we analyzed years later and it was clear to both of us that he would have been better off had he stayed with his house buying program. There was diversification, lower risk, etc., and the total of her estimated assets would have been nearly as high.

Add to this one more ingredient from a very wise broker from Witchita, Kansas, Colby Sandlian (another SEC friend) who says only make your property work once—meaning finance it once and then never again. Keep it free and clear.

Thanks for Talking Story with me.

STRATEGY 105

Don't Drop Your Price If ...

There is a trap that many people fall into and an easy trap it is. When a market is falling or a real estate parcel has lost what the world calls value, remember—the benefits may not have diminished. Vying between these two worlds of value and benefits is tricky but can be rewarding if you understand it.

SITUATION	1. You have a house on the market to sell at $1,000,000. The market is softening and the tendency is to drop your price in order to find a buyer. See Strategy #103. 2. You drop your price to $900,000 and it still doesn't sell and then you go to $800,000 or maybe $700,000. 3. Bear in mind now that you are dealing in the world of value when dealing in dollar signs and not in benefits. The benefits of this house have not changed from the time you had it priced at $1,000, 000 to the time it is priced at $700,000. It still has the same number of square feet, the same roof, the same school district, etc. So the benefits have not changed, but the value has. But now you are moving to a different arena—the exchange market. 4. Think before you lower the price. If the only way you are going to be able to move this house is in an exchange within the circle of people who deal in benefits, dropping the price to $700,000 means you have given up a great deal of your equity position. Once you have dropped the price you usually cannot recapture it. You can go to un-priced, but the records and tracks are there for anyone to see when they do their due diligence.
POSSIBLE SOLUTION	If you think the market is gone or is too low for you to accept, then do not change your price from $1,000,000. Leave it right there and move away from the value/price world into the benefit world. Don't give up your equity to please a realtor or a market. Control your fortune. Lowering your price is a waste of time and equity if there is no cash buyer within your range of acceptance. Lowering the price will eventually hurt you. Leave it at $1,000,000 and go for an exchange.

STRATEGY 106

Over-Trade: a Viable Technique for Moving Equity in a House

The over-trade is a reversal from the norm (see Strategy #169 Vol. 7) of selling a house, going down and out in exchangors vernacular, and going up instead, exchanging it into something of higher value. As you go up, the importance of what you are leaving (the back side of the exchange) or exchanging becomes of less importance. More importance is given to what you are going into, or into the more expensive property. The higher in price you go the less importance the property you are leaving becomes. Any problem around the back side (house) becomes of less importance.

SITUATION	1. You have a house on the market to sell at $1,000,000. You have 2 loans, $500,000 and $100,000. There is an equity of $400,000 2. The $100,000 note is becoming due and payable and there is no market to refinance at this time and there is no sales market.	Price: Loans: Equity:	$1,000,000 500,000 100,000 $400,000
POSSIBLE SOLUTION	1. Consider an over-trade or exchanging this up. You have a partner or an associate who also has a property he would like to get moved. It is a commercial building, valued at $2,000,000 with a $500,000 loan and one where it would be very easy to borrow the $100,000 you need to retire the loan coming due on your property. 2. You form a joint venture and combine the two properties: You now have (hypothetically) a total of $1,900,000 in equity with still $100,000 loan coming due. 3. The joint venture exchanges up into a $5,000,000 property where you owe $3,100,000. The party taking your two properties will have to retire the $100,000 debt coming due but that is insignificant because of the size of the deal and the source of the needed funds is within the deal. He can borrow the $100,000 on the building your partner or associate is bringing in. By trading up, the problem becomes smaller in relationship to the size of the deal.	Price: Loan: Equity J.V. Equity: Up Trade Loans: Equity:	$2,000,000 500,000 1,500,000 $ 400,000 1,500,000 $1,900,000 $5,000,000 3,100,000 $1,900,000

STRATEGY 107

Strategic Withdrawal (Default) on SFR Loans not Un-common

Morals and mores are changing! A true story.

SITUATION	1. John Doe has always dutifully paid his bills and socked away money for retirement. But recently he defaulted on the mortgage on his home, even though he could afford the payments. 2. Mr. Doe paid $385,000 for the two-bedroom in 2006, when prices were still surging. Comparable homes are now selling as low as $200,000. At 66, the retired psychologist doubted he'd see his investment rebound in his lifetime. Plus, he said he was duped into an expensive loan. 3. The way he sees it, big banks that helped fuel the mess all got bail-outs, while small fry like him are left holding the bag. No more. 4. "There was not a chance that house was ever going to be worth anywhere near what my mortgage was," said Mr. Doe, who is now renting a few miles away after defaulting on the $310,000 loan. "I haven't cheated or stolen." 5. Time was when Americans would do almost anything to hang on to their homes. But that commitment appears to be fraying as more people fall behind on their loans while watching the banks and lenders that helped trigger the financial crisis return to prosperity. 6. If he stays in the property, he will pay out another $110,000 in losses plus substantial interest on a negative equity.
POSSIBLE SOLUTION	Strategic Withdrawal (Default) or keep paying? That is the question each person has to answer for himself.

Price Paid:	$385,000
Owes:	310,000
Loss:	$75,000
Price Paid:	$385,000
Value:	200,000
Potential Loss:	$185,000
Cardinal rule of business: ***Cut your losses!***	
Potential Loss:	$185,000
Actual loss:	75,000
Additional loss if he stays	$110,000

STRATEGY 108

Short Sale in SFRs

In real estate, a short sale means that, upon sale, there is not enough money to pay off the loans. The sale proceeds are "short" the needed amount to un-encumber the financial obligations tied to the property. A real estate short sale should not be confused with a securities short sale whereby the investor sells the stock having not owned it and is therefore "short" the stock and has to borrow the stock from an independent source in order to make delivery to the entity to whom the investor has sold the stock.

SITUATION	Because the proceeds in a short sale fall short (pun intended) of the amount needed to pay off the loan obligations, the seller must get the approval from the lenders (creditors) because the lenders will not be made whole upon sale.	Example: Short Sale Price: Loans: Negative Equity:	SFR $1,000,000 1,200,000 ($200,000)
POSSIBLE SOLUTION	1. Once approval has been granted by the lenders, the transaction proceeds pretty much as would any other real estate transaction with the added need for the lenders approving everything along the way. 2. What has happened in short sales is that it can take months – many months in some cases – before the lenders grant approval for a short sale. This strings out the seller and can sometimes cause other financial ramifications. 3. The lenders are under absolutely no obligation to grant permission for a short sale, thereby choosing to take the property back, assuming they proceed with the foreclosure process.	Lender receives: Lenders Loss: Credit:	$1,000,000 ($200,000) Possibly affected. Things change, but currently not as bad as bankruptcy.
NOTE	The short sale is time-consuming and the deal could still be pulled down the road if the lender finally decides against the short sale.		

STRATEGY 109

When You Can Use Performance Mortgages in Buying SFRs

We have been beating the Performance Mortgage drum for seven or eight years now and it seems like finally there is an awakening taking place. More and more people are seeing the absolute necessity of using these mortgages both as buyers and lenders. There are other examples of this strategy in Volume 4 of this series.

SITUATION	One advantage of using this type of mortgage or T.D. is that it totally eliminates the possibilities of foreclosure. Over time it has been very difficult to get recognized lenders to see the light but private investors are moving into this arena. In effect it makes the lender a joint venture partner and sharing in the potential profits of the real estate deal but doing so from a safety first position of being the owner of the first trust deed or mortgage. We will show here its possible using in an SFR acquisition where the SFR is to be held as a rental and investment property. To exemplify the performance aspects we are going to make it a 100% loan. You can structure it any way you want.
POSSIBLE SOLUTIONS	You are buying a $200,000 SFR to use as a rental and you expect the rents to be $1,500 per month ($18,000 per year) and the expenses at 40% ($7,200) and $10,800 spendable cash flow or a 5.4% return on the $200,000 invested. You offer this out to private investors to put up the $200,000. They are in effect joint venture partners, as they receive one-half of the net rents during the holding period. Upon future sale they get their money back first and 50% of the profits. They carry the risk that if values fall they take the loss, but they never can lose it all. As rents go up their payments also go up. You can, of course, change these percentages any way you see fit.

STRATEGY 110

Don't Buy Houses In Your Own Name

It is important to protect yourself, and your first step is to hold title to your real estate, and often other assets, in a fictitious name. This can be in a business trust, a land trust, a partnership, an LLC, a Corporation or any other vehicle directed by your legal counsel and acknowledged by your tax counsel.

SITUATION	Recognize that for the average person real estate represents the single most expensive item he will buy during his lifetime. Business-wise that also means it is your greatest exposure to risk. In any business deal you must have an exit strategy—a back door. How do you get out of "it" if after all your planning you were wrong? There is not and never will be anyone "out there" who is going to protect you, except you. Therefore, if you listen to the crowd, the newspaper, the radio or TV you very well may be damaged if the market turns. The bad things that can happen are a list as long as your arm. They are talking as we speak about bulldozing thousands of houses in Detroit, the eleventh largest city in the U.S. The bureaucrats can change your entire life with one vote.
POSSIBLE SOLUTION	If you treat business like business and own your real estate in a business form, if something goes wrong you can close your business, take your loss, walk away and not be damaged beyond your investment. There are many things the average person does not understand, like judicial foreclosures that allow lenders to come after other assets you might own. If you have to take title in your own name, use an exculpatory clause in the debt instruments that your attorney can draw for you. It will read something like this: "The property herein is the sole security for the debt."

STRATEGY 111

Use Gold & Silver to Offset (and Eventually Pay Off) Your Loan on an SFR

We have been advocating this play for the last few years and continue to do so. Please also see Strategies #59 & #83 for other gold & silver techniques. Because of its importance we are considering doing a book on the variety of their uses, in concert with real estate, when hyperinflation comes calling. A loose consensus of opinions pegs hyperinflation as being when inflation is 50% per month or 600% per year.

SITUATION

One of our major western cities is said to have, as of this writing, 81% of their SFRs upside down or mortgages over value and the market is still dropping. One possible way for the owners of these houses, who will probably never see the value relationship change in their lifetimes, can still win is by using the strategy suggested herein. This obviously could also be a good strategy for those not up-side down.

Chart showing hyperinflation vs. gold & silver prices in Germany in years noted:

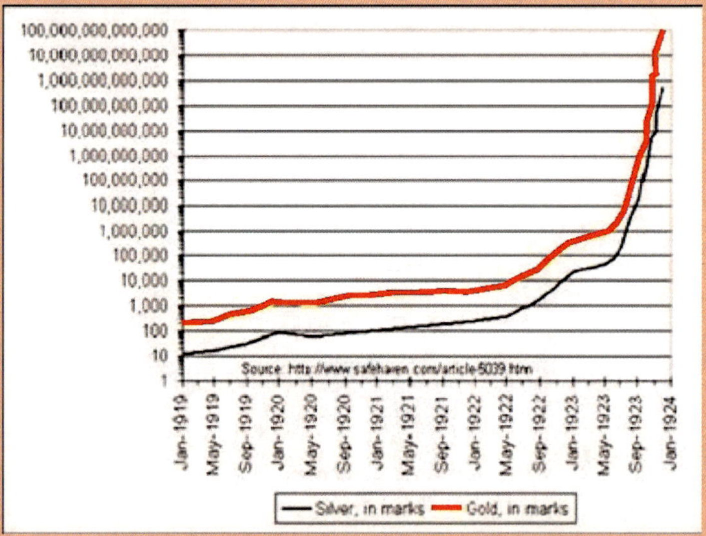

POSSIBLE SOLUTION

If the mortgage on your SFR is $200,000, beg, borrow or steal $20,000 cash (10% of loan) and buy gold and silver. When hyperinflation hits, the G & S prices will rise rapidly, your mortgage is static and will remain unchanged. When the G & S reaches the amount of your loan, sell it and pay off the mortgages. Keep one eye on taxes as it is a taxable event.

STRATEGY 112

If You Have a F/C House (or a long equity), Refinance it Now and Buy Gold, Silver or Other Inflation-Resistant Assets

The hardest part of this strategy is to move against all the belief systems you have held for many years. Paying off the mortgage was sometimes the life goal of our mothers & fathers.

SITUATION	1. Mental toughness and radical changes are difficult bedfellows. 2. 99.9% of us have never experienced the ravages that come with hyper-inflation. We can, however, read history and not have to re-live it, but it takes some serious mental preparedness. 3. If your study of history shows you that having the capital tied up in your home, which is giving you peace of mind, but the same capital might beget you 10 or even 1000 to 1 if it were placed in some other hard asset like gold and silver when hyper-inflation hits, then a tough new thought has to be entertained, and perhaps action is needed.	
POSSIBLE SOLUTION	1. I am a serious believer in the right to bear arms. Let's compare this hyper-inflation problem of borrowing out one's home equity with the four steps to the defensive use of firearms. WHITE is when conditions are normal, no action is necessary. YELLOW is walking down a dark street at night. We need to be alert. ORANGE is when a man is following you down that dark street. RED is when the downstairs window is broken during the middle of the night. 2. Defensive firearm use is different than how we were trained in the military or when we have been hunting. The key is never point the gun unless you are going to fire. Don't hesitate or ask questions, just fire. That takes mental toughness. In 60 plus years I have only been at code RED once & this phrase was paramount in my mind: "If I point it, I am going to shoot it." I am not going to point it at some kid stealing tires off my car as I am not in danger. That is not code RED. 3. You figure out what code RED is for you when it comes to hyper-inflation, and recognize that if you are going to borrow out that house equity, you have to borrowed it before you get to code RED. At some point it may be too late.	When re-financing obtain only a fixed rate loan. When hyper-inflation hits, you can pay off the unwanted mortgage with cheap, cheap, cheap dollars.
NOTE	Visit www.steelesstrategies.com to use the Hyper-Inflation Wheel.	

STRATEGY 113

Buy 1, 2, 3 or More SFRs & Form an Assisted Living Business

Zoning requirements are a key to this business. Different areas and different cities have zoning laws to control the use of houses. For instance, some allow up to six people using a home for assisted living purposes. We are using this factor in the example below.

SITUATION	Using 3-bedroom-and-den homes (two people per bedroom), you can accommodate six people in each house as an assisted living facility. The more bathrooms, the better. The den serves as a communal area with the television, etc. The number of units you have depends on the quality of the service you can offer. Using a nurse to dispense pills and having a driver for the van for shopping trips, doctor visits, etc. all play a role. This can also be done with just one person or with a couple. Usually you can find a price structure that allows you to be below the going rate in a standard assisted living facility. Every area differs. The nicer the area, the higher the price. Small facilities can possible offer more personalized service but this of course depends on management.	Price: $4,500 ea X 6 per house = $27,500 per month Income x 3 SFRs = $81,000 per month Consider long-term leasing facilities also. Consider using this technique if you have a larger house than you need and can use one or two bedrooms to create income. The population is getting older. There will be more and more need for facilities.
POSSIBLE SOLUTIONS	If the going rate in an area is $6,000 per month for a care facility, then $4,000 or $4,500 per month in a small facility should certainly find a market. Many people use this program to supplement their retirement and others use it as a full fledged business. I saw one grouping by one owner who owned three (3 bdr.) houses on one cul de sac and the advantages were many in that he could use one driver, one manager which was also a nurse, for all three properties. One business opportunity broker has suggested that one manager can comfortable handle five of these small facilities.	

STRATEGY 114

Sell, Trade or Donate a Percentage of Interest in Some SFRs

There was a time when an SFR was just too small an item to warrant holding title when the asset was geographically out of your area. This is no longer the case. Also there can be other than geographical reasons to divide the equity interest in an SFR.

SITUATION	Not too many years ago the mean average 3-bedroom house was $35,000. If it had a 50% mortgage the equity was only $17,500 and the rents were also low. The equity was just too small to fool with if you lived in California and the house was in Texas. Today that house is perhaps valued at $300,000 – $400,000 and thousands of houses are well over a $1,000,000. The potential significance of SFRs has moved from almost a nuisance category to one that can represent a lot of wealth. A 50% equity can represent a lot of dollars and potential. However, the nuisance factor has not changed any. It is difficult to monitor or manage smaller properties from afar. Couple that with the fact we are now moving more and more into the international market, that distance factor adds to it possible language differences, etc.	To me it is almost always worthwhile to have a local partner of some nature in joint ownership or profit sharing when the property is afar. Management is probably one of the best recession-proof businesses there is but there are professionals that know a lot more about it than I do. Management and monitoring are two different things. The later being much simpler.
POSSIBLE SOLUTION	If you have an associate, a broker, an attorney or other contact who is qualified and located in the area of the SFR asset, it can really be worth your while to trade them, sell or even donate a percentage of ownership in that particular vehicle to eliminate the nuisance factor. They are on the spot and can handle the monitoring and make decisions and provide solace where needed. Even on a local basis, if you want freedom from management and to set up your life to be more free for creative work or travel, giving someone a percentage of interest in the vehicle or in the profits is often a smart way to eliminate the brain drain that goes with management.	

STRATEGY 115

Diversify SFRs to Maximize Returns

There is massive wealth in this world. This money wants to work. It is trying to find places where it can do work and produce benefits and make profits. That is capitalism. Socialism produces nothing. It consumes (Ludwig Von Misis). The more you can open up your area of take geographically, the more chances for opportunity there are. When political systems create an environment where capital can work, money and jobs flood to that direction. It is like creating a vacuum in a sea of taxation. Remember that all systems are political and when they start to change from capitalism to socialism you have to move your assets. Don't fight the truth. As Nike says, "Just Do It." That is why you must diversify. For instance, right now there are no real estate taxes in Panama on new construction for 20 years. This helps your capitalization rate and means you can own condos or rental units there and make a larger profit. But as sure as the sun is coming up tomorrow, a new socialistic politician will come into the mix someday in Panama and you will again have to move assets. It may be 10 years or 50 years, but it will happen. Diversification is paramount. Don't fight the system, it will drive you nuts.

SITUATION	Let's say that you like single family residences as an investment. So you set up a target of owning 100 of them. You brainstorm this (see Volume 7) and develop a plan and continue to refine it as needed. Build into your plan the information above. Here is a possible plan: While you are acquiring your first 10 SFRs in one country you are researching for your next country so that by the time you have your hundred houses you end up with maybe 1/3 in each of three countries. Be sure you have researched all laws regarding ownership in any country in which you invest. Please note, that the political climate will change. Don't fight it. When you see that happen, and you will be far more cognizant than 99% of the populace, then sell or trade out and move your SFRs to another country or political arena.	Don't fight the problem. No political system is forever because the moment people find out they can vote and receive entitlements or benefits from their votes, capitalism will break down. "Vote With Your Feet." Move your assets. See strategy of that name in Volume 9.

STRATEGY 116

Educate Yourself about Owning SFRs

If you believe that you would really like to own SFRs as an investment, then it is up to you to find the instructors or teachers to help you get there. Public education has one type of school (with a few exceptions noted). Schools teach you how to become employees, not how to run businesses. We really need two school systems as we need one to teach employees and one to teach entrepreneurs. Someone has to create the jobs for the employees. Most teachers are employees themselves, not entrepreneurs. That means you have to find a mentor and ferret out the education yourself.

POSSIBLE SOLUTIONS

There are several ways to go about starting your educational process. You can start by building your first house yourself. Get the hammer and nails and just build it out of pocket, meaning pay for it as you go.

Another way is to build it yourself but get a loan and you be the contractor.

Another is for you to be the developer, get a loan, hire a contractor and work with him to build the house.

I started by getting a real estate license and using my commission as the down payment along with some ingenuity to get into title on an existing home, and then did the old fashioned fix-it-up routine.

Today there are seminars that can help and a lot of books on the subject. Seminars are really good if they are taught by teachers that actually ply their trade. That way they are bringing knowledge into the session today that they used yesterday in the field.

If you happen to be in a house ownership position right now that is untenable, as so many are with mortgage over value, and so forth, bless it, take all the learning you can out of it and move on. Get another house and do it right. Think it out for yourself and make your own decisions. There are thousands of opportunities world-wide.

You also do not have to start at the bottom.

You can start by including someone with land in a partnership and start out by building a group or tract of houses and maybe keeping one or two for yourself.

If you make your first deal a good one, it will set a tone for the rest.

STRATEGY 117

Retirement Ploy Using SFR

Sell the building only (not the land underneath) to your children or future heirs for nothing down and keep the land. Deed out slowly a percentage of the equity at $10,000 each per year, in compliance with gift tax laws.

<table>
<tr><td>CAVEAT</td><td>There are a variety of different laws relevant to this structure and they are subject to change. It is the concept you should try to grasp here and then work with legal & tax counsel so that the structure is right.</td><td rowspan="3">SFR
$300,000

Building $100,000 value

Land $200,000 value

Building purchased at $500 per month

Land leased at $1,000 per month.

Tenants pay rent to children

Children make two payments to you totaling $1,500 per month.</td></tr>
<tr><td>SITUATION</td><td>You own a house that you have rented. It is free and clear and has a value of $300,000. Rents net, after expenses and taxes, $1,500 per month and you use this income as part of your living expenses.

The house is older but on valuable land. The tax assessed ratio of land and building show 66% land value and 33% building value.

You have three children or future heirs.</td></tr>
<tr><td>POSSIBLE SOLUTIONS</td><td>You sell the building only (not the land) to the children for $100,000 for nothing down with no or a low interest rate (counsel can advise you regarding imputed interest rate requirements) and payable at $500 per month.

The children lease the land from you at $1,000 per month. At this point you have recaptured the $1,500 per month income you started with. In the agreement you actually deed this land (value of $200,000) out to the children at $10,000 each (total of $30,000 per year) but you retain a life estate on the income total of the amount of the land lease ($1,000 per month).

The net result of this is that you are retaining the cash flow from this property for your lifetime but the children are going into title basically tax fee one bite at a time. This is a conceptual strategy. Design it so it fits your situation.</td></tr>
</table>

STRATEGY 118

You Have 1,000 Things in Other People's Stuff (OPS) to Use as a Down Payment into SFRs

We have tried to exaggerate a little here to make a point. SFRs are the smallest improved items available in the real estate market. At any one time there are millions of them on the market for sale or trade. Probably 95% of the brokers dealing in the retail market only sell these SFRs with a cash down payment. At any time there is an interruption in either the cash market or the credit market, these sales tend to stop and there is a clean-out process where 25% to 50% of the brokerage fraternity fall out. The other 5% of the market is open to trade and making deals that do not require cash. This percentage can move down during good economic time and rise considerable during the tougher times. This is the arena where you can acquire SFRs for investment if you wish.

SITUATION	We have all heard the acronym OPM meaning Other People's Money. Real estate uses this in most transactions. One way or another there is money involved in most real estate deals, and the buyer is either borrowing it from a conventional lender or a private lender.	Every property held for investment is potentially an OPS item for you.
POSSIBLE SOLUTIONS	There is another acronym, OPS, meaning Other Peoples' Stuff (besides money). You can negotiate to borrow someone else's vacant lot and use it as your down payment. That is OPS. Our Vol. 10 in this series is entitled "Half the World is Vacancy." There are literally thousands of things or "stuff" going unused in our world that can be used as down payments into SFRs. There are two major points that are worth noting here: 1. Spend your time locating the SFR property owner you can deal with first and then find the OPS. Finding the property owner who will deal with you is harder than finding the OPS, so do the hardest part first. 2. You have to be the flexible one in the transaction. You can't go shopping with OPS like you can cash. You have to be flexible in what you buy and where you buy it. The more flexible you are the better you will do.	Those holding property for investment are deal makers in some way and can be approached as a potential OPS source for you. There is literally no end to the source of OPS which opens up avenues for you.

STRATEGY 119

Stretch Geographically to Acquire SFRs if Necessary

Sometimes you are lucky and you can buy SFRs that make investment sense right in your home town. Most of the time it is more difficult than that.

SITUATION	As we are writing this there are many cities in the U.S. that have over 50% of the homes that have mortgages over the value of the homes. And you must couple that with the knowledge that the prices of homes are being artificially held up through manipulation, so conditions are actually worse than they appear, as the free market can't work and give you clear investment signs. Banks have not been permitted to fail, mortgages not foreclosed on, etc. It is not just a national problem but it also permeates the world. Here in the west some nice cities, Modesto, Las Vegas, and Phoenix, just to name a few, have this problem. Would you buy investment SFRs in these cities now? Probably not.	Stay out of any areas where there are conflicts of any nature, high unemployment, school enrollments falling, etc. Look with favor on college towns, those with civic amenities like museums, art festivals, bankers that have been in the same chair for 20 years, etc.
POSSIBLE SOLUTIONS	Are there cities in other parts of the U.S. where statistic are much better? Yes. Absolutely. How about picking a nice town of say 30,000 people in Nebraska, Colorado or Kansas that is agriculturally based? Manufacturing plants in bigger cities have moved to China or India towards cheaper labor, while food products will always be needed. Stretch even more and think "International." Get as close to the 1% rule as you can but don't make it the only factor. That is, 1% of price per month in rents. A $100,000 house that rents at $1,000 per month would be the perfect house economically. Other factors definitely count. Panama with no taxes on new SFRs for 20 years works very closely. Florida with high insurance rates make it difficult.	You have definite need for a well-established real estate management firm with competition. Long term stability.

Strategy 120

SFR Wellness Rentals

We refer you also to strategy #226 in Volume 10 regarding Wellness Units, and we will also make a prediction as we have watched these micro changes over a lifetime and know how they develop. Maybe 10 years from now this strategy will be just be getting a good toe hold in the real estate world. 20 years from now it will be commonplace. In the meantime some fortunes will be made by those who are aware of the potential and get in on the ground floor.

SITUATION	You can see the change in consciousness in every direction concerning wellness. Organic foods, non-smoking rooms, explosive use of herbs vs. medicines, medical professionals switching to the field of naturopathy and some clinics acknowledge that at one time most things used in the medical world were alternative medicine so they are becoming more open to new thoughts while still relying on science.	Specializing makes you an authority which begets higher prices. I'll put on my long range thinking hat and predict that you will see wellness cars in the future. If you go back and reread Strategy 113 in this Volume, and couple that with the Wellness concept, you can open what could be a fantastic business with your SFRs.
POSSIBLE SOLUTIONS	To create a Wellness House from the ground up is expensive. It could add as much as an estimated 25% – 30% more to construction costs. At the time of this writing I have no experience in building these but reasonable knowledge about designing remodels or rentals, and I am very familiar with the companies that have head starts in this field. Their growth is very impressive and their results are becoming historic. Every time you see someone with a health problem, there is a serious chance he can be improved or corrected by living in a wellness environment—meaning the elimination of contaminates and surrounded by the correct air system, drinking the right water, strengthening his immune system, and so forth. By converting SFRs to Wellness Houses for rentals, you will be able to obtain much higher rents. Starting with the basics, you get rid of the rugs and go to hardwood floor, change the air system and water system, paint, etc.	

STRATEGY 121

Become a Teacher & Speaker on SFR Acquisitions

By becoming an authority on the subject several things will happen. You will become involved in the acquisition of SFRs because you will become well-versed it the acquisition techniques, you will meet investors and partners that will want to follow your lead and you will have product brought to you by those wanting to market them.

SITUATION	Teachers & speakers that know their subjects are always in demand in real estate or business. The profits from teaching a seminar can be rewarding but the real profit comes from the connections and the business opportunities that are derived from it.	Use this book to teach a seminar to either peers, home owners, or investors. If you are working with clients or partners, the smarter they become the easier your job is. Teach seminars for profits. Deal in the now. Be a speaker at realty boards, exchange meetings, civic clubs, conventions, colleges, Chambers of Commerce, title companies, etc.
POSSIBLE SOLUTIONS	The other enormous benefit that comes from this is that you have to really study your subject matter in order to present it logically to others. This work and knowledge become second nature to you and it is at your mental finger tips as you need it in plying your trade. If the acquisition or selling of SFRs is an important part of your business and planning, then by speaking or teaching about the techniques you will know what really works and what is marginal. You will develop simple little plans that work over and over. It becomes easy. As you learn your subject matter better than anyone else around you, your confidence shows through. People become comfortable that you can deliver the solution that is needed and more and more opportunity is brought to you. And last but not least is that both your peers and potential clients or partners want to do business with you. No one likes to waste their time and people like to deal with closers.	

STRATEGY 122

Motivation is a Motivator in SFRs

I have seen clients so highly motivated about the acquisitions of SFRs that it was paramount in all their thinking. All their waking hours were spent in thinking about how to acquire another unit or get more income out of the ones they had.

MOTIVATION	One common technique used is to rent out bedrooms in a house to increase the overall income. Some will even rent out two to a room, often acquiring units just outside of cities where the zoning requirements were not as strict. In one city in Southern California, it is said that there are as many as 20 people living in a three bedroom house. It is probably true of more than one city. I had one client who was 80 years old and had accumulated houses for about 20 years, so she started when she was about 60. She actually had two houses moved onto a vacant land parcel for rentals when she was 80. Another highly motivated younger client decided to trade his SFRs into a motel, and then expand his motel operations by using the creation of wealth formula (see Volume 1). He was so highly motivated that when his first motel would sell out for the night he would actually make up his room and rent it out and go outside and sleep in his car. He owns a lot of real estate today. Motivation can move aside road blocks.	One highly motivated client who acquired many SFRs explained to me his motivating philosophy. He said he wanted to get paid for the rest of his life for the work he did today. So he worked to make his SFRs prime rental units and he planned to keep them forever and let them produce. He did a remarkable job.

STRATEGY 123

Sell Out the Reverse Cash Flow in Rental SFRs

It is always better to have a property that carries itself financially. That means that it earns enough from rentals to cover any mortgage payment and all expenses. Anything above that, of course, becomes spendable income.

SITUATION	There are a lot of SFRs that cannot be rented for enough to carry all their costs and pay the mortgage. Sometimes these SFRs are worth keeping. For instance, they might be in the path of growth, you might be in the process of plottage (acquiring contiguous properties for future development), they might be in line for an upgrade in zoning, etc. Let's make the assumption that this is a $500,000 SFR. You have trading in $200,000 in other equity and you have a $300,000 mortgage. The property has an overall negative cash flow of $1,500 per month including mortgage payments and all expenses. You do not want to service this negative cash flow.
POSSIBLE SOLUTIONS	Bring in a partner. She can actually come into the partnership with no front end investment. Her requirement is that she pay into the partnership $1500 per month. This offsets the negative cash flow. She will be receiving tax shelter depending on how you structure the transaction. Other terms and conditions you should design to work for both parties. Perhaps the investor's payments drop as the rents go up, etc. The percentage of ownership received depends on what is negotiated and acceptable.

STRATEGY 124

Hitting Singles With SFRs

I got this title from my son who has created and run a more than successful company for 15 to 20 years making residential loans using Dick Reno's & C. Charles Chatham's counseling techniques. He had played a major role prior to that in the acquisition of a lot of SFRs. I don't know the number but somewhere around 40 to 50 of them. He was a student at one time of a couple of men, Jack Miller & John Schaub, who taught a seminar called, "Making it Big in Little Deals."

SITUATION	Again the benefits on the small SFR shows through in a recessionary type market. The commercial market is totally frozen as we write and while it certainly isn't what it use to be, loans can still be had on SFRs. Politics certainly plays a role. There are probably 100 to 1 - SFR owners to every owner of a commercial or industrial building. If I were a politician I would probably like to help the sector that controlled 100 votes vs. the sector with 1 vote.	With proper financing almost any SFR can weather a recession. It is doubtful you will get recession-proof financing (like Performance Mortgages) from a conventional lender so look with favor on owner financing or private mortgage money. 3-way deals are good ways to set up this financing, see Vol. #6
POSSIBLE SOLUTION	Additionally the risks are lesser in a $300,000 to $400,000 house vs a $3,000,000 building. The tax complication can be minimized. If you need cash you can sell off one or two houses and not a major holding like a shopping center. If you acquire your SFRs in the wrong place no one can help you (think Detroit) but if you have structured your financing right and things go bad you can just lower your rents and work your way through it. Others with bad financing will be gone. Hitting singles make sense today. SFRs use to be $30,000 average, now around $300,000, as we move on in inflation we will see $3 million average and when it is hyperinflation time, you pick the number.	

STRATEGY 125

Foreign SFRs

When I first started in real estate I sold houses within roughly ten miles of the office. When I got into commercial real estate and businesses, this increased to cover my city area, and when I found the exchange market it expanded further to include the state and the national market. When I lived overseas, then the expansion into the international market came naturally. The opportunities when you add the world to your marketplace are just unbelievable.

EXTRANJERO

À L'ÉTRANGER

国外

ABROAD

BUITENLAND

VERKEERSBUREAU

There are 205 countries & territories, all with different opportunities:

See our Vol. 9 / International.

I spent several weeks in England a couple of years ago, and at one point visited with the president of a 600-year-old real estate family company with major holdings in downtown London. His company was building 5-star hotel properties in Asia and houses east of the Adriatic Sea where he said they had found a pocket where there were five buyers for every seller. My guess was he was in the area of Kosovo, Bosnia and Herzegovina. His other comment was that he would not put a nickel into the current real estate market in England or the United States at this time. Thinking foreign came naturally to him.

When I lived in Spain, prior to the Olympic games and World Fair there, the government was giving land free to qualified developers and furnishing them with no-interest loans to build hotels and motels to accommodate people along the new freeways that were being built for those events.

We have mentioned in other strategies within these pages that Panama is giving a 20-year moratorium on real estate taxes on new construction to entice people to move to Panama. When you plug no taxes into a real estate capitalization sheet, it mean owning condos or rental houses there makes economic sense.

There are hundreds of new opportunities out there.

The international market is as close as the internet.

When you worked in just your local marketplace that is all you thought there was. The same thing is true when you work in just your nation.

There is always someplace where a positive opportunity is waiting.

BONUS STRATEGY 125-A

When to Buy Real Estate Again

This strategy comes from a note that I sent to some close personal people on 5/7/10. It represents my own personal opinion and it shows how to analyze your holdings in gold and silver instead of dollars. As an admitted 40 year gold bug, I will paraphrase Mahatma Gandhi as my defense against a lot of comments over the many years: first they ridicule you, then they debase you, then they demean you and then you win. I will guess that 1 or 2% of the readers would have believed this 10 years ago and I will probably get 20% today. The Course In Miracles says it all when it states that it is a required course. The only thing that is optional is when you take it.

You are maintaining your assets with a base in free and clear real estate, commodities, precious metals and stocks representing the same. Every day there are some economists, news pundits, real estate boards, T-V Investment Panels or talking heads on the stock channels that tell you the depression is over, and in real estate the brokers are advertising, "It is a buyers market, jump in."

Forty years ago I was advocating in my seminars buying a 4-plex in Germany rather than in the U.S. to get the same rents but better purchasing power on the currency. Here is a least a guide as to when to go out of the hard stuff and back into houses or encumbered real estate (it won't have to be F/C then):

First a major point: Stop denoting real estate in dollars. In 2001 a median-priced home in the U.S. cost 601 oz. of gold. That was the time to get out and stay out. Today it is 153 oz. of gold, so houses have now really dropped 75% from their high regardless of what the pundits say regarding value in dollars. In 1980 it took 86 oz. of gold to buy that house. In 1970 I was not using gold as a standard but silver, and it took 1 bag of silver (715 oz.) to buy that house – approx $35,000 in dollars at that time.

When houses get back to 70 – 90 oz. of gold, a drop still to come of about 50% from where they are now (see above) it will be time to sell some of your G & S and go back into houses. In today's dollars that would be buying houses just under $100,000 (gold is at $1,200 oz.) but at that time, if we hit hyper-inflation, houses might cost $1,000,000 or even 10 times that in paper dollars—but pay no attention to that.

No one will want houses by that time and the market should be glutted. In a soft market 5 & 10% down will control a lot of real estate and with positive cash flow. Everyone will think you are nuts for buying, just like they all thought we were a little off when we started to say, "Don't buy."

NOTES

300 STRATEGIES FOR MAKING
REAL ESTATE & BUSINESS DEALS

VOLUME 6

STRATEGIES
126 – 150

Multiple Exchange Philosophies, Formulas & Strategies

ROBERT W. STEELE

Foreword by Madge Davis

OUTSIDE THE BOX & INSIDE / OUTSIDE THE COUNTRY

300 Strategies for Making Real Estate & Business Deals

Outside the Box & Inside / Outside the Country

VOLUME 6

Strategies 126 – 150

MULTIPLE EXCHANGE PHILOSOPHIES, FORMULAS & STRATEGIES

by Robert W. Steele

Foreword by Madge Davis

Design, Layout & Graphics
Victoria Vinton
Coyote Press Graphic Communications
www.coyotepressgraphics.com

VOLUME 6
CONTENTS

Introduction

Foreword: Madge Davis, SEC

Strategy	Title
#126	Using Multiple Exchange to Facilitate Breaking Up a Partnership
#127	When to Formalize the Multiple Exchange Avenue
#128	The Logic of Multiple Exchanges
#129	Idea Tracking
#130	Client Selecting First Leg of Multiple Exchange
#131	Multiple Exchanges Spawned By Smaller Groups
#132	Taker Tracker Form
#133	The Easiest 3-Way Exchange There Is
#134	The In-Lieu-Of Formula
#135	Double In-Lieu-Of
#136	Trading Into a Performance Mortgage
#137	Multiple Exchanging on One Property
#138	Multiple Exchange Going Up: Using Zeckhendorf – Dornbush Concepts
#139	Multiple Exchange with Broker Buy Out
#140	Missouri Waltz #1
#141	Missouri Waltz # 2
#142	Definancing via a Multiple Exchange
#143	Escrow Clockwise – Pass Deeds Counterclockwise
#144	Cowboy Auction— Recreation
#145	Cowboy Auction — Professional
#146	Credits Represent Delayed Multiple Exchanges
#147	BLM Multiple Exchange — Gov't Exchanging
#148	The Continuous Multiple Exchange
#149	Multiple Sale and/or Exchange of a Business
#150	International Multiple Exchange — the Easiest Way

INTRODUCTION

Multiple Exchanges

The introduction for this book is probably the most important one I will try to write. The trick herein will be to get the reader, who has not done multiple exchanges, to grasp the genesis of how multiples work and actually why they work. It is almost like there is some hidden force that propels them to a conclusion.

Does this all sound a little eerie? Maybe it is. In a standard sale you trade a common denominator called cash for a physical property that you can see and touch. Even in a barter deal you can see the horse being traded for the sacks of grain you can touch. But that is not so in a multiple exchange.

It is a common expression to say you are trying to "get to the table," meaning that in a business discussion people bring to the negotiation table the things everyone involved in the deal has to deal with, and you try to maneuver these items into a transaction that works for all parties.

The difference at the start of a multiple exchange is that not only is one of the ingredients (properties or assets) not at the table, but neither is the principal and/or the agent representing that unknown ingredient. One major part of the solution to the exchange is not at the table when you start. How can anyone be really serious about a deal like this, and more important, why would someone put up the time, energy and the capital it takes to make this unknown thing happen?

It can be made to sound rather futile can't it? And it is if you pick the wrong ingredients at the beginning. Part of what we hope to show in this book is how to pick ingredients (assets, principal & agent). If you make the right selection at the start, this is like passing a basketball to two or three other hands to get to where you want to go and score. A multiple exchange sometimes can get you to a conclusion faster than you can ever get it done in a two-way exchange.

If you make the initial choices right, a multiple exchange starts to build to a crescendo with all the elements of team play. Everyone wants to see it completed and there is a give and go attitude that develops like in no other type of transaction, but the first time you do it, it is all based on faith. It can be a little scary, as can all new things, but once you recognize the latent power of doing multiples you will become a cheer leader of the process.

My associate, Chet Allen, who is mentioned in several of these books says, "Bob, in doing some of these deals it is like diving off a diving board into a waterless pool and knowing that by the time you get down there, there will be water in the pool." At some point you learn to believe that there will always be water there if you make the right start. Momentum and the quality of the players produce the results you want.

Good luck,
Robert W. Steele

Madge Davis, SEC

Foreword

I am most pleased to have the chance to write this Forward for my friend, Bob Steele. I am inactive now but he and I closed a lot of multiple real estate exchanges together. We were both trained by Richard R. Reno of San Diego as were many other real estate brokers. Many of us belonged to the Society of Exchange Counselors, a group formed by Richard. He believed that multiple exchanges were a marvelous way to solve real estate problems if you worked with brokers that understood the philosophy.

I discovered early on that if I could get the multiple exchange started and moving so everyone was cooperating, it almost moved itself to the final closing. I did some multiples with Bruce Howie, another SEC. We would bring the first two clients of a multiple exchange into a meeting at the office at nights and the four parties would brainstorm the next move. The clients loved it and it was very effective as they would come up with other properties to add or broaden their horizons as to what they would accept. It was a great team. I guess you could say it was almost contagious. Everyone wanted the deal to go. We always made it work.

Bob and I would start a multiple and meet for breakfast every Monday morning until it was completed and plan our week and what each would do about getting another leg to the multiple. Pretty soon there would be another broker at the breakfast meeting as we added legs to the deals. We never failed, in my recollection, to close one we started.

While we often did five-way exchanges, we did one together that was really different. We started one with a Double In-Lieu-Of. This means that neither client would close on the other person's property, but the benefits changed and made it a worthwhile start. There were going to be a lot of details in this one, so we actually opened an exchange escrow with no one accepting anything. The escrow agent who handled the deal was smitten with the idea and could not have been more helpful. She had closed several deals for us in the past. We knew the minimum number of legs would be four, but it ended in three months in a five-way exchange with two other brokers in the deal with us, Yavonne Nasche and Chuck Callison, both SEC brokers. I had two of the five legs in that transaction.

Bob really knows what he is doing when it comes to multiple exchanges, so if you want to learn from someone that really knows how to do it, read on.

God Bless,
Madge Davis SEC

Editors Note: As a complement to Madge, I will use one of her Multiple Exchanges as the first one in this book. She has always been very proud that she never had an investment client leave her fold as she always put their interests first. The example I'll use was with one of her clients, a major developer in Southern California. She did a lot of exchanges for this one company.

STRATEGY 126

Using Multiple Exchange to Facilitate Breaking Up a Partnership

This in one example of a multiple exchange I did with Madge Davis, the author of the forward to this book. She did many exchanges with this same developer client.

SITUATION	I had a listing on a large older commercial building in downtown Long Beach, California built before the 1933 earthquake and it had no steel used in its constructions so it was illegal to renovate it without steel. All the upper floors were empty, but the commercial units on the street were all occupied and under lease by a major restaurant and a clothing store plus others. You could not move the tenants out. The earthquake had shaken the building one inch onto the contiguous property so it had to come down and the title company would not insure a new owner. We tried leasing the one inch but it was not acceptable. It was a prime corner in the city. The owner, my client, was a trust representing 10 owners. They had been trying to sell it and break up the trust for several years as clients wanted to divide their interests. Madge Davis' developer client had a subdivision of residential lots. His company was very capable of tearing down the old and building a new building on this prime site.
POSSIBLE SOLUTIONS	She wrote me an offer for vacant lots for the building. Her client was willing to wait until the commercial leases expired in four or five years and then build the new building. My clients were willing to compromise on their price to get Madge's client to allow the title company to write title insurance around the lot line violation. Four of the members of the trust agreed to accept and close escrow on the lots. Four of them didn't but allowed us to re-exchange the lots for them into four other properties in multiple exchanges which they did accept. Two of them were wards of the court so we got cash offers for them from other members of the trust to facilitate the deal which the court approved. The transaction closed with several lots, one building and four other miscellaneous properties, all improved. An important ingredient here was that the lots were neutral. They were an easy place to just hold their equities

STRATEGY 127

When to Formalize the Multiple Exchange Avenue

It is important to understand this point. You might be offered several exchanges for a property at an exchange meeting. If all of them fail to solve the problem you are working on you cannot formally go into a multiple exchange position with all of them.

SITUATION	A formalized multiple exchange posture, in my vernacular, is when the two brokers commit to getting the job done. Obviously, one client has to be fully satisfied with one end of the exchange. There is one important hidden point here. The other broker is the key. You can waste a lot of time and money trying to do multiple exchanges with brokers or principals that don't deliver. In the previous example, Strategy #126, I had a broker who knew how to make deals on the other side, and she had a real estate professional as a client with whom she had done several deals before. All critical ingredients were right. It took her professional client to look past all the problems with my listing and see the potential of it long term. My client's position was improved immeasurably in that the lots being offered were really a direct solution for some of them, and a viable means to an end for the others. We could not close in a two way exchange but all aspects of my clients' problems were improved and now there were two brokers working to solve what amounted to about a half a problem, moving out part of the lots into something acceptable to some of my clients. The lots were many times easier to move than the building I started with.	Questions: Is the other side (broker or principal) really excited about making this multiple exchange work? Is the In-Lieu-Of portion of the agreement, both property and client, easier to work with vs. what you started with? To really formalize your effort do not be afraid to open an escrow even before you have the last leg.
POSSIBLE SOLUTIONS	So to formalize or initialize the multiple exchange action you should have: 1. One client completely satisfied 2. A broker on the other side of the deal that is knowledgeable and capable. 3. The property taken In-Lieu-Of along with the circumstances is substantially easier to exchange (a better vehicle) than what you had to begin with. 4. The client who is In-Lieu-Of is reasonable and capable. If any of these pieces are missing, don't start the multiple. If they are all there you have an excellent chance of closing.	

STRATEGY 128

The Logic of Multiple Exchanges

Thirty to 40 years ago multiple exchanges were used more often than they are today, as new strategies and formulas have developed whereby transactions can be closed in two way deals. However, I am still of the opinion that the easiest exchange to make in real estate or business is to start with a multiple exchange, to wit:

SITUATION	1. **Property:** It is very easy to find the first leg of a multiple exchange. All you need is for one person to say, "I'll take that property in exchange for my property." It is easy to find this first step; however, you need to know that the overall exchange aspects and prognoses are improved by this move. Is it going to be easier to find a fit with this new property and the owner who is still searching? 2. **Owner or client In-Lieu-Of:** In this second step you have a hypothetical owner of the property that is In-Lieu-Of. Everything should be improved with this step or you should not be in this multiple exchange. By this I mean that the hypothetical owner of the property should be bringing more motivation, flexibility or other assets to the table and making the hoped for exchange easier. If it would make the exchange more difficult, do not enter into the first step. 3. **Other principals or brokers:** It is critical that you get the multiple exchange started with others who will carry their share of the load. If they are clients they must be well-counseled.
POSSIBLE SOLUTION	**Example of a good start to a multiple exchange:** a) You are a broker and your client has a nice commercial building, fully rented, but a small equity that is in the form of a large 2nd TD coming due. The owner needs to get into a neutral position and eliminate what is causing him stress. b) Another broker with whom you have had previous dealings and you know is a good broker, has a builder client that she has done several deals for, and he has some rental houses that carry their mortgages and have a positive income. Her client can also add cash and is looking for development land in exchange for his houses. c) All of the ingredients are here for a successful multiple exchange: You write the other broker an offer that you will take the houses and your client locks down on this step. Her client accepts In-Lieu-Of the broker finding another property for her client. Here are the salient points: Her client has the cash to pay off the second coming due on the commercial property which makes it more acceptable into the marketplace. She is a professional and knows what she is doing and she has a long-term relationship with a client who knows what he is doing, and now he has two brokers working to find the third leg for the exchange when before there was only one broker. Everything has improved and the odds just went up that this deal will get done.
NOTE	On multiple exchanges, enter escrow clockwise and pass deeds counterclockwise for tax reasons.

STRATEGY 129

Idea Tracking

This is a derivative of the Forced Relationship Brainstorming technique. I developed this form for my own use both at exchange meetings and for my own brainstorming. It forces me to consider the exchange possibility between two clients and then to use different formulas. There is no end to the possibilities. Thanks to Ron Bowden, SEC, a friend, for this design of the technique. On a scale of 1 to 10, this rates 9 as a functional tool that delivers deals that close.

There are over 5,000 ideas on this page

IDEA TRACKING

Client or Package

Broker	Package								Ideas/Thoughts

Formulas and Questions:

1. Would I take this?
2. Would he take mine?
3. Could two of mine take his?
4. Could I take part of his?
5. Is there a 3-way on the page?
6. Do two other brokers match in a 3-way?
7. Exchange - Buy Back
8. Leasehold
9. Share of wealth
10. Subdivide
11. Thief
12. Definance
13. Creation of Wealth
14. Exchange and Lease-back
15. Un-Built building.
16. Refinance
17. In-Lieu-Of
18. Use of personal Notes
19. % of interest.

Courtesy of R.W. Steele and Richard Reno Educational Foundation

STRATEGY 130

Client Selecting First Leg of Multiple Exchange

This is a technique I stumbled on by accident. I was looking for a two way exchange and it resulted in a three way. I used it routinely after the first discovery. In my opinion it is a good way to enroll a client in the process and often will give you an insight into possibilities you had not considered and it delivers transactions.

SITUATION	Real Estate exchange groups meet periodically so their members may exchange products for themselves and/or their clients. The members of the groups submit what they refer to as "Packages," which are one-page flyers about the property or asset they wish to exchange. A broker or principal may have from one to ten Packages to present to the group. Usually these Packages are pre-assembled into a binder (called a book), indexed by the broker's or principal's last name, or crossed-indexed by price, etc. Many times there can be two or three hundred Packages and they can run from $50,000 to several million of dollars in price. Originally, exchange meetings were set up for the brokers or principals to ply their exchange trade and there were only professional exchangors at the meetings. There was no education, as it was the place where the professional went to work, not to learn. Very few guests or newcomers to the business were permitted. As time went on these exchange meetings morphed into both educational and marketing sessions where there were a lot of guests, education was part of the program, and many of the packages became cash sales packages, development packages, and represented by individuals who did not really understand exchanging. The properties became the important ingredient instead of the owners of the assets. I often would let exchange clients go through one of the books to see what might be acceptable to them. The problem was that often the properties they would pick out would not be ones looking for an exchange, and/or they would be ones controlled by a broker who did not know how to exchange. It usually turned out to be a time waster.	It is very difficult to walk an uninitiated person through an exchange. An exchange is an extremely simple process but it is based on benefits and not value. Numbers and dollar signs are important but so are benefits. Benefits control exchanges and dollar signs control sales. Mixing them makes it very difficult.
POSSIBLE SOLUTIONS	One time I took the book apart, selected just the Packages controlled by brokers who were good exchangors, and let my clients only look at those and "Voila," I ended up closing a nice transaction in a three way exchange.	

STRATEGY 131

Multiple Exchanges Spawned By Smaller Groups

Let me validate this title by the observation of two professional exchangors who did a lot of multiples. Madge Davis, the broker writing the Forward in this books, says "Give me eight to ten brokers who know how to exchange and have counseled clients, and I'll give you multiple exchanges all day long." Ken Johnson, another professional, said, "With not over twenty exchangors at an all-day session, you will have multiple exchanges."

SITUATION	The benefit of larger exchange meetings is that there is a lot of inventory. Inventory is good. It means there are a lot of Packages with which to work. It also means, however, that there are time constraints as a person can only be allowed a small amount of time on the podium as there are so many packages that have to be presented. There is little if any time for brainstorming the problem, if there is one. It also means something else. If there are 100 brokers in the room and each one represents 10 clients, then when you're "Pitching" your Package from the podium your situation is hypothetically connecting with 1,000 possibilities through the brokerage fraternity present. Here again, as you will note throughout this book, does the quantity theory override the benefit theory? Are there more deals initiated and closed by a large meeting, vs. a smaller more benefit- oriented meeting where a lot of time is spent on each package?	The large meetings and the small meetings provide different sets of benefits. In good times the larger meetings probably move more real estate. In tougher times, when the multiple exchanges play such an important role, probably the smaller meetings produce more deals and for sure more multiple exchanges.
POSSIBLE SOLUTIONS	One of the benefits of the smaller meeting is, of course, having the time to brainstorm solutions which beget offers and also beget multiple exchanges. You have the time at a smaller meeting to explore three- and four-way possibilities, and the brokers are able to ask the questions they need answers for in order to lock down on a transaction. Larger meetings usually have what is called a "break out room" where a broker may go after presenting, and where people can join him or her and further explore a Package. These are good and serve as a place where some brainstorming can be done in a smaller group setting. There is one truism that comes from shedding light on this subject matter. Seldom do you ever see a multiple exchange come from a large meeting.	

STRATEGY 132

Taker Tracker Form

Form for looking for a multiple transaction courtesy of Ron Bowden

TAKER TRACKER FORM

This is neither an offer nor acceptance - merely an idea of how we might identify a multi-leg exchange

FROM: **PHONE:** **FAX:** **EMAIL:**	**TO:** **PHONE:** **FAX:** **EMAIL:**
MY CLIENT: **PROPERTY:**	**YOUR CLIENT:** **PROPERTY:**

TAKER: My client may be a taker for your property. If we can't do a two-way exchange, I may be able to help deliver one of the properties listed below which have indicated that they are takers for my property. Please forward my property package and this list to anyone who has what you want, but who is not interested in your property. You may have better luck finding what you need with my property or one of the properties listed below and we'll have a multi-leg transaction.

MULTI-LEG POSSIBILITIES: I have received the following taker proposals:

	TAKER #1	**TAKER #2**	**TAKER #3**	**TAKER #4**
Description:				
O.V. $				
Loans $				
Equity $				
Agent				
Attached	☐	☐	☐	☐

	TAKER #5	**TAKER #6**	**TAKER #7**	**TAKER #8**
Description:				
O.V. $				
Loans $				
Equity $				
Agent				
Attached	☐	☐	☐	☐

NOTE: This list of takers is neither an offer nor acceptance. It is intended to stimulate discussion between us about potential multi-leg transactions. Under no circumstances shall this proposal be considered a contract or part of a contract. My property will not be withheld from the market unless our clients agree otherwise in a written and executed long form exchange agreement. If you have any questions, please ask.

STRATEGY 133

The Easiest 3-Way Exchange There Is

This is a 3-way exchange that almost can't miss and works for everyone. It takes two things: A taker on the front end who will take the first asset and a person In-Lieu-Of who is reasonable for what will be acceptable to close out the exchange. Understand this strategy and you are armed to make an offer on any property that will support rental income regardless of inflation or deflation. It is an excellent tool for both the lender and the payor. There would be no foreclosures if everyone used this strategy.

SITUATION	I am going to use, in this example, the one item that is probably the most difficult item there is to exchange: An owner-occupied single family residence. The reason is that people are more emotional about their home than they are with an investment property. I normally will not get involved with trading an owner- occupied residence for this reason. I am going to use a $300,000 house in Florida as the example. It is free and clear in a good residential district. The owners want to relocate to California and move this equity there and are willing to accept other things, not just a house.
POSSIBLE SOLUTION	You are willing to buy this house on your terms and rent it out as an investment. You offer them nothing down and a Performance 1st TD back against the property for $300,000. It is a Performance Mortgage (see Vol. 4) and will recite that it will pay the holder of the Note ½ of the net rents (after all expenses) from the property as interest for a period of 20 years at which time the Note is due and payable, plus at any time the property is sold they are to receive their $300,000 back first, plus 1/2 of any net profit over $300,000. As rents go up their income will increase. If the house brings in $2,000 month rent and expenses are $700 month, they would receive $650 (1/2 of the net of $1300).
CONCLUSION	Normally sellers will not accept this offer as the buyer has put nothing down, but there is little or no risk that there will ever be a foreclosure because it is a Performance Mortgage and engineered for our modern world. However, the easiest thing to do is put the offered Note & TD (or mortgage) into the exchange market for something in California. You will get lots of offers for a first TD that brings in some income now & potentially share in profits of a higher price later, and one that they don't have to risk foreclosing on. This is an excellent piece of paper and much, much, much, easier to trade than is the house in Florida. It is a very simple three-way transaction. I sincerely hope the redundancy in the last sentence will be heard. This is the easiest multiple-leg transaction there is, in my opinion.

STRATEGY 134

The In-Lieu-Of Formula

Phrase to use in acceptance: "This offer is being accepted provided the brokers, clients or principals herein are able to re-exchange what is being offered In-Lieu-Of something satisfactory to the undersigned, within 90 days."

SITUATION	1. There is a need here to recognize a truth: Many times it is easier to make a three-way exchange than a two-way. They are many times much purer. 2. The advent of two things has made the three-way exchange a seldom used tool over recent years. a) The Starker Law cases provided that you could use cash in the middle of an exchange with a facilitator, so during the inflationary period of fiat currency and inflation, the need for using three-way exchanges diminished appreciable (#1031). b) The development of many new strategies and formulas did likewise.
EXAMPLE	1. Present a situation or a property to a group. Ask the group who will take what is being offered regardless of what they have to exchange. 2. These offers are written. First see if there is anything acceptable in a two-way exchange, bouncing the idea against various formulas. 3. If not, then take one of the items offered and see who will trade for it. Offer the things being offered to the first party and if any of them is acceptable you have a three-way exchange. 4. It is not complicated and at the first step the motivation and intensity increases as three of the four parties are ready to close; two brokers and one principal.

STRATEGY 135

Double In-Lieu-Of

A Madge Davis Formula

Proving the power of cooperation in the world of exchanging, Madge Davis engineered Double-In-Lieu-Of multiple-legged transactions. The cooperation between practitioners proved her point.

TECHINQUE	The concept in a multiple exchange—that cooperation between brokers or principals, coupled with concentration, can get an exchange done—is never proved more convincingly than in a Double-In-Lieu-Of Exchange. The shortest possible exchange would be a 4-way.	A does not take B B does not take A A takes B In-Lieu-Of B takes A In-Lieu-Of
MADGE DAVIS	She had a philosophy that a counseled client or sophisticated principal could take a variety of things as long as the problem they were trying to solve was properly defined. By going into an in-lieu-of situation, where both she and another broker committed to doing the transaction, the impetus and concentration helped manifest the deal.	A, becoming the hypothetical owner of B's property, changed the problem surrounding B's property which made it much more tradable.
EVERYONE WINS	Even though there are still two problems to solve, the one very difficult problem was mitigated by hypothetically putting in a new owner.	
IN MY CASE	The author did one Double-In-Lieu-Of with her. It closed in a five-way exchange with two other SECs, Yavonne Nasche and Chuck Callison.	
CONCLUSION	Nothing happens until someone does something. In the one I did with Ms. Davis, she wanted to open the escrow without either party agreeing to take the other's property. She was right: The concentration helped make it happen.	

STRATEGY 136

Trading Into a Performance Mortgage

You or your client become principal

LOCATE PROPERTY THAT WILL EXCHANGE	You locate an asset that you would like to own, property A. A standard item would be free and clear, improved and rentable or income-producing even if only modestly. This is an excellent strategy if you are open to international transactions as many foreign properties are free and clear. Let's be exact, it does not have to be free and clear but it facilitates the transaction if it is.	$1,000,000 F/C house or other property that can be rented and professionally managed.
HYPOTHETICALLY STRUCTURE PERFORMANCE MORTGAGE	You hypothetically structure a Performance Mortgage against this property that would work for you, e.g. $1,000,000 first TD secured by this property payable at 50% of the net rents monthly or quarterly, due in 10 or 20 years. When due, the property has to be sold and the beneficiary of the TD gets his or her money back first, and 50% of the net profits above the loan.	You are the buyer of this property with nothing down. You will owe $1,000,000 in a first TD that can never be foreclosed on as long as you make the agreed to payments.
EVERYONE WINS	You now go into the exchange market looking for something that will trade for the $1,000,000 first TD and for something that will satisfy the original owner. All of these transactions are like three way deals: The owner is taking the Performance Mortgage In-Lieu-Of.	For those that live in the world that nothing down is a sin, consider that this TD is a thousand times safer than any standard loan. C will not get hurt. Don't live in the past.
CONCLUSION	A gets C C gets B B gets A	

STRATEGY 137

Multiple Exchanging on One Property

Richard R. Reno had a chapter in his book called The Seven "Cs." One of those "Cs" stood for the word **continue.** ***This means that very often out of exchanges one or more of the properties needs to be or can be exchanged again. In other words, continue exchanging. This was exemplified in our Orange Coast California Exchange Group over about a three year period when one property was traded, I think, seven or eight times, the first few in the course of business. Later it became an "in family" joke and was done just for fun. The "C" point is there, however, and well proven so be aware of it. In a way it is a delayed multiple exchange***

SITUATION	**SWEET HOME, OREGON** A single family residence (SFR) in Sweet Home, Oregon was exchanged in the course of a larger exchange transaction. The house was rented. Upon closing the tenant was notified in the course of business as to who the new owner was and where to send the rent checks.	The joke in the exchange group was that every time the tenant went out to the mail box there would be another letter saying, " I am the new owner of the house. Please send me your check." The laugh aside, millions of dollars worth of delayed multiple exchanges are made because of the "C" philosophy. Be cognizant of its power.
THE "C" IN ACTION	The new owner of the houses did not want it and put it back on the exchange market (note Reno's "C" philosophy) The property was exchanged again and the tenant re-notified as to where he/she should send the rent check. This new owner also did not want the house as it was just taken as a means to an end. The house went back on the exchange market and was again re-exchanged. Again the tenant was notified, etc. etc. etc. It is, of course, a little humorous and did become a joke as people would ask, "Who owns Sweet Home now?" In a sale of real estate, when it is over, it is over. In an exchange, that is quite often not true. One party often wants to re-move one or more properties.	

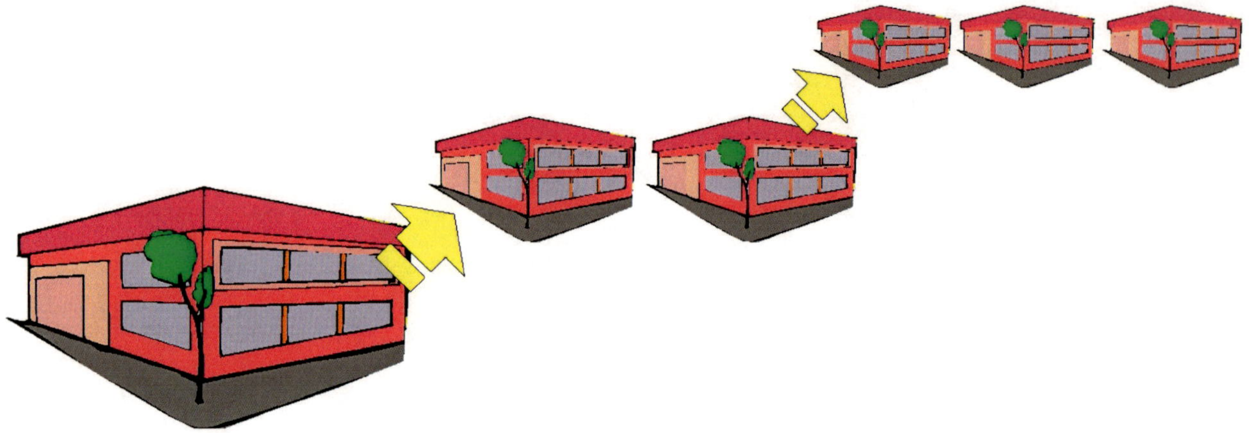

STRATEGY 138

Multiple Exchange Going Up Using Zeckendorf – Dornbush Concepts

Zeckendorf developed a formula he used with insurance companies in New York. Sturgis Dornbush, SEC used this same formula multiple times with industrial clients.

SITUATION	1. Zeckendorf wanted to buy a building occupied by an insurance company. They wanted a larger facility. 2. There were no buyers for their building except Zeckendorf and he didn't want to use money.
POSSIBLE SOLUTION	1. He found another larger building occupied by a larger insurance company. They also wanted a larger facility. He traded the smaller building into the larger one and continued the multi-exchange until he found another building for the second company. 2. He continued the trade process going up until his real estate commissions totaled enough to allow him to purchase the first building. 3. Sturgis Dornbush was working the same formula in the mid-west with industrial buildings and did several of these transactions.
CONCLUSION	In all multiple exchanges, at some point, there are enough commissions earned to buy out one property and close the deal if the real estate brokers are amenable to this.

STRATEGY 139

Multiple Exchange with Broker Buy Out

By the time you have entered into a 3-way exchange commitment, the brokers, if there are brokers in the transaction, have started to accumulate real estate fees that could be used, if necessary, to purchase one of the properties. By the time it is at a 5-way exchange, you almost always have accumulated enough to guarantee a closing as the brokers could buy out one leg if necessary.

SITUATION	Assume that all the real estate commissions are at 6% and there are three legs in a multiple exchange including properties of \$2,000,000, \$3,000,000 & \$4,000,000 for a total of \$9,000,000. The total commissions at this point would be \$540,000. If you would add a fourth leg to the exchange of \$5,000,000 the total would be \$14,000,000 and the total fees would be \$840,000. By the fifth leg, if you added a \$6,000,000 property the total would be \$20,000,000 and the fees \$1,200,000.
POSSIBLE SOLUTION	With \$450,000 in fees or equity position, the brokers can usually figure out a way to buy one of the properties and close out the transaction. If you get to the five-legged position from in-field work, everyone is usually anxious to see it finished as perhaps considerable time has elapsed, and often some compromises on values and or prices can be negotiated. If the 5-way comes basically out of one meeting, it is pretty well worked out right from the beginning and if there is a broker buy-out, it has been engineered into the deal right from the start.

STRATEGY 140

Missouri Waltz #1

This is the old formula that later was accentuated by two court cases, the Starker Cases, and it then became known as the 1031 Exchange. The 1031 is, in fact, not an exchange but a delayed sale and has nothing to do with exchanging. The Missouri Waltz on the other hand is an exchange subject to one property selling out. The 1031 exchange comes from the other direction: It starts with a sale of one property and the funds are held in an escrow and then another property is purchased to the satisfaction of the buyer but in compliance with certain rules.

SITUATION	The entire exercise must be recognized for what it really is. It is a man-made bureaucratic manipulation of the market. It makes sense to exploit these as long as one can, but recognize at some point in time it will be changed because it is man-made. It is like the entire 1031 law which allows a tax deferred exchange and moves an artificial tax thing called a book basis from one property to another. It is all artificial. People get trapped when they rely just on a government-sponsored program because I can guarantee you it will be cancelled at some point, and some people will be looking for chairs when the music stops. You can actually get to the point where you believe it is real. As of this writing (2010) thousands of brokers and clients are stuck in the 1031 exchange belief and of course the cash sale market is not functioning, so the people have been led down a trail that has dead-ended. Properties are being foreclosed, clients are losing their equities and brokers are failing out because they believed entirely in one government ruling.
POSSIBLE SOLUTION	The simplest way to solve or resolve these transactions is to first make an exchange that makes economic and personal sense, and then come back and look at the tax consequences and structure to minimize same. The transaction should stand on its own feet first without tax considerations (IMO).

Strategy 141

Missouri Waltz # 2

The Missouri Waltz needs to be in this book because, even though the laws have changed because of court cases, they are man-made laws and they will change again sometime. The difference is that in what is known as the 1031 exchange, the sale of property to facilitate the exchange happens at the beginning, whereas in the Missouri Waltz, the sale happens at the end. I have included two samples of this accomplished by two brokers who have been mentioned before, Chet Allen, who did the first one, and Madge Davis, who wrote the forward for this book, did the second one.

SITUATION #1	**This started with the broker listing 47 fourplexes in Florida. The owner had the need to solve one financial problem but wanted a tax-deferred exchange with the balance that would also improve his cash flow. It took approximately four months to complete. The fourplexes were exchanged into separately owned shopping centers in Florida, Arizona and Idaho. The fourplexes were all sold, including 14 exchanged and other escrows closed.** **The net result of this was titles changed on 64 properties from coast to coast, 35 principals were involved, 13 brokers and 14 different lenders. A title company and escrow company with extra staff were employed five weeks to handle the closings and recordings were handled at 11 am Eastern Time, 9 am Mountain Time and 8 am Pacific time in order to close concurrently. $13,000,000 in escrows closed which would equate to over $100,000,000 in today's dollars.**	When we see these types of transactions go together it makes you wonder how many other transactions are missed because we don't see the "possibilities." You can see and perhaps sense the underlying techniques, formulas and strategies applied by the brokers herein to make these transactions come together.
SITUATION #2	This one started when the broker listed a mobile home park for exchange in Redlands, California. The owner wanted an exchange into Idaho. The park had separate titles to each mobile home lot within the park. They located a nice office building on a lake in Idaho as the first step and that owner wanted an exchange into Colorado. All exchanges were made subject to selling out a total of 192 of the lots in the Redlands park to generate the cash needed to negotiate the rest of the exchanges. A separate broker was brought in to accomplish these sales. It took 14 months to complete. It survived a divorce, a bankruptcy and two deaths in the sale of the lots but those were all replaced and the escrow closed in 14 months.	

Strategy 142

Definancing via a Multiple Exchange

An exchangor's connotation of the word de-finance is "to remove any obstacle that impedes a transaction." Not just moving loans off a property. As an aside, you will also see the un-built building formula come into play in this transaction.

SITUATION	A developer client, in combination with an investor partner, had developed two large combination office and industrial buildings in Newport Beach, California. They were fully leased and producing nice income. Newport was growing into a big city and the developer decided he wanted to raise his children in a smaller community. He would like to trade these buildings into something that could support him and his family in that type of a milieu. At an exchange meeting I found a three-story general store in a small mountain community in Northern California, where the owner wanted to retire and the Newport Beach properties fit him just fine as they produced the income he wanted. The problem developed when the partner of my client in the two buildings decided he did not want to move his equity into the mountains.
POSSIBLE SOLUTION	We were able to answer the problem by finding another lot about two blocks from the two buildings which the developer client was able to obtain. He designed a building to go on it agreeable to the partner, located a tenant and built the building. On closing, we traded the new building to the partner for his half interest in the two buildings, and then traded the two buildings for the general store. It took about 7 months to complete the escrow. De-finance is just about the opposite of the Creation of Wealth formula. We tried various things before using the un-built building formula because they would have been faster. We offered the partner a second TD on the mountain property and then offered him the land lease under the mountain property and then offered him other property owned by the developer client. Nothing worked until the idea evolved about the un-built building. He was very happy with de-financing into that position. There were three legs in this multiple exchange.

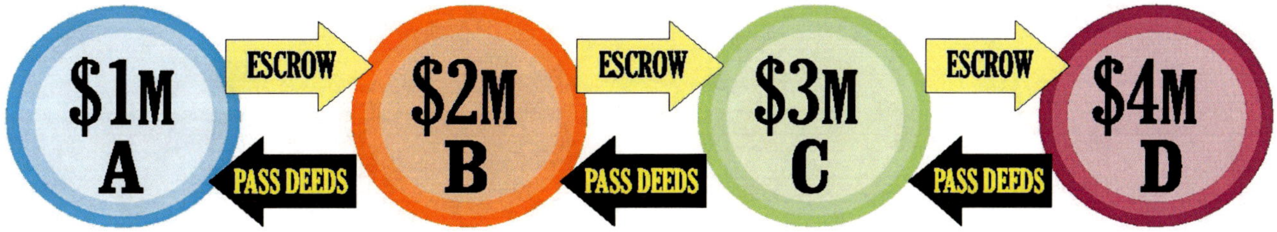

Strategy 143

Escrow Clockwise – Pass Deeds Counterclockwise

Again the importance of this has to do with government rules which, like most man-made rules, will someday be changed. Using the concept that in order to have a tax deferred exchange you have to have like property held for use or investment and receive no cash, no boot and no mortgage relief in the transaction, then this method of escrowing makes it rather simple to understand.

SITUATION	Assuming that all the real estate represented above qualifies for the tax deferred treatment then the only party subject to tax consequences is D.
POSSIBLE SOLUTION	A passes her deed direct to B. B to C and C to D. A, B & C have tax deferred treatment. D passes his deed direct to C and goes into title momentarily into C and passes the deed to it C. He takes the C deed the same way and passes it to B. He takes the B deed the same way and passes it to A. Prior to the two Starker Law cases, this is the way the multiple exchange business worked. After the Starker Law cases, what became known as a 1031 exchange came into being, where money was used to accomplish this transaction and they simply sold one property and moved the cash through an intermediary into the new property. Now with the advent of the depression, cash money has again become dear so this multiple exchange and escrowing strategy will come back into play.

STRATEGY 143
Multiple Exchange Escrow
Escrow Clockwise – Pass Deeds Counterclockwise

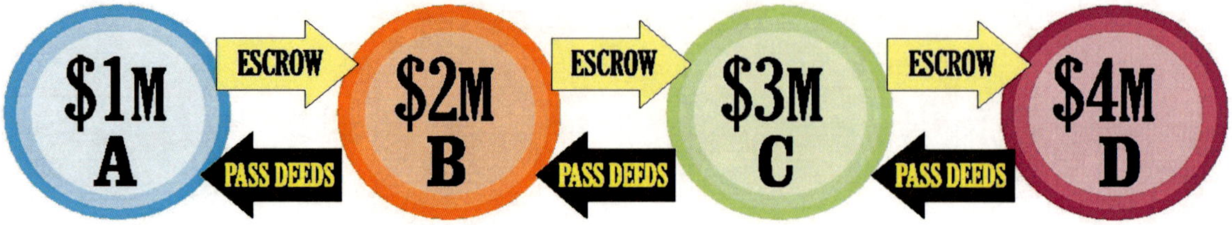

STRATEGY 143-A
Middle Corp

Charges a 1% or more fee to all for services rendered.

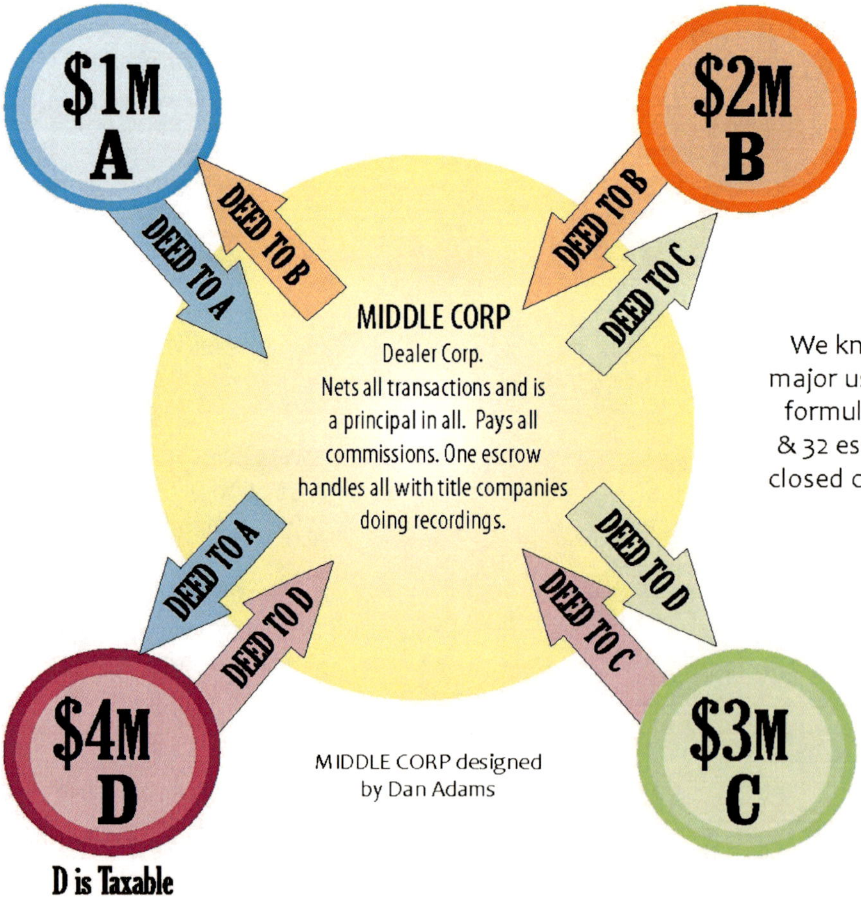

We know of two major usages of this formula where 28 & 32 escrows were closed concurrently.

STRATEGY 144

Cowboy Auction - Recreation

For recreation at some real estate exchange meetings we have an evening Cowboy Auction. This is authentic personal property exchanging, where "vacancy" (unused assets) items are traded with no middle men and a plethora of small multiple exchanges take place. No financing is allowed.

SITUATION	A offers his rifle for trade. B offers to trade a painting for the rifle, C offers some gemstones, D offers two weeks at her timeshare, E an equity in a 1994 pick-up truck. F wants B's painting, not the rifle and will trade a computer. G will take the two week timeshare time with one day's consulting. This goes on until everyon in the audience has had a chance to offer on anything that has been offered in. Then A gets to choose anything that is on the board, because indirectly, either through a 2-way, 3-way, 4-way, or X-way exchange, everyone is a taker for A's property. There is no worldwide Cowboy Auction. However, experienced exchangors can connect the dots if they have the individual pieces to the puzzle.	The author herein had a gorgeous grand piano obtained at a cowboy auction traded for some asset I no longer remember. Here is homework for the reader: What do you have that is a real asset that you no longer have a use for? Would you trade it at a cowboy auction for something else?
POSSIBLE SOLUTION	The successful exchange professional can determine that if A (the rifle owner) will take G's consulting that a creative transaction can be put together that satisfies everyone's needs and wants. G takes D's timeshares, D takes A's rifle , A takes G's consulting. THERE ARE SEVERAL KEYS THAT MAKE THE COWBOY AUCTION WORK, OVER AND OVER AND OVER. EVERONE HAS THE INTEGRITY TO TELL IT LIKE IT IS AND PERFORM. THEY SAY WHAT THEY WILL DO. IF THEY DON'T WANT THE RIFLE, THEY JUST SAY NOTHING. AND THERE IS NO FINANCING ALLOWED AND NO CASH IN THE TRANSACTIONS. IT IS PURELY BASED ON BENEFITS.	

STRATEGY 145

Cowboy Auction - Professional

WAEX, World Asset Exchange.com, does professionally what is done on a recreational basis by exchangors. The rules are similar but the numbers are larger and it is a for profit company that provides this service for a reasonable fee. Think a cross between E-bay and a Cowboy Auction. Internet & e-mail auctions are run on small sizes under $1,000,000 and larger deals $1,000,000 and over. All items must be free and clear. No financing alowed.

SITUATION	**Under $1,000,000** A puts up a $350,000 f/c house in Costa Rica B company offers $50,000 per year for 7 years of apples from apple farm operations in Oregon. C offers F/C lots in Redding, California D offers $350,000 in pre-paid dental services in Trade Credits in $5,000 increments E offers $350,000 partnership interest in a commercial building fully leased in Denver, Colorado. **Over $1,000,000** A (small hotel chain) offers their $3,000,000 in F/C hotel rooms good for three years for trade or any fractions thereof. B offers $1,000,000 in restricted company public stock for $1,000,000 of the hotel rooms and would use the rooms as gifts for employees and places for salespeople to stay. C offers $3,000,000 in pre-paid radio advertising time and would sell hotel rooms via ad specials on the radio in markets outside hotels area. D offers $3,000,000 in vacant seats at soccer stadium and would package other empty seats as a promotion for their soccer teams.
POSSIBLE SOLUTION	It is 100% incumbent upon the players to say what they will take and be willing to close on that agreement. WAEX professionally monitors the process and keeps it moving in the right direction.

STRATEGY 146

Credits Represent Delayed Multiple Exchanges

Google says it has 28,600,000 web sites about Trade Credits. If you are into exchanging or creative business of any form, is there just maybe something in this Trade Credit thing that you should know about?

SITUATION #1	On a single piece of paper you write, "The bearer of this instrument is entitled to one eight-hour day of physical labor from the undersigned." And you sign it. This is a Trade Credit. You trade this document to me for a sack of flour. I have your Trade Credit. I trade it to Jane for painting a room in my house. Jane now has your Trade Credit. Jane wants some yard work done. She calls you and you work a day in her yard and she gives you back the Trade Credit, marked paid.	Trade Credits can be very simple or they can move right on up the line to being very complex. While a one page labor Trade Credit is sufficient it might take a 10 page Trade Credit to establish a one year credit for the use of a hotel room in a five star facility. Can you perform on $1,000,000 in Trade Credits or 100 times that amount? They are the epitome of the Creation of Wealth formula.
SITUATION #2	You are an attorney and you charge $500 per hour or $4,000 per day. You make up 10 Trade Credits, each for one day of your time (total 10 x $4,000 = $40,000) and you trade it to me for the down payment into a little $200,000 rental house. I trade your Trade Credit on for a used car, vacation time in Hawaii and a vacant lot, plus I use a day of your time (one Trade Credit) to get my affairs in order.	
SITUATION #3	You are a farmer growing corn. You issue five Trade Credits, each good for $100,000 worth of corn at market value. The first Trade Credit is due in one year, the second one in two years, etc. You have a total of $500,000 in Trade Credits to trade and you trade them for a yacht. The Trade Credit due in five years might be multiply traded a half dozen times before it is time to collect.	
SOLUTION	Is there any end to this wealth creation? No. Is there risk? Yes. Anyone can die at any time. Accept the risk or don't play. NOTE: See Volume 12 our special book on Barter & Trade Credits.	

STRATEGY 147

BLM Multiple Exchange – Government Exchanging

Two-way exchanges are common place with the government. There are some multiples done. This example was from the archives of an Oregon SEC broker, Kenneth A. Johnson.

SITUATION	It is probably best to initiate this example by first explaining the general format of a standard two-way exchange with the BLM, that often will use cash and the Missouri Waltz formula (see master index) to accomplish its goals. This is not what is often called a 1031 exchange, as the Government does not seem to have a tax problem in their dealings. BLM stands for Bureau of Land Management, a government operation that includes handling of range land and other holdings. The two-way exchanges I have been involved in have all been centered around cattle ranch operations, but the government exchange program is very diversified. Wherever there is land owned by the government, there are exchanges being made. The government agencies do not need cash to make exchanges so using assets (land) does not interfere with their budget programs. They have lots of land to work with.	Government ends up with the parcel on the Snake River in Idaho. Ranch owners end up with the parcels they wanted to own within their ranch boundaries. Owner of Idaho parcel received cash. All escrows recorded concurrently These multiple parcel exchanges can work anywhere a government wants to buy.
SOLUTION	In a large ranch in ranching country, the government will often own a small amount of land within the borders of the ranch. The owners would often like to have title to these parcels but the government can't sell them without multiple bids, etc. so the technique is to have the rancher buy something else, another parcel of land say that the government would like to own and exchange it, without any money in the deal, for the parcel the rancher wants to own. A very slow process. I have had these exceed two years in time. Kenneth Johnson did his multiple parcel exchange in the reverse of the norm outlined above. The government wanted to buy a certain large parcel of land on the Snake River in Idaho for a boat launching ramp facility, etc. but they didn't have money to make the purchase. He got the offer signed to make the acquisition subject to the government being able to exchange into it. He then went to many ranchers to find ones that would like to own government holdings within their borders. He got offers for cash purchases on these. When he had enough of these offers, everything was escrowed to close concurrently. The government ended up with the parcel they wanted by exchanging many small parcels into it and these were all sold out in the escrow so that the owner of the Idaho parcel walked out of the escrow with cash.	

STRATEGY 148

The Continuous Multiple Exchange

I have met some ingenious real estate people in my life but no one open my eyes more than an SEC broker, George Hoover, when he initiated and put together a long multiple exchange he labeled the Continuous Multiple Exchange. Part way through the process he converted it to an un-priced transaction and he said he could have kept it going forever. This exchange showed me the tremendous power of the un-priced concept which is so hard for people to grasp.

SITUATION

Hoover had a listing on some dormant free and clear land in California which was next to impossible to sell as there was no market. The client wanted to convert this to something producing income which again is a very difficult thing to do. (Please note that in our current market, 2010, we have a market conditions in which countless land parcels are sitting dormant and this type of formula might apply).

For example purposes we will call the value of the California land $1,000,000. He was offered an exchange for a commercial building in Florida priced at $1,000,000 with a $200,000 loan on it and an equity of $800,000. There were some problems with the building. The client not only wanted out but also a geographical move to California. The client was willing to take Hoover's land and give his client a $200,000 1st TD back on the California land on favorable terms and payments.

SOLUTION

From this offer Hoover conceived his plan: He had his client accept the $200,000 carry back 1st TD on his own land but took the Florida building In-Lieu-Of. (See master index for this formula). At the same time he took the price off the Florida building and made it un-priced (any price agreeable to the seller). He then went back into the market to re-exchange the Florida building into anything anywhere that would allow him to carry back a 2nd TD for his client on the Florida building.

He was offered a small farm in Nebraska where the owners were retiring to Florida and they had cash to fix up the Florida building. Their farm was free and clear and valued at $550,000 and they agreed to give Hoover's client a $250,000 2nd TD on the Florida building.

Again, Hoover's client accepted the 2nd TD on the building (he now had $450,000 in TDs) but took the farm In-Lieu-Of and Hoover kept exchanging until he got his client $900,000 in TDs and Hoover took the remaining property for his fee — but Hoover did not stop. He kept exchanging the new property and each time taking another TD for himself as profit. He did say he could have kept it going forever as he was flexible enough to take things any place in the country

If you are afraid of work don't do this. This took Hoover about three months to get his client's problem solved.

Client started with $1,000,000 in land and ends up with $900,000 in various TDs producing income.

Hoover took a real estate asset for his fee and kept producing TDs and income for his profit.

He made four or five additional trades before he closed it out.

STRATEGY 149

Multiple Sale and/or Exchange of a Business

I first saw this used in England. It makes so much sense.

SITUATION	A company that made gift basket packages (fruits, chocolates, etc.) wanted to establish its same business in England. It was an excellent business and would have lent itself to franchising or international marketing, but the owner did not want the hassle of management.	Zeckendorf, a real estate legend of the past, said he always tried to sell a building for six times what a broker said it was worth. He sold sandwich land leases under the building; he would sell and lease back an elevator, etc. The same is true of this formula. A $1,000,000 sale can be turned into a $10,000,000 sale with a little ingenuity and in this case by going international.
POSSIBLE SOLUTION	The broker devised a plan which allowed them to sell the business multiple times, and he later entered into the field where he exchanged some of the businesses. As an example, he sold the business into France with non-compete clauses for England and the other countries. He had the buyer come into England for training and had all of the equipment lined up to be purchased. The new business owner was fully trained and sent back to France to open up operations independently. The England owner sent representatives to France to help select the building to lease, buy and install the equipment and initiate sales and then come home. They did not sell the business once, they sold it many times and later opened it up even more and started exchanging it.	

STRATEGY 150

International Multiple Exchange – the Easiest Way

Elsewhere in the book you will find the formula I call the Easiest Multiple Exchange. This same formula, when dealing in the international market, is not as easy as the one intra-national but, it facilitates and in my opinion, it makes for the easiest international multiple exchange. The TD or Note created in this first step of the exchange is many times easier to exchange than is the physical property, but I will certainly listen to your arguments. You will also find this mentioned in our Vol 9, International Exchanging under TD Exchange.

SITUATION	You own a $1,000,000 house in France. It is free and clear. You would like to sell it and repatriate the funds to the U.S. The sales market in France has dried up and a sale does not seem possible. You would be willing to exchange the house in France for some other asset in the U.S., but people are reluctant to make the exchange because of management responsibilities of owning this house, even if it is a rentable asset and therefore potentially income producing.	Investors are much more prone to own debt internationally than they are to own assets. If you are a broker or facilitator, you can be the initiator of this type of an exchange and end up owning the properties that, while heavily financed, are great income producers because of the Performance Mortgages.
POSSIBLE SOLUTION	Have a local (France – perhaps a management company) entrepreneur offer to buy the house on a Performance Mortgage. Hypothetically, say this is nothing down and a $1,000,000 first mortgage back payable at a rate of 50% of the net spendable per month with certain due dates, etc. (see Performance Mortgages). The norm might be that on future sale of the property, the beneficiary receives his $1,000,000 back first, and 1/2 of any profits over that amount. Now, in the In-Lieu-Of position, you exchange the $1,000,000 mortgage and note into something acceptable to you in the U.S. There are a lot more people who would accept the 1st TD or mortgage on the house in France than would accept the house, as there is no management responsibility when owning the debt. The person in the U.S. now does not have to take the house in France. Get legal counsel, because in some countries individuals cannot own debt, so it may need to be structured in a corporation or company.	

NOTES

300 STRATEGIES FOR MAKING
REAL ESTATE & BUSINESS DEALS

VOLUME 7

STRATEGIES
151 – 175

The Art & Science of Brainstorming

Obtaining Ideas not Available Through Conventional Thinking

ROBERT W. STEELE

Foreword by Nancy Steele

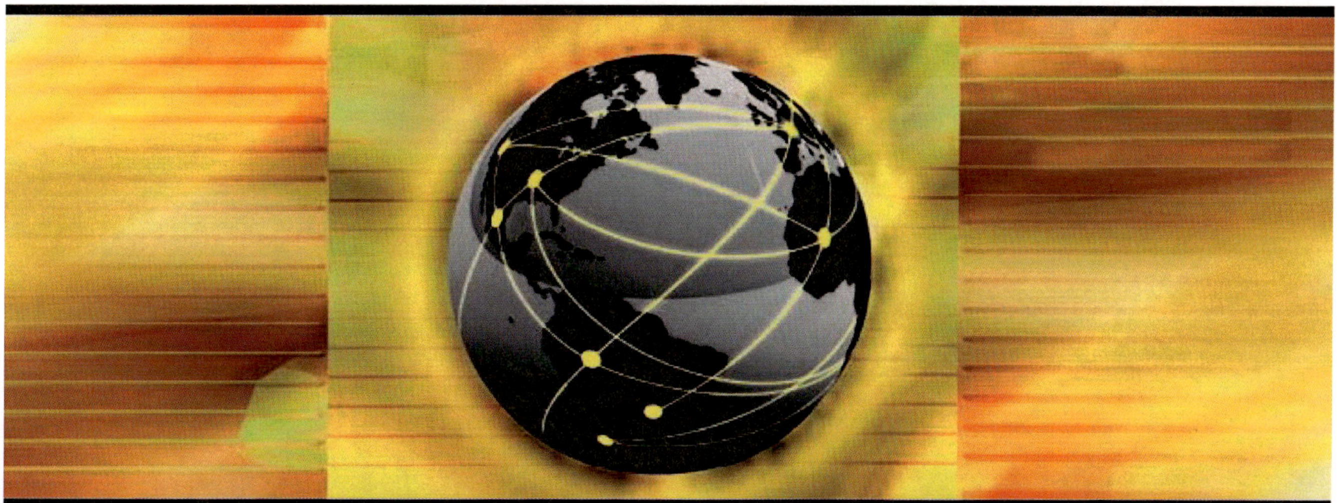

OUTSIDE THE BOX & INSIDE / OUTSIDE THE COUNTRY

300 Strategies for Making Real Estate & Business Deals

Outside the Box & Inside / Outside the Country

VOLUME 7
Strategies 151 – 175

BRAINSTORMING: THE ART & SCIENCE

Obtaining Ideas Not Available Through Conventional Thinking

by Robert W. Steele

Foreword by **Nancy Steele**

Design, Layout & Graphics
Victoria Vinton
Coyote Press Graphic Communications
www.coyotepressgraphics.com

VOLUME 7
CONTENTS

Introduction
Foreword: Nancy Steele

Strategy	Title
#151	The Five (5) Steps to Brainstorming
#152	Assessing the Situation
#153	Defining the Problem
#154	Brainstorming the Problem
#155	Use of the Subconscious
#156	Using Judgment
#157	Signs Following
#158	Idea Tracking
#159	Killer Thoughts
#160	Forced Relationship Technique -
#161	Best Ideas Come Last -
#162	Quantity Breeds Quality
#163	No Limitation to Creativity
#164	Deferment of Judgment
#165	Group vs. Individual Ideation
#166	The Gordon Technique
#167	Don't Drive With Your Brakes On
#168	Hitchhiking and More
#169	Reversal Brainstorm
#170	Set a Deadline When Brainstorming
#171	Association of Ideas
#172	Dr. Osborn's Rules for Brainstorming
#173	The Moveable Brainstorm
#174	Diversification in Brainstorming
#175	Brainstorming as a Way of Life

INTRODUCTION

The Art & Science of Brainstorming

Obtaining Ideas Not Available Through Conventional Thinking

This book and its strategies and formulas represent a major key to potentially unlocking the creativity that is within you. This is not something invented by the author but is the result of the studies of two men who were the pioneers: Dr. Sydney J. Parnes and Dr. Alex Osborn (and also their students) who ran hundreds of tests so that we might hitchhike on their efforts. It is also the result of the author's participation as both a member of groups brainstorming and as the moderator of these types of groups. These latter examples were from the real estate exchange market and were not theoretical but actual business transactions "in process."

The mind, to say the least, is awesome. If we can extract just a little more from its capacity, we have moved in a positive direction. Hopefully this book will help prove that anyone can learn to create at any age and that there are no restrictions or limitations to what can be done. The world really is ours. It makes no difference what your targets are, brainstorming can add a dimension that you can't get in any other way.

The trick of course is to use the knowledge. The easiest way to learn it is to use it; so perhaps a good place to start is now. Take anything you are trying to solve, place it in your mind and start brainstorming it as you read this book. By the time you finish the book you will have some new ideas about how to solve your problem. It is mechanical and it will produce ideas that you have never thought of before.

Good luck.

Robert W. Steele

Foreword

by Nancy Steele

Brainstorming As Lifestyle

My name is Nancy Steele and I have spent a good deal of the last 29 years brainstorming with Bob. I now cannot imagine living my life without this valuable tool in my tool chest. But it hasn't always been that way for me!

My career was as a schoolteacher. I can remember faculty meetings, committee meetings, PTA meetings and lunchroom conversations where the exercise was to come up with as many ideas as possible within the allotted time and the person who had the most ideas was the most respected. That was the exercise. There was never any notion of doing anything with these ideas as we were, somehow, trained to believe that the drill was in the process.

Shortly after I met Bob and we realized that we were going to be making a life together, we started brainstorming. I can remember our first session sitting in my living room in Westlake Village, California. It was a beautiful day, we had wonderful music playing and were sitting with our tablets on our laps. We had a wonderful time brainstorming about our future life together and its endless possibilities. Bob laid out the fundamentals for the brainstorm before we started and away we went. As I recall the brainstorm went on for several hours and when we finished we had an impressive list of exciting possibilities. After we reread these aloud I suggested that we go get something to eat whereupon Bob looked at me with a curious smile and said, "But we're not finished!"

I had no idea that one ever did anything with all of those ideas. From my experience we were through after we thought them up and went on with our lives until the next time we'd decide to brainstorm and then repeat the process. WRONG. From there we went into the selecting and then activating stage which was putting the best idea(s) into action. What a concept and did it ever work.

From this first brainstorming session our lives changed in the most fantastic and astounding ways. Over the years, I don't believe we have ever made a major decision without brainstorming it out first and then putting the results into form. This goes for both our business and private lives. We have developed a routine whereby we go to the nicest place we can think of (such as a lovely hotel or a beautiful beach) and conduct our brainstorming session in that inspiring atmosphere. It works like a charm, is a tremendous amount of fun and I have learned that the implementation is the best part of the process.

When Bob asked me to write the introduction for this book, I felt a little intimidated because I am not really a business person. But I do know that brainstorming works—and it's very fortunate to learn it from a person such as Bob who has mastered the art. And now you, the reader, will have the same advantage I've had (more or less). I know that if you study and work with this book you will master the art also, and I can imagine that both your business life and your personal life will benefit and grow as mine has.

Best wishes for your new life and enjoy the process. Oh…and please don't forget the implementation. That's the best part.

Nancy

STRATEGY 151

The Five Steps of Brainstorming

The following techniques are based on the studies of Dr. Sidney J. Parnes and Dr. Alex Osborn, the grandfathers of brainstorming, and their students. Depending on their purpose in the studies, they used three to seven steps. Our knowledge of the real estate exchange market led us to define this in the following five steps. Also included within are my own observations from having used these techniques extensively for the last 30+ years.

The Art and Science of Brainstorming – Obtaining ideas not available through conventional thinking.

1. **Assessing the Situation:** This boils down to extensive research, keeping your own counsel and not becoming opinionated.
2. **Defining the Problem:** The importance of this cannot be over-stated. Almost without exception, the consensus of all studies shows that this is the single most crucial step leading to a successful brainstorm & subsequent conclusion.
3. **Brainstorming:** Your choices of arriving at a creative solutions to a problem are:
   (1) a business meeting, if available
   (2) individual ideation
   (3) a group brainstorm, if available
4. **The Use of the Subconscious in Brainstorming:** This requires the element of time elapsing. As anxious as one might be to "get to the solution," this is the step which may unleash the answer you are looking to find.
5. **The Use of Judgment in Selecting the Best Ideas & Activation:** At this point you will have as many ideas as you want. Hundreds if you want them. The time has come to be analytical and critical and combine ideas, etc. and end up selecting the best one and then activating it.

Once you have developed confidence in your ability to properly use brainstorming, it will fit naturally into your life and your lifestyle.

You will find the process is so simple that things from your daily life will filter through the system automatically.

It will also cause you to seek out others who use this technique, as the power of group brainstorming can only be used when there are other knowledgeable minds available.

STRATEGY 152

Brainstorming: Assessing the Situation (Step #1)

The first step in brainstorming a problem is to assess the situation. In one word it is research. You can not properly move to the second step, defining the problem, until you have completed this assessment.

SITUATION	1. What are the known facts? 2. No ideas are wanted here. 3. Avoid seeking opinions. 4. Don't become opinionated. 5. Seek – questions, questions and more questions. 6. You assume that there is at least one area in which you do not have the sum total of all current knowledge. 7. Assume a posture of intelligent ignorance and do not produce ideas. 8. Search for key factors. 9. Personal investigation.	Keep this to yourself. Do not seek advice. Become one with the problem.
RESEARCHER	Researcher trained a flea to jump when he said jump. Removed one of the six legs & it still jumped on command. Removed one more leg & it still jumped on command. Did this through the first five legs. Removed sixth & last leg & it did not jump on command. Researcher wrote his conclusion: ***When all six legs of a flea are removed it loses its power of hearing.***	If you do your research incorrectly you will not get the situation properly defined, and that will lead to the wrong conclusion.

STRATEGY 153

Brainstorming: Defining the Problem (Step #2)

The second step in brainstorming is by far the most important step.

Steam Shovel-type problem: This is the entire picture of the problem which includes the client, the vehicle (property) and all the surrounding circumstances.

Spade Problems: These are the multitude of small isolated problems within the steam shovel problem. Many times by solving the majority of these smaller problems the big problem disappears.

SITUATION	1. With a feeling of finality. 2. With a sense of irrevocability. 3. If you define the problem wrong you will solve the wrong problem. Whenever a broker or principal presents a creative offer that is designed after a brainstorm and it is not acceptable, it means that the person defined the problem wrong (or circumstances have changed). 4. One researcher felt that this section was so important that he suggested that all problems should be defined up to 77 different ways. His purpose was of course to emphasis the importance of this step. 5. If defined wrong a good idea will die because it was born in the wrong world. 6. In defining stay away from habits. Just because you solved a similar problem one way, don't presume that this one will work out the same way. 7. Keep reworking your definitions until you are positive. 8. Check each word for meaning. Stay away from adjectives. Get a clear definition of the problem.	Treat the definition as though you were creating something new. You are defining all the reasons why someone could object to the solution that you would bring to the table. If A is true then so is B. If there is no objection to your definition, then what you bring to the table will be an acceptable solution to the problem.

STRATEGY 154

Brainstorming a Problem (Step #3)

This is the real fun of brainstorming. Business meetings are okay and individual ideation is great, but if you have an association with others who know how brainstorming works and you can find yourself in a group brainstorm milieu, you are most fortunate.

SITUATION	1. You have completed steps #1 and #2: Assessing the Situation & Defining the Problem. 2. The normal step at this point, within a company, is to have a business meeting about what to do with this situation. The standard things you know how to do would be explored and normal decisions would be reached. 3. If you are versed in brainstorming, this is the point where it comes into play.	
POSSIBLE SOLUTION	1. It costs you nothing but time to brainstorm the situation. If you use individual ideation (the ideas from only one mind), I can guarantee that you will generate countless other ideas to go with those you thought of at the business meeting. 2. If you have a group that affords you the opportunity to utilize group brainstorming, you can get a plethora of ideas that you could not get either through the business meeting or individual ideation. 3. This is the uniqueness of the real estate exchange business in that it can provide this group brainstorming opportunity, in which members of the group give freely of their time and knowledge to help each other solve situations. Some problems are extremely complicated. 4. It is obvious that the first two steps of brainstorming need be completed prior to taking the time for the group. It is also obvious that a property or vehicle that is only on the cash sales market does not have to go through these steps. If, however, there is no cash sales market or other problems exist that make the property not readily saleable, then exchanging, including the brainstorming, come into play.	**IMO (In My Opinion):** A nice brainstorm can be had with as few as two people if they know how it works. Three to five can give you a great brainstorm. 15 and up to 20 can be Utopia if they know what they are doing. Above that the effectiveness seems to fade.

STRATEGY 155

Brainstorming: Use of the Subconscious in Creativity (Step #4)

To maximize the benefits of the creative process, the subconscious needs to be brought into play. With the assessment of the situation, the definition of the problem and the actual brainstorm behind us, it is now time to let the process work in our subconscious.

SITUATION	1. You have garnered many ideas and possible solutions to the problem from your business meetings, individual ideation and brainstorming. 2. With the problem fresh in your mind, as are the many ideas developed to this point, it is time to let the subconscious do its work. 3. Soak – let the problem soak in your mind. 4. Relax – think about something else. 5. Simmer – let the problem and the new ideas simmer.	We hardly ever consciously use our subconscious mind. It just may be the best tool we have.
RESEARCHER	1. File Clerk – imagine your mind has a file clerk and you have instructed him to search through your mind files for other ideas that could be used in solving this problem. As these come up add them to your brainstorming list. 2. Fantastic computer – One of the authors said it would take a computer the size of the Empire State Building to house all the information that is in your mind. 3. Having faith in the power of the subconscious will build over time. The information that you seek is probably already there. One example of this hidden power that I saw in the studies was as follows: a) People were placed in a strange room. b) After they left they were asked to list the things that they had seen in the room. c) The average listed was 20 to 30 items. d) Later they were placed under hypnosis and they listed 200 more items. The subconscious picked up 10 times more than the conscious mind.	Creative thinking gives us a marvelous chance to actually witness it in operation. You will get ideas coming out of the subconscious pertaining to the problem you are working on for about a week.

STRATEGY 156

Brainstorming: Using Judgment in Creativity (Step #5)

Through the first four steps of the brainstorming process you have deferred judgment. Now you have a long list of possibilities in the form of ideas and embryo ideas. Now is the time to use judgment and select the best idea and activate.

SITUATION	1. You now have before you a list of perhaps 100 ideas and it is the time to select the best idea. 2. Initially you will find this task a little daunting, but as you learn more about the process from usage, the first part of the judgment process can be completed rather rapidly. 3. Many of the ideas may be acceptable as they were the consequence of aiming at a single target, but one of them is best. Your search is now to find the best idea and activate it.	It only takes one idea to unlock a problem. Sometimes, if the problem has multiple spade problems, then you need to watch for more than one idea Really be critical at this stage and be analytical.
RESEARCHER	1. Many times you can combine two or more ideas to develop a prime thought. 2. Play percentages. 3. Group pressure can sometimes be wrong. If you are convinced that your idea is sound, then proceed. 4. Look for the good and bad effects of the idea at the same time. 5. It's choosing and using the ideas that really count. 6. While you are in the conscious mode and using judgment, you will find that as you read ideas they will germinate other ideas that are perhaps a modification of the one you are reading. Write the new idea down as it may be the one you are looking for.	

STRATEGY 157

Brainstorming: Signs Following (Step #5)

Will you get signs that you have made the right decision? Yes! Are you sensitive enough to read these signs? Hopefully, yes.

This is a process that I have developed for my own usage and it has proven to be very helpful. There needs to be an awareness concerning thinking—linear (sequential) vs. non-linear (non-sequential). Non-linear tends to be more creative and freer. In general I have found this most beneficial.

Even though you have completed all segments of your brainstorming and you have implemented your plan, you are not yet finished. This is probably the most sensitive time. As soon as you have implemented the plan, actions and reactions begin. There are a lot of old sayings about this like, "The proof is in the pudding," or as stated above, "For every action there is a reaction."

There will always be signs following your implementation, 100% of the time. Are you sensitive enough to pick up on them and/or are you so bull-headed that maybe you plow ahead when the signs come back negative?

As an example, here is a current one I am working on as an example. Market conditions at this time are mostly frozen in my business of real estate. In concert with an associate, I have been developing strategies to free up equity in land that is good but has no market. I brainstormed using different formulas and ideas and came up with creating soft paper and trading the paper rather than the land. I used interest only, 10 years or longer and at a low interest rate of 1 or 2%. This was based on TIGRS, STRIPS (bonds), and low interest CDs. I took two listings at $1 million plus and had them entered into the marketplace along with other test listings.

Example of signs following: Three months later offers are still coming in on the paper. I got another one yesterday. Initially people were trying to negotiate on the terms and conditions, but that has stopped now. In Chase Bank yesterday I saw a sign quoting and promoting a CD at 1.6% interest.

I am considering these as signs following. This low interest rate paper is acceptable in the current marketplace even though I have never seen this low a rate on a TD or mortgage in 40 years of real estate. We can now use the equity in this land during the down market via the Creation of Wealth formula (see Vol. #1).

After you have implemented your creative idea, stay cognizant and watch for signs following showing that you are right.

STRATEGY 158

Idea Tracking

This is a derivative of the Forced Relationship Brainstorming technique. I developed this form for my own use both at exchange meetings and for my own brainstorming. It forces me to consider the exchange possibility between two clients and then use different formulas. There is no end to the possibilities. Thanks to Ron Bowden, a friend, for this design of the technique. On a scale of 1 to 10, this rates 9 as a functional tool that delivers deals that close.

IDEA TRACKING

There are over 5,000 ideas on this page

Client or Package

Broker	Package								Ideas/Thoughts

Formulas and Questions:

1. Would I take this?
2. Would he take mine?
3. Could two of mine take his?
4. Could I take part of his?
5. Is there a 3-way on the page?
6. Do two other brokers match in a 3-way?
7. Exchange - Buy Back
8. Leasehold
9. Share of wealth?
10. Subdivide
11. Thief
12. Defiance
13. Creation of Wealth
14. Exchange and Lease-back
15. Un-built building.
16. Refinance
17. In-lieu-of
18. Use of personal notes
19. % of interest.

Courtesy of R.W. Steele and Richard Reno Educational Foundation

STRATEGY 159

Killer Thoughts in Brainstorming

Anything that stops the flow of ideas in a brainstorm is a Killer Thought!

PRECONCEIVED THOUGHTS	1. These are taboo when brainstorming. If you have a preconceived idea about a person or a thing, it will cause your brainstorming session to be contaminated. 2. It is the same with everything from religion to the food we eat. For true brainstorming you must let the juices flow. There can be no absolutes.
KILLER THOUGHTS	The moment a broker says, "My client won't do that," the broker is stating to you that he is a filter in this deal. The channel is not opened to the client. The other thing that is happening is that the person who puts the idea into the brainstorm that has just been "killed," her mind goes on the defense and is trying to justify what she said and is no longer creatively contributing to the brainstorm.
WHITE HATS AND BLACK HATS	To emphasize this concept, two brokers, George Hoover and Chuck Chatham, once took two sailors' hats to an exchange meeting. One hat was dyed black and the person wearing that hat was the one to raise "Killer Thoughts" during the exchange meeting. The person wearing the white hat always had positive input. The concept grew for a while and anyone coming up with a "Killer Thought" had to wear the black hat until the next person made a similar mistake. It did make you become aware of what you were saying.

STRATEGY 160

Forced Relationship Brainstorming Technique

You probably unknowingly use this now.
It is an extremely powerful and easy technique to generate ideas.

SITUATION	1. This is probably the tool I use the most as it works so well in self-ideation. This is also called the Forced Object Technique, the Catalogue Technique (the Sears & Roebuck Catalogue works great) or the Book Technique. 2. You are brainstorming and want to create ideas that you would not be able to get in a normal business-like setting. This technique is used routinely by many in the advertising business, but seldom utilized in the real estate and business marketplaces. It is guaranteed to develop all the ideas you could ever hope for.	
POSSIBLE SOLUTIONS	Force the idea between two unrelated objects. 1. **Example** (I have used this for years in classroom settings and am constantly wowed with the ideas that people can come up with in a group brainstorm): Consider yourself a chair manufacturer. You would like to develop a new line of chairs within a certain budget and you have exhausted your normal channel of ideas. Using the above set of circumstances, force the idea against unrelated objects and see what kind of a new chair idea comes back to you. 2. **First bounce it against a light bulb:** You will get an immediate flow of 5 to 10 to 20 ideas from a group. Anything from a glass heating chair, a chair hanging from the ceiling, to a chair with a built in light and an electric chair. If you are moderating, be cognizant that when the flow starts to slow down, you need to change the object. In this instance, let's ask the group to now bounce the question against a glass of water and the flow of ideas will start again. 3. If your business is real estate, you have just taken title to an apartment house, and you want to do some upgrading or maintenance, perhaps do a brainstorm before you spend your money. You will get many ideas that you would not get otherwise.	Brainstorming is free. Can anyone come up with a reason why people don't use it? With just a a little effort anyone can master the process.

STRATEGY 161

Brainstorming: The Best Ideas Come Last

This is true in a brainstorm and at exchange meetings or any other long drawn-out business or personal meeting. The best ideas will come after you are thought out.

RELATIVE NUMBER OF GOOD IDEAS FROM A BRAINSTORM

78% more good ideas come from the second half of a brainstorm vs. the first half.

When the group starts to "run down" the moderator should say something like, "Give me one more idea!" People start to force out ideas and all of a sudden the flow will start anew.

Whoever holds back even the glimmer of an idea is defeating the purpose of a brainstorm.

Borderline ideas that would not come out in a business meeting have a chance to come out.

A brainstorm should be wild.

It should be free-wheeling.

A brainstorm should creative a Pavlovian condition in a permissive atmosphere.

If you attend an exchange meeting, be the last one to leave the room. The best ideas come last. If it is a multiple day event, stay for the last day and work until the last minute. If the numbers above mean anything, your chances on the last day may be up to 78% higher than they were the first day of the meeting. This is hypothetical as to my knowledge no test has been run on this possibility, but my experience tells me that it could be in that range.

STRATEGY 162

Brainstorming: Quantity Breeds Quality

In the average gold mine it takes four tons of ore to get one ounce of gold. The same is true when ideating. You need a quantity of ideas in order to get one good one.

RELATIVE NUMBER OF GOOD IDEAS FROM A BRAINSTORM

QUANTITY BREEDS QUALITY and DEFERMENT OF JUDGEMENT are the key ingredients of brainstorming.

Osborn & Parnes Example:

The need for quantity was demonstrated in an idea-finding session we conducted for a group of Air Force officers. The problem presented for their joint attack was unusual in that the answer was already known. This was the problem:

If 700 miles of outside telephone wires were so coated with frost that long distance calls could not be made, how would you restore normal service as fast as possible. This emergency actually arose in the state of Washington in November, 1952. Local telephone men solved the problem by flying helicopters over the wires. The downdraft from the blades quickly blew off the frost, and long distance service was restored in record time.

We were fearful that the officers might know about this actual case. Luckily they did not. They started shooting ideas as fast as could be stenographically recorded. As Airmen, they would most likely hit upon the helicopter solution, and they did. BUT—here's the point—they suggested 35 other ideas before they hit upon the proven answer. The helicopter solution was their 36th idea. They would have missed the proven solution if they had of stopped at 5, 10, 20 or even 35 ideas.

If this had been a group of other than Airmen, this might have take many times that number of ideas to arrive at the right one.

STRATEGY 163

There Are No Limitations To Creativity

The ability to be creative can be learned by anyone at any age.

SITUATION	1. Creative brain power does not require higher education. 2. It is thought that your capacity for creative thinking stops during the middle teens. 3. Creative problem-solving can be learned by anyone at any age. 4. If you judge and evaluate as ideas are brought up, the person who is questioned will be more concerned about defending his position than he will be in thinking up new and better ideas. 5. Humor in brainstorming is important.
RESEARCHER	1. The location of where you brainstorm is important. Place yourself in a milieu that is comfortable and supporting. Personally, for joint brainstorming with another person, I like a nice place, e.g., Hyatt Regency in the U.S. or Puerto Banus in Spain. If individually, sometimes at the ocean, but also at a library, depending on what I might be working on. Much of the material for one of the books in this series—about using stock formulas in concert with real estate—was developed in a joint brainstorm I was doing for a corporate client with an associate, Chet Allen, and was initiated in the lobby of the Beverly Hills Hotel in Los Angeles. 2. Exchange groups, meeting in nice places, have the same effect. 3. Have the courage to throw out the idea of "Limburger Cheese" during a brainstorm. This is completely off the wall as far as any problem you might be trying to solve, but I use it. What it does is to remind me that I am suppose to be wild and non-conventional when brainstorming. You can not have a problem in your mind and say "Limburger Cheese" without getting some thought back. The forced relationship technique works with any word.

STRATEGY 164

Brainstorming: With Deferment of Judgement

Please make note of the following: It is critical to understand that if you learn how to defer judgment when creating ideas, you will become far more creative than you ever thought possible.

HOW DEFERMENT OF JUDGMENT ENHANCES INDIVIDUAL IDEATION (DURING THE SAME PERIOD OF TIME)

This is telling us that during a normal business meeting you are not getting 90% of your good ideas to the table. We are so very cognizant of not making a fool of ourselves that we will not throw out long shot ideas or things that do not fit the norm. However, when we are doing individual ideation there are no mores holding us back. Let the juices flow.

Here is what happens to the mind when working on a problem:

The left circle represents the different ideas you are throwing at the problem. Then along comes an idea that is outside the circle. A wild idea! What happens is your mind jumps over and starts building ideas around the wild idea or new thought.

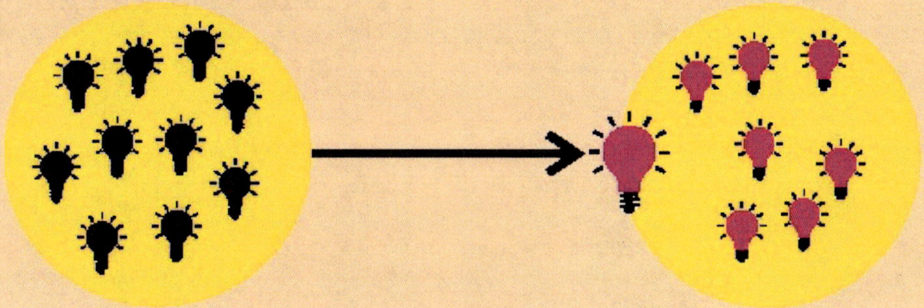

STRATEGY 165

Group Brainstorming vs. Individual Ideation

If you have the opportunity to use group brainstorming you should definitely take advantage of it. If you are in a group that doesn't use this technique, you are not taking advantage of the possibilities you have— you're not hitting on all cylinders.

PRODUCTION OF GOOD IDEAS IN THE SAME PERIOD OF TIME

It is obvious from these numbers that whenever you have a group that knows how to brainstorm you can create unlimited ideas that you simple cannot extract when you have only one mind to work with.

NOTE: This above information was from tests run by Dr. Parnes and Dr. Osborn or their students. The individual in this instance is not using creative brainstorming, but just the standard or normal thinking patterns we use every day. When an individual is versed in creative brainstorming, he or she can obtain a plethora of ideas from using the proper techniques.

E.g., Forced Relationship Technique, etc.

STRATEGY 166

The Gordon Technique

This is like Richard R. Reno's un-priced listing concept. The Gordon Brainstorming Technique is for purists. It is the ultimate technique for free-flowing ideas. Think of charades in understanding it.

YOU ARE NOT LOCKED TO ONE FORM OF BRAINSTORMING	William J. Gordon of the Arthur D. Little Company, a research and consulting firm in Massachusetts, developed a technique which carries his name. At the time we were teaching this brainstorming class, their company had a unique service in the invention and design section. They would invent a product for a fee. They claimed that they had never failed in an assignment. Gordon's concept was and is still revolutionary. The big difference is that no one but the group leader (moderator) knows the exact nature of the problem under consideration.
UNLOCK POTENTIAL FOR A CLIENT OR PARTNER BY TEACHING THEM BRAINSTORMING HAVE THEM READ THIS BOOK	Teaching a client or partner some of the brainstorming techniques can have major rewards for all concerned. Hitchhiking on the Gordon Technique—except in this case no one knows where the brainstorm is heading—get the client to agree, after learning how to brainstorm, to have a go at creating ideas for things the client might do with assets that are completely different than things they once thought of. The benefits of having a client read this book would be that they would not be fixated on one solution when they can see so many more are available. You will help open boundaries for them like they have never been opened before, and make your job much easier.

STRATEGY 167

Brainstorming: Don't Drive with Your Brakes On

Deferring judgment is very important in brainstorming!

BRAINSTORMING WITH THOSE THAT DON'T UNDERSTAND THE PRINCIPLES IS DIFFICULT	The following is a good explanation of brainstorming. The essence of the brainstorming principal of deferred judgment is to allow a given period of time for listing all the ideas that come to one's mind regarding a problem, without judging them in any way. One is to forget quality of the ideas. Quantity only is stressed. Defer judgment when brainstorming: a. Don't drive with your brakes on when trying to think up ideas. b. Don't get rid of your brakes. c. The stronger your motor gets, the stronger your brakes must be. d. But don't try to use both at the same time. Don't try to think at the same time you are trying to create: a. Yogi Berra always swung at the first pitch b. Manager, yelling at him: "Think before you cut at the ball." c. Next time up Yogi took three called strikes. d. Manager: "What happened?" e. Yogi: "How can you think and hit the ball at the same time?"
TRY NOT TO BE JUDGMENTAL OR LOCKED TO HABITS	Because we usually live in one particular political arena, we do not even think that what is not normal or not legal in one area can be very normal and legal in another area. Sometimes all we have to do is change an area or country and the problem is solved. It is not always necessary to solve the problem as you see it, but to change the circumstances around the problem and the problem goes away.

STRATEGY 168

Brainstorming: Hitchhiking and More!

One idea begets another!!

SOMETIMES YOU CAN HITCHHIKE ON WHAT IS SAID AND ACTUALLY SOLVE A DIFFERENT PROBLEM FROM THE ONE YOU ARE WORKING ON.

THIS IS SIMILAR TO WHAT HAPPENS IN THE GORDON TECHNIQUE: "NO LINEAR THINKING" IS THE RULE

This is one of the benefits of group brainstorming.

Every time someone suggests an idea the other members of the group treat the thought like the forced relationship technique and this often gives birth to another new idea.

This is called hitchhiking.

It is the association of ideas.

That is why if you hold back even a glimmer of a thought you lose the possibility that that thought just might be the catalyst idea that sparks the idea that will solve the problem.

At a meeting where people are versed in brainstorming, the ideas will come so fast that they cannot be written down. It is always good for the presenter to have a tape recorder going so she can capture even the most remote of ideas.

If you maintain a list of the various brainstorming formulas in front of you as someone is presenting a problem, it will help you hitchhike as you can bounce what is being said against the various formulas to also get new idea.

STRATEGY 169

Reversal Brainstorming:

What is left is the sculpture.

1. I really like this technique within a brainstorm. A reversal per se is a common tool of brainstorming. Whatever the problem is, you turn the problem around 180° and see what kind of ideas it produces. And of course there are partial turns, also.
2. In every brainstorm, the leader or moderator can often start a whole new flow of ideas by suggesting a reversal.
3. The referral above to the sculpture is going back to the saying that "The sculpture is already within the marble and that the artist is merely removing the excess rock to free it."
4. I particularly like the Reversal when you are brainstorming a new business or project. I do this in sections, including being sure to brainstorm the back door, or how to break it up if it is not successful.
5. I brainstorm out every possible reason I can think of why the business or project might fail. I really exhaust this list. Then I come back and find the counter for each of these reasons that it might fail. If each of these reasons cannot be countered, I don't do the project.
6. In other words I take out, or counter in some way, all the reasons why it can fail and what is left should be something that will not fail.

FOR INSTANCE:

You have a client who wants you to sell some land for him: Ask him that if you could get him the money, what would he buy? This opens up the possibility of an exchange and makes him think like a buyer, and whereas sellers are often on the defense, this changes the posture to offense. You are now writing offers, not just waiting for someone to write to you.

STRATEGY 170

Set A Deadline When Brainstorming

This will tend to push your mind into action

BRAINSTORMING A SITUATION MAKES YOU SLOW DOWN.

SLOWING DOWN MAKES ONE DO A MORE THOROUGH JOB.

SETTING THE DEADLINE HOWEVER KEEPS IT MOVING AND BRINGS IT ALL TO A CONCLUSION.

1. Doing the research can differ with different situations but let's say again we are real estate brokers and we are taking a listing on an investment property.
2. We estimate we can have all the facts and data gathered within one week. We set the time frame and the mind usually gets it done on time.
3. Once the data is collected we have to define the problem and then brainstorm it so let's say that will take one more week.
4. A normal time for me on any brainstorm of significance is one week for the subconscious to work and I actually calender that day to make the decision, as I say, usually one week from the conclusion of the brainstorm.
5. I know this date is coming and that means the decision is coming and it just prompts the subconscious mind to get cracking and come up with some more answers.
6. Does it work? Yes, with the obvious caveat of not every time. It has, however, substantially changed my life many times. I use the technique in business and personally.
7. We never make a major family move without doing the complete brainstorm. We have lived in various parts of the world doing various things all as the result of brainstorming.

STRATEGY 171

Association of Ideas

These three circles explain graphically what is happening in a brainstorm.

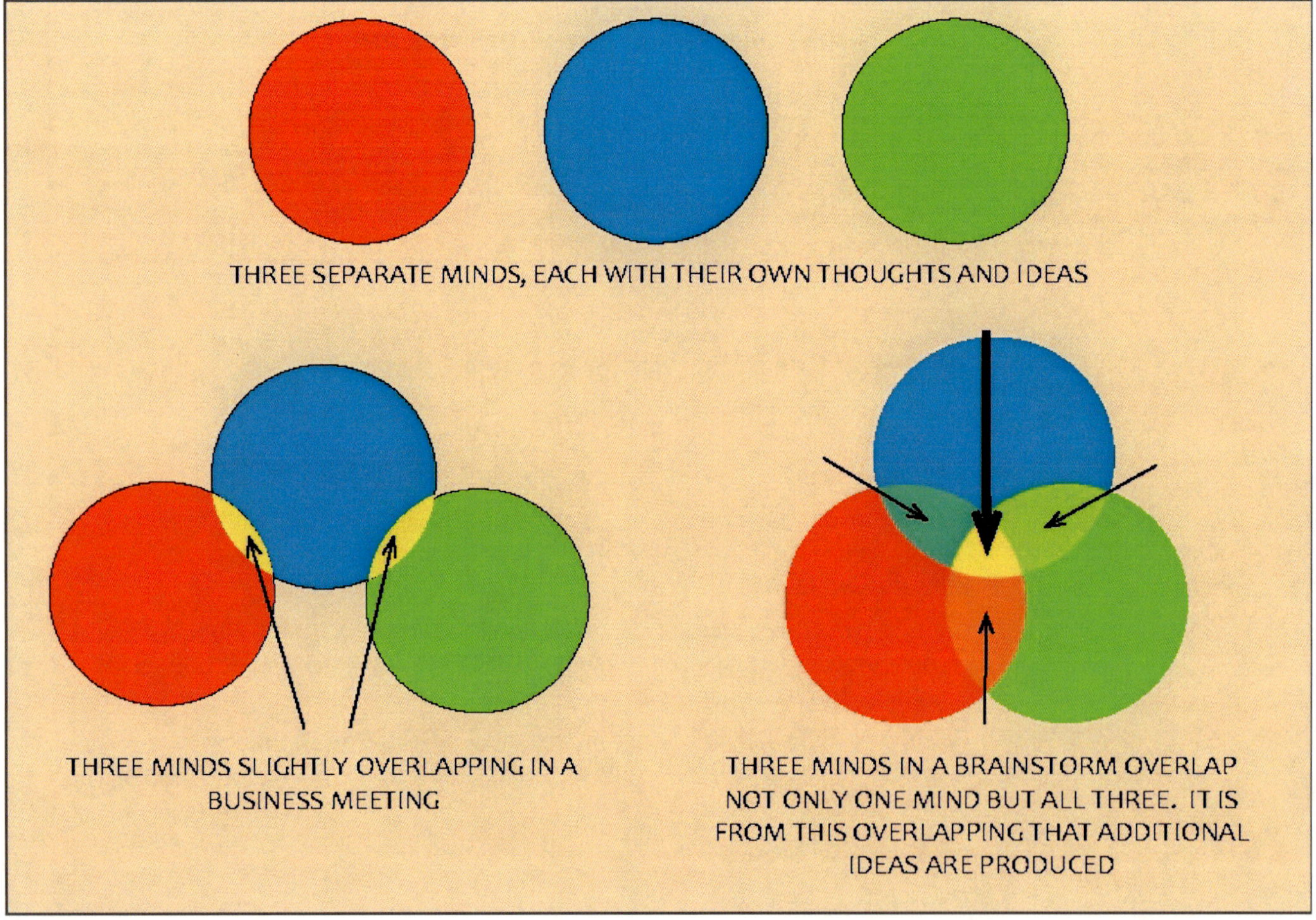

Strategy 172

Dr. Osborn's Rules for Brainstorming

He just used nine items to break down a problem. As a leader or moderator, by suggesting these different items to a group you can shift the minds onto another plane and a new flow of ideas should develop.

SITUATION	Can you put the situation to other uses? (Like if it were a building, changing it to a condo-type unit or assisted living)	
ADAPT	1. What else is it like? 2. What other ideas does it suggest? 3. Modify 4. Magnify 5. Minify (subdivide) 6. Substitute 7. Rearrange 8. Reverse 9. Combine If you have 20 people in this brainstorm each of these items above will connote something different to each mind and will germinate a thought that is different than anyone else's. Wrigley said, "When two people in business agree on everything, one of them is unnecessary!"	Moderating a brainstorm is not like running a business meeting where you possibly demand attention and/or control. It is more like playing a violin. You are trying to pull the best music or ideas out of the minds before you. Within those minds are ideas that you want to extract.

STRATEGY 173

The Moveable Brainstorm

Like Hemingway's* Moveable Feast*, this is a group brainstorm that travels.

SITUATION	You have completed the research and defined the problem, and you are by yourself. This means the brainstorm will be through individual ideation. You know the rules and how to make this work but there is one more dimension that can enhance it. The definition of a sample situation is that you have some money that you want to invest. For this purpose use what you feel comfortable with: $10,000, $100,000 or $1,000,000. Let's agree on $100,000. This is risk capital and we want to invest this into something that will give us five to one return in one year at a risk ration of three to four. What we are saying is that we recognize it is a stretch to find something that will change this from $100,000 to $500,000 in one year and still not be buying the Brooklyn Bridge. We recognize the risk and will accept some, but not real, long shots.	One of the big advantages of this type of brainstorm is the diversification of the people involved. These participants can be a spectrum from your banker to your barber.
POSSIBLE SOLUTION	We write this definition on a 3 x 5 card, put it in our shirt pocket or purse and move on. When we meet people in our normal walk of life, we ask them the question that is on the card and listen to their answer: You are using the movable brainstorm here. You then write their ideas on your 3 x 5 card and move on. Then you ask the next person, and the next, etc. This Moveable Brainstorm is also a nice supplement during the week that you are letting the problem soak in your subconscious from a standard brainstorm.	

Strategy 174

Diversification Can Enhance a Brainstorm

(Dr. Parnes & Dr. Osborn)

but Knowing How Brainstorming Works Trumps All

(Robert Steele)

Parnes & Osborn ran hundreds of tests to prove their theories. Likewise I have been in hundreds of brainstorms concerning real estate and can speak with a certain amount of authority about that aspect.

SITUATION	Acknowledging what we have studied to this point, it is easy to understand how the diversification of people can enhance a brainstorm. In an office setting combining people in a brainstorm that come from different divisions within a company adds this diversification. Tests that were run included having the president of the company in a mix with engineers, accountants, secretaries, janitors and salespeople. You can also add to this mix, male, female, older people and children. All will give you a different slant. All of the problems submitted by the leader or moderator connotes different things to each person which developed a different approach to a problem.	Hopefully this book will be helpful to those wanting to effectively brainstorm. If each person who was not familiar with how brainstorming works would read this book before the brainstorm, it could be very helpful.
POSSIBLE SOLUTION	The problem I have found with the diversification aspect is that in each instance you have to teach the people how to brainstorm or to separate a problem into small or spade-size problems so they are confined to a small area. When people do not know the fundamentals of brainstorming it can cause a rift in the procedures as Killer Thoughts come in from different directions and those doing it don't realize what they are doing. The most effective brainstorming I have seen is when all the participants know how the system works and are uninhibited enough to throw out the wild ideas necessary to stimulate the thinking of others. Knowing how this works is what I have found to be the key.	

STRATEGY 175

Brainstorming: As a Way of Life

If I had to pick 10 things that have had a positive effect on my life, brainstorming would be one of them.

I am advocating brainstorm as a part of one's life. The knowledge of brainstorming and actually using it has affected my life in many ways that I feel are positive.

I researched brainstorming approximately 40 years ago in order to include it as part of my seminar on creative real estate, and I became fascinated with the possibilities of using the technique for other things.

I have seen some remarkable things happen because of brainstorms and I have a world of confidence in the process. It has affected the way I educated my children, to the countries I have lived in, and to the towns or cities within those countries.

It has affected my choice of friends, my spiritual bent, the business I will do and the business I won't do, my politics and what my plans are for tomorrow.

My wife is really good at it and knows how to extract the maximum from the process. I have some business associates who have incredible minds, and it is a pleasure to interact with them in a brainstorm.

I was and am most fortunate to belong to the Society of Exchange Counselors, a real estate society, that has within it many people who know how to brainstorm and develop ideas. You can enter into a transaction with one of them and have every confidence that it is going to work out well. I have seen many transactions close that without brainstorming would have never happened.

It is a rather simple process once you learn it, so it is easy for things you are working on to be processed through a brainstorm mentality. It can become a tool that can enhance both one's personal and business life.

NOTES

NOTES

300 STRATEGIES FOR MAKING
REAL ESTATE & BUSINESS DEALS

VOLUME 8

STRATEGIES
176 – 200

Real Estate & Business Counseling

ROBERT W. STEELE

Foreword by Steven L. Cropper

OUTSIDE THE BOX & INSIDE / OUTSIDE THE COUNTRY

300 Strategies for Making Real Estate & Business Deals

Outside the Box &
Inside / Outside the Country

VOLUME 8
Strategies 176 - 200

REAL ESTATE & BUSINESS COUNSELING

Robert W. Steele

Foreword by Steven L. Cropper

Design, Layout & Graphics
Victoria Vinton
Coyote Press Graphic Communications
www.coyotepressgraphics.com

VOLUME 8
CONTENTS

Introduction

Foreword: Steven L. Cropper

Strategy	**Title**
#176	Counseling and Exchange: History and Evolution
#177	Becoming a Counselor Takes Time
#178	Information to Obtain Through Counseling
#179	The Client Needs to Be Eyeball to Eyeball; Property Can Be Anywhere
#180	Other Counseling Techniques
#181	Pre-Counseling Techniques
#182	Counseling Time
#183	Counseling and Control
#184	Assess Yourself vs. the Deal
#185	Setting Fees as a Consultant or Broker
#186	Are All Legs Under the Table?
#187	The Don't Wanter is a Key to Many Transactions
#188	Counseled Clients Tell You Their Truth
#189	Value, What is It? Is It in the Eye of the Beholder?
#190	Value of an Asset in an Exchange
#191	Would-Ya-Takes
#192	Counseling Is an Individual Thing
#193	People in Hell Want Ice Water
#194	Head 'em West 'Til Their Hat Floats
#195	DFTP—Don't Fight the Problem
#196	Miscellaneous Counseling Techniques
#197	Counseling May Unearth a Good User
#198	When You Have Exhausted All Possibilities, Remember This: *You Haven't*
#199	Entitlement Syndrome: Call a Spade a Spade
#200	Counseling for Escrow

INTRODUCTION

You can be a great real estate sales person by doing exactly the same thing year after year. This applies to both residential and commercial real estate. It can actually become a numbers game: If you call 40 people a day every day, or the equivalent of this, you will become successful, in terms of dollars, at real estate whether you are dealing in brokerage or buying and selling on your own account. In order for this sales effort to work, there needs to be financing available because it is credit that makes this market turn. If you had to give this market a name, you might call it a good real estate market or a Seller's Market.

The common denominator is cash. It means one thing to one person and it means something else to the other and neither party cares what the other does with it.

There are two ways of marketing real estate and the above is one way. This second way is one that works in both the good market and the one you might call a bad market or a Buyer's Market. This is the type of market that doesn't have easy financing or one that may be beset with political regulations that stifle, slow or kill the process.

In this latter type of marketing the motivation to transfer title by sellers is actually much higher than in the first market but the majority of investors or brokers are not familiar with how to connect with this desire and use it to consummate a real estate transaction. It is anything but a numbers game as it requires slowing down and counseling with what is termed a seller. It requires finding out what the motivation really is and to see if there is another way to solve it via exchanging the property or using creativity in some other way to circumvent the heavy and very difficult processes of trying to turn the equity into cash.

Counseling does not change the requirement to know about the nuts and bolt of the real estate itself. This is just the ABCs of real estate and this information is required in any transaction. But, that is where almost all real estate people stop. It is where counseling begins. Long before there were dollars there was trading and exchanging. It is based on two things; motivation on what you are leaving and desire for what you are going into. If the motivation to get rid of a property is extremely high the owner is referred to as a Don't Wanter.

This book, then, is about how to counsel with people to find out about what this motivation is and if it will be possible to solve this without actually turning the equity into cash, which in many cases in a Buyer's Market can't be done. Our newspapers, at this time, are full of discouraging articles: One just stated that 81% of the mortgages on houses in Las Vegas were upside down. The mortgage is over the value. The average real estate broker is still trying to sell into this market. The counselor is not. The commercial shopping centers are having a bad time with vacancies and the average broker is still trying to sell something that is not saleable at certain times.

Counseling can not solve all of these problems but many can be solved if the clients will understand what has to be done to get them solved. One of the key ways is to counsel with the person that has the problem.

Hopefully this book on counseling will help open the eyes of those willing to learn another approach to real estate.

Steven L. Cropper

Foreward

I am honored to have the opportunity to write the forward for this particular book on Counseling. Bob and I are close friends and have crossed paths, professionally and repetitively, for many years and we have lived through many of the changes in the marketplace. In all this time one thing has never changed and that is the core needs of the clients we facilitate in the structure called "real estate exchange business." The availability of dollars in the market may change, and politics may go amiss but people still are hurt in many ways and often trapped in situations that most brokers cannot solve.

As counselors the rewards from our sides of the desks are tremendous. Our lives are really free: We have no open houses to attend and we have no floor time requirement, we may have clients in other countries and we have the chance to travel and create a life style that suits us as individuals. But, at the same time, if we are not professional in our approach to counseling our clients, we can waste hours of time going down the wrong trails and not solving their problems which means, of course, that we do not go to escrow and our cash registers do not ring.

But with counseled clients they do ring and when they do we have two blessings, our fees can be really large and we can have the satisfaction that many brokers never experience and that is that we have unlocked and solved situations that really do change people's lives.

Counseling, in my mind, is the major key in helping to solve these problems. I am very tough about getting counseling right and that is probably why Bob asked me to write this forward. I will simply not waste my time or that of my fellow brokers by taking on a client that is not realistic. I refuse to accept clients that WANT something. I am looking for clients that DON'T WANT what they have. This is just 180 degrees from the norm. In our kind of transaction it is this DON'T WANT that is the motivator. They want out of the situation they are in. Note I did not say their real estate I said their situation. The real estate is just incidental to the deal as it is their situation that needs to be changed.

When you come from this side of the ledger you will, through your counseling and actions, develop a respect with the client applicant first, and potentially the client later, that can last throughtout many years and many transactions. I keep it very professional: I do not give away free advise, I have very little patience with a client applicant that does not tell it straight, I restrict the amount of time that is spent in discussion that is not germane, I never go to the client applicant's home for a meeting, I am not interested in inspecting her real estate and I use my own forms for listings and offers that are unlike Realty Board forms that require me to do things I do not want to do and am not capable of doing.

If the client applicant motivation is not there, I turn down the applicant. If after the person becomes a client and they do not perform, then I feel very comfortable in firing them. I just let them go. I am not working for someone who will not perform so it is always best to unearth this as early in the counseling process as possible.

On a local basis I want the client in a positition where we can meet face to face. I really like them to be within a short driving distance to my office. However, I also deal internationally in Viet Nam, China and the Philippines, and while many meetings are face to face, a portion of my business is via phone and electronically. I am even tougher in counseling with my international clients than I am on the local ones and they have to fit a very narrow profile for me to work for them as international mistakes can be very costly.

Counseling is a personal thing. Take from my suggestions above and from those that Bob reveals to you within this book and then build your practice to fit you, your personality and your environment.

Come live the good life. Good Luck.

Steven L. Cropper

STRATEGY 176

Counseling & Exchanging: History & Evolution

In 1955 Richard R. Reno headed up the Exchanging and Counseling division in CAR, California Association of Realtors. At their first meeting in Fresno, he had five people attend the meeting. A few years later at the CAR convention he had a full day session in Los Angeles with 2,100 in the room. I have had Exchange Seminar classes with as low as 20 people to over 200. I co-sponsored Exchange Sessions with Cliff Weaver, SEC at the CAR meetings in Northern and Southern California in which there were standing room only crowds. I doubt today that we would get even the 20 people. The motivation of people is so infused with entitlements that the crying urge to learn and improve is no longer a part of out culture. Am I reading it wrong? Time will tell.

COUNSELING	Over a period of time the real estate industry has opted for franchise real estate—where well-trained personnel do a certain structured work ethic to perfection, which through advertising, open houses and door knocking for listings, they can become successful financially. It works when the underling credit market is supportive. The moment this support evaporates, the foundation is gone. They are intentionally not trained in any counseling activity as it is not necessary when the dollar controls the transaction. Politics unfortunately plays a heavy roll in this as entitlements tend to hold people where they are both physically and emotionally. When employment ceases in an area, welfare keeps the populace in place rather than the people going to where the jobs are. The same seems to be true within the framework of real estate. People continue to look to the sales market with short sales, etc., while they are slowly dying on the vine as problems are stacking up all over that could be solved via counseling and exchanging. In our area alone, one firm that was averaging 40 sales a month and a volume of approx $40 million a month are now still doing 40 sales a month but the volume has dropped to $12 million.
NOTES	The realtors could be re-educating themselves into a very exciting exchange market but instead are failing into other more menial jobs, welfare and living off the assets of their estates. There is a huge need for counseling and problem-solving but without motivation it's nada.

STRATEGY 177

Becoming a Counselor Takes a Little Time

It can't be done in one month but it can be in three to six months. Read and study and practice. Take some seminars and think people not property. Yes, know the property, but that is not the major issue. It is mundane. The basics remain unchanged. The real estate is inanimate. It is the people that count in counseling, and no matter how BIG people might think they are, they are all 100% human. If you are not going to be able to control a client applicant, then move on and head 'em west. You can't solve everything. Don't loose your existing clients if you are currently in the real estate business. Go slowly. C. Charles Chatham, a noted counselor of the past, made the transition in one month but he never suggested that others try it. He had been in real estate 20 years, but he said it was really just the one year done over the same way for 20 years. He had learned nothing beyond the first year, and in counseling it was new and innovative every day. Life was much better. He was 60 and he said he didn't have time to waste.

COUNSELING	Counseling is where this business of Creative Real Estate and Business begins. If you are a principal or an agent you need to be able to unearth the problem and deal with the people. The underlying real estate remains unchanged from every other form of selling but the counseling leads you to solutions based on the people that own the real estate, not the property itself. You have to counsel to get there.
IT'S ABOUT THE PEOPLE	Following is a portion of a letter I received regarding Volume 1 of this series of books from a reader who expresses this extremely well: "Bob, I am not an old guy but I have to tell you that this whole set of strategies has shaken me up. The concepts have made me realize that I need to open my eyes to looking at buying and selling and marketing in new ways. It's not that the fundamentals are so different—due diligence, paperwork, and people. They are essentially the same. But the tools and the way they are being used are different. For an old architect-construction guy like me, I would liken the strategies to using new tools with old materials—e.g. hammers have been replaced with nail guns and power hammers, but the nails haven't changed much."
NOTES	The real estate hasn't changed much. Spiritually we know there is an outer, human world and an also that there is an inner world within us—what we think and feel. What happens in the inner world governs what takes place in our outer world. Counseling speaks to this inner world and the outer vehicle, Real Estate, just comes along for the ride.

STRATEGY 178

Information to Obtain Through Counseling

This is a guide list. You will have to develop the specific things you need depending on the requirements of each individual client case.

COUNSELING

Listen with your inner ear as the client answers questions. Drain the information from the client so you don't waste your time going down the wrong road. If there is more than one client be sure each person participates

1. The date, owner's name (exact), addresses, occupation, family status, etc.
2. Complete description of the property or properties owned and how title is vested.
3. When and how was the property acquired and what is its basis and was the property previously on the market, and if so under what circumstances?
4. Is a tax deferred exchange desirable; is client classified as a dealer and is there a potential tax on forgiveness on mortgage?
5. What can the property the client doesn't want do for someone else? Is it crankable? Does it have good depreciation possibilities, etc?
6. Just what is the problem at hand? Appreciation, income, depreciation? How much of what is desirable?
7. Is there a time element and is the client ready, willing and able.
8. Is there a third party involved?
9. Does the client have money for expenses and/or other properties that might be assets, and does he have personal property that might be utilized?
10. Does client understand initiating with a talking paper with weasel clauses?
11. If income property is involved will the client manage, lease or what?
12. What is client's financial and income status and about how much tax is he paying?
13. Will the client stay in the state of mind of a Don't Wanter rather than act like a Buyer?
14. By whom was the client referred and what is the fee basis to be when the practitioner makes the final decision of whether to handle the problem or not?
15. It is important to understand that if the practioner takes on the problem and finds that, when presenting offers to this client he tends to change into a buyer, then the practitioner should be fully prepared to get rid of the client.

With the exception of a few things where I keep these notes personal, I usually have clients sign the counseling session notes and make them a copy for their files.

STRATEGY 179

Client Needs to be Eyeball to Eyeball – Property Can be Anywhere

There is neither East nor West, Border nor Breed nor Birth
When two strong men stand face to face though they come from the ends of the earth.
Rudyard Kipling

This is a catch-all strategy. The point is that this is still a people world. I have spent 40 plus years in the business and there is no substitute for looking a person in the eye and working out either the deal or the problem. For last 30 years I have seen computers trying to take over the business, and they are just not a substitute for meeting people face to face. Computers and telephones just don't have body language.

COUNSELING	Counselors have different guidelines. Some say that they want their clients to be within 75 miles of their offices.
IT'S ABOUT THE PEOPLE	Others that fly their own planes open that area up dramatically. I lived in Spain but had occasional counseling sessions in San Francisco as a central point for meeting clients. More and more counselors in the international arena have clients in various countries. I have found that after you have closed escrows with clients or partners over a period of time, a great deal of the work can then be done remotely, as everyone knows when to counsel and when to brainstorm. Trust develops so the deals can go together based just on the words of the people. I have flown from Los Angeles to Mazatlan, Mexico for one day just to be eyeball to eyeball to put together a deal. I had a partner fly to Spain for one day to see me and complete a deal. Cliff Strand, who wrote the forward for the Stock & Real Estate book in this series, flew with me for one day from Los Angeles to Portland, Oregon to go eyeball to eyeball with an attorney to get a deal done.
NOTES	You can take away our faxes, phones, computers, e-mails, websites, airplanes, cars, busses and trains but if you will just leave us the people, we will make deals.

STRATEGY 180

Other Counseling Techniques

I believe that the best way to accomplish counseling is the one-on-one or face-to-face exchange of information and probing for motivations. There are several other ways of counseling and I am sure that there will be new ones developed in the future. I will note one that I have used and one that I know about, both of which have been successful.

COUNSELING	1. I found that when I had a major client who needed a lot of counseling but was someone whom I thought had the ability and the assets to do some serious exchanging, I would send them to Dick Reno's six-day class. Other counselors don't necessarily agree with me on this because they think the client is being taught too much, or they will go do it themselves, or they will hook up with one of the other realtors. I found this was not the case. They always returned fully understanding where I was coming from. I did a lot of business using this approach. I also sent a couple of them to Chatham's Six-Day Counseling course, and if they were in the business world I sent them to Art Hamel's Three-Day Business Opportunity Seminar. 2. My son, a mortgage banker, used a variation of Reno's and Chatham's counseling technique in his mortgage company by developing a specialized telemarketing company that delivered the leads to a counselor. That counselor worked with people on the phone, sometimes for only a week or so, but often for a month or even a year, before they were actually ready to close the deal and apply for the mortgage. At that point it was just a two-hour session to put the deal in escrow. When he implemented this counseling system, he went from 40 salespeople down to just himself with a full office staff for back up, but raised returns from 2% to 5% and closed 865 million in mortgage sales over 15 years. Counseling made the difference. 3. If I am counseling with scientists, engineers, CPAs or the like I always use numbers. They love numbers. If they are in sales, the entertainment or music world, etc., I stay away from numbers and deal in philosophy.

Strategy 181
Pre-Counseling Techniques

Counseling is ongoing. It is not difficult to counsel via the media. I actually call it pre-counseling. There are a lot of tools that can be used for pre-counseling.

COUNSELING	1. Each time you do something of any consequence in your field of endeavor, consider how you can make use of it in your pre-counseling. For instance, you attend a seminar on exchanging, should that be your business, and you write a short article about it and send it to the real estate editor of your local newspaper(s). You send him a letter saying "For Immediate release" and you recite your credentials so that he can see that people in their marketing area would be interested in this information.
	2. This pre-counsels people in the area, and someone reading the article can quite possibly make your phone ring. Secondly, you use a copy of the article to start your "scrap-books" for the lobby of your office, for people to read while they are waiting to see you. Again a pre-counseling tool.
	3. You then build a collage of these articles for your web site and let it build. You give talks on your subject matter to the Lions Club or the Chamber of Commerce and these are recorded the same way. Very soon you have built a network of pre-counseling tools. They all lead to direct and indirect referrals.
	4. You can write articles about your subject, and don't be afraid to write a book about your specialty. I often use this series of "300 Stratgies…" books as part of a counseling tool, as do others. If you are going to be talking to a resort owner about trading some of his vacancy, consider sending them our Volume 10, *Half the World is Vacancy*. It will definitely pre-counsel them, which merely equates to getting some of the blinders off their eyes so they can start to see that other options from the norm do exist.
	5. Become a true authority in your field. Don't agree with the masses, do your homework in depth so that you know your subject better than anyone else, and then be sure that shows through in your pre-counseling. Learn how to brainstorm and brainstorm how you can pre-counsel, and then counsel in a new and better way.

STRATEGY 182

Consulting Time

SITUATION	1. Assess your thinking capacity: Little, medium or big. Same with the people you deal with. Same with all things in your life. 2. If you earn $500,000 per year you are probably in the medium category and your time is worth approximately $2,000 per day. Convert this to benefits and it means you probably can't afford to work on little deals. 3. Maybe you need to eliminate everything that brings in less that $100,000 per deal or benefits that approximate what that might mean to you.
POSSIBLE SOLUTION	1. Don't spend your time on people or things that do not make you feel fulfilled 2. If you are dealing with a person who only has a capacity to think at a certain level, don't present to him things that are out of his stretch zone. 3. Present a $10,000,000 package at a National or International Marketing session and present a $1,000,000 package at a Local Meeting.
CONCLUSION	Use your time wisely.

STRATEGY 183

COUNSELING AND CONTROL

Counseling leads automatically to either control or disassociation, with the opportunity to re-associate at some later date.

COUNSELING	1. Counseling is: a) Listening to what is being said and to what is being implied. b) Advising potential clients, partners, or those you are doing business with what the current market conditions permit you to make happen. 2. Counseling is not: a) Getting picked up in the attributes of a parcel of land or a business opportunity. b) Telling the client how great you are.
POSSIBLE SOLUTION	1. If you analyze what you are being told by the person you are talking to, and match that against what is actually happening in the marketplace, you will have an idea as to what can be done under current conditions. 2. At the same time you are trying to analyze whether or not this person has the capacity and the malleability it will take to close a deal. 3. Early in my life as an exchangor, I paid for three or four major clients to go to Dick Reno's Six-Day Exchangor class in order to get counseled. It was the complete way to get the job done. I did a lot of business with these people. I have used books to help in counseling. The more a person understands the more flexible she becomes.

STRATEGY 184

Assess Yourself vs. the Deal

If the shoe doesn't fit...

SITUATION	1. Assess what is important to you: Peace of mind, cash, cash flow, ego, stature, geography, your time, etc. 2. If it is a business deal, assess what it is going to cost you in money and time: If, as a broker, you take ten listings a year, your overhead is $100,000 per year and you work an average of 2,000 hours a year; it means that for you to sign on a listing as a broker with a client, it is going to cost you $10,000 in cash and 200 hours. Is the deal worth this investment? 3. In the above situation, who is taking the risk in this deal, you or the client?
POSSIBLE SOLUTION	1. Unless there are extenuating circumstances, at least know what you are doing and don't waste your time. 2. Don't be locked to a percentage. If the listing will only generate $10,000 with a 5% fee, quote a 15% fee or something else to make it worthwhile, or don't do the deal. It is your option alone as to what you will work for.
CONCLUSION	1. You are only working on things that profit you. If you don't make a profit you won't be here tomorrow to help the next person. 2. If you can't find things that produce a profit, go fishing or to the beach or go to a seminar.
NOTE	If you are entrepreneurial there are thousands of things to work on and invest your money and time on and there will be a thousand new ones tomorrow. There is never an end to opportunities.

STRATEGY 185

SETTING FEES AS A CONSULTANT OR BROKER

Base your consulting fees on the amount of actual time spent with the client plus any work or preparation and expenses required on your part. Base your contingency fees on the degree of difficulty. A free & clear house should be easy but a free & clear house with a tough restrictive client can be difficult. Is it a 5%, 10% or 15% fee or more, or should it be a flat fee?

COUNSELING FEES	There are a lot of favorable things to be said about setting a flat fee for a contingency fee. Remember this fee is based on the client's ability to close as well as to deliver a title to a property that can be closed. The degree of difficulty, I believe, is the paramount thing to consider and the difficulty is just as likely to be the client as the property. I make sure the client knows and understands this during the counseling sessions. I have purchased some art in my lifetime and I once asked an artist how long it took him to paint a certain painting. He reflected for a moment and said, "About eight hours and 20 years." The same is true when you are setting a consulting or contingency fee. The resolution may seem simple on the surface, but the expense and time it took to accumulate the knowledge to make it work is what is being paid for. I have mentioned elsewhere in this series of books that if you are a broker, then at the end of each year take the sum total of all your overhead and divide it by the numbers of listings you took during the year — then you can ascertain what it cost you to take on a client's problem. If your business overhead was $100,000 for the year and you took on 10 clients that year it cost you $10,000 to sign your name to a listing. If your overhead is $200,000, then it cost you $20,000 (average). If you first act as a consultant on a time basis and then you change to a contingency fee basis, be sure to draft a document that both you and the client sign so there is no miscommunication.
NOTE	Some of the best listings you ever get are the ones you did not take. I really like to fish so sometimes I say to myself, would I rather take on this problem or go fishing? If the answer is fishing, I don't take the problem.

STRATEGY 186

ARE ALL LEGS UNDER THE TABLE?

When counseling you are wasting your time if all the people who are in title to the property are not there for the counseling session. This obviously cannot apply to corporations needing board approval of major decisions, but the concept remains true. The biggest waste of a counselor's time is to not having all influences at the counseling session.

CONSULTING	The easiest way to be sure you have all the signors at the counseling session is to require that they furnish you with a copy of a title policy (if it is real estate being discussed). This shows exactly who is on title. I like to furnish them with a list of things to bring to the session so I don't have to wonder about details. At the first counseling session, which, if it doesn't go well, will probably be the last, I like to get the major details about the property out of the way so I can get to their personal situations and the motivation. If their personal desires are impractical or a relationship of trust and respect cannot be developed, then having all the facts about the property is superfluous. The time in gathering them has been wasted. With everyone in the room as the session is going on, then everyone is being counseled at the same time and the progress is forward. You do not have to go through it again and again and again. If you find out in pre-counseling (before they get there) that their brother or someone else has a controlling influence on their decision, even if his name is not on the title, you must request that he be there or don't have the session. If someone can influence the signing of documents, they need to be there. If an attorney is germane to the future signing, I like to have a visit with her, even if it is just by phone, to get a sense of who she is and what her thinking might be about an exchange. Many of them have no idea why an exchange might be useful or necessary.

STRATEGY 187

The Don't-Wanter is a Key to Many Transactions

There is a basic difference between an exchange and a sale.

SITUATION	1. The motivations in a regular sale are hidden within the cash in the transaction. While everyone values cash in a different way, it is still a common denominator. In an exchange, where there is no cash or minimal cash, then the desires of the participants are often very visible. 2. There is another very significant factor in an exchange that is often either visible or just below the surface. The motivation of the participants can be on either the front side of the exchange (what they are receiving) or on the back side (what they are getting out of). 3. When there is a high degree of motivation on the back side of the exchange, that participant is said to be a Don't-Wanter. From my experience this is the key to many exchanges. She is highly motivated and brokers will often state that this person is a #8 (on a scale of 10) Don't-Wanter.
POSSIBLE SOLUTION	1. In counseling it is important to get at the key reason people are transacting business when you are considering a structured transaction and not a normal sale. If you can uncover the person's Don't-Want, why he wants out of the property, you have found the key to the transaction. Now it is a matter of finding the opposite side and putting it together and you will have a completed transaction. 2. Note the difference in the backside motivation between the following examples: a. A person losing his property to a foreclosure scheduled to be complete in 30 days. b. A free and clear house rented at a high rate. c. A person who has just inherited a motel a thousand miles away in a very bad section of a city and the person has no understanding of how to run same. d. A wealthy person owning an industrial building leased for 20 years to Coca Cola. 3. Numbers 1 & 3 are highly motivated on the backside of the exchange and would be considered as a high number Don't-Wanter, maybe a 10 on "a" and a seven on "c". They definitely want out of what they own. The higher the number the easier the deal is to get together

STRATEGY 188

Counseled Clients Tell You *Their* Truth

They tell you the truth as they know it. They understand that the more you know about them and their situation the better chance you have of making a transaction that benefits them.

COUNSELING	1. Usually when the client applicants come to you, they do so with the idea that they will be asking you for help in selling or exchanging their property. To them at that first meeting, they usually think that the discussion will be about the real estate or other assets. 2. They are not usually completely open about the information they give you, even about the property. A good question is to ask them first to tell you everything good about the property, and then tell them you need to know everything bad about it. People will be making inspections at a later date and you don't want to find out the negatives that way. You want to tell those who are making inspection or doing due diligence what they are going to find before they find it. 3. It is, of course, the people who are key here, so it is very important that they arrive at a point in the counseling where they are willing to share their innermost thoughts with you. There must develop a sense of trust for this to happen, because if you cannot reach this point you cannot find out what is the primary motivation, so you are in essence shooting blind in trying to arrange an exchange for them.
POSSIBLE SOLUTION	If what they would like to happen is impossible or difficult in the existing market, you are far better off to tell them this, If they cannot live with that, then do not waste your time trying to get them to that point. Once they reach the point where you actually believe that what they say is what they actually feel about a situation, you are very close to having the deal done. You just need to find the vehicle that solves that set of circumstances.
NOTE	Trusting someone comes hard for most people. Sometimes a lot of time can be wasted trying to get to that point. If you set appointments up for a limited time period, e.g. one hour, then they realize they must keep the meeting going and you will eliminate some chaff.

STRATEGY 189

Value...What Is It? Is it in the Eyes of the Beholder?

Three brick masons were laying bricks and they were each asked what they were doing: One said, "I am building a wall." The second one said, "I am building a church." The third one said, "I am earning $20 per hour." They each saw value in a different way.

You will find the Exchange Counselors Definition of Value below substantially different than that of the real estate society as a whole. It is important in counseling that a client applicant understand this connotation. If they don't you may never get your deal done.

COUNSELING	1. Value has been described as a relationship between persons and things desired. It does not have substance or form. It is a mental concept. It exists in the minds of people. The measure of the so-called value of a thing is the amount of sacrifice which will be made to gain control of the rights or of the use of the thing, such as money or asset price which will be paid for its possession. 2. Real Estate cannot have value in the strict sense of the term. This is the reason that value cannot be an attribute (an inherent quality) of any object. Value is a relationship between the desirous persons and the thing desired. The mere existence of a thing is not sufficient to cause the emergence of value. 3. Value must be related to persons. When it is said that the value of a residence is $300,000, it does not mean that its mere existence is the cause of the price. The price must be related to someone. Thus the statement that a residence is worth $300,000 simply means that the rights of ownership (to someone) is worth that amount.
FURTHER COMPLICATION & A SOLUTION	When they enter the exchange market, the "price" tends to fade in importance as value moves away from the denominator of cash and moves toward benefits. Benefits start to affect the price-conscious more than the dollars. The more the exchange client can recognize that it is benefits he is after, the truer he can analyze the value to him of a property. The value is personal, not generic.
NOTE	The California Supreme Court says: *Value is the highest price in terms of money, if exposed for sale for a reasonable time to find a purchaser, buying with knowledge of all the uses and purposes to which it is best adopted, etc.* Most of these of these points are not even remotely applicable to exchanges.

STRATEGY 190

The Value of an Asset in the Exchange Market

This has also been known a the Ladder of Value, but all the names are a derivative of a counseling tool, developed by Chet Allen years ago, to allow a client in counseling to visually see how their asset stacks up in the exchange marketplace. The locations of these rungs in the ladder will vary over time and market conditions, and as we move more into the national and international markets. So modify them as needed for your particular counseling endeavor.

LIST OF ASSETS: Please note these are real estate oriented. If you're in the barter world create a list that exemplifies your market at a particular time.	• CASH • NNN LEASES • PAPER (TDs, MORTGAGES, etc.) • FREE & CLEAR HOUSES (easy to borrow $) • ENCUMBERED HOUSES • FREE & CLEAR INCOME PROPERTY • POSITIVE CASH FLOW INCOME PROPERTY • BREAK EVEN INCOME PROPERTY • FREE AND CLEAR LAND • PERSONAL PROPERTY • NEGATIVE CASH FLOW INCOME PROPERTY • ENCUMBERED LAND	Please note that this list changes with the market. At one time NNN leased property was more valuable than cash. When cash is in shorter supply it moves to the top.
	In counseling this type of a chart allows the client to visualize where her property might fit in the market. If she has a negative cash flow income property and wants to move up to a positive income cash flow property, what can she do to move up the list? Can she add cash, is she willing to solve a geographical problem for someone else and take her exchange in a different state or country? What can she do to make it feasible? If she wants to exchange encumbered land for a free and clear house, what are her chances?	

STRATEGY 191

Would-Ya-Take?

If properly used, the Would-Ya-Takes can be a great counseling tool.

COUNSELING	1. At the appropriate time during a counseling session, while exploring options, you might ask a client applicant, "Have you ever thought about trading for a motel?" There are many reasons for this: It places a new thought into the arena; it allows the person to react to perhaps an alien thought and you can judge that reaction; it will indicate how open to new ideas the person might be, etc. 2. Another question might be that you know of a situation some distance away—such as an apartment house halfway across the country—and you ask if the person might be interested in something like that. You will get an immediate reaction to whether or not geography and distance might limit their take area. The wider this area of take (acceptance), the more chance there is of finding the right solution. 3. You might say that you have a client with some private schools that might be an exchange opportunity for the client applicant's property. "Would something like that be of interest?" From the reaction to this you will get a picture as to their interest or not in a business opportunity. 4. Would-Ya-Takes are used to explore avenues that the person probably has never thought of while at the same time giving you a chance to actually see their reaction to these possibilities. If the person is thoughtful in analyzing these various options vs. being extremely closed and didactic about what is acceptable, this could affect your decision as to whether to take on the client or not.
NOTE	Would-Ya-Takes help you analyze the client applicant's range of acceptance. The one about distance lets you know if the person would be willing to make inspections on something that is some distance away. Ten or twelve Would-Ya-Takes will beget a lot of information.

STRATEGY 192

Counseling is an Individual Thing

Be yourself. It is a mutual conference with someone. Advice is sometimes not wanted but counsel is. The client applicant does not know what the market is like. He reads the paper and listens to the talking head on TV and to his friends, but your market is different. The terminology of having a controlled client does not derive from controlling his decisions, but from counseling with him so he understands the market, what can be expected from you and what is expected from him. The wide swings of emotion and time wasting has been eliminated. Your knowledge and connections within the marketplace are leading him to his solution and he realizes it. You cannot be a pompous professor or a browbeater and be a good counselor—keep your ego out of it.

COUNSELING

In counseling there are certain patterns but having the desire to help people solve situations is paramount. They have to give you the information and the tools in order for you to do the job.

I used to half jokingly say that every time I took a course on counseling I came back and redid my office.

Many counselors pattern their offices after the legal profession: tastefully decorated, plaques on the walls, high back chair, etc.

For many years in Newport Beach, California, I shared offices with eight other real estate brokers and investors. Each individual had a private office, and we shared a conference room and secretarial, reception and bookkeeping staff. I have been at times in my own facility, and in small one or two person facilities, and I found this group of nine independent counselors /investors was probably the best arrangement. We shared the expenses but not the pot. Each person brought certain specialties to the table and you could reach out and get what you needed within your own facility. We knew not only our own clients' situations but those of our constituents, so many transactions happened because of the association.

Other counselors prefer to operate from their own single offices, some from their homes and some do their counseling in the nicer hotel lobbies. Part of my studies included learning body language, and I found using a desk for counseling precluded me from seeing the bottom half of a person's body, so I prefer a more relaxed arrangement like a davenport or comfortable chairs.

Other types of counselors, who are investors, spend a lot of their time counseling with real estate brokers to try to understand if they have good enough control to deliver a viable transaction.

STRATEGY 193

People in Hell Want Ice Water

When people want impossible things there is always an agent or broker who will waste his time trying to deliver the impossible.

SITUATION	1. There are a lot of cases of this, but let's use someone wanting a cash sale when there is no cash market. 2. You as a broker, or possibly an exchangor, tell them there is no cash market, and ask if they would consider exchanging. They say, "No, we need a cash sale." 3. If you are a broker you might say, "OK, I'll do the best I can," and take the listing. Both parties waste time and money.
POSSIBLE SOLUTION	1. Between steps two and three, the broker or agent or principal should try to do some counseling. Ask the client how, if there are no cash buyers in the marketplace, they are going to sell for cash. 2. If something can't be done, it can't be done. From the agent's point of view it is better to use the other formula, "Head 'em West 'til Their Hat Floats," or sow a seed that will bring them back later. For example, "Please go ahead and list your property with (name your competitor down the street) and if they are not successful in selling, come back to me and I will try to exchange it for you." 3. When they come back they will be more attuned to what is real and will have eliminated the impossible requirement.

STRATEGY 194

HEAD 'EM WEST 'TIL THEIR HAT FLOATS

Arbitrarily let's pick a number — 90% of the situations in real estate and business are not worth your time, so the maximum situations you have to pick from are 10%. I am not saying that if you are a retail real estate broker not to take a quantity of listings. I am saying that if you are interested in a somewhat selective life don't take on situations where the other side of the transactions is difficult to work with.

SITUATION	1. When you are counseling someone or even in a pre-counseling mode the attitude might be one of, "The quicker I decide not to get involved in this deal the quicker I can get on to doing something I want to do." 2. There are many signs that you can pick up in counseling that are red flags that tell you not to get involved with this person or in this situation. The thought often goes through my mind: Would I rather be helping this person or going fishing? 3. Some of the salient things you might watch for are those that play the victim role. The world has mistreated them. Others are those that have a best friend that is great advisor. Another one is they have three other partners: Remember that each partner has a spouse and an attorney and a best friend advisor, that totals well over 10 people before a decision can be made.	Head 'em west 'til their hat floats. Head 'em west... Head 'em west...
POSSIBLE SOLUTION	1. Of each degree of difficulty you might consider raising the fee or your profit structure. At some point you might consider that it is just not worth the potential anguish vs. the potential reward. 2. There is always one more deal right behind this one. The trite saying does come into play: "Some of the best deals you ever make are the ones you turn down."	If you are closer to the east coast, head 'em east...

STRATEGY 195

DFTP: Don't Fight the Problem

The problem is what you are looking for during your counseling sessions. When you unearth it don't fight it. Just let it be. It is no different than any other professional problem solver be it medical, legal, financial or other discipline. Stay just a little bit remote.

COUNSELING	This is the same as any other brainstorm. Try not to be judgmental regardless of what the problem is. The client applicant usually wants a rapid fix. You know from your previous work that just because a problem was solved one way for a previous client, it doesn't mean this one will always have the same pattern — no two owners are alike. It is really important to not jump to conclusions here, as you must continue to probe to find out how to bridge the gap between the individual and the perceived problem. You are not so much looking for an answer as you are looking at the capability of the owner and how he can assist in solving the situation. When you later present this situation to your associates looking for a solution, you will be asked questions that can only be answered if you know a lot about your subject. If you have a real depth of information and present it more as a situation than a problem, you may be surprised at where the answer might come from. Once you know your subject, if someone says that no one could ever solve that problem, DFTP, let it flow off as water off a duck's back. DFTP – move on. Some years ago a group of very successful exchange brokers had a corporation by the name of DFTP. They would trade into problem situations just to solve them and make a profit.

STRATEGY 196

Miscellaneous Counseling Techniques

Once you take on a client the counseling never stops. Each time there is a contact of any kind there is ongoing counseling.

COUNSELING	Counseling with offers: During counseling sessions you have advised clients that you will be writing offers on their behalf subject to their approval, so it is important they arm you with the knowledge it takes to write offers that will be acceptable to them. Here is the verbiage and how it is handled: *This offer is subject to final written confirmation and written approval of and by the undernamed.* Then print their name. You can sit at your desk and write offers all day. When you have your next meeting with them present these offers plus the ones you have obtained in the field, and as you present them you are finding out more about what will motivate them. If you solve their problem and they do not accept it, it may be time to re-evaluate your association with them. Please remember that the truth is only momentary and situations change. Continuous counseling keeps you current with these changes. Do not leave your virtual desk or your hotel lobby desk or wherever you do your counseling to meet with them. Don't go to their offices or home; they should come to *you*. Wherever your place of business is, that is where you do business. Do not inspect the property they list or the property they go into. The only time you check it is when you intend to buy it. Do not use the real estate industry's standard forms such as listing or offer forms. They obligate you to do things that you do not want to do or are not qualified to do. You are not an appraiser or an attorney or an accountant. Tell them to use those professionals if they wish, but you are not capable nor wish to help them in those areas. Listening is an art form. Hear their words during counseling but listen for the inner meaning. Watch the body language. Some people counsel without the desk between them just to see their body language.

STRATEGY 197

Counseling May Unearth a User

We have mentioned the importance in counseling of listening with the inner ear—understanding the feelings behind the client's words. When you counsel, your practice will expand, as will you, to the point where you are not just a citizen of an area or a city or state or even a nation, but a citizen of the world. As you expand geographically so does your confidence, and so do the opportunities for those you counsel. Many times their objectives can be magnified by the knowledge you bring to the consulting table.

COUNSELING	I am going to use three examples here but there are many of these. I am going to discuss "unearthing a user." My first experience was counseling a couple where the man, about 40 years of age, was an engineer and had been employed by a local company for 15 years. The couple wanted to trade a small investment property for a larger one to grow their estate with more leverage. In the course of counseling I could sense, not hear, that he was unhappy in his job but stuck because of responsibilities.
WATCH FOR A POTENTIAL USER	I explained to them that they might open up their vista a little by entertaining the idea of running their own business using the real estate as part of it. For instance, when you own a motel you not only own a piece of real estate that can make you maybe an 8% return, but the business within the real estate can maybe make you a 20% or better return. I asked them to consider that for the next session. They agree and became quite enthused by the idea. I ended up exchanging them into a lighting fixture store, building and business. They became a user of the real estate and over the years they became very wealthy and I think maybe acquired seven or eight other properties from me. I had another man with a small 40-unit apartment house who started out with the idea of just trading up. He also liked the idea of perhaps trading into a business. I sent him to Art Hamel's Business Opportunities Seminar before I would go on with the counseling. He came back enthused and with an idea. He started acquiring motels, three in a series of within 75 miles of each other so one manager could manage all three. We used the Creation of Wealth formula to keep expanding his ownership. He is national now. A third man who I had been trading into rental houses decided, likewise, from a counseling session and we started by trading 10 or 12 of his houses into a mobile home park, and this is still his business to this day. He is now international in scope. Users have additional value as they will put up their time and energy to go with their equity.

STRATEGY 198

When You Have Exhausted All Possibilities, Remember This: *You Haven't*

When counseling, remember that there is usually one area where you do not have the sum total of all available knowledge. If you fail to get the answer to all possible facets of the equation, that just may be the one missed item that causes you to waste a lot of time and the cause of the job not getting completed.

COUNSELING	If people skip over a question or skirt around it, then you must probe to see if that unknown thing might affect an exchange or make the effort to find it a waste of your time. They might want an exchange just to get away from the neighbor who dumps garbage over the fence every night. Or perhaps the property will be under the flight pattern of a new airport going in. You do not care what the problem is, you just need to know what it is so you can deal with it. Part of counseling is being intuitive: If one of the two parties being counseled makes a snide inference toward the other, then is it something to delve into. Maybe explore trading for two properties rather than one. You might spend six months finding the right deal for them and then have a divorce negate all the work and expense. If people are reluctant to bring you a certain document or you suggest that you should call their accountant or attorney and there is a little tension about it, then there may be a definite reason you should do so. Also, people may not realize the importance of you having certain facts and data, and the fact that they are not forthcoming is that they did not recognize the importance.
NOTE	When everything is on the table and above board then getting to the solution is much easier. You must be able to eliminate the hedging through counseling or you are going to waste your time. If you are counseling on an hourly basis, which you are qualified to do, then time is not a critical factor. On a contingency basis, it is.

STRATEGY 199

Entitlement Syndrome: In Counseling, Call a Spade a Spade

There is a tendency throughout the world today for people to think that they are owed something by someone, often the government. The entitlement programs used by politicians to gain election have at least some of the people believing that they are owed something, and that men are not just created equal but they have the equal rights to all things even if they have not earned them. In counseling these people are creating new obstacles and in most cases should be headed west until...

COUNSELING	We have been watching on TV the people in Greece rioting as their country is plagued with financial problems. They have become very angry and unruly. They voted for and elected politicians who promised them wonderful entitlements with wonderful welfare benefits, free medical service, 30-hour work weeks, retirement at age 50 with full income, etc. All these entitlement are now going away because someone has to pay for them. Picture if you will one of these Greek rioters across the desk from you in a counseling session. Her belief system is perhaps that the banks have no rights to foreclose on his properties. It was really the mortgage banker's fault who agreed to a loan that was beyond her capacity to pay... that she is entitled to keep and own her vacation condo in Hawaii, etc. Picture the word "Victim" tattooed on her forehead. These people need help, but if their first thoughts are that it is not their fault, and if you as a counselor cannot rein them in to see the error of their philosophy then, "Begone." You are going to waste your time and listen to their complaints over too long a period of time. Also, if they are blaming the mortgage banker for their own stupidity, then if there is ever a little hiccup in some future real estate or business deal you might handle for them, then it is going to be your fault and it is probably better to send this nice client applicant down the street to your competitor.

STRATEGY 200

Counseling for Escrow

This is a guide list. You will have to develop the specific things you need depending on the requirements of each individual client's case.

COUNSELING FOR ESCROW	1. An exchange escrow is different from a cash sale, as there is a deposit made in money into an escrow on a cash sale when it is opened. In the case of an exchange this is not true, as the deed for the other property is the consideration. As a broker, I recommend that each client be required to make a deposit into the escrow to cover costs of title work, etc. when the escrow is opened. This could be $5,000 or $10,000, but it is good business on many levels to have this requirement. 2. If there is a T.D. being created in this escrow, and if your client would like to minimize the escrow cash requirement, you can use the following verbiage in the escrow documents: *"There are to be no cash adjustments to actual balances on encumbrances. Any differences are to be adjusted in the amount of paper being created in this escrow."* 3. If you are a broker, I would suggest you use the following clause to control the escrow: *"These instructions and related documents shall not be changed, amended or altered in any way without the expressed consent, in writing, of the brokers involved."* 4. Clause to consider using when client or participant agrees to accept a property without first inspecting it: *" _____ has agreed to acquire and accept property described as ______ without first seeing and inspecting it and is doing this based on his (her/their) own judgment and decision and are accepting the liabilities inherent therewith."* 5. If you are a principal or a broker carrying back paper in this escrow, consider using this or a similar alienation clause: "This trust deed is given and accepted upon the express provision that should property herein described, or any part thereof, be conveyed by trustors either voluntarily or by operation of law or further encumbered or an agreement of sale entered into by trustors for the sale of said property, or leased, without the written consent of the beneficiaries, then and in that event, all sums secured hereby shall at the option on the beneficiaries become immediately due and payable."

NOTES

NOTES

300 STRATEGIES FOR MAKING REAL ESTATE & BUSINESS DEALS

VOLUME 9

STRATEGIES 201 - 225

Blending Your Real Estate, Business & Life into the International World

ROBERT W. STEELE

Foreword by Alexander J. Krem, BA, MBA, JD

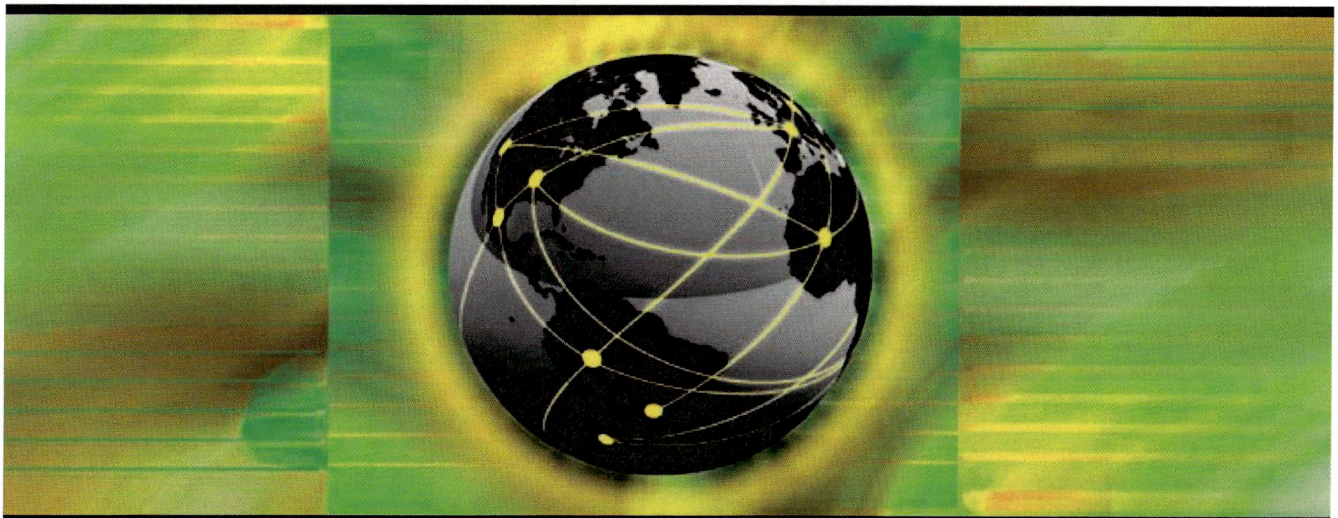

OUTSIDE THE BOX & INSIDE / OUTSIDE THE COUNTRY

300 Strategies for Making Real Estate & Business Deals

Outside the Box & Inside / Outside the Country

VOLUME 9

Strategies 201 – 225

BLENDING YOUR REAL ESTATE, BUSINESS & LIFE INTO THE INTERNATIONAL WORLD

Robert W. Steele

Foreword by Alexander J. Krem, BA, MBA, JD
University of California, Berkeley

Design, Layout & Graphics
Victoria Vinton
Coyote Press Graphic Communications
www.coyotepressgraphics.com

VOLUME 9
CONTENTS

Introduction

Foreword: Alexander J. Krem, BA, MBA, JD

Strategy	Title
#201	Think International
#202	St. Kitts & the Chinese Market
#203	Gibraltar & the Spain Market
#204	Zimbabwe
#205	Vote with Your Feet
#206	Falling Dollar
#207	Virgin Vacancy Ploy
#208	Butterfly Effect
#209	Japanese Carry Trade
#210	Liquefying Mineral Assets
#211	Derivatives #1
#212	Derivatives #2
#213	Inflation
#214	Hyper-inflation #1
#215	Hyper-inflation #2
#216	You Can't Play Baseball in a Hurricane
#217	DMI International Wheel
#218	Soft T.D. Exchange
#219	Panama Trader Traces
#220	International Trading Opportunities
#221	Friday is International Day
#222	Wholesale Trade Credits
#223	International Cold Calling
#224	Reasons to do International Business
#225	Where Did This Dirt Come From?

INTRODUCTION

Blending Your Real Estate, Business and Life Into the International World

This book and its strategies and formulas represent part of the opening salvo of the creative real estate exchanging and business marketplace of the United States moving into the international marketplace. Currently, this being the beginning of 2010, there are approximately 100 creative real estate and business exchange groups in the United States meeting one to two days per month. There are two main national associations of creative thinkers that meet for marketing purposes: The Society of Exchange Counselors with approximately 100 members, that has been in business for approximately 50 years, and the National Council of Exchangors with approximately 300 members, that has been in businesses over 30 years. These groups meet three to six times a year for from three days to a week to do creative business transactions between themselves and their clients.

There is also the CCIM group, Certified Commercial Investment Member, with approximately 12,000 members that deal in sophisticated transactions under the umbrella of organized real estate but dealing primarily in the numbers business and not necessarily in the creative thinking arena.

The newest company, Deal Makers International S.A., which is designed specifically to operate in the creative international marketplace, is opened to both investors and entrepreneurs of all natures. These marketing meetings, currently scheduled for five-day tenures, will be held throughout the world in any country that is receptive to free enterprise.

Alexander J. Krem, BA, MBA, JD

Foreword

Bob Steele is an extraordinary man, an athlete, a natural leader, visionary and creative genius who spends most of his mental life thinking outside the box and coaching others to do the same. He sees events in a remarkably broad context and recognizes subtle patterns and trends that most fine minds miss altogether.

Volume 9 of his excellent Steele 300 Strategies focuses on the international marketplace and provides practical, clever and often provocative ideas for prospering in the new "Flat World" of the future. The world is changing dramatically and Bob gets it. No longer does the U.S. have the tallest buildings, the largest companies or the greatest opportunities. Like Horace Greeley's famous advice to "Go West, young man," Bob advises us to "Become Citizens of the World." For many reasons, the foreword thinker will want to evaluate Bob's excellent ideas and consider which are appropriate for self and family.

Clearly and simply, he presents the advantages of multiple passports ("one of the greatest gifts you can give your child") and foreign residence ("vote with your feet") and outlines strategies to achieve each. He discusses, with more wisdom and clarity than government officials or university academics, the awful truth about inflation and presents strategies to benefit from this inevitability.

Anyone who believes that Detroit will once again become a major car manufacturing center, that the Washington Monument or the Empire State Building has a pre-ordained right to be the tallest structure in the world, that the American middle class will determine international consumer habits, or that Uncle Sam will have the will and wit to fix his many problems, need not read this book or benefit from Bob's clear ideas. For the rest of us, who acknowledge which way the wind is blowing and who welcome the great opportunities that the future will provide, this is a must read.

Alexander J. Krem, BA, MBA, JD (University of California, Berkeley)

Founder, Admiralty Investment Group of Companies, Worldwide School of English, Alameda Capital LLC, and more. Advisor to the Asian Development Bank, World Bank, International Finance Corporation, National Science Foundation, US Congress, numerous foreign governments, domestic and international companies. Former resident of Egypt, Germany, Japan, Mexico, New Zealand, the UK and the US, with banking and legal experience in over 75 countries and (most important) wonderful daughters who are truly "Citizens of the World."

STRATEGY 201

The International Child

Potentially one of the greatest gifts you could give your child

SITUATION	1. You recognize that the world is inter-related in many ways and that this is the mega-trend of the future. 2. People give hours and hours of thought and thousands of dollars to what will help their children the most. 3. Where should they go to school? More and more are getting away from the "dumb down" public education and opting for home schooling or private or foreign schools. 4. What languages should they learn? (If you need help on this how about Spanish and Mandarin Chinese?). Check the demographics.
POSSIBLE SOLUTION	**Probably the best thing you could ever do for your children is to *have them born in another country*, thus immediately giving them the right to a second passport in the future (see Strategy 202). Will they use it? There is no way to know at this time but people pay a lot of money for this privilege and you have accomplished this for your children in rather a simple way.**
CONCLUSION	1. Open up the world for your children. They may do something with it, or not, but you have opened the door to them to a future that few others have. 2. Do your homework and select the right country(s).
NOTE	The reason this formula is first in this book is to try to get the student's or reader's mind open to where we are going. There is no point in trying to stay conventional when you are trying to look at all the options the world has to offer. Know the formulas, strategies and options, then make informed decisions.

STRATEGY 202

ST. KITTS + VALIDATING FORMULA #201

One of many examples

Real Estate Play between St. Kitts and China and other parts of the world:

In case you haven't heard of the program, it's one of the oldest economic citizenship models in existence. An interested applicant must invest $350,000 (plus government and legal fees) in a government-approved real estate project, as well as undergo a background and medical examination.

If accepted, the applicant will be awarded with citizenship in the Federation of St. Kitts and Nevis. Since the island-nation is a Commonwealth country, as a former British colony, St. Kitts' citizens enjoy visa-free travel to the UK and the European Union.

Real estate developers build nice homes in St. Kitts, approximately $700,000 average, and sell them in China. The Chinese want to be able to travel internationally with ease, and this is something that is simply not possible with a Chinese passport. There are far too many visa requirements, making staying somewhere for more than a couple of weeks problematic. The St. Kitts economic citizenship program provides an excellent passport for them and their family members.

There are thousands of islands in the Caribbean, 700 in just the Bahamas group, and all of these island countries have separate governments. All of those have different laws and all have a real estate market. Each of them has a separate real estate and business play of some nature. The opportunities and the real estate markets are endless.

The entire country of Gibralter is in this photo taken from an airplane. Spain is under the airplane. You can just see Africa across the strait. As a point of interest they have to close the main road into Gibralter from Spain every time a plane lands or takes off as the road crosses the runway.

STRATEGY 203

GIBRALTER + VALIDATING FORMULA #201

One of many examples

Real Estate Play between Gibralter and Spain

There are thousands, probably hundreds of thousands, of corporations, companies and trusts domiciled in Gibraltar. It has fought off domination from many sources over many years. Battles of all nature have raged here. There is an ongoing battle with Spain over this airport which was built out of the slag from the tunnels that honeycomb "The Rock." The runway goes out into the ocean to the right of the picture. Spain has sealed the frontier (border) many times to press the issue. Obviously, Spain wants to own or share the airport.

While a British protectorate, Gibraltar fiercely protects its independence.

It is hard to believe but some countries have taxes on profits made in real estate and business that exceed 50% and sometimes into 90% and in extreme examples to 100%. Also people sometimes would like privacy. A common technique in Spain (and other countries too) is to hold title in a Gibraltar company, where there are minimal tax consequences, and then when it comes time to sell the real estate, the corporate officers sell the company that owns the real estate and not the real estate itself. For example a developer in Spain building a 100 unit condominium project might have 100 Gibraltar companies, each one owning one condo.

STRATEGY 204

ZIMBABWE

Real estate for sale at pennies on the dollar

Real Estate Play between Zimbabwe, Detroit, et. al.

Zimbabwe is used here as an extreme example of hyper-inflation and the resulting chaos of devaluing a currency (any relationship to the dollar is coincidental) and the devastation it is causing the real estate market. One accepted connotation of hyper-inflation is 600% inflation per year or in simple terms 50% a month. Zimbabwe was at 5,000% inflation in Aug. of 2007 and at 100,000% in April of 2008.

Printing currency in 100,000-denominated Zimbabwe fiat notes had to give way to million dollar bills and then billion and then trillion. Now any currency may be used.

Zimbabwe real estate has no marketplace. Pennies buy you dollar values. These ultra-extreme examples are happening all the time when you enter the international marketplace. With these markets, created almost always via the corruption of governments, comes opportunity.

Detroit, the 11th largest city in the U.S., now does not have one supermarket in the entire city and they just tried to auction off at a tax sale 9,000 properties and houses, some as low at $5,000 each. In many cases they had "no bids." Opportunities abound in this world but you won't find them if you stay on your front porch. Part of my children's education was on college boats going around the world to teach them that the world was bigger than just where we lived.

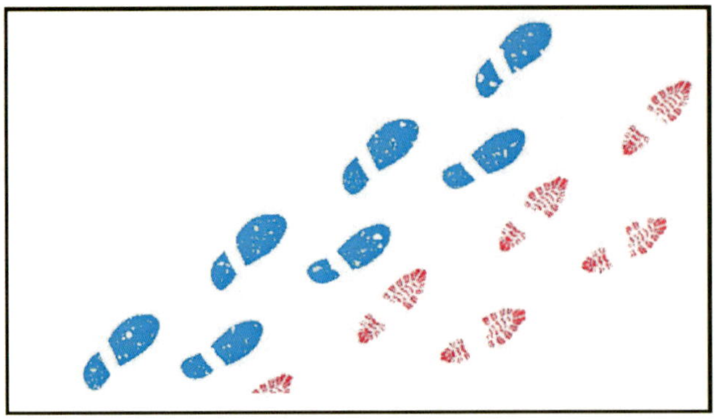

STRATEGY 205

Vote With Your Feet

A Lifestye Formula: Live where it's nice and profitable

SITUATION	True story: I was driving with a broker friend I had done lots of business with in Laguna Beach, California. I was stopped at a traffic light and across the street was a girl with dyed bright red hair standing straight up, wearing a large nose ring, tattoos and clothes to match. My broker friend also noticed her and said he was sorry to tell me but that was his daughter. He said she was in with a bad crowd and he could do nothing about it.	I know that later she OD'd on drugs. Laguna Beach is a beautiful place but when you have a problem, get away: Vote with your feet.
SOLUTION	The broker could easily have moved 20 miles north to where we lived in Newport Beach. We did not have that problem there. Fifty miles south he could have moved his family to La Jolla where people lived in a nice place without those problems. Countless options are open to all of us every day and for every decision.	If you wish to live where mosquitoes eat you up and business is done at McDonalds, it is your choice.
QUESTION	Why do people live where the environment is unfriendly to what they want to do with their life? It is easy to understand why some would like to live away from civilization in the wilds of Alaska—it's because they want to. But to live where you do not want to live or do not feel safe or prosperous doesn't make sense. You are either stuck in your mind or under a political system where you can't move.	Vote with your feet: Move.
TAKE CONTROL	If the market goes bad, or the political system goes bad, or the monetary policy goes bad, or the river floods you out, or your real estate market turns into a war zone, or they put in rent controls, vote with your feet: Move. If it means going out of the city or the state or the nation, do it. Control your own destiny and don't be a victim. If you want to be a socialist, fine and if you want to be a capitalist, fine. Just get in the right milieu, in a beautiful place to live—and work, if you are a capitalist.	Vote with your feet: Move.

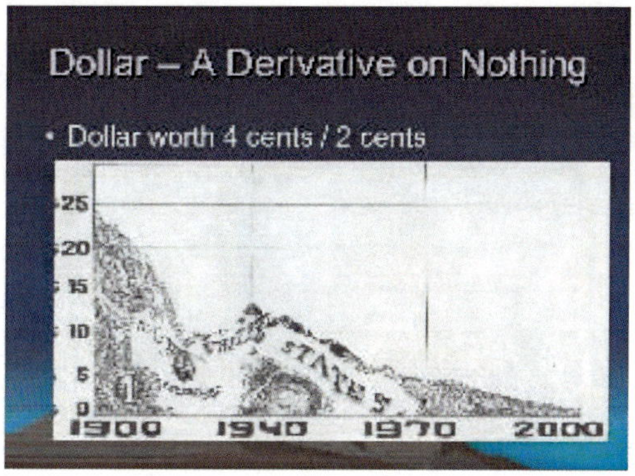

STRATEGY 206

The Falling Dollar

Wake up America!

SITUATION	1.	Does it really make sense to work and save something that is well on its way to being valueless?
	2.	Explain to me and yourself the logic of saving or trying to accumulate an item that is worth less and less every day.
	3.	Do you think you have been lied to by someone? Would it make sense to consider thinking this out for ***yourself***?
POSSIBLE SOLUTION	1.	Deal in benefits rather than currencies.
	2.	Obviously you may have a learning curve to move through.
	3.	Now might be a good time to move in this direction and away from old paradigms.
CONCLUSION	1.	Eliminate everything in your portfolio that is denominated in dollars if you can, e.g. bonds, trust deeds, dollar savings, etc.
	2.	Educate yourself and do your homework.
NOTE	Consider broadening your marketing arena to include international & other medias of exchange.	

STRATEGY 207

Virgin's Vacancy Ploy

Richard Branson's formula used to help build Virgin Music Stores

SITUATION	1. England's Sir Richard Branson wanted to start Virgin Music Stores world wide. 2. He had the desire but not the capital to get through the start-up periods when opening each store. 3. He actually called his group together to brainstorm the problem.
POSSIBLE SOLUTION	1. They used several techniques to avoid having to pay for things during the start up period. 2. One thing he did was to located people that had vacancy problems in their retail commercial outlets. 3. He would agree to lease the property if the first three months of the rental were free. He would not budge from this requirement. It was a deal breaker. They leased store sites all across England, Europe and then the world with this formula.
CONCLUSION	1. He said he missed some very nice retail outlet sites because of this but he also got some very nice ones. 2. Virgin Music became one of the largest music companies in the world.
NOTE	Vacancy represents an opportunity—always.

STRATEGY 208

International Butterfly Effect (Google this): If "A" is true then so is B!

If the butterfly flaps its wings in China, will it alter the course of the hurricane in the Caribbean?

How the Expansion of the Panama Canal affects the real estate market in Houston, Texas – Plus Plus Plus

INTERNATION-AL EXAMPLE AS WE SPEAK	1.	This is "A": In 2009 a ten-year expansion project was started on the Panama Canal. Currently 40 ships a day transit the canal at an approximate cost of $200,000 each, $8,000,000 a day, $3 billion in fees paid to Panama per year. This will soon be 120 ships a day or $9 billion a year.
	2.	This is "B": 1,800 miles away in Houston, the closest U.S. port to Panama, there is a rush on warehouse space in anticipation of the Panama Canal expansion project.
SPECIFICS	1.	Houston prepares for Panama Canal expansion: Warehouses, holding everything from beer kegs to frozen chickens, crowd the roadside along Highway 146 south of Houston. A ferocious building boom is adding acres more. Many of the ships carrying goods to the U.S. will dock in Houston and unload for further transit.
	2.	Retailers like Wal-Mart and Home Depot have already snatched up land around the Houston ports. Houston is the closest U.S. port to the Panama Canal and U.S. imports from East Asian Nations are valued at approximately $410 billion.
	3.	The Houston port will spend over a billion to expand its Bayport Container Terminal and will buy giant cranes appropriate for unloading post-Panamax cargo ships.
PLUS FOR REAL ESTATE BROKERS:	1.	This is "A Plus": Panama now has such a large income that they pay from 25% to 50% of retirees' meals eaten out, airplane tickets, and so forth. The Country of Panama actually reimburses the retailers who extend the discounts to the retirees. Retirees are moving into Panama by the thousands.
	2.	This is "B Plus": Real Estate sales and exchange brokers be aware of a huge movement of residential and commercial properties as retirees relocate their assets into Panama.

STRATEGY 209

Japanese & Now U.S. Carry Trade!

International Geography & Distance Provides Opportunity

SITUATION	1.	Japan's economy has been in the tank for over 10 years. Interest rates are as low as 0%.
	2.	A small percentage like ⅛ or ¼ charged for buying or selling the currency.
	3.	Question: How to take advantage of this low rate?
SPECIFICS	1.	This is called the Japanese Carry Trade: Borrow large sums of money from Japan. Borrow: $100 mil Costs: ½ pt Earn: 3 pts. Profit: $2.5 mil
	2.	Convert Yen to U.S. Dollars
	3.	Buy U.S. short term treasuries, (notes, bonds, etc) yielding 2 to 4%.
CONCLUSION	1.	Sandwich the yield spread of a net of 1 to 3%
	2.	Billions if not trillions of currency is traded in this manner.
NOTES	1.	Distance and markets provide many opportunities not only for currencies but for real estate also.
	2.	As of this writing the U.S. Dollar is now being used in the carry trade because of the artificially low interest rates.
	3.	The distance factor: It is probably easier now to sell Montana lots in China than it is to sell them in Montana as, rest assured, there are people in China who would like to own something outside of their own country.

STRATEGY 210
Liquefying Mining Assets

Proven Assets are determined by geologists. They are factual. In mining, particularly in hard rock mining, it takes a long time and a lot of money to extract minerals. If the assets are real, we can create against them.

SITUATION	1. An exploration company has proven reserves of 10 million oz. of silver. The market is $15 an oz. and extraction cost is $5 an oz. They have a net asset value in this of $100 million dollars. Price: $150 M | Cost: $50 M | Equity: $100 M 2. They need $5 million dollars in cash for operating expenses to see them through until they can get roads built and the infrastructure established. 3. Miners usually go to banks and hedge some of their deep storage minerals to raise capital. This presents a problem for both management and stockholders of the mining company as the banks usually want the loans paid back in either dollars or oz. of the product, whichever is the dearer. It is conceivable that the mine might have to pay back five or even 10 times the borrowed amount if the minerals appreciate rapidly. Mining is a global business. Minerals, from all over the world are critical to everyday living. You can use the Creation of Wealth formula in any currency and make an exchange for assets in any other country of your choice.
POSSIBLE SOLUTION	Have an exchange broker list the right to create up to a $10 million loan against the proven assets and exchange the paper into a real estate asset where the miners can borrow the $5 million and pay it back without having to hedge some of their product.
CONCLUSION	The mining company ends up with $5 M cash and a $5 M equity in a parcel of real estate. They have an unhedged loan.
NOTES	1. Distance and markets provide many opportunities not only for currencies but for real estate also. 2. As of this writing the U.S. Dollar is now being used in the carry trade because of the artificially low interest rates. 3. I.E. the distance factor: It is probably easier now to sell lots in Montana in China than it is to sell them in Montana as rest assured, there are people in China that wold like to own something out side of their own country.

STRATEGY 211

DERIVATIVE #1

BENEFITS, BENEFITS, BENEFITS, BENEFITS

Derivatives, partially from the sub-prime mortgage market, play a significant role in the perfect storm raging in the U.S. and International economic and monetary markets today: 2009.

Believe it or not, the neat little pile above is $1 million dollars (100 packets of $10,000). You could stuff that into a grocery bag and walk around with it.

Fiat currency: We still think of it as real and it plays tricks on our minds. If it is worth two cents on the dollar and if you think you are a millionaire you are really worth $20,000. Real estate and other hard assets are real, we know that. Could we start to think in benefits rather than dollars?

STRATEGY 212

DERIVATIVE #2

While a measly $1 million looked a little unimpressive, $100 million is a little more respectable. It fits neatly on a standard pallet...

Now look at the number of pallets above. Ladies and gentlemen... I give you **$1 trillion dollars...** ***see the little man in the left hand corner? (And notice those pallets are double stacked.)***

So the next time you hear someone toss around the phrase "a trillion dollars"... that's what they're talking about.

Derivatives: The total number the government reports is **ONE QUADRILLION: ONE THOUSAND ONE HUNDRED and 44 TRILLION to be exact. (1,144 of the above display)**. Approximately one-half of these are said to be Credit Default Swaps (CDS) and the ones where the notional value becomes real value when they default. Payment is then dependent on the loser's balance sheet to have the ability to pay. AIG, Bear Sterns and Lehman Bros. were losers. Internationally I give you Iceland & England as failure examples from these CDS derivatives. Those that received bail out money watched it go in their front door and out their back door to pay off the winners of these derivatives. Were you a real estate or business pawn somewhere in this game because you didn't see the whole picture?

APPROXIMATELY THREE TRILLION DERIVATIVES HAVE FAILED TO DATE. How many are left to fail? 500 trillion maybe?

Derivatives are just part of the perfect storm. Let's look at hyper-inflation next and then let's bring in the formulas and strategies to help ease the problems, protect our assets or generate profits on both a national and international level.

STRATEGY 213

Inflation

Inflation is a monetary event and not an economic one.

It is one of the ingredients of the perfect storm brewing for the world economic and monetary market.

SITUATION	**INFLATION:** Our monetary policies play a major role in inflation in all countries. Pick any area you want but let's just use Europe today: a) Cost of a single fare on the London Underground (the Tube) in 1957 was 1.5 cents. Now $7.80. **Increase of 51,900 percent.** b) Cost of three course dinner at Munich RathsKeller in 1957 was 40 cents. Now $25. **Increase 6,150 percent** c) Cost of one night at Paris' Hotel du Pantheon in 1957 was $3.00. Now it is $219. **Increase of 7,200 percent.** d) Cost of admission to Athens Acropolis in 1957 was 30 cents. Now it is $15.60. **Increase of 5,100 percent.** e) Cost of a half-day sight-seeing tour in Rome in 1957 was $2.20. It is now $79. **Increase of 3,491 percent.**
POSSIBLE SOLUTION	1. Position one's assets so as to take advantage of the forces. Try not to buck the tide but try to know and understand the fundamentals.
	2. Is it better to owe money or to be receiving it?
CONCLUSION	Know your fundaments during inflation so you will be positioned right when hyper-inflation pays a visit.

STRATEGY 214

Hyper-Inflation #1

There are many opinions as to what this is.
One common one, that we will work with today, is that hyper-inflation is when prices increase at a rate of 50% per month or more.

SITUATION	1. Fundamentals: There are supposedly 3,800 examples of fiat currency in the history of the world. According to historians, none has ever lasted. Hyper-inflation in one country now (Zimbabwe) is exceeding 100,000% per year. 2. Officially, inflation in the U.S. is very low. The government has stopped posting M3, which tells how much currency is being printed by the government and is in circulation, so there is no public guideline. 3. Shadow Statistics.com, a private company which includes M3 statistics, will tell you (for a fee) that inflation is substantially higher than what the government is reporting. 4. For today's purposes let's look at the market as if hyper-inflation were going to happen and how we should be structuring our asset holdings and what type of transactions we should be making.
POSSIBLE SOLUTION	Use hard assets as an insurance policy such as gold and silver. Back up all mortgages and debt with 10% to 20% in G and S. Loans are static. When hard assets appreciate to the am't of the debt, pay it off. In this case you hold the insurance premium.
CONCLUSION	See Hyper-inflation #2.

STRATEGY 215

Hyper-Inflation #2

This is a very important subject matter for those with investments. What formulas and strategies are there and what could be developed to protect assets and/or make profits with the knowledge of what might be coming?

SITUATION		As outlined in Hyper-inflation #1
POSSIBLE SOLUTION	a)	Use hard assets such as gold and silver as an insurance policy. Back up all mortgages and debts with 10% to 20% in gold and silver. Loans are static. When hard assets appreciate to the amount of the debts, pay them off. In this case you hold the insurance premium.
	b)	Consider TIGR's and STRIPS to back up these loans. See Formulas (Government Bonds)
	c)	Diversify holdings 1) Into foreign market 2) Think safety 3) No one between you and your money
	d)	Acquire rural land where you can grow items.
	e)	Structure debt with Performance Mortgage concepts. **Buy everything you can with this structure.** See Formula (Performance Mortgage).
	f)	Brainstorm
	g)	Brainstorm
CONCLUSION		Huge gains and losses will probably occur. Having some insights at this time could help you lean in the direction of those that gain.

STRATEGY 216

You Can't Play Baseball in a Hurricane

Or - Stay off the floor when the elephants are dancing

SITUATION	Don't join the thousands of people that say, "But that is all I know. I want to just play baseball." If you can't play baseball you can't. Don't go down saying that is what you want to do and the world is at fault for not letting you do it. In a down market think of all the architects, civil engineers and on ad infinitum that can't do what they were trained and educated to do.	Hello Reality
ANALYZE YOUR CHANCES	Your chances of success in these markets are minimal. Yes, there are opportunities available but also remember that more and more very capable entrepreneurial souls are also looking for these scattered opportunities and they will bid them up.	Keep looking for the niche or shifting through ashes
THE FROG GETS COOKED	We all know the story of the frog in the heating water. CHANGE YOUR BALL PARK (OR DANCE FLOOR). If you are provincial and stay in one arena your chances are considerably diminished. It is a big world and the negative forces do not permeate every corner.	Re-read *Illusions.* There is a beautiful world outside your entrapment. Think International.
DON'T TRY THE IMPOSSIBLE!	Many political arenas are becoming socialistic and if you want to know the true denotation of the word "Impossible" it is very easy to exemplify when trying to do entrepreneurial business in a socialistic milieu. It is "impossible" They have different rules.	You can still play baseball but do so in a different ball park. Go international.
HOW POSITIVE	Notice how positive you become when you start thinking internationally. You are on the offense, not the defense.	

Strategy 217

DMI International Wheel

Diversify Diversify Diversify

True economic and political freedom is as follows:

STRATEGY 218

T.D. Exchange

Soft paper makes it easier to cross long distances or borders

SITUATION	In a very slow real estate market it is sometimes difficult to turn an equity into cash without suffering a substantial equity loss. For instance, let us say you wanted to move some equity into another country. You can't find a cash buyer for your property at a fair price and you can't find someone in the foreign country who will exchange properties with you.	You own $2,800,000 F/C land
ALTERNATIVE	Consider the compromise of creating a soft TD against your property and exchanging that, rather than the real estate. Let's assume you own a $2,800,000 parcel of land free and clear. Offer to create up to $1,400,000 (50% of supposed value) TD bearing interest at 2% and all due in 10 years in exchange for something in the foreign country agreeable to you.	Create up to $1,400,000 soft TD for trade.
CONCLUSION	People on the other side of this transaction do not have to take in land or property in a foreign country. They end up owning a TD that provides an income of $28,000 year. They have no management or other real estate-associated problems.	Trade for foreign real estate.

STRATEGY 219

Panama Traders Trace Motivated Clients

Know your market: World wide conservatives are moving away from socialism and inflationary markets

SITUATION	World wide entrepreneurs, investors and price-conscious individuals are moving away from the dictatorial and socialistic markets as are those who cannot live in the higher priced countries.
POLITICS	In Panama a great many people are moving in from Venezuela and out from under the dictatorial and socialistic rule of Hugo Chavez. Also you are seeing a migration for similar reasons from Columbia
INFLATION DRIVEN	Ex-patriots are moving in large numbers from Canada and the U.S. to get away from the inflationary prices coming from the over-creation of fiat currencies. You can live in Panama for as little as $1,000 per month. That's not a good living but a passable one. For $2,000 or $3,000 a month one can live reasonably well.
CONCLUSION: PANAMA TRADER SEES	Additionally expats are arriving from Holland and throughout Europe, many Latin American countries, China and Korea. Couple this with the expansion of the Panama Canal and you start to understand why Panama will become the capital of Latin America. We can envision a country built as a solid city across the 80-mile isthmus.

STRATEGY 220

International Exchanging Is the Way

Gandhi's dictum: "First they ignore you. Then they ridicule you. Then they fight you. And then you win."

SITUATION	Read a U.S. newspaper or listen to the TV or radio and chances are you will hear something negative about our economy, business and real estate. If that is not the case by the time you are reading this, I can guarantee that such will be the case somewhere in the world. Stuff happens, as they say.
SOLUTION	With the advent of the Internet and the airplane there is no reason you have to be locked into doing business close to home. Originally, I sold houses in a radius of primarily five miles of my office. Then I started to branch out. I have been pushing the exchange business toward the international arena for 30+ years. The European Union and the South American Mercosur are trading blocks that open up tremendous opportunity for real estate and business entrepreneurs. There is a world of opportunity out there. Emerging Asian markets, with over a billion people with discretionary income, are looking for opportunity. The Persian Gulf and major pockets throughout the world have wealthy investors looking for opportunity. Even the Russian investors and markets are sending wealth into the world.
EXCHANGE BROKERS	There is a huge untapped demand for these services for trading properties internationally.
TAKE CONTROL	Look for opportunity and solutions in the international market place.

STRATEGY 221

Every Friday is International Day

Here is a simple strategy that comes from a brainstorming session.

We guarantee results.

QUESTION	How can a person who has never been international in his thinking and has no international connections turn the corner and become international in scope? If the person only has one language to work with and has never been outside of their home country, how can he possibly make the transition into the global world?
SOLUTION	Take one day a week, we picked Friday, and do nothing but think *international*. That is all you have to do. The pieces will start to drop in one at a time. You will start reading the right things, meeting the right people and suddenly the world will begin to open up. You will find that your thoughts the rest of the week will start to convert things you normally do to having a wider scope...a bigger playing field.
BOOTS ON THE GROUND	The next thing you know you will be landing in another country, going to an exchange meeting in another country, talking to a foreign entrepreneur about a transaction. It is like any journey, there is always that first step. Friday is your first step.

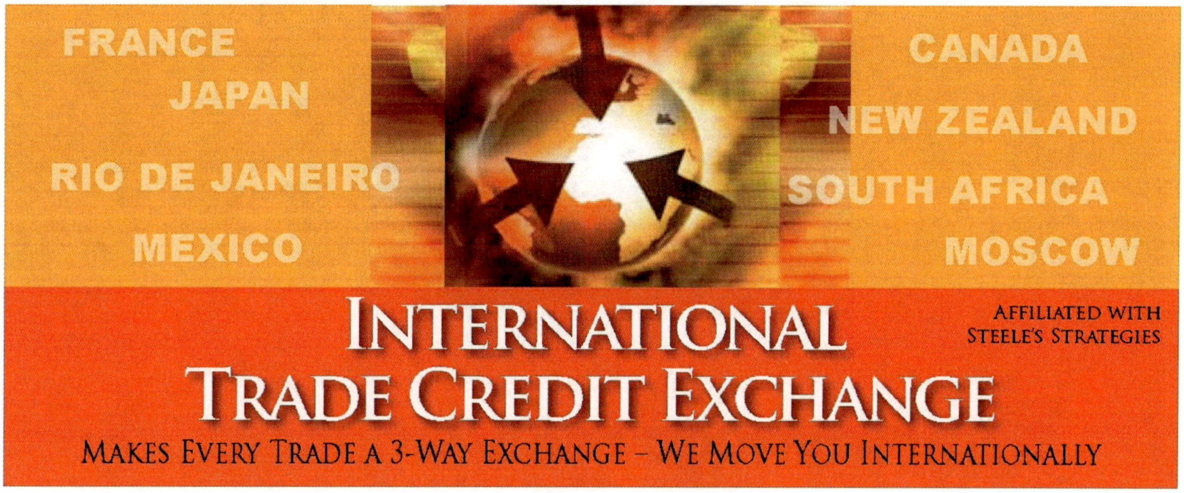

STRATEGY 222

WHOLESALE TRADE CREDITS

$100,000 to $1,000,000 minimum sizes

In a marketplace where things are really backed up, as we are experiencing in 2009, and because there are a myriad of reasons why it is so congested, it is a good time to assess your position and the options open to you.

By the time you read this the correction may have already happened, but someplace in the world humans have caused some other catastrophic problem (s). Unwinding problems can result in nice profits.

I am showing herein an example of structuring being done in an international milieu where liquidity is a problem. There was an old established formula many years ago in the SEC group were a multiple exchange of 3, 4 or 5 ways (often referred to as "legs") could result in enough in brokerage commissions being earned that the brokers could buy out one leg and close the transaction if they had to.

The SOS Trade Credits, depicted herein, is just a sophisticated way to facilitate a multiple exchange and effect the same desired results. These things are impossible to do without having controlled assets or clients and without knowing something about the art of brainstorming.

Trade credits are an excellent way to cross borders as they soften, not circumvent, the various currency issues.

A little creativity can open up tremendous opportunities.

STRATEGY 223
International Cold Calling
Don't do it the way I started. There are easier ways.

QUESTION	I can remember two wasted weeks years ago in England knocking on doors trying to find someone that had some idea what real estate exchanging (my business) was all about. I also tried libraries, all kinds of government offices and facilities and on and on. There was no internet or cell phone, etc., at that time but there were international attorneys and things of that ilk that I did not use.	
SOLUTION	International Attorneys (best) and CPA-type people doing international accounting are good connections. In England, had I known, there are also 500 year old companies and family cells that deal in real estate world wide. Phone that international attorney in a country of your choice and tell her you are interested in making investments in her area and watch the connections develop.	
INTERNET	Spend a day on the internet and you can walk away with many international connections. As an entrepreneur you will know when an opportunity shows itself. If you are a builder or developer of houses I can promise you that someplace in the world right now there are five buyers for every seller.	
CRAIG'S LIST	How simple it is today: Plug in Craig's List. Pick a country where you speak the language and start making connections. Pick out a third world country and the information in your brain becomes potentially very profitable.	
HOW POSITIVE	Notice how positive you become when you start thinking internationally. You are on the offense, not the defense.	

STRATEGY 224

Strategy – Reasons to Go International

How long is a piece of string?

QUESTION	The more complicated the civilized world becomes the more reasons there are to think internationally. When we mention motivating things remember that also nothing is black or white. There are many layers to most problems. Take the preservation of wealth. You could probably write a library full of books about this one subject.	
SOLUTION	Let's do a little brainstorm on this one item. Let us say that the preservation of wealth refers to real estate holdings in one country and the owner is concerned about having all their eggs in one basket and would like to diversity into two or more countries. The 1031 law is not applicable in international exchanging but if there is no real estate market available where you can sell in one country and buy in another, you can still exchange equities without going to cash. There is a huge movement of people between countries. Exchanging is a tool that works.	
OPTIONS	What are some of the other reasons to want to move equities or assets or their persons from one country to another? More favorable tax treatment, labor costs are lower, living costs are less, weather is better, politics are better, opportunities are better, education is better and on and on and on.	

STRATEGY 225

Where Did That Dirt Come From?

Perspective and value are in the eye of the beholder

SITUATION	The following are two true stories originating form the history of the SEC, Society of Exchange Counselors, and both pre-internet:
	1. A broker, Chuck Callison, of Newport Beach, California, wrote an offer to exchange a vacant lot in Newport Beach for a property represented by another broker, George Hoover, in Glendale, California. The lot, being free and clear, did solve Hoover's client's problem but Hoover wrote Callison and asked him, "What does the lot look like?" Callison sent him an envelope full of sand. 2. Art Alwen, a broker, offered some vacant land in one state to another broker, Bert Spear's client, for an asset in another state in exchange. It solved Speer's client's problem but the client wanted to know what the vacant land looked like. Bert took him across the street and showed him a vacant lot. He said, that is what vacant land looks like.
SOLUTION	Both transactions closed.
CONCLUSION	The above two examples covered first intrastate and the second one interstate. If you picked up a handful of dirt in one country and a handful of dirt from another country, could you tell which was which? Real estate is real estate, no matter where it originates. They may build the buildings a little differently and they may speak a different language but a roof is just a roof no matter what country it is in.

He has taught his **Creative Real Estate Course** one or more times in the following locations:

Alaska:	Anchorage	
Arizona:	Phoenix	Scottsdale
California:	Anaheim	Bakersfield
	Carmel	Chico
	Costa Mesa	Eureka
	Irvine	Long Beach
	Los Angeles	Monterey
	Newport Beach	Palm Desert
	Palm Springs	Pismo Beach
	Red Bluff	Redding
	Riverside	Sacramento
	San Bernardino	San Diego
	San Jose	San Luis Obispo
	Santa Barbara	Santa Monica
	Santa Rosa	
Colorado:	Denver	Grand Junction
Florida:	Clearwater	Tampa
Georgia:	Atlanta	
Hawaii:	Hilo	Honolulu
Idaho:	Boise	

Illinois:	Chicago	
Iowa:	Des Moines	
Kansas:	Wichita	
Maryland:	Bethesda	Tysons Corner
Massachusetts:	Boston	
Minnesota:	Minneapolis	St. Paul
Missouri:	Kansas City	
Montana:	Billings	Missoula
Nevada:	Las Vegas	Reno
North Carolina:	High Point	
Oregon:	Corvallis	Eugene
	Lincoln City	Medford
	Portland	
Texas:	El Paso	
Utah:	Park City	Salt Lake City
Washington:	Seattle	Tacoma

NOTES

300 STRATEGIES FOR MAKING
REAL ESTATE & BUSINESS DEALS

VOLUME 10

STRATEGIES
226 – 250

Half the World is Vacancy

CHESTER W. ALLEN & ROBERT W. STEELE

Foreword by Robert E. Baines

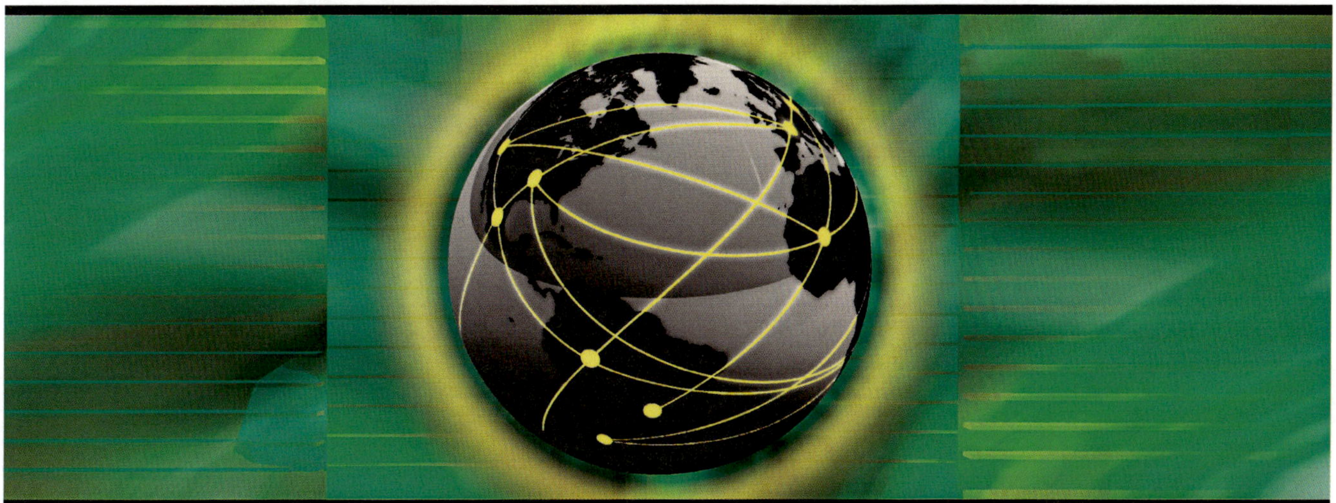

OUTSIDE THE BOX & INSIDE / OUTSIDE THE COUNTRY

300 Strategies for Making Real Estate & Business Deals

Outside the Box & Outside the Country

VOLUME 10

Strategies 226 – 250

HALF THE WORLD IS VACANCY

Obtaining Ideas Not Available Through Conventional Thinking

by Chester W. Allen & Robert W. Steele

Foreword by Robert E. Baines, BA, JD

Design, Layout & Graphics
Victoria Vinton
Coyote Press Graphic Communications
www.coyotepressgraphics.com

VOLUME 10
CONTENTS

Introduction
Foreword: Robert E. Baines, BA, JD

Strategy	Title
#226	Turn Vacancies into Wellness Units
#227	Virgin's Vacancy Ploy
#228	The Un-Built Building
#229	Vacant Air Rights & Mineral Rights
#230	Use of Consignments Fills Commercial Vacancy
#231	Personal Notes in Vacancy Exchange
#232	Subdivide the Vacancy
#233	Give Away the Vacant Building
#234	Trade Credits
#235	Apartment House with Many Vacancies
#236	Trade Credit for Special Hotel Vacancy
#237	Create Your Own Credit Card to Fill Vacancy
#238	Open-Ended Note Tied to Insurance Policy to Soften Assisted Living Payments & Fill Vacancies
#239	Create Open End Reverse Mortgage to Fill Assisted Living Vacancies
#240	Combining Strategies to Fill Assisted Living Vacancies
#241	Trading Vacant Lots for Corporate Stock with a Put Option for Additional Trades
#242	Trade Credit to Help Fill Shopping Center Vacancies
#243	Create Low Percentage Land Lease and Exchange for Higher Yielding Asset
#244	Create Low Percentage Land Lease On Vacant Land (or Under Buildings) and Exchange for Trade Credits
#245	Resort Hotel/Motel Vacancy Problems & Seminars
#246	Vacancy Equals Equity, #1
#247	Vacancy Equals Equity #2
#248	Trade Vacancy for Equity in Business
#249	Give Vacancy to Charity
#250	Use Vacancy as Investment Security to Generate Income
#250A	Bonus: Rent or Trade Your Vacancy via Telemarketing
#250B	Bonus: Hotel Vacancy for Semi-Retired
#250C	Bonus: Trees for Vacancies, etc.
#250D	Bonus: A Vacancy in Your Mind Can Be Good
#250E	Bonus: Sandwich Vacancies for Profit

Half the World is Vacancy

by Chester W. Allen, SEC, CCIM. EMS

Well, maybe not half. But then again, maybe more than half. About 40% of the world's hotel rooms remain empty every night. Airlines are running about 65% full. There are millions of square feet of vacant industrial, office and retail space. And land – at least half of the world's privately owned land lays fallow. And then we can add in unbilled hours for attorneys, architects, engineers, doctors, dentists and other professionals. Thousands of freight cars, trucks and cargo ships are deadheading every day. Newspapers, magazines, radio and TV stations have capacities far beyond what they are using – all are vacancies.

Bob Steele, Mike Stewart and I were walking the 184 mile Thames Path across England last summer and began talking about vacancies. Like so many things in life, until one seriously begins thinking about something, we remain unconscious about hundreds of things we encounter every day. My wife will see and identify flowers on our walks, while I am off in my head about something else. But once we began to think about vacancies as a potential business opportunity, we began to see vacancies everywhere.

On our walk we stayed in hotels where we were the only tenants. We ate at restaurants 10% full. We attend movies in theatres 90% empty. Stadiums are filled to capacity only a few days every year. Harbors are filled with boats seldom used. The yellow pages are filled with products and services not being sold or being used to capacity. These are all vacancy.

Okay, so we can make the case that there is a lot of vacancy in the world. Maybe not half, but maybe more. So what!

Let's start to think about the cost of vacancy. If a hotel could go from 60% occupied to 80%, and fixed expenses run 40% and cleaning and laundry add 10%, net income would triple with this 50% vacancy reduction. It costs almost nothing more for an airplane, bus or train to run full as running half empty. So, almost all vacancy reduction is pure profit.

THE UNRECORDED ASSET

Companies, when compiling their balance sheets, do not record vacancy as one of their assets. The 40% of the unused hotel room nights, the billions of dollars in un-acquired advertising, the ship's non-billed deadheads, and the phone companies' unused capacity never appear on anyone's books as assets. Consequently these assets are not a priority in corporate consciousness. Yes, hotel management constantly attempts to fill the vacant rooms, and newspapers and magazines spend millions on salaries for sales people to sell space. The corporate mentality is to reduce vacancy and obviously it would be a poor business decision not to do so.

The real issue is that businesses view vacancy only as a liability. Corporate thinking seldom goes beyond "What can we do to reduce vacancy."

A paradigm shift is needed to fully appreciate the vacancy opportunity.

Let us begin by broadening the view of vacancy to include all usable assets that are not providing income, reducing costs, or adding net worth.

In order properly evaluate their potential, using the above criteria; we need to make the distinction between Vanishing Assets and Hard Assets

Vanishing Assets are those that, if not used in a timely fashion, disappear entirely. The list is quite long. The aforementioned non-rented hotel rooms, the radio program un-interrupted by commercials and the hours not billed by the law firm are examples of vanishing assets. Tomorrow, today's lost potential revenue has no value. It has vanished

Hard assets have ongoing value, whether used or not. They can lose perceived value if not used. A building, half rented has less value, based on income, than the same physical property, fully rented. But the building will retain some value, even if 100% vacant.

Some hard assets have lost nearly all of their value. There are desert airfields covered with obsolete airliners, and the waters of Suisun Bay, near San Francisco, has scores of derelict merchant ships.

The list of both Vanishing Assets and Hard Assets is about a long as our imaginations will take us. We will start with Vanishing Assets. Assets that will disappear with time, if not used, include:

- Rooms (hotel, cruse ship);
- Seats (airline, stadium, concert, theater);
- Advertising (print, radio, TV, internet, phone);
- Shipping space (truck, rail, boat air)
- Services: (legal, engineering, consulting, architectural, literary, medical)
- Products: (spoilage)
- Real estate rental space: (residential, office, industrial, retail).

ASSET ENHANCEMENT

It serves no purpose to write a book that merely points out that there are vacancies. Or even that these vacancies are often overlooked as real assets. That is about as useful as pointing out that we are having a recession or that stock values are decreasing. What is important is our understanding that while there are vacancies, they can be useful in helping create profit, reduce loss, or bring pleasure.

Perhaps all industries have forward thinking groups that research the non-performing or under-performing asset problem.

In real estate, there are organizations that specialize in solving non-performing asset ("vacancy") problems. While the traditional real estate brokerage and advisory community have used cash as the only asset enhancing commodity, national groups like the Society of Exchange Counselors ("SEC") and National Council of Exchangors ("NCE") have solved innumerable problems for property owners and investors throughout the world using assets other than cash. The co-author of this book, Bob Steele, wrote a classic One Hundred Ways to Make a Real Estate Transaction, One of Which is Using Cash.

The SEC and NCE organizations meet nationally (and sometimes internationally) eight times a year throughout the country, while dozens of regional and local "exchange groups" meet monthly in scores of locales. What these groups do is to use one party's non-performing (or poorly performing) assets to acquire assets better suited to the owner's situation or tastes.

While most organized groups have previously limited their venue to real estate, there is no reason why the same creativity and formulas used by these professionals can not apply to non-performing assets ("vacancies') of all types. A vacancy is a vacancy, whether real or personal property.

A new, broader thinking, group has come into being to assist a world that is half vacancy. Believing that the same creative formulas and brainstorming can solve not only real estate problems, but those of businesses, International Vacancy Exchange ("IVX"), and World Asset Exchange ("WAX") were born.

To better understanding what is effective and what is non-productive, the exchange professionals have learned, by trial and error, the traditional ways of marketing challenged or hidden assets, doesn't work. In the case of real estate, they have proven that real estate is not a property business, but a people business. One man's lemon is an ingredient for another man's lemonade. An effective professional will not attempt to market a challenged asset without a thorough understanding with the property owner as to the owner's goals and capabilities. What is a liability to one owner can be an asset to another.

The two major challenges for effective asset enhancement are: 1) for the professional and principal to be in agreement as to the principal's goals and potential solution's reality, and 2) interacting with other qualified professionals to provide both takers for the principal's asset and locate the asset acceptable to that principal. These often are not the same asset. If they are, the result is a two way transaction. A takes B's asset and B takes A's asset. The magazine trades advertising for hotel rooms, and the hotel owner has advertising.

All transactions must benefit all parties. The above exchange benefits both parties as the cost to the hotel owner for advertising is almost nothing. If the owner is exchanging rooms that won't be rented anyway, the only cost is some laundry and a few minutes of housekeeping and front desk time. For this the hotel owner will be acquiring an asset that may fill up many rooms with paying customers. The advertiser can send friends, family, customers and employees on vacation, or use the rooms as promotional assets to increase circulation.

To be successful, in every transaction, each party must acquire benefits that outweigh the liabilities. Sometimes the benefit is just getting away from stress. Some types of asset ownership are stressful to most people. An apartment complex occupied by drug dealers and gang members requires a very special type of owner. Most of us would exchange for almost anything to get out of this ownership. But there are others who, if they can creatively acquire a potentially profitable asset, will revel in the challenge.

Successful asset enhancement precludes the "needle in a haystack" approach. The client who will only close if they can acquire a 2,000 square foot blue house on Maple Street in Key West Florida is a waste of time. Yes, a transaction like that may have closed once, and will likely do so again 12 years from now.

Some assets (vacancies) are more marketable than others. Some owners are more motivated than others. In general, assets that are more liquid (convertible to cash) are more easily marketed. Assets with positive cash flow are preferred to those with no cash flow, or those that require a periodic infusion of cash ("eater"). At one time, for real estate, we put together an "Order of Property Desirability". The idea was to determine who should be generally motivated to be a taker for what. In general we felt that those lower on the scale would be motivated to take a property higher on the scale. The challenge to the professional is to provide additional or offsetting benefits to the party moving down the list. This is where the asset enhancement professional's experience is critical. This is where Bob Steele's 250 formulas are priceless.

REAL ESTATE ASSETS

Real estate takes many forms: Land, Houses, Apartments, Retail, Office Buildings Industrial, Storage, Hotels, Motels RV Parks, Mobile Home Park, and many others. It can also take different forms. There are air rights, mineral rights, leases, timber, and even view corridors. Some types of real estate and some rights are more in demand than others.

As an example, identifying what most consider to be the most to least valuable is our Order of Property Desirability list. This is a real estate priority list, but the same concept is being used for all types of vacancy.

This list was created for the average real estate investor to illustrate desirability in an average time. Let's examine each of these property types and why they are where they are on the list.

1. **Twenty five year, single tenant building, triple net leased to Bell Telephone, at a 14% cap rate with full CPIs, and a 6% assumable loan.** Unless there were extenuating circumstances, such as environmental issues, this property is worth more than 100% cash. People with cash would compete for this asset, perhaps offering twice as much as the quoted value. Nearly anyone on the list below this property would be a "taker" as it could easily be converted to cash, probably at a profit.
2. **Cash**: Real estate and businesses values have long been measured by the amount of cash they can bring as income or will sell for on the market. Most people disposing of an asset want to go to cash because of the variety of choices cash can give them. Everything on this list is measured by the amount of cash the asset is worth and the ability to get to cash
3. **Free and Clear House**: This asset rates right up next to cash because of its ability to be converted to cash. There are far more buyers for houses than any other type of real estate. Absent a buyer, lenders will loan on a house sooner than any other type of real estate, with higher loan to value percentages. A homeowner normally can get a lender to loan 80% of the value of a house, while only willing to lend 75% on commercial and 50% on land.
4. **Free and Clear Income Property**. This also rates near the top of the list because of the positive benefits. Income and free and clear are very positive real estate features
5. **Cash Flow Income Property**. Another desirable asset.
6. **Paper**. The desirability of promissory notes will vary with the return on the note, the payments, and the security for the note. A high yield first mortgage with solid security can rate very high on the list, while a fourth position mortgage on a vacant, crumbling building or nearly worthless land can drop to the bottom of the list.
7. **Free and Clear Development Land.** During boom times this can be near the top of the list, with developers throwing cash at the asset.
8. **Free and Clear Personal Property.** This also can vary as to desirability, dependent on the asset itself.
9. **Break Even Income Property**. No positive or negative benefits.
10. **Free and Clear Cold Storage (Warehouse) Land**. This asset has no real present value, but also has no huge negative features.
11. **Negative Cash Flow Income Property**. This asset costs money to own, but may have a use for somebody.
12. **Negative Cash Flow Development Land**. Except to a developer-user this land only has negative benefits.
13. **Negative Cash Flow Cold Storage Land**. This is last on the list. It is an asset that costs money to own, and has no present day value.

When attempting to maximize the value of an inventory of assets, step one is to identify all assets, present and future value, and then design a strategy to use those not being used to acquire an asset of more use to the owner. The above chart, and Bob Steele's formulas are tools that can be used to acquire usable assets.

PERSONAL PROPERTY HARD ASSETS

While we have spent decades marketing real estate assets, and some personal property, such as partnership interests, most hard asset personal property has been marketed via straight sales or auctions. Almost everywhere, except on very small items, cash is the means of exchange. The father of a friend was once manager of Hudson's Bay Company stores north of the Arctic Circle in Canada, where the main method of the Eskimos doing business was for them to bring in skins for store credits, used to acquire goods. This is one examples of the few modern day marketing where some currency is not being used. Or is it? In reality this is not a direct barter, either. In this case the store credits are the currency. The Eskimos do not directly a trade a skin for a case of soup. The store places a value on both items, making a profit on both.

Swap meets are not really swap meets. Swap meets are places where things are paid for in cash. One must go back in history, before someone created the perception that gold, or shells had a tribe wide, or universally wide value, that true barter took place.

And barter in the days of cave men and early civilizations had some interesting forms, some of which we use today. A great hunter would trade his prowess with a spear for a place by the fire and a woman of his liking. Today an actor, athlete or writer trades his/her celebrity for invitations to fancy balls and other perks.

For recreation, at some real estate exchange meetings, we have an evening Cowboy Auction. This is authentic personal property exchanging, where "vacancy" (unused assets) items are traded with no middle men and no currency of any kind, involved. A offers his rifle for trade. B offers to trade a painting for the rifle, C offers some gemstones, D offers two weeks at her timeshare, and E, an equity in a 1994 pick-up truck. F wants B's painting, not the rifle and will trade a computer. G will take the two week timeshare time with one day's consulting. This goes on until everyone in the audience has had a chance to offer on anything that has been offered in. Then A gets to choose anything that is on the board, because indirectly, either through a 2 way, 3 way, 4 way, or six way exchange, everyone is a taker for A's property.

There is no world wide Cowboy Auction. However, experienced exchangors can connect the dots if they have the individual pieces to the puzzle. The successful exchange professional can determine that if A (the rifle owner) will take G's consulting that a creative transaction can be put together that satisfies everyone's needs and wants. G takes D's timeshares, D takes A's rifle and A takes G's consulting.

Using formulas and experience: idle and under performing boats, planes, trucks, cars, ships and trains can be put to use. Businesses assets such as excess manufacturing capacity, unused retail space, un-booked service hours, and internet times can be used to acquire needed assets, formerly requiring dearly needed cash.

Professional Services are vanishing assets. The attorney, engineer, architect, doctor, and environmental specialist's un-booked hours are forever lost. As of course are: unused hotel and cruise ship rooms; airline and stadium seats; radio and TV time; and vacant cargo space

Commodities are hard assets, some with only future value. While minerals already mined may have an immediate cash market, minerals in the ground still have value, as do yet to be planted agricultural products and young timber.

Some assets can be created, or changed to another form. Stocks, publicly or privately traded, LLC interests, partnerships, created notes and mortgages can be used to acquire usable assets

Talent is an overlooked asset. A yet to be created painting could be used to pay for gallery space. Writers get advances on their books. Why not: a yet to be written song. The creative exchange professional would put some conditions on these assets, but they are clearly assets.

World Asset eXchange (worldassetexchange.com) is being developed to be a true venue for trading non-productive assets ("vacancies"). Following the successful real estate format, developed over 50 years by the Society of Exchange Counselors, World is creating an on-line asset exchange to use their professional expertise and the formulas that follow in this book to make vacancies productive.

Half the world is vacancies. Half of the world's assets are non-productive. Assets valuing trillions in Dollars, Euros, Pesos and Yen, sit non-productive.

Let's enliven those assets.

Robert W. Steele SEC

We would like to share with you the Vacancy Formulas & Strategies on the following pages.

Robert E. Baines, BA, JD

Foreword

Bob Steele and Chet Allen's book lives in the realm of magic. It is deceptive. One is first struck by the book's superb organization, the beautiful graphics and illustrations, and the ultimate clarity of it all. They are not pompous professors, purposely making complex things more obscure to somehow enhance their own value as the interpreter of it. They are true masters of communication-real communication. They have taken complex situations from two lifetimes of profound experience and reduced them to the simplest possible language and concepts. Its deceptively simple.

And, it is not grand theory. It's all very real and practical stuff. Bob and Chet have lived each and every one of these formulas. Each formula has been grounded and fine-tuned in the arena of life and business, springing from a necessity to fulfill diverse needs.

And this isn't a book about winning at any cost. They have always strived to create win-win transactions that work for everyone involved. Their integrity comes through so clearly in each page of this book.

Bob and Chet have lived their lives pushing, with each transaction, beyond where things have ever gone before. They are used to living on that ever expanding edge in the realm of magic. They now share with the reader their lifetimes of experience, reduced to the most clear and readable concepts

This is one of those rare books that so engages the mind that further readings will take the reader deeper and deeper into, not only an expert knowledge of real estate and deal-making, but into the realm of the reader's own creativity. It opens the possibility, for the reader, of beginning to live in his own realm of magic. There is nothing that the mind can conceive and believe that the mind can't achieve. This book is a great step into the infinite world of possibilities.

One of the beauties of this book is that you can apply it anywhere and everywhere. You have 80 acres of unsellable land with a large annual negative cashflow. You are worried about being able to live on your retirement. This book will show you how to create the results you want. One can also take these concepts and work to solve global poverty and lack of food, energy or the national deficit. No limits.

I have long admired Bob Steele and Chet Allen. Not only are they among the smartest and the most creative people that I have ever met, but they also care about people and about service. This book is part of their service, to share with the reader the experiences of two well-lived lifetimes, not just of success after success, but of success grabbed again and again from the mouth of failure, due to their ability to think way outside the box. Two great men. One great book. Reader, take advantage of it.

Robert E. Baines, BA, JD

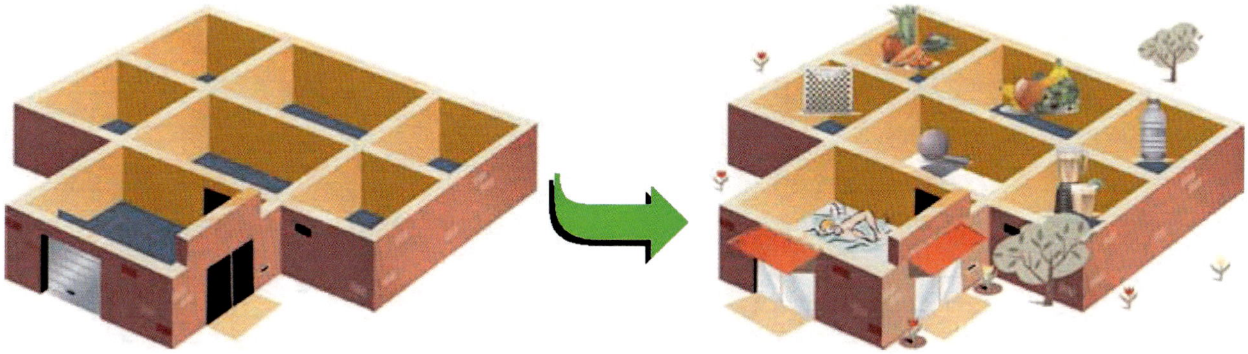

STRATEGY 226

Turn Vacancies into Wellness Units

Create wellness rooms in hotels, motels, resorts, assisted living facilities, trains, cruise ships, condos, apartments, office buildings, etc.

COMMENT	Macro planning is difficult but micro events are relatively easy to see coming and they can play a role even to the point where they can help fill vacancies. For instance, cultural changes are hard to plan for as they are so slow in developing: e.g. some social groups are very slow to turn. Some, even today, are stuck back in the 7th to 19th centuries. But social consciousness shift can happen over a shorter, maybe 25, 50 or 100 year span of time and can be planned for. For instance, smoking has changed in the western world and now the percentage of smokers is less and non-smoking rooms in hotels and so forth are the norm. Likewise other things are subject to consciousness change in our western societies like the acknowledgement concerning organic food that is showing up in more and more grocery stores, restaurants, etc. How can you use some of these micro changes to help fill vacancies?	Convert some of your vacancies to Wellness Units. Advertise & charge extra for these rooms. Convert existing clientele to higher rates and/or obtain new clients. Sell mer-chandise from the rooms.
SITUATION	You own a nice hotel and while you have a modest vacancy factor you would like to lower it.	
POSSIBLE SOLUTION	Consider converting a few of your rooms to Wellness Units. More and more people are becoming conscious of wellness programs even to the point that occasionally you will hear of a developer considering building wellness houses. The cost of building and furnishing Wellness Units is considerable higher than the norm. But existing structures can be converted, if even on a modest scale initially. They will definitely attract clientele and some of your regular clientele will be willing to pay more for a room that is design with wellness in mind. Using certain tiles or hardwood floors, the right paint, the rights beds, having the right water, air filtration, etc. converts a room to a wellness unit.	
CONCLUSION	Having wellness rooms helps your advertising, and a tasteful sign on the check-in counter, or offering these accommodations at the time of reservation, will help sell them. Another big plus is that these clients are possible buyers of wellness merchandise that can be sold from the rooms by the hotel menus on the TV screen in the rooms, or with printed information in the room.	

STRATEGY 227

Virgin's Vacancy Ploy

Richard Branson's formula used to help build Virgin Music Stores

SITUATION	1. England's Sir Richard Branson wanted to start Virgin Music Stores world wide. 2. He had the desire but not the capital to get through the start-up periods when opening each store. 3. He actually called his group together to brainstorm the problem.
POSSIBLE SOLUTION	1. They used several techniques to avoid having to pay for things during the start up period. 2. One thing he did was to located people that had vacancy problems in their retail commercial outlets. 3. He would agree to lease the property if the first three months of the rental were free. He would not budge from this requirement. It was a deal breaker. They leased store sites all across England, Europe and then the world with this formula.
CONCLUSION	1. He said he missed some very nice retail outlet sites because of this but he also got some very nice ones, and he saved a lot of upfront capital. 2. Virgin Music became one of the largest music companies in the world.
NOTE	Vacancy represents an opportunity—always.

STRATEGY 228

The Un-Built Building

This can work on anything where you dream the dream and then create the item.

SITUATION	1. Abel is a developer and he has land to build on. Have the building designed, have it costed or bid, as the case may be, and then sell, exchange or lease the building as though it were completed. Even though it is in an un-built building, it can be marketed. If you are exchanging, an obvious exchange would be to exchange it for another parcel of development land. 2. Many high-rise buildings and shopping centers are developed this way but this formula can apply to almost anything: businesses, farms, ships, etc. 3. When you are in a down real estate market you can use this formula by going through a middle step. Say you are developing a small apartment complex. The credit market is difficult and you cannot get enough of a loan to build the building. Perhaps use the Un-Built Building formula and exchange the equity into a crankable or borrowable building, like an SFR, where you get enough cash to complete the building by borrowing on the house. You need to handle the paperwork allowing this to happen.
CLOSE	It is suggested that the builder and future owner go over all the plans in a fine tooth manner and make any corrections and/or additions that are necessary, initial same, and then the plans go into escrow. Any further changes then require a change agreement and payment as required. Escrow closes after notice of completion is filed on the building. I learned this the hard way.

STRATEGY 229

Vacant Air Rights & Mineral Rights

Look up, and look down!

SITUATION	1. We are often made aware of the value of mineral rights (looking down). We had a broker friend who made us aware of it. He was a broker in Eastern Oregon. He had a client from Texas who bought thousands of acres of vacant land from him and had him resell the land but retain the mineral rights. The broker later started collecting mineral rights himself and owned literally thousands of acres of mineral rights. We later retained mineral rights on properties we traded out of in Long Beach, California and made a secondary profit by selling same to an oil company. 2. We seldom, if ever, think about the value of air rights. We first became aware of the value of air rights when Zechendorf created them and then developed those rights over the Penn Central Station in New York. 3. We later realized that had we retained the air rights over several of the residential properties we had owned in Newport Beach, California, we could have profited as they later became high rise locations.
POSSIBLE SOLUTION	1. Whenever going out of title to property, always try to build in the retention of mineral and air rights. For instance, in a residential transfer you might state that the air rights are retained above 35 or 50 feet. All title companies have the verbiage for retaining mineral rights, allowing or disallowing slant drilling, etc. 2. Commercial locations, beach fronts, islands, railway right-of-ways, etc. all have potential value by retaining air rights and mineral rights.
CONCLUSION	You have immediately created something that didn't exist before, and therefore you have created a value. You can sell or exchange that value.

STRATEGY 230

Use of Consignments Fills Commercial Vacancy

This formula helped build a major retail chain in Canada.

SITUATION	1. Abel has a 2-unit retail commercial property with one vacancy. He can't find a renter. 2. He will lose the building as he can't pay the mortgage with just one unit rented. 3. There is no sales market for the building.
POSSIBLE SOLUTION	1. He decided to fill the vacancy with his own company. He went to other stores in the area and made a consignment arrangement with them. 2. He would pick up at night, in his truck, items that they wanted to get rid of. It didn't matter whether it was clothing, hardware or groceries—anything that the other merchants no longer wanted and that he could obtain on consignment at a price where he could resell and make a profit. 3. He advertised things at very cheap prices. If they didn't sell, he returned them to the other stores. If they did sell, he paid the other merchants for them.
CONCLUSION	1. He saved his building. 2. He developed a retail chain store with outlets all across Canada.
NOTE	1. The glass is always half full.

STRATEGY 231

Personal Notes in Vacancy Exchange

Probably the ultimate in the Creation of Wealth formula is the creation of personal notes.

SITUATION	1. You own a 500-unit resort hotel on Maui and you are running 40% vacancy. That's 200 rooms a night vacant, and at $200 per night that is $40,000 daily times 360 days is $14,400,000 a year and $43,200,000 over 3 years. 2. You have an exchange broker working for you on exchanges for the hotel. What else might you do?	Vacancy Loss per: Night: Year: 3 years:	 $40,000 $14,400,000 $43,200,000
POSSIBLE SOLUTION	1. Consider taking personal notes for vacations at your hotel in concert with travel agents or radio stations. You set the requirements at a minimum of a 700 point FICO score and terms payments over three years (soft interest or no interest). 2. $200 per night @$200 is $1,400 per week 3. Payment on note $38.89 per month for 3 years. 4. Do the math: it generates $218,400 in cash flow over three years for each room where you use the personal note concept. 5. Average vacation is closer to two weeks than one. Average sale $2,800.	Price per Week: Payment Per week: 36 weeks: 2 weeks: Payment:	$1,400 $38.89 $1,400 $2,800 $77.78
CONCLUSION	1. Consider using travel agents in areas where normally your hotel does not get business. 2. Trade for radio time and advertise this special on the air.		
NOTES	Go on the offense whenever possible.		

STRATEGY 232

Subdivide the Vacancy

IVX (International Vacancy Exchange) research found in just one internet marketing site over 200 industrial buildings of 400,000 sq. ft. or more 100% vacant

SITUATION	1. Markets change for a variety of reasons. 2. Products designed for one market and one time may become obsolete and buildings go vacant. 3. There is no or little sales market
POSSIBLE SOLUTION	1. Divide into smaller spaces is one possible solution. 2. Break hospitals with vacancy problems into per- floor units for rental or condo units. 3. Divide floor space into storage unit areas. Lines on the floor. Fence it in. 4. Buy small businesses you can put into part of the spaces or trade your vacancy for part interest in the companies that will fill the vacancies. 5. Divide into mini-warehouse units.
CONCLUSION	1. Change character of building 2. Go on the offense
NOTES	1. Don't get hung up on price as it probably will lock you to the building. 2. It is a previous problem you are fighting now. The error, if there was one, was made before, not now. Is your mind better off working with this problem or moving on to one with a more positive and profitable outlook. 3. People can spend years fighting a problem when they could have replicated the asset several times over had they been spending their time otherwise.

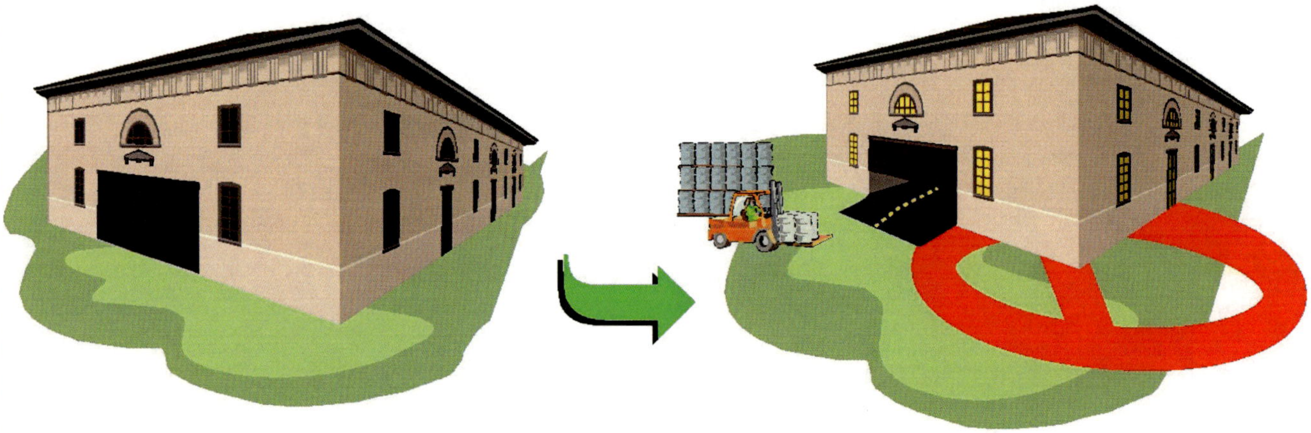

STRATEGY 233

Give Away the Vacant Building

Keep the land under it to circumvent the reverse cash flow.

SITUATION	1. You own a 400,000 sq. ft. warehouse. It is free and clear but also it is vacant and has been for a year. You can not afford the maintenance and taxes. 2. You have it on the market to sell but there are no takers.
POSSIBLE SOLUTION	1. Locate a company that wants to downsize. 2. Agree to sell them the building only (not the land) for nothing down, or on an insignificant trade, and you keep the land. 3. You can offer them a very low land lease rate or a moratorium for an extended period, etc. 4. You can offer to pay for part of the taxes for a period. 5. You can reverse this and find an investor for the land, acquiring it for no down, and you keep the building and pay a percentage of the rents for land lease (performance land lease) when you get it rented..
CONCLUSION	Anything to mitigate the income loss.
NOTES	Go on the offense whenever possible.

STRATEGY 234

$250 Trade Credit©

G.S. Consultancy

We specialize in helping companies and individuals protect themselves from the effects of the Falling Dollar.

"Projection: Over 30% of the people will lose the majority of their assets in the coming recession!"

Wake up! Stop listening to the spin. Protect yourself. Our company is one possible solution for you. Please phone for consulting service. "Inflation is under control", Right!

Food prices up 44% last year.

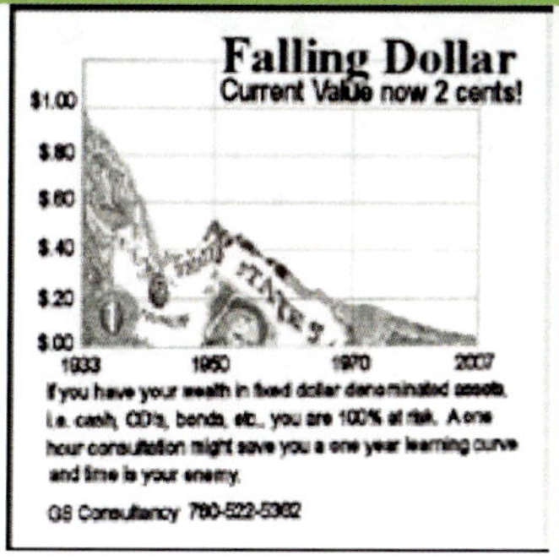

	Past Price	Price Now	% increase to date	Projected Price
USA				
Gasoline, per gallon	.09 cents	$3.00	Increase 3,333 %	$50.00 /gal.
Bread, per loaf	.10 cents	$2.00	Increase 2,000 %	$50.00 /loaf
Dinner for two	$1.50	$60.00	Increase 4,000 %	$500.00 dinner for two
EUROPE (in dollars)				
Fare on London Tube	1.5 cents	$7.80	Increase 52,000 %	$150,00 /fare
One Dinner, Rathskeller	.40 cents	$25.00	Increase 6,250 %	$250.00 /dinner
Pantheon Hotel, Paris	$3.00 / night	$219.00	Increase 7,300 %	$3,000.00 /night
Admission to Acropolis	.30 cents	$15.60	Increase 5,000 %	$200.00 /admission

SAMPLE TRADE CREDIT

Number ________ Date Activated ________ Expiration Date ________

This Trade Credit, when properly authorized and exercised, entitles bearer to $250.00 worth of telephone consulting service by G.S. Consultancy, subject to terms and conditions, and by appointment.

TERMS AND CONDITIONS:

1. Expiration date means that this Trade Credit (T/C) expires on this date and can no longer be used.
2. Any change of ownership via assignment in this T/C is to be processed through G.S. Consultancy (GS).
3. There is a 5%transfer and/or processing fee when T/C is exercised by bearer or is transferred via assignment to others.
4. All cash expenses incurred by GS in providing this consulting service, if any, shall be paid by bearer of TC.
5. The consulting service hourly rate shall be the standard rate charged by GS at the time this TC is exercised by bearer.
6. This TC is activated when signed and dated by authorized personnel of G.S.
7. Consult your attorney and tax consultant about the ramifications of using trade credits.

Authorized	Bearer Check: Exercising ☐ Assigning ☐	Transfer and/or Assign Trade Credit to:
Date Activated: / Expiration:	Name:	Name:
G.S. Consultancy	Address:	Address:
By:		
Signature:	Phone:	Phone:
Address, Email, & Phone:	Email:	Email:
	Date:	Date:
	Signature:	Signature:

STRATEGY 235

Apartment House with Many Vacancies

Modify usage to solve problems.

SITUATION	1. Initially we saw this with a 20-unit apartment house that had 15 or 16 vacancies. 2. Units had deferred maintenance. Owner lived out of state and the person he hired to manage was obviously not doing a very good job. 3. The owner had a mortgage with a high constant, meaning high payments, so if he lowered rent to prevailing market prices there was still going to be reverse cash flow.
POSSIBLE SOLUTION	1. He traded the apartment to someone who had free and clear land. 2. The new owner installed an Registered Nurse as the manager and combined two units into a day nursery for small children. 3. He filled the swimming pool with sand and made a massive sand box. 4. He ran ads for tenants who were single parents needing day care services for their children and filled the units at higher than normal rents which included the day care service for their children right where they lived.
CONCLUSION	1. Original owner ended up in free and clear land that solve the reverse cash flow and management problems. 2. New owner substantially increased the value of the assets by using creativity.

STRATEGY 236

Trade Credit for Special Hotel Vacancy

Specific hotel/motel design for long term guests so part of the cash requirement is met.

SITUATION	1. Abel owns a 200-unit hotel and is running 50% vacant (100 rooms). Rooms average $300 per night. 2. He estimates his transient tax and maid service costs at about $15% or approximately $50 per night. 3. There is a very soft rental market 4. These certain cash costs must be met for each guest in order for the hotel to be viable.	Price:	$ 300 ea
POSSIBLE SOLUTION	1. Discuss the problem with a trade credit broker. 2. It is decided that the trade credit broker will design 50 trade credits, one each on 50 different rooms, based on a price of $250 per night each or $90,000 for a three year period. These will be aimed at corporate users or individuals who would like to live in the hotel full time for the three year period. Zoning must comply. User of each T/C will have to add $50 per night or $1,500 per month. 3. Exchange the Trade Credits.	Price: Nights: Each Year: 3 years 50 T/C	$ 250 ea $ 360 yr $ 90,000 $270,000 $ 13,500,000
CONCLUSION	1. $90,000 T/C are now exchanged into any asset agreeable to owner of hotel or motel complex: Examples, corporate lettered stock, land, advertising or ? 2. Transaction is good for three years	Users:	Pay $1,500/mo in cash & $7,500/mo in trade
NOTES	1. Users get hotel living at a price they can afford 2. Hotel gets vacant space occupied. 3. Trade credit broker charges for design of credits and trading them.		

STRATEGY 237

Create Your Own Credit Card to Fill Vacancy

This is another variation of the creation of wealth formula

SITUATION	1. You own a 500-unit resort hotel on Maui and you are running 40% vacancy. That's 200 rooms a night vacant and at $200 per night that is $40,000 daily times 360 days is $14,400,000 a year and $43,200,000 over 3 years. 2. This is a variation of the personal note formula.	Loss per Night: 1 Year: 3 years:	$40,000 $ 14,400,000 $ 43,200,000
POSSIBLE SOLUTION	1. You can create your own in house credit card that can only be used at your hotel. You can compete because you can add things others won't do; e.g., you can offer a free rental car or a percentage of your hotel bill such as a 20% deduction to help pay for the air fare for 2 people. 2. You can add a plethora of things to help direct the vacationer to your hotel rather than someplace else. 3. You can offer low or no interest. 4. You can offer a period of time, 6 months or a year at no interest or before first payment is required.		
CONCLUSION	1. Consider using travel agents in areas where normally your hotel does not get business. 2. Trade for radio time and advertise this special on the air.		
NOTES	Go on the offense whenever possible.		

STRATEGY 238

Open-Ended Note Tied to Insurance Policy to Soften Assisted Living Payments & Fill Vacancies

Specific design for Assisted Living complex so part of cash requirement is met.

SITUATION	1. Abel owns a 200-unit assisted living complex and has 50 vacant units. 2. One reason he feels locked to his price is a fear that if he lowered prices for new tenants, he would have to lower his existing prices for units already rented at $6,000 per month. 3. There is a very soft rental market. 4. There are cash costs that must be met for each tenant.	Price:	$6,000 ea
POSSIBLE SOLUTION	1. Discuss the problem with an exchange broker. 2. It is decided to use open-ended personal notes tied to the assignment of interest in a client's life insurance policy. The client will pay $1,000, $2,000 or $3,000 per month in cash of the $6,000 guest fee and the unpaid portion will go on the open ended personal note with assignment of the life insurance. It is further guaranteed of course by whoever signs the personal note.	Price/mo: Cash: Bal: To Ins:	$6,000 3,000 $3,000 $3,000
CONCLUSION	1. Exchange broker locates clients. 2. Client obtains the assistance needed within the price range they can afford, in cash.		
NOTES	1. User gets assisted living at a price they can afford and the rest paid later from proceeds of the insurance policy. 2. Assisted Living facility gets vacant space occupied.		

REVERSE
MORTGAGE

STRATEGY 239

Create Open End Reverse Mortgage to fill Assisted Living Vacancies

Specific design for Assisted Living complex so part of cash requirement is met.

SITUATION	1. Abel owns a 200-unit assisted living complex and has 50 vacant units. 2. One reason he feels locked to his price is a fear that if he lowered prices for new tenants, he would have to lower his existing prices for units already rented at $6,000 per month. 3. There is a very soft rental market. 4. There are certain cash costs that must be met for each tenant.	Price:	$6,000 ea
POSSIBLE SOLUTION	1. Discuss the problem with an exchange broker. 2. It is decided to create a reverse mortgage on a real property owned by the client or a benefactor. Reverse mortgages are open ended so they can increase in size as assets are used up. The client will pay $1,000, $2,000 or $3,000 per month in cash of the $6,000 guest fee and the unpaid portion will go on the open ended reverse mortgage in favor of the assisted living facility.	Price/mo: Cash: Bal: To RM:	$6,000 - 3,000 $3,000 $3,000
CONCLUSION	1. Exchange broker locates clients. 2. Client obtains the assistance needed within the price range they can afford, in cash.		
NOTES	1. User gets assisted living at a price they can afford 2. Assisted Living facility get vacant space occupied.		

COMBINATION

STRATEGY 240

Combining Strategies to Fill Assisted Living Vacancies

Creating a new solution.

COMBINING	Combing an Open End Mortgage with a Reverse Mortgage & with the Creation of Wealth you create an Open End Reverse Mortgage to fill assisted living vacancies.	Create an open ended trust deed & note secured by real estate to cover the cost or partial cost of a resident in an assisted living facility. This can be secured by their home or other property.
OPEN-END MORTGAGE	An Open End Mortgage is one whereby additional funds, capital or principal can be added to a note / mortgage and be cover by the existing paper work.	
REVERSE MORTGAGE	A Reverse Mortgage is one were a principal sum is lent and no payments are made until a certain something happens, like the death of the borrower. The Interest during the holding time accumulates and is added to the principal owing.	As expenses are incurred they are added to the balance on the note which is growing just like a reverse mortgage note grows.
CREATION OF WEALTH	Creation of Wealth Formula is one where a TD/Note is created without their being cash funds involved in the loan. The combination of these three creates the solution seen in strategy known herein as ***Create Open End Reverse Mortgage to fill assisted living vacancies.***	Upon future sale of the property, the note is retired.

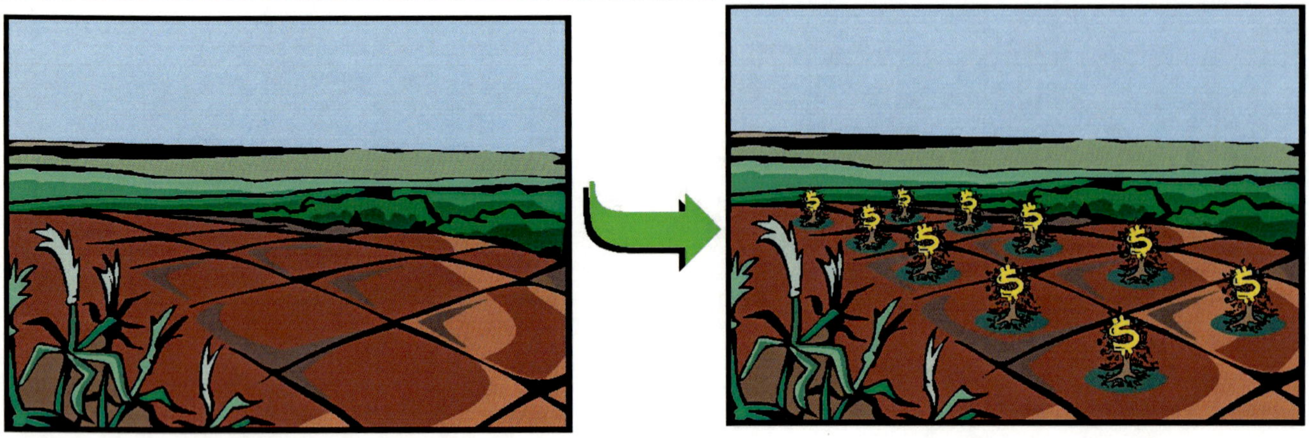

STRATEGY 241

Trading Vacant Lots for Corporate Stock with a Put Option for Additional Trades

Lots can be added to corporate balance sheets and lot owner has an opportunity to put dead equity into service and an opportunity to further leverage profits.

<table>
<tr><td>SITUATION</td><td>1. Property owner has 30 F&C lots at $20,000 each – Total $600,000.
2. The owner is not willing to bet all $600,000 on a public or private company but does want to get the equities working.</td><td rowspan="4">We are making the assumption here that there is no active sales or development opportunity for the lots at this time – or that the owner is a player and wants to take risks in order to achieve larger profits.

The PUT option gives the risk-taker a way to mitigate the downside.</td></tr>
<tr><td>POSSIBLE SOLUTION</td><td>Stock company agrees to take ten lots at $20,000 each in exchange for $200,000 in preferred stock (200,000 shares at $1.00 per share) and give the land owner a PUT (option) to exchange his other 20 lots at the $1 preferred price for a period of 18 months.</td></tr>
<tr><td>RISK TO OWNER</td><td>Downside is $200,000. The loss of partial if not all the value of the 10 lots.</td></tr>
<tr><td>UPSIDE</td><td>The upside is huge! If the stock goes to $5.00, the owner would realize three million $3,000,000 for his lots.</td></tr>
</table>

STRATEGY 242

Trade Credits to Help Fill Shopping Center Vacancies

It takes a little ingenuity but it pays off with a full shopping center.

<table>
<tr>
<td>SITUATION</td>
<td>1. We are currently in a situation where the economic forecasts become gloomier and the potential recovery date predictions go farther into the future & the need for interim solutions intensifies.
2. Dozens of our best known retailers are going under, leaving hundreds of thousands of mall square footage dark.
3. Will this result in hundreds of shopping centers going under? Very possibly.</td>
<td rowspan="2">Remember, you do not have to spend the trade credits just on the shopping centers or office buildings.

There are all kinds of other things that can be acquired, from dental services to resort vacations.

At one time in history, barter and exchanging made up a part of everyone's daily life. It is conceivable that those times might be returning. Being receptive to this change could prove beneficial.</td>
</tr>
<tr>
<td>POSSIBLE SOLUTION</td>
<td>1. One of our associates owns shopping centers and office buildings, and has managed to use "trade credits" for services or other opportunities.
2. The trade credit tenants may make the difference between holding on to an asset, or losing it in hard times. He keeps them afloat in hard times by accepting trade credits in lieu of cash rents, then spending the credits for services. His shopping centers probably would be 50% vacant without the trade credit tenants, and although he can't pay the property taxes with trade credits, he is able to keep the parking lot clean, lawns cut, and plumbing fixed by using contractors willing to take trade credits
3. Many times you can trade direct for services but sometimes it is better to employ the services of trade credit companies.</td>
</tr>
</table>

STRATEGY 243

Create Low Percentage Land Lease and Exchange for Higher Yielding Asset

Treat the land as though it were vacant. Consider that all lands under buildings are inactive. All they do is physically hold the building. If you treat this land under a building as an under-utilized asset you can use the equity in a higher calling.

SITUATION	1. You own a shopping center with a value of $4,000,000. 2. You have a first loan of $2,000,000 and therefore an equity of $2,000,000. 3. The land under the shopping center is valued at $1,000,000 or 25% of the total value. 4. You have a reasonable return on the project but you are aggressive and would like to increase your net worth.	Start Value: Loan: Equity: Exchange out land from under center: Equity now:	$4,000,000 2,000,000 2,000,000 $ 1,000,000 $ 1,000,000
POSSIBLE SOLUTION	1. Consider creating a long-term, low-percentage-rate land lease by exchanging the land under the shopping center into some other vehicle you want and then leasing the land back. We suggest a long term lease of 30, 50 or 100 years. Using a 2% rate as an example, the payments on the $1,000,000 valued land would be $20,000 per year. 2. You try to make the exchange into something that will return you 6%, 8%, 10% or perhaps a business where you can make 20%. 3. Can it be done? Many people want out of properties and passive income is acceptable as is a CD in a bank delivering 2%.	Land lease pmt/yr: New Income per year: 6% 8% 10% 20%	$20,000 $60,000 80,000 100,000 200,000

STRATEGY 244

Create Low Percentage Land Lease on Vacant Land (or under buildings) and Exchange for Trade Credits

This is the same process as Strategy #243 except the lessee exchanges his equity into trade credits (albeit often in anticipation of a three way exchange).

The basic fundamentals are the same as #243.

SITUATION	Same as Strategy 243		
POSSIBLE SOLUTION	1. You can use the land exactly as above or this can be vacant land. We will use here $4,000,000 in vacant F/C land. 2. The land lease rate can drop to as low as 1%, and it can include future subordination for development, offers divisibility and will usually require at least a partial three-way exchange to complete—the latter because the owner of the credits will need to know that they can be traded for something of value or an opportunity.	OPTIONS 1% land lease rate Sub-ordination Divisability Usually 3-way transaction	

STRATEGY 245

Resort Motel/Hotel Vacancy Problem & Seminars

Modify usage to solve problems.

SITUATION	You or your client become the owner of a large resort motel with a restaurant and bar. The facility does very well during the summer months but does very poorly in the winter season.
POSSIBLE SOLUTION	Organize an educational seminar program for the winter months which will not only sell the vacant rooms but also help to keep the restaurant and bar active. Price the seminar with the rooms included, compromising as you need to, to make it happen.
CONCLUSION	1. You develop higher cash flow. 2. Motel/hotel is occupied on a year round basis. 3. You can maintain better staff control and a higher caliber of employees because they have employment year round.
ALTERNATIVE	Let's assume you have a 4-month winter season. You can consider leasing your entire motel/resort to a seminar company for the winter and just take off and enjoy a 4-month vacation.

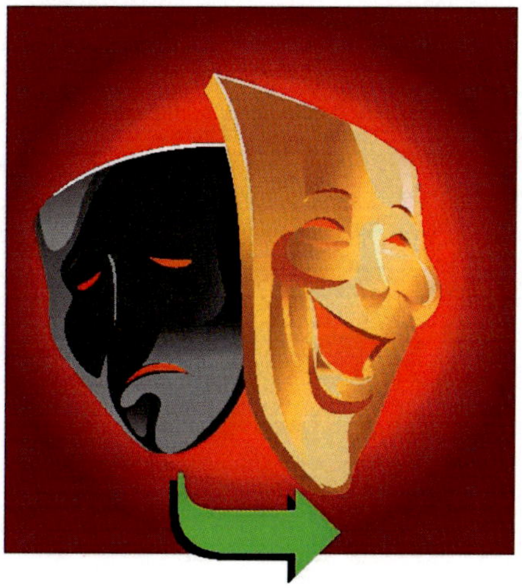

STRATEGY 246

Vacancy Equals Equity #1

SITUATION	1. You are negotiating to go into title on a 20-unit commercial building. 2. There are six vacancies each at $2,000 per month. This represents $24,000 per year each or $144,000 per year in vacancy.
POSSIBLE SOLUTION	1. As part of the negotiation offer the seller prepaid leases of three of the units for a period of five years, which represents $360,000 equity, as part of the acquisition price. 2. You perhaps should build into the offer that this seller would have the right to sub-let these three units at any price he or she wanted, but probably with your concurrence as to who the tenants are. 3. Rentable space is an exchangeable equity.
CONCLUSION	You have eliminated 50% of your vacancy problem.
ALTERNATIVE	1. The Irvine Company in Orange Country, California, a huge real estate company holding million of dollars in land leases, was purchased by a buyer who took the land leases the seller owned to a consortium of banks and used these leases to borrow the money needed to buy the company. 2. Buying with debentures—notes on the company you are buying or merging with—is a standard ploy, and you buy said company out of the profits that the company earns.

STRATEGY 247

Vacancy Equals Equity #2

SITUATION	1. You are negotiating to go into title on a 20-unit commercial building. 2. There are six vacancies each at $2,000 per month. This represents $24,000 per year each or $144,000 per year in vacancy.
NOTE	I have structured the following as a broker, to reach a compromise that was agreeable to both parties.
POSSIBLE SOLUTION	As part of the negotiation both buyer and seller are working to rent up the vacant units as the offer states that the seller pre pay leases on all the vacant units as follows: 1. The first three months seller guarantees all six vacancy rents. 2. The next three months seller guarantees rents on five vacant units, etc., so by the end of 18 months the seller no longer has any guarantee. 3. In addition, each unit that is rented, whether by the seller or the buyer, the lease back is modified to eliminate one unit from the leaseback.
CONCLUSION	You have negotiated a situation where both the buyer and the seller are working to fill the vacancies.

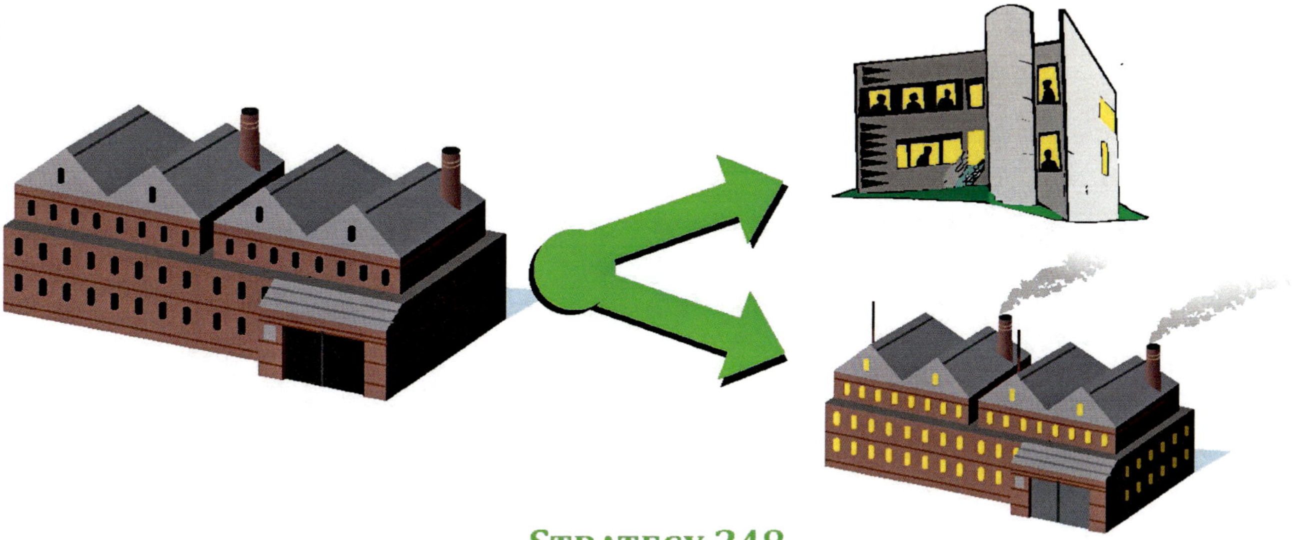

STRATEGY 248

Trade Vacancy for Equity in Business

SITUATION	1. You have a large industrial building that has been empty for three years. 2. There is a well-run business in your neighborhood that is in a building much smaller than yours. They could use more space to grow their business. They are paying just about half of what the rent would be on your building.
POSSIBLE SOLUTION	1. Offer to have them take over your much larger building on a long-term lease for the same rental price they are paying for a smaller facility, and you take stock in their company for the difference. 2. Assuming your building is free and clear, you might offer to exchange them your vacant building for stock in their company. They end up paying no rent.
CONCLUSION	1. You have converted your vacancy into stock. 2. Something else beneficial happens here that we often miss: The time you spend thinking about the vacant building is negative think time. Once that is resolved, one way or the other, you can move on to positive things.

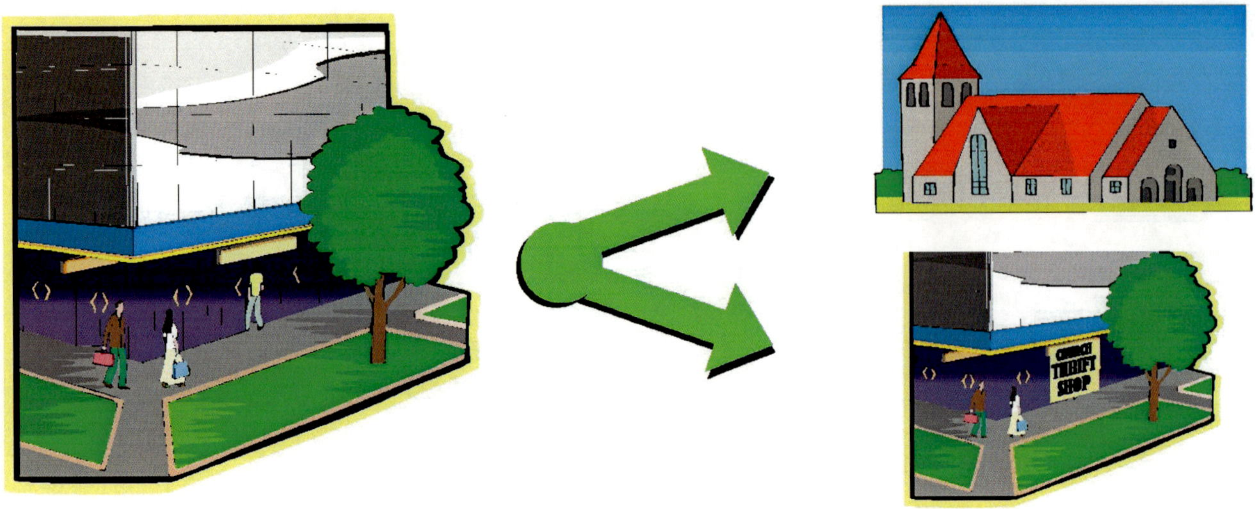

Strategy 249

Give Vacancy to Charity

SITUATION	1. You own a nice commercial condo that has been vacant for a long time. The prospects of renting it are slim. 2. Your church would like to have a storefront where they could sell used clothing.
POSSIBLE SOLUTION	1. Consider donating your vacancy to them (not the building) for either a period of time or until you can locate a renter. 2. The facility might show better if it were occupied and the church might help on the taxes or pick up the maintenance and or take over management, etc.
CONCLUSION	1. Your accountant might look into the possibilities of some sort of a tax benefit for you. 2. I used this once in a small strip mall for a client and put the church into just a small part of the facility. They did help us find two other renters for the balance of the space.

STRATEGY 250

Use Vacancy as Investment Security to Generate Income

SITUATION	1. One client is looking for a signer to secure a letter of credit. Substantial income can be derived from an international business transaction and that transaction can be recreated three to four times per year. Needs $250,000 initially for letter of credit, moving up to $1,000,000 over time. 2. Another client has a $1,500,000 free-and-clear land package in a trust for a retiree who needs income to live on. There is no market for the land.
POSSIBLE SOLUTION	1. Set up an equity line of credit for the first transaction with the $250,000 loan against the land to secure the letter of credit. The person wanting the letter of credit agrees to pay a 5% fee, over and above the cost of borrowing the money, for a 90-day period of time. 2. The land owner earns $12,500 each time the process turns over. 3. If it turns over four times during the course of the year, he nets $50,000 towards the living expenses of the retiree in the trust. 4. These can sometimes be turned over six to nine times a year. Use dead assets as security for letters of credit can deliver income.
CONCLUSION	Income provided for retiree.

STRATEGY 250-A

Bonus: Rent or Trade your Vacancy via Telemarketing

SITUATION	You own a nice building that is vacant and has been for some time and there is no indication that the situation will change in the near future. You have tried to rent it and the real estate brokers have tried to rent it. There just does not seem to be a market at this time.
POSSIBLE SOLUTION	1. Analyze what you could use in your life. Brainstorm this out (see Vol. 7 in this series of books if you don't know how to brainstorm) and come up with a list (maybe 100 items) that you could use, and then whittle that down to three or four main things. 2. Then get on the phone and find a trade. Or hire a telemarketer. You can find many through Craig's List who will work from their homes. If each caller talks to 40 people a day, you will come up with some possibilities of tenants or trades.
CONCLUSION	1. You can trade either the vacancy or the building. 2. We traded a vacant building just like this taking in pre-paid gasoline over three years from a station owner.

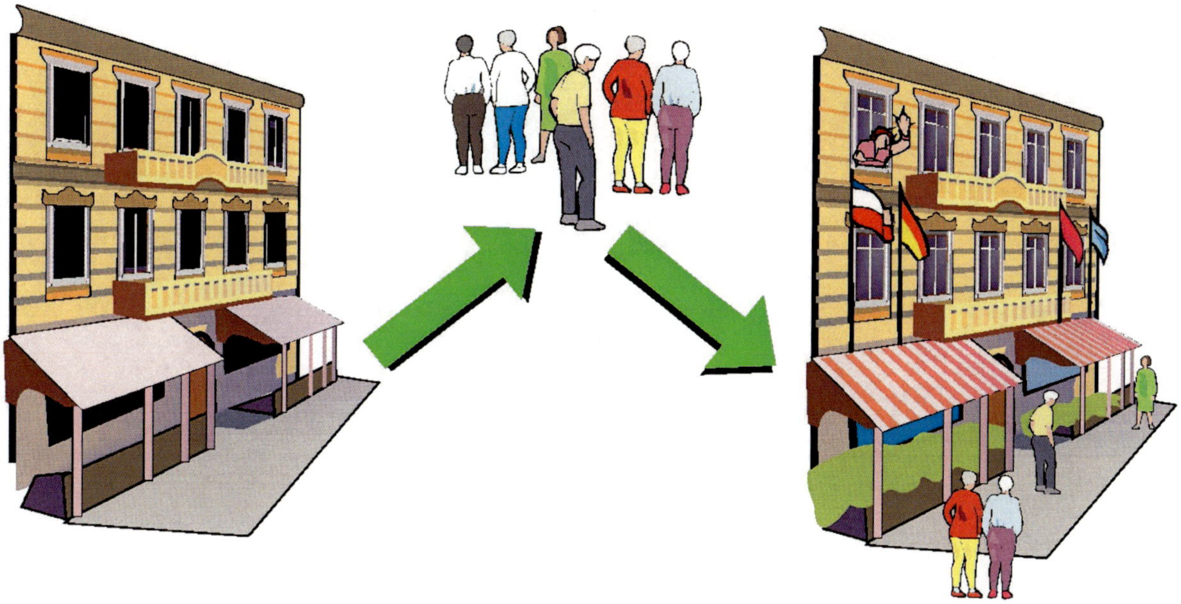

STRATEGY 250-B

Bonus: Hotel Vacancy for Semi-Retired

SITUATION	1. You own a nice hotel and while you have a modest vacancy factor you would like to lower it. 2. You have a nice two room suite with kitchen and because the rack rate is high it is vacant most of the time.
POSSIBLE SOLUTION	1. Consider exchanging the vacancy in this unit for a period of years. If the rack rate is \$100,000 a year, consider putting it on the exchange market for a pre-paid period of five years, or \$500,000. 2. This makes a nice exchange for someone who likes the refinement features of living in a hotel with the accompanying maid service and other amenities.
CONCLUSION	You need to negotiate the transit tax or room tax, etc.

STRATEGY 250-C

Bonus: Trees for Vacancies, etc.

Filling vacant land with trees, nurseries, etc., to generate income from vacancies and change character and add value.

SITUATION	You have vacant land. You might be holding land for appreciation or it may be that there is no sales market for the land right now.
POSSIBLE SOLUTION	1. Consider planting the land with trees that can be marketed: Xmas trees, palm trees , etc. 2. Consider forming a nursery and planting flowers and shrubs. 3. Consider renting your land to someone else who has a nursery, and you will accept some of his products for the rent. 4. Consider subdividing the land into plots that people can rent for growing their own gardens. 5. Consider roadside vending operations for agricultural products. 6. Consider growing sod for sale.
CONCLUSION	Etc., etc., etc!

STRATEGY 250-D

Bonus: A Vacancy in Your Mind Can Be Good

It is sometimes beneficial to create a vacancy in your mind – getting rid of your vacancy problems in the human world may free up your mind to do something positive.

SITUATION	You own a land parcel that you have been trying to sell for a long time. You have it priced at \$1,000,000. The market has been falling and the sales have stopped and you are not at all sure about your price but you paid \$1,000,000 for it and you don't want to have to take a loss. It has a loan of \$800,000 that is eating your lunch. Or... You own a shopping center that is losing tenants right and left and it has now gone into reverse cash flow and there do not seem to be any answers on the horizon. Or... You own a motel or hotel that is now running 70% vacant and you are using savings to make the loan payments.
POSSIBLE SOLUTION	Try the strategies in this book first. The bulk of the problems can be resolved or mitigated via these strategies. However, people will sometimes spend years of their lives working on a vacancy problem that, had they given the property away or walked away and spent those same years recreating the asset, they would have been better off. Consider health and well being when thinking about your vacancy problems.

STRATEGY 250-E

Bonus: Sandwich Vacancies for Profit

Over 30 years ago I wrote my first book. In it was this very strategy. It remains today a great technique on how to use OPM (other people's money—their assets) and realize a profit.

EXAMPLES

While I lived in Newport Beach, California I still rented a beach house there ever summer for a couple of weeks or a month as it was nice place to vacation. While with a client/friend soaking up sun one day, we spotted a beach house for rent that was substantially under-market and they wanted a year lease. We made them an offer for a five-year lease at even lower terms with the right to sublet. It was accepted. We gave the listing to a broker who handled weekly rentals and netted about $2,000 per month profit for five years. We sandwiched the lease.

A chain supermarket vacated a large store. The chain was responsible for the lease for several more years. It had been sitting empty for about a year. A successful grocer in a neighboring town was located and he was asked how much would he pay in rent for the vacant store if he could name his own price, which he did. We went back to the chain making the payments and offered them approximately $10,000 per month less for the remainder of their lease with the right to sublet. They negotiated it down but we were able to establish a nice sandwich profit.

This is the same thing can be done with vacant office spaces, hospitals, industrial buildings, almost anything.

Chester W. Allen, SEC, CCIM, EMS

Chester W. (Chet) Allen, SEC, CCIM, EMS, Stanford economics graduate, is experienced in all areas of real estate exchanging, brokerage, development and building. He has closed in excess of $110,000,000 in real estate transactions, mostly exchanges, involving individuals, corporations, lenders and foreign investors in locations from coast to coast and border to border.

As a broker, Mr. Allen is the only winner of both of the nation's two highest commercial real estate awards, Most Creative Commercial-Investment Transaction and Most Creative Exchange (64 properties, 35 principals, 14 agents, and 12 lenders). Other honors include four times winner of Most Outstanding Commercial/Investment or Exchange Transaction, California; Counselor of the Year, National Society of Exchange Counselors; and induction into Exchangor's Hall of Fame.

He has exchanged regional shopping centers, office buildings, condo projects, bank foreclosures, notes, boats, trade credits, land, apartment complexes, horses, retail centers, and self storage projects. Allen is a Member and past president of the Society of Exchange Counselors (SEC) and holds commercial real estate's highest designation, Certified Commercial Investment Member (CCIM).

Mr. Allen has been, on three occasions, a guest lecturer at Stanford University. He has authored and conducted nationally accredited seminars including *Developing & Syndicating, Analyzing Investment Properties, The Secrets of Successful Exchanging* and *Exchanging from A to S*. His book, *The Guide to Becoming Real Estate Rich* is available on-line at iuniverse.com. and amazon.com.

NOTES

300 STRATEGIES FOR MAKING
REAL ESTATE & BUSINESS DEALS

VOLUME 11

STRATEGIES
251 – 275

Combining Real Estate and Stock Strategies

ROBERT W. STEELE

Foreword by Clifford L. Strand, SEC, EMS

OUTSIDE THE BOX & INSIDE / OUTSIDE THE COUNTRY

300 Strategies for Making Real Estate & Business Deals

Outside the Box & Outside the Country

VOLUME 11

Strategies 251 – 275

COMBINING REAL ESTATE & STOCK FORMULAS

Robert W. Steele

Foreword by Clifford L. Strand, SEC, EMS

Design, Layout & Graphics
Victoria Vinton
Coyote Press Graphic Communications
www.coyotepressgraphics.com

VOLUME 11
CONTENTS

Introduction

Foreword: Clifford L. Strand, SEC, EMS

Strategy	Title
#251	PUT #1 (Option) Using Real Estate
#252	PUT #2 (Option) Using Real Estate
#253	Stock Traded for Real Estate but Not Income
#254	Covered Call (Option) in Stock Vernacular
#255	Covered Call #2 (Option)
#256	The Double or Nothing Contract
#257	Variable Purchase Price of Real Estate Based on Performance
#258	Disappearing Trust Deed
#259	Real Estate Owner Keeps the Eat
#260	Stock for Installment Sale
#261	Stock for Geographical Trade (or Multiple Exchange)
#262	Mitigating the Downside
#263	Growing a Corporation Partially with Real Estate
#264	REIT — Real Estate Investment Trust
#265	Crop Futures Strategy
#266	Stock Exchange with the Option to Buy Back
#267	Developing Internal Exchanging Department within Corporation
#268	Major Trader Obtains a Seat on the Board
#269	Public Company Trades Stock for Expense Items
#270	Derivatives of Real Estate
#271	Trading Stock for Space
#272	Upsiding Currency Land
#273	Charitable Trust Alternative
#274	Funding Corporation with Real Estate
#275	Stock For Troubled Paper
#275-A	Middle Corp Escrow

INTRODUCTION

Combining Real Estate & Stock Formulas

Using and/or combining real estate & stock formulas and strategies together can sometime create a double win situation. It is paramount to understand that you are working within two very exacting disciplines. They each have rules and regulations that have to be followed. When you use a strategy from one discipline totally within the other discipline then just one set of rules apply but if you combine the two in one transaction then both sets of rules will apply.

If you are transacting with or for a Public Company, the accountancy needs to be involved in the decision making processes as GAP may come into play. Also the question of, "How does the relationship of a new acquisition affect other phases of the accounting process?" must be addressed.

With these caveats accounted for, then there are some excellent things that can be accomplished by having the knowledge of how to work with both real estate and stock. You can create leverage where it wasn't available before and you can solve geographical problems. When you recognize that actually square miles of real estate are nonproductive or underproductive but they are still assets that can enhance corporate balance sheets and there is leverage available in stock that can enhance real estate situations then there are opportunities for exchange.

The REITs, Real Estate Investment Trusts, have certainly shown one way that the two can be combined (see Strategy No. 264 in this book). When someone finally combined these two in this form, it opened up avenues for literally billions of dollars in transactions. Many hotel and motel chains are owned by corporations as are shopping centers and ranches. In each of these cases, there are two plays going on: One is real estate and one is stock. While real estate investors usually like real estate, there are those that think stock is the better play. It is possible to have both at the same time.

Regardless of what your personal preference might be, if you do not have some knowledge of both disciplines you may be missing an opportunity. If you take the time to learn both you may find that many new doors open. Hopefully this book will open some of those doors for you.

Good reading.

Robert W. Steele

Clifford L. Strand, SEC, EMS

Foreward

We often forget the role Securities (Stock) can play in real estate transactions. Public Companies, Real Estate Investment Trusts, Hedge Funds, Pooled Asset Funds and the like use a variety of security instruments to improve their asset base. Often stock is used to acquire real estate for portfolio or investment purposes, sometimes for corporate Headquarters, sometimes in a merger, sometimes to diversify and hedge against loss and also simply as a means of growing a portfolio with Hard Assets; yes Real Estate is a hard asset.

While serving as the President of a small Real Estate Investment Trust and later as the CEO/Chairman of a small "Public" real estate investment company, we often would issue a class of convertible preferred stock in direct exchange for real estate, or into a single asset LLC or Corporation for 51% controlling interest, thus we were able to build our asset base and grow the company. Doing this allows the company to acquire assets without using cash, while giving the recipient liquidity at some point upon liquidation of the stock. This method can also be a valuable tool in the splitting up of partnerships and multiple owner entities such as corporations, TICs and LLCs. There are ways of minimizing or deferring taxation while dissolving ownership and giving liquidity.

Securities (stock) are highly regulated by the Securities and Exchange Commission and the States Securities regulatory agencies. One must always be in compliance. Auditing and accounting issues can arise since public entities must comply with GAP accounting principles, which are sometimes not real estate friendly. Once one understands the process it's not really complicated to do it the right way.

I first met Bob Steele in the late 1960s. I was instantly drawn to his creativity and "out of the box" thinking, and he became a mentor to me and a friend. One of my earliest transactions with Bob Steele involved a building in Portland Oregon owned by a Public Company that I was representing. The transaction was difficult, with multiple parties influencing the transaction. Bob's out of the box thinking, finding solutions and relentless pursuit drove the transaction towards a successful win/win closing.

I am glad to see Bob writing again, developing new ideas and strategies, and passing along the new with the proven to a new generation.

It's an honor to be associated with Bob Steele and to have been asked to write this forward.

Clifford L. Strand, SEC, EMS

President, The Capital Companies

STRATEGY 251

PUT #1 (Option) Using Real Estate

This is a great formula for growing a corporation and a high leverage opportunity for a person or a company willing to take a higher risk for a higher reward.

SITUATION	A corporation would like to increase its capitalization and would like to use real estate as part of that base. Therefore it would benefit them if they could exchange their stock for it. A property owner has a subdivision of 100 F&C (free and clear) lots at $50,000 each. Total value $5,000,000.
COUNTER-PROPOSAL	The owner is not willing to bet all $5,000,000 on a public or private company, but he likes the business plan of the corporation and thinks it is going to be a winner. He is willing to take some stock for his equity in the lots.
UPSIDE/ DOWNSIDE	They reach an agreement and the company agrees to take in 20 lots in exchange for $1,000,000 in preferred stock (1,000,000 shares @ a value of $1 per share) and give the land owner a PUT (option) to exchange his other 80 lots at the same $1-per-share preferred price for a period of 24 months.
BENEFITS	The maximum downside is $1,000,000. That is based on the corporation's stock going to zero. The upside potential is huge! If the stock goes to $5.00 per share, the owner would realize $25,000,000 for the lots. The owner may exercise the option and exchange in the other 80 lots and receive an additional 4,000,000 preferred shares, for a total of 5,000,000 shares, at a value of $5 per share—or $25,000,000 in value.
NOTES	There is no leverage in the free and clear lots. The leverage is created on the stock side of the transaction, not the real estate side. The risk is obviously that the stock can go to zero in value whereas the real estate seldom if ever goes to zero. The upside potential, while accompanied by a higher risk, provides the leverage for the much higher potential. ***The thrill of the hunt is also a legitimate benefit.***

STRATEGY 252

PUT #2 (Option) Using Real Estate

Formula to mitigate the risk and/or leverage the upside using a stock formula and for growing a corporation.

SITUATION	A corporation would like to increase its capitalization and would like to use real estate as part of that base. Therefore it would benefit them if they could exchange their stock for it. The owner of the real estate likes the business plan and the management of the corporation.
TRADE MADE	The owner has a \$200,000 F&C parcel of land and two heavily encumbered houses, \$400,000 each with \$250,000 in loans on each. The owner trades land for stock at \$1.00 per share (a total of 200,000 shares) and receives a Put Option to trade the SFRs (houses) free and clear for stock at the same price for 24 months.
UPSIDE/ DOWNSIDE	Downside is \$200,000. That is based on the lowest the stock could go to, zero. Upside is huge! The owner is trading \$800,000 in F/C houses for 800,000 shares of stock at \$1.00 per share. At \$5.00 stock the owner would net \$4,500,000 (\$5,000,000 less the \$500,000 to pay off the loans on the two houses).
ADDITIONAL BENEFITS	Obviously the stock can be worth less than \$5.00 in 24 months but it can also be worth a lot more so there is no fixed top to this transaction. The bottom is set at a maximum loss of \$200,000.
NOTES	There is no leverage in the free and clear land and the 2 houses have a small equity and probably reverse cash flow. The leverage is created on the stock side of the transaction, not the real estate side but by using the Put Option the real estate owner is actually leveraging the debt on the two houses. ***Again the thrill of the hunt is also a legitimate benefit.***

STRATEGY 253

Stock Traded for Real Estate but Not Income

This is an excellent strategy for growing a corporation via a real estate trade and it is an outstanding way of making a geographical exchange. It has many facets that can be negotiated in so many directions. Also it is a nice way to break up real estate partnerships, divorces, etc. The cash flow can be divided to suit the needs of the transaction. THE LEASEBACK MAKES THE PROPERTY MANAGEMENT FREE.

SITUATION	The owner has a $1.000,000 office building with a $600,000 loan. The building has a net cash flow spendable of $50,000 per year. The building is in Florida.	Building: Loan: Equity:	$1,000,000 600,000 $400,000
KEEP THE INCOME	A California-based corporation trades the owner $400,000 in stock ($1 per share) for the equity and lets the owner lease back for a period of time (1 to 10 years), giving the owner all the cash flow (negotiable). In this cited instance there is no interruption in the owner's cash flow income.	Shares of Stock:	400,000 at $1 each
LEVERAGE	If the owner is willing to roll the dice on a public company where he likes the business plan and the management, his upside may be much greater than holding the building equity, and at the same time the building equity is added as a plus to the corporate balance sheet. If stock moves to $5 per share he has increased his equity 5-fold.	At $5 Value, Stock is at value of $2,000,000	
AUTHOR'S NOTE	Whenever you move from one field of endeavor to another, you will find there are new strategies and formulas available. The same thing is highlighted when you move assets into the international arena and each country has different laws. You can do some things legally in one country that are illegal in another. All kinds of avenues open up, but be sure and do your homework on the laws in each place.		

STRATEGY 254

Covered Call (Option) in Stock Vernacular

(Note this is the same as Strategy #250 in the Vol. 10 under a real estate title.)

SITUATION	Client #1 is looking for a signer to secure a Letter of Credit. Substantial income can be derived from an international business transaction and that transaction can be recreated three to four times per year. She needs $250,000 initially for the Letter of Credit, moving up to $1,000,000 over time. Client #2 has substantial real estate holdings totaling several million dollars, but is always interested in leverage and creating more equity and/or income from his holdings.
POSSIBLE SOLUTION	Set up an equity line of credit for the first transaction with the $250,000 loan against one or more of client #2's holdings to secure the Letter of Credit. Client #1, wanting the Letter of Credit agrees to pay a 5% fee (negotiated), over and above the cost of borrowing the money, for a 90-day period of time. Client #2 earns $12,500 each time the process turns over. If it turns over four times during the course of the year, he grosses $50,000. These can sometimes be turned over up to nine times a year which at the above numbers grosses to client #2 - $112,500. You are using existing assets as security for letters of credit to deliver extra income. In the stock market Client #2 is putting up existing stock at a fixed number (price), like an option, and receiving an option premium paid in cash by Client #1. If the stock rises and exceeds this strike price Client #2 has to sell the stock at the strike price to Client #1. In the real estate market, if there is a failure it would be settled in cash rather than the transfer of real estate assets (more like a settlement in the Futures Market).
NOTES	Each time a Letter of Credit is issued client #2 receives $12,500 or actually 5% of the Letter of Credit amount. This strategy is often used to fund motion pictures. One client might be used to put up the assets to raise the money for the U.S. distribution for the film. Another client might be used for funding the distribution of the movie in Argentina and another one for the VCR distribution in Europe. Using the assets without actually going out of title is leveraging exactly like the covered call.The settlement is different.

STRATEGY 255

Covered Call #2 (Option)

Using stock in the acquisition of real estate with the right to negate transaction based on future conditions.

SITUATION	Real Estate owner has $1,000,000 in free and clear land. Stock company wants to add assets to its balance sheet. They offer 1,000,000 shares of stock at $1.00 per share. Real estate owner likes the business plan of the stock company and the management team but is still hesitant to make the transaction.
POSSIBLE SOLUTION	An offer is drafted that mitigates, at least in a substantial part, the potential problems: The real estate owner will have the option to buy back her real estate parcel for a period of time, three years. The option is designed so that if she buys it back in the first year, the price will be 110% of the original sales price. It can be paid for with the stock received (at acquisition price), and/or cash, or any combination thereof. The second year the option price will be 120% and the third year 130%. (The increase is to allow for potential growth in the value of the real estate.)
BENEFITS	The original landowner can get back into title to the land for a period of time and only suffer a minor loss if the stock does not work out. At the same time, the corporation is going to make a profit one way or another if they make a deal. No one is wasting time. The future market conditions will determine the outcome.
NOTES	Free and clear land has zero leverage. By moving into speculative stock your risk goes up substantially but your leverage also goes way up. It is easy to see $1.00 stock go to $10 or $100 per share in a short period of time but it has some real risks. It is almost impossible to see the land go to $10 million or $100 million during the same time frame. The covered call (option) lets you play both sides of the street. ***The thrill of the hunt is also a legitimate benefit.***

STRATEGY 256

The Double or Nothing Contract

If the stock goes to zero you lose. If it doesn't, you double.

SITUATION	Real Estate owner has $1,000,000 in a free and clear building. Stock company is a start-up company and needs to raise its asset base and capital. If they can trade stock for real estate it will increase their asset base. They offer 1,000,000 shares of restricted stock at $1.00 per share. Real estate owner likes the business plan of the stock company and the management team but is still hesitant to make the transaction.
POSSIBLE SOLUTION	An offer is drafted that compensates for, at least in a part, the higher risk: In two or three years, or when the stock becomes fully trading, the number of shares will be adjusted upward, if necessary, to reflect double the building value at the acquisition time, even though newly issued shares might also be restricted. Example: Owner is receiving 1,000,000 shares of stock. At the two or three year mark, if stock is selling for $1.00 owner receives an additional 1,000,000 shares. If selling at $2.00 or above, no additional shares. If at 50 cents, 3,000,000 additional shares. The contract is designed so if the stock is viable the owner of the real estate is going to get double his value for the real estate. If stock goes to $5 or $10 a share, real estate owner is a big winner.
DOWN-SIDE	If the stock goes to zero, it is time to go fishing.
NOTES	Free and clear land or buildings have zero leverage. By moving into speculative stock your risk goes up substantially but your leverage also goes way up. It is easy to see $1.00 stock go to $10 or $100 per share in a short period of time but it has some major risks. It is doubtful that you will see the real estate go to $10 million or $100 million during the same time frame. The double or nothing contract lets you play both sides of the street. ***The thrill of the hunt is also a legitimate benefit.***

STRATEGY 257

Variable Purchase Price of Real Estate Based on Performance

This formula can be used for multiple purposes regarding the value of the real estate. If the property is in the path of growth and a fast appreciation is expected, this formula could allow the real estate owner to participate in part of the future real estate upside.

SITUATION	Real Estate owner has $1,000,000 in free and clear land. It is dead center in the middle of a growth pattern. Stock company is a solid company that wants to increase its asset base, would like to own the land, and is willing to trade its stock at market value for the title. The landowner is willing to make the deal, but is reluctant to leave the future growth potential available to him if he holds onto the land.
POSSIBLE SOLUTION	An offer is drafted that compensates, at least in a part, the leaving part of this growth equity on the table. The parties agree to have an appraisal run now to determine the value of the land, and the stock company will pay, in stock, the appraised amount at the market value of its shares. At the end of three years, the property will be re-appraised. If the price is the same or has dropped, the deal will stand as made. If the price of the property has gone up, the land owner is to receive additional stock to represent one-half of the appreciation amount.
NOTES	This agreement can be secured by a T.D. if desired. T.Ds are normal associated with being the security for a note. They can also be security for an agreement. This TD or agreement may be considered as boot, tax-wise, and it is also a potential asset and therefore is an exchangeable or tradable item...

STRATEGY 258

Disappearing Trust Deed

When you are dealing with a combination of real estate and stock, the future price or value of both commodities often comes into play. In this instance, the T.D.'s actual balance will be decided by events that have not happened yet.

SITUATION	Real Estate owner has $1,000,000 in a free and clear building. The stock company would like to own the building, but the owner is reluctant to risk her entire equity. Real estate owner likes the business plan of the stock company and the management team but is still hesitant to make the transaction.
POSSIBLE SOLUTION	An offer is drafted that compensates, at least in a part, for the higher risk: The stock company uses 500,000 shares of stock at $1 per share for the down payment into the building giving back to the owner a $500,000 carry back T.D. payable on terms and conditions agreeable to both parties After a certain period of time, say two or three years, if the stock has doubled or greater, then the TD is conveyed without further compensation. If the stock has increased 1½ times, the T.D. is reduced to reflect the growth in the stock value.
DOWNSIDE	The landowner risks just one-half of her equity. The stock company is a winner if the stock goes up in value.
NOTES	Real estate owner is out of real estate and into stock. This formula lends itself to geographical moves for the real estate owner as she can re-trade or multiple exchange (in-lieu-of) this offer into other real estate. The real estate owner mitigates the downside in exchange for possibly not receiving all of the potential growth on the stock. ***The thrill of the hunt is also a legitimate benefit.***

STRATEGY 259

Real Estate Owner Keeps the Eat

This is a possible method of a landowner freeing up equity in a real estate parcel that is eating (has reverse cash flow) but has real equity. It can also be improved property.

SITUATION	Land owner owns a \$500,000 parcel of land with a loan on it of \$150,000. It has a reverse cash flow of \$15,000 per year in payments and taxes. The stock company is willing to take the property and acknowledges that the equity is there, but does not want to accept the eat (reverse cash flow).
POSSIBLE SOLUTION	The stock company offers to pay \$500,000 in stock for the property providing the landowner will continue to make the payments on the loan and pay it off over time. The property owner agrees, and further agrees to put the \$500,000 in stock up as additional security that the loan payments will be made as scheduled. The stock company adds the land to its asset base and the landowner now has stock that he believes will appreciate more than the land would have. In addition, he has something that is probably easier to exchange on into something else. If he could find a f/c house that would trade for the stock he could, in the transaction, borrow \$150,000 on the house and pay off the loan on the land.
NOTES	This kind of step sometimes leads automatically into a three way exchange. Where the encumbered land was so difficult to move, the stock company is not afraid of the transaction because they are retaining the control on their stock until the encumbrance has been paid off.

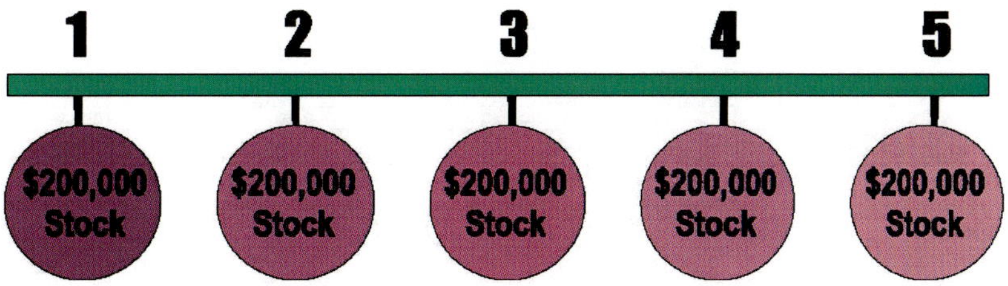

STRATEGY 260

Stock for Installment Sale

Stock for Down Payment plus stock for ongoing annual payments. This can mitigate risk and is another potential tax saver.

SITUATION	Owner has $1,000,000 in free and clear land. The stock company would like to trade stock for the property. The owner likes the idea of the stock, likes the company and management but would like to mitigate the risk and minimize tax consequences
POSSIBLE SOLUTION	The stock company agrees to pay the owner $200,000 down in stock at market price and $200,000 per year in stock for four years in annual payments. The structure here is open to a variety of avenues. Interest on the first TD carry-back loan of $800,000 can be paid in cash or additional stock, or can be with no interest charged (always opened to imputing possibilities). The stock can be transferred at market value at the time payment is made, or negotiated for the price of the stock at the time that the deal was struck. The owner has several options open. He can trade the $800,000 first TD, he can trade any one or all of the $200,000 payments, or he can trade the stock he has. The stock company can book the asset if the accountancy agrees.
NOTES	This transaction is also a good one with improved property and again with multiple payments there are more avenues opened for trade.

STRATEGY 261

Stock for Geographical Trade (or Multiple Exchange)

Stock used to initiate a geographical transaction with multiple parts.

SITUATION	A California-based owner has Florida property producing $50,000 per year positive cash flow. The owner would like out of the Florida property but would miss the cash flow. The stock company would like to trade stock for the property to increase its asset base.
POSSIBLE SOLUTION	The owner likes the idea of the stock, likes the company and management but would sorely miss the income from the Florida property. The stock company agrees to exchange stocks for the equity and pay the owner for a period of years from $25,000 per year to $50,000 per year which is, in essence, paying the owner all or part of the cash flow from the property. This can be done via a corporate debenture (note), or as a consulting fee, or as part of the purchase price. It can be for a period of one year to twenty years. It can be structured so the payments stop if the owner re-trades the stock, or structured so it continues if the stock is traded. The owner of the real estate can now keep all or part of the trade, or can exchange all or part of it. The stock company adds the property to its asset base.
NOTES	A stock company usually is more flexible than an individual owner. Property in other states or countries are often okay particularly if professional management is available. There are probably thousands of corporation that have the ability to trade their stock for real estate that do not know that the opportunity is available.

STRATEGY 262

Mitigating the Downside

For a particularly desirable property, stock company agrees to issue additional shares should value drop below a given amount.

SITUATION	A mining company wanted to raise capital and did not want to work with a bank loan, as the banks wanted the loan repaid based on minerals being mined at a market price of minerals at the time the loan is made. If minerals triple in value, the stockholders would be suffering a loss. They preferred to raise the capital by trading treasury stock for free and clear real estate, and then financing the real estate.	Property: Stock: Loan:	\$3,000,000 \$3,000,000 \$1,500,000
KEEP THE INCOME	Stock was offered for a free and clear apartment building which was acceptable to the owners. The stock would not become free-trading and could not be sold for approximately two years. It was agreed that if the stock fell below the price that they took it for, additional stock would be added to bring it up to the price first stated. If the price was above the original number the owners realized an additional profit. The mining company was able to borrow the money they wanted from a new real estate loan. The problem for a mining company, such as a precious metal gold mining company, is that when it borrows from a bank, the bank likes to get paid back in product if it thinks the product will appreciate. In the instance of gold, many gold companies, and therefore their stock holders, took serious losses when the banks got paid back with ounces at \$300 per oz, when the actual price had risen to \$1,000 per oz. Even to this day they may be better off to trade their stock for real estate and borrow on the real estate. Things change, but currently that is the case. Some mining companies lost many millions by hedging their production ahead which cost the stockholder huge looses.	Stock company (mining company) issues \$3,000,000 in treasury stock & ends up with \$1,500,000 in cash from the loan less expenses plus \$1,500,000 in real estate equity. The real estate owner ends up with \$3,000,000 in stock with an upside possibility plus additional stock if the price on the stock should drop.	

STRATEGY 263

Growing a Corporation Partially with Real Estate

There are billions of dollars in real estate equities lying idle. If some of these assets were inside of corporations they would have a positive effect on the balance sheets and give the corporations assets with which to work.

SITUATION	One of the easiest formulas is to issue $200,000 in stock in exchange for $100,000 in an asset like real estate, plus $100,000 in cash. This gives the stock company a $100,000 asset on their books and $100,000 operating capital.
POSSIBLE SOLUTION	It is the same formula used thousands of times by hard money lenders (and even conventional lenders when they are smart enough to use it) when they have a foreclosure in real estate. If the hard money lender has foreclosed on a $100,000 parcel of land, he has a private lender client who is in title to the property via the foreclosure. That client is usually looking for income, and now has his cash tied up in the property that was foreclosed on. The ploy, and this formula, is for that client to add $100,000 more cash and the hard money lender finds someone who wants $100,000 cash, and tells them they will make the loan wanted but they have to also take the $100,000 parcel of land. In that case the $100,000 in land plus $100,000 in cash is traded for a new $200,000 mortgage. As I said, thousands of these types of loans are made. It is called a "must take." You must take the land in the deal. Growing the corporation is the same formula, except instead of trading in $100,000 in a foreclosed-on real estate asset, the person with the cash is getting stock. The player is also different. The player is profit-oriented rather than a lender.
NOTES	The mission of the corporation changes from trying to find people to buy their stock to people that have a problem they are trying to solve with their real estate holdings or other assets. The corporation agrees to take these holdings in exchange for company stock if the owners will add cash. Quid pro quo.

STRATEGY 264

REIT — Real Estate Investment Trust

Billions of dollars in real estate equities are inside REITs.

SITUATION	A REIT is a tax designation for a corporation investing in real estate that reduces or eliminates corporate income taxes. In return, REITs are required to distribute 90% of their income, which may be taxable, into the hands of the investors. The REIT structure was designed to provide a similar structure for investment in real estate as mutual funds provide for investment in stocks. Like other corporations, REITs can be publicly or privately held. Public REITs may be listed on public stock exchanges like shares of common stock in other firms. REITs can be classified as equity, mortgage or hybrid. The key statistics to look at in a REIT are its net asset value (NAV), adjusted funds from operations (AFFO) and cash available for distribution (CAD). REITs face challenges from both a slowing economy and the global financial crisis, depressing share values by 40 to 70 percent in some cases.
POSSIBLE SOLUTION	REITs can exchange their treasure stock for real estate. The public identities are easy to read as they have a market through the exchanges. The private REITs do not have this easy- to-read market and it is more difficult to trade their stock.
NOTES	Mega billions of real estate are within the REITs and their pass-through tax savings make a readily saleable package. Management is always the key and as evidenced by the drop in the values recently they are not always managed by the smartest of people. More and more the computer black boxes are programmed to make decisions based on what has happened, not what is causing things to happen.

STRATEGY 265

Crop Futures Strategy

If the commodities brokers can use futures so can the real estate brokers or principals. There is literally no end to how far this particular strategy can go. It is truly open-ended.

<table>
<tr><td>COMMODITIES MARKET</td><td>Futures can be used by those wanting to protect a buying or selling price for some time in the future. The farmer growing corn can pre-sell his crops at a price now to insure the price in the future, if she thinks the market may go down. In this instance the futures is a hedge.</td><td rowspan="3">Building value $2,000,000.

$2,000,000 in tomatoes delivered at $400,000 worth per year. In this transaction the building was at a fixed price and the tomato price floated with the market. It can be designed both ways, either fixed or floating on either side.

This futures formula is a derivative of the Creation of Wealth formula, see Volume 1 plus it also moves into the stock market or commodities market, see Volume 11.</td></tr>
<tr><td>COMBINING WITH</td><td>It can also be structured so it guarantees a delivery some time in the future even though the price may change to a new market price but the delivery of product is guaranteed.</td></tr>
<tr><td>REAL ESTATE MARKET</td><td>Actual example from our files: Client exchanged tomatoes from a farm in California for a Big Box Building (old White Front Store) in Oregon that was leased. It was for a floating quantity of tomatoes delivered to the crop buyer, selected by the farmer, at the rate of 20% of the building's value per year for the next five years. The building price was delivered at a fixed price but the tomatoes were delivered at market value at the time that their delivery was made direct to the wholesaler on behalf of the building owner.

Building owner gets fixed price on building. If price of tomatoes goes up during the coming four years, the tomato farmer makes additional profit because he delivers fewer tomatoes. He would lose if the price drops because he would have to deliver more. Tomato farmer had no interest to pay on loan by negotiations. There was actually a small $200,000 loan on the building which was paid off out of the first delivery of tomatoes.</td></tr>
</table>

STRATEGY 266

Stock Exchange with the Option to Buy Back

Land with great potential several years out is exchanged for stock and the landowner negotiates options to buy the land back. If land does increase, the option is exercised. This is win-win. If stock and land both increase in value, owner wins on both plays.

SITUATION	Again, this exchange exemplifies that motivation can be on either the front side of the exchange (what you are going into) or the back side (what you are exchanging out of). Usually there is motivation on both sides but one side predominates. A typical example of this situation is someone with a $1,000,000 land parcel free and clear. It is in the path of growth and is increasing in value at 5 to 10% per year and as a new street and a lot of building is planned for the area, the owner believes some faster appreciation is in the future. But the owner is a mover and just holding the passive land is not exciting enough. He is being offered stock for the land and likes the company and the management of the company
POSSIBLE SOLUTION	He counter offers that he will accept the $1,000,000 in stock providing they give him an option to buy back the land at a price that is increasing at a 5% a year constant for a period of 7 years. That means that the first year to exercise the option and buy the land back it would cost him $1,050,000. In the 7th year it would cost $1,350,000. If it did appreciate to $2 or $3,000,000 he would exercise his option and make a profit. The stock company agrees to the transaction and the deal is done. The owner now has two items: The $1,000,000 in stock and the option. Either or both can be further exchanged. The stock company has valuable land on their books and if the option is exercised they will make a profit.

STRATEGY 267

Developing an Internal Exchanging Department within a Corporation

Any corporation of any size or consequence should consider the following strategy. Also, all cities, counties and states should consider this.

SITUATION	I have often wondered why corporations did not develop an internal exchange or trading department as there are so many options open to a corporation. They have preferred stock, common stock, debentures, notes, bonds, etc. that they can trade. They can trade their products, they can trade their future products. They can trade and barter for services and assets, and literally on and on. You certainly cannot use a standard purchasing agent for this. There are many avenues open to the corporation to acquire personnel that understand exchange and barter and there are many classes and seminars on the subject.
POSSIBLE SOLUTION	There are societies and clubs that have educational forums and there are marketing sessions, often a week long where you can ask for what you want and offer what you have for trade. It is like the fur traders of old coming to the fort, except now it is exchangors and traders with computers and a plethora of things to exchange, not just furs. A corporation could even outsource this department to an existing exchange organization. Many exchange brokers represent corporations but almost always they could go a lot further than they go. A newspaper or media company could easily develop a trading department and actually expand the company's business multi-fold. Companies that own sports organizations could add millions and maybe billions by exchanging those empty seats in their ball parks and arenas. There is absolutely no end to the opportunities for a trade and barter department in a corporation.
NOTES	Any hotel or resort with 500+rooms could easily support an Exchange Department. International cruise lines could fill some of those vanishing vacancies in, no one knows how many, staterooms. A Barter Department for either of these two entities could perhaps trade that surplus production and get full dollar value for it if they knew the formulas and techniques.

STRATEGY 268

Major Trader Obtains a Seat on the Board

An investor with a large asset, for example real estate or other, who would like to change the direction of her holdings, can use the following strategy to obtain control or augment the status of a small public company via an exchange of assets for stock and a position within the company.

SITUATION	The owner of a high rise building with good cash flow and equity of approximately $10,000,000 is looking for an opportunity. By profession, this owner is a CPA with public company experience and this asset is the major holding in her portfolio.
POSSIBLE SOLUTION	The owner is approached by an agent representing a merger and acquisition firm (MA) about a small public company. The company has an excellent chance to expand an already successful product line, but it needs a stronger financial statement to get the financing it needs. The merger and acquisition agent suggests an exchange of the real estate building for stock in the public company, and that the company then borrows on said real estate to obtain the cash it needs for the product line expansion. After full due diligence, the owner of the building agrees proving she is made the Chief Financial Officer (CFO) of the company. The transaction goes together and the building owner becomes a major stock holder in the company.
AUTHOR'S NOTES	1. I have seen this formula work very well. I have also seen a couple of other situations which should be noted. In one case the due diligence showed the building owner that the president of the company was not smart or strong enough to run the organization, so she would only make the deal if she could be president. The existing owner would not allow that and the deal fell apart. She was right as eventually the company did fail because of management. 2. I have also seen a case where the building owner received such a large portion of the stock of the company that after the newly energized company was really off and running, he maneuvered the situation whereby he ended up with control and ousted the original owners. Indirectly the building owner does not lose all of the control on his building as the corporation, which he is a part of, still owns it.

STRATEGY 269

Public Company Trades Stock for Expense Items

Improves accounting ratios and $1 million trade may have a positive impact

The following is an opinion of this type of trade from the CFO of a banking corporation, specifically at this author's request.

Banks live and breathe by their risk-based capital ratio. The calculation for same is obtained by dividing risk-based capital by risk-weighted assets. In the current economic environment, this particular ratio has come to the forefront due to the increase in impaired assets (increasing the risk-weighting of assets, or the denominator) and poor financial results negatively impacting capital (reducing the numerator). To correct this situation banks must either raise new capital or rid themselves of the bad assets.

Focusing on capital, if a bank were to trade stock for some of their larger expenses they could achieve the goal of increasing the risk-based capital ratio. Let's take an example where a bank incurs a $1,000,000 expense for advertising. In a typical transaction the accounting entry would be to record the expense for $1,000,000 and issue a check for same. Assuming a 40% tax rate, the result on the capital ratio would be as follows:

Capital (equity) is reduced by the negative after tax earnings of $600,000. Cash has a zero risk-weighting (no risk associated with cash), so there is no change to risk-weighted assets in the denominator. The result is a net decrease to the capital ratio resulting from the reduction in the numerator.

Now, let's look at a transaction where a bank decides to issue stock to the advertising company vs. paying cash. The same reduction of $600,000 occurs to capital for the after-tax advertising expense, but it is offset by a $1,000,000 increase to equity when the stock is issued. As such, there is a net increase to capital of a net $400,000. No assets are involved in this particular transaction, therefore there is no impact on the denominator. The result from this transaction is an increase to the risk-based capital ratio. The downside, of course, is the dilutive impact to the current shareholders.

(Dollars in 000's)	**Dollars**
Capital ratio before transaction	
Capital	$ 5,000
Risk-weighted assets	$ 45,000
With advertising expense	
Capital	$ 4,400
Risk-weighted assets	$ 45,000
Trade stock for advertising	
Capital	$ 5,400
Risk-weighted assets	$ 45,000

Author's note: Said dilution effect may or may not be offset to some extent by the benefits received from the advertising.

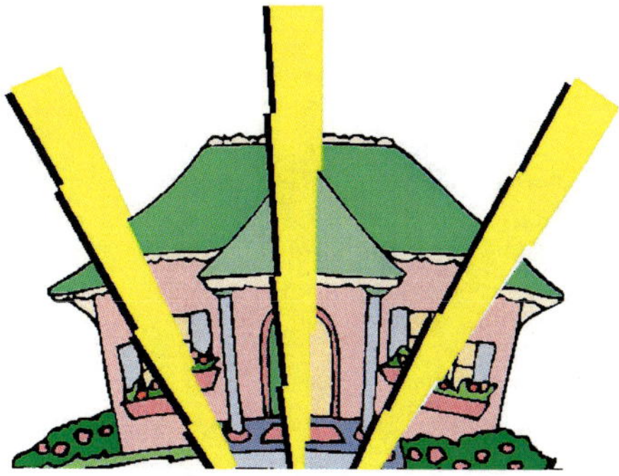

STRATEGY 270

Derivatives of Real Estate

While real estate is often the underlying asset, it can be represented by a plethora of different derivatives from stock to mortgages to sub-prime mortgages that have been sliced and diced and packaged in a variety of forms, ad infinitum.

SITUATION	1. A real estate owner, which can be an individual or a company but we will use a company in this example, may control the physical real estate but: 2. The mortgage on this real estate may have been owned by a bank that made the loan, 3. Or the loan may have been sold into the secondary market where it was bundled with a number of other loans and, 4. Then resold to another identity where a percentage of the bundled loan package that is represented by the lowest risk were resold to one company at a superior price and, 5. The portion of the highest risk sold to another company at a lower price and, 6. One of these buying companies was in one country and the other was in another country and, 7. The company that owned the real estate then sold the land under the building, subject to the existing mortgage to another company and leased the land back and, 8. Then the company issues and sells more stock and so the ownership of the real estate becomes more diversified and, 9. Then the company leased the real estate to one party and the air rights to another company, with an option to buy them back.
POSSIBLE SOLUTION	Recognize that all of the above varied identities, assets and instruments are derivitaves and have an economic play of some sort. Some of the plays are more important than the real estate itself if you listen to some of the players. The simple days when a person bought the homes for cash or paid them off is, at least in the United State, basically over. Add to the above the tremendous force placed on the real estate market by the political arena, and it really gives you a distorted picture of what might be real. Political donations & lobbyists representing all of these factions play a role.
NOTES	Stock companies, whether in the form of REITs or others, will continue to own a major portion of the market. Smaller companies have an excellent chance to take advantage of the laws and statutes that are developed through major expenditures by the bigger players. A tightly run smaller company has an excellent chance of being successful because a variety of avenues are open to it that individuals don't have.

Strategy 271

Trading Stock for Space

This is a very common formula.

SITUATION	This is a relatively easy formula to use. When a young corporation is expanding and capital is tight, it is relatively easy to find vacant buildings, offices or commercial spaces that will exchange at least part of the vacant space, that the corporation can use, for stock.
POSSIBLE SOLUTION	If you approached the owner of a vacant space which has been vacant for a long time and asked if he would consider exchanging the vacant space for part interest in a company, he usually will say, "Tell me about the company." In other words, he wants to get that space occupied somehow. For the corporation, it is often prudent to ask for an option to buy back the stock if you want to eliminate the dilution effect by buying it back later. If you do, it is the equivalent of deferring your rent or lease payments. A corporation owning a nursery can expand in this manner by leasing land for other nurseries, and also the corporation can tie in an option to buy the property as well as buy back their stock. The corporation has a plethora of other things that it can augment its exchange offers with, and you can see a number of them listed in Strategy #267 within this Volume.
NOTES	We refer you to our Volume 10 – *"Half the World is Vacancy"* for you to get a peak as to how much vacancy there is in this world. It is extremely easy to trade good company stock for vacancy if you are realistic & flexible in your requirements.

STRATEGY 272

Upsiding Currency Land

What has a better chance of going up in value: Company stock or currency land?

SITUATION	Please see Volume 2 in this series for more information on Currency Land. Currency Land is esoterically synonymous with what is also called Trading Sardines. These are items that are definitely assets if looked at one way, or in the case of vacant scrap land, they might be considered a liability as they have no functional use and taxes must be paid on them. This land can be on the top of a mountain, in the middle of a desert, under the flight pattern, and even land from war zones that have suspected wooden land mines or other unpleasant possibilities.
POSSIBLE SOLUTION	At the same time, there is a market for this type of property in the field of problem solving. For example, would you rather have your $100,000 equity in some free and clear currency land or a house equity that you are going to lose because you cannot pay your mortgage and there are no buyers? You will take the Currency Land every time so you have a place to "hold" your equity until you can re-exchange it into something you can use. If a stock company can trade for some of this type of land, it can strengthen the Assets side of its books if the accountancy is in accord. An exchange for stock for this land lets the land owner diversify his interest and perhaps opens up three-way exchange possibilities.
NOTES	There are millions of acres of Currency Land and lots throughout the U.S. and the world. There are thousands of corporations trying to strengthen the assets side of their ledgers. Stock for land often makes sense. Where there usually are no comparable values with this type of land, prices are often very flexible which can leave room for profits.

STRATEGY 273

Charitable Trust Alternative

A trust doesn't want property being offered because of debt, management, geography or whatever. Stock is third leg and management-free for the trust.

SITUATION	Charitable trusts are often offered assets without geographical limitations. The assets are many times far away and sometimes are not items that can be managed by the trust. People donate or will property and assets to their churches or former colleges, and these items can sometimes be in the far reaches of the globe.
POSSIBLE SOLUTION	A corporation can offer to exchange stock for these assets to either solve the problem, whether it is geographical or managerial, and/or to facilitate a three-way exchange by moving the stock into other assets that the trust can use. It the stock can be preferred and paying dividends, it may be worthwhile for the trust to just retain the stock. Most major universities and institutions have a department that handles these donations and they are very interested in helping people make decisions along these lines. The use of stock can be a handy tool in some of these transactions as it allows there to be some division of assets, whereby a certain heir might take stock and another take the charitable tax deduction and so forth.
NOTES	Tax and legal counsel are recommended as there can be some nice tax advantages available sometimes for the donating party and/or their estates.

STRATEGY 274
Funding Corporation with Real Estate
This is one way to fund a corporation.

SITUATION	This is a formula often used to fund a corporation. Principals in the company put assets into the company and take stock for their equities. These assets can be cash, of course, but also other things, such as real estate that can be used for purposes of capitalization. It is wise to have appraisals, or at least a broker's opinion of value, to substantiate the exchange. It is also possible to exchange stock for other assets in the open market as it allows one to grow the company faster. For instance, a company that owns motels might incorporate its holdings into a public company and then it would be able to use some of its stock in future acquisitions of motels.
POSSIBLE SOLUTION	A corporation can be funded in some unique ways with outside assets: Land under buildings can be exchanged for stock and leased back, and on terms and conditions that are very different, such as one percent of air or mineral rights. Even prepaid leases on vacancy can be used, if approved by the accountancy, and the corporation is able to use the space in some way.
NOTES	Legal and tax counsel should be used in these funding procedures to be sure all the bases are touched. Tax basis and so forth need to be established, and you need to be sure you have not flagged a tax event or at least be cognizant of it if you have.

STRATEGY 275

Stock For Troubled Paper

There is often bad or difficult paper in both the business market (chattels) and the real estate market (trust deeds & mortgages). A public company set up to handle these types of assets can do quite well.

SITUATION	When real estate markets are dropping there are a lot of mortgages and trust deeds that are delinquent and troubled. Sometimes there are loans over the value of the real estate. Even the cost of foreclosing is very expensive today and it is time consuming and can be unpleasant. In the business world the same thing is true which results in delinquent chattel mortgages. These can be secured by equipment, rolling stock, machinery, boats, airplanes, etc.
POSSIBLE SOLUTION	Companies set up to handle these problems can do quite well, and if they happen to be a stock company, they can often trade stock and/or stock and part cash for these underwater or difficult assets at favorable prices—because the owners do not want to spend the time and the money to solve the problems. This can also sometimes solve or mitigate geographical problems for lenders as the cost and distance factors enter into play. Legal-based companies (with in-house legal talent) are naturals for this type of service business and the stock is a neutral asset when used and can be held or re-traded by the recipient.
NOTES	$1,000,000 in troubled paper can often be bought for just a few cents on the dollar. Stock can often be used as all or part of the purchase price.

STRATEGY 275-A
Middle Corp

Charges a 1% or more fee to all for services rendered.

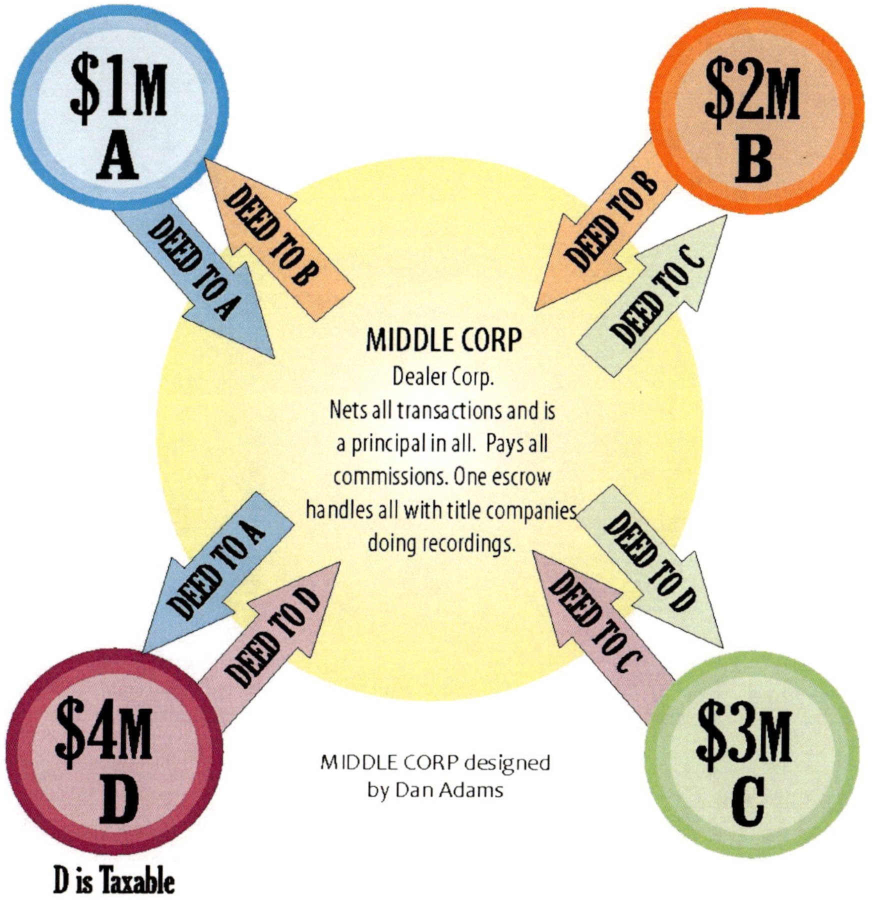

We know of two major usages of this formula where 28 & 32 escrows were closed concurrently.

NOTES

300 STRATEGIES FOR MAKING
REAL ESTATE & BUSINESS DEALS

VOLUME 12

STRATEGIES
276 – 300

Barter, Exchange & Trade Credits

ROBERT W. STEELE

Foreword by Ron Moser

OUTSIDE THE BOX & INSIDE / OUTSIDE THE COUNTRY

300 Strategies for Making Real Estate & Business Deals

Outside the Box & Inside / Outside the Country

VOLUME 12
Strategies 276 – 300

BARTER, EXCHANGE & TRADE CREDITS

by Robert W. Steele

Foreword by Ron Moser

Design, Layout & Graphics
Victoria Vinton
Coyote Press Graphic Communications
www.coyotepressgraphics.com

VOLUME 12
CONTENTS

Introduction

Foreword: Ron Moser

Strategy	Title
#276	**Barter – The One-On-One Trade for Goods or Services**
#277	**The Birth of the Trade Credit**
#278	**Trade Credits #2 – Basic Trade Club**
#279	**Three Options: Direct Barter, Direct Trade Credit, or Trade Club Trade Credits**
#280	**Crop Futures Strategy**
#281	**Trade Credit for Hotels**
#282	**Trade Credit for Assisted Living**
#283	**Printing Your Own Money #1**
#284	**$250 Trade Credit©**
#285	**Printing Your Own Money #2**
#286	**Printing Your Own Money #3**
#287	**International Trade Clubs**
#288	**Starting & Running a Trade Club**
#289	**Breakage in Trade Credits**
#290	**Outlaw Dates on Trade Credits**
#291	**Holder in Due Course of Trade Credits**
#292	**Trade Credits Can Represent a Delayed Multiple Exchange**
#293	**International Trade Credits #2**
#294	**Trade Credits to Help Fill Shopping Center Vacancies**
#295	**Barter & Trade Credits on the Internet**
#296	**Becoming a Trade Credit & Barter Broker**
#297	**Trade Credit Trade**
#298	**Multiple Barter Trades**
#299	**Bartering Education**
#300	**300 Trade Credits for 12-Volume E-Book Set**

INTRODUCTION
Barter, Exchange & Trade Credits

I have been in the real estate exchange business for over 40 years. Years ago, when I was living overseas, I became cognizant that international real estate exchanging was more difficult than in the U.S. for a lot of reasons, not just because of language barriers. Each country had different laws and, like those in the U.S., they were constantly changing. This alone made for a very steep learning curve. Add to that the fact that there were no exchange brokers in all of these various countries who knew the laws, and it made for an almost impossible situation.

I discovered something then that I have seen developing rather slowly but is now starting to speed up. Barter, the exchange of goods and services, worked very easily between foreign countries and crossed borders with a minimum of difficulty. There were people well versed in the mechanics of moving these goods internationally. And of course, the best part for me was the fact that almost all the formulas, strategies and techniques that were semi-unique to the real estate exchange business also worked in the barter business. The transition then from exchanging real estate to exchanging barter was rather simple.

The real estate market today, 2010, also borders on being extremely difficult. Exchanging is perhaps one of the best methods of moving within this market but because the market is so manipulated by political forces it is almost impossible to know what a true market value might be. Buyers think the market has farther to fall and sellers are being led to believe that the bottom is in, and as Kipling said, "... ne'er the twain shall meet."

While this is happening, goods and services are piling up unused in huge quantities. Airplanes are stacking up, ships are dead-heading back to home ports, professional people have thousands of un-billable hours and the list can be as long as your imagination.

Barter is a full-fledged important business today. Google barter and you will find thousands of companies in the business in one form or another. Barter is a perfect business for exchangors, investors and brokers to move into, and as mentioned above, all the knowledge gained in one arena works in the other. The transition is simple.

This book is aimed at helping to make that transition. You will find the same techniques used here in barter situations that you have worked with for years in the real estate exchange business. The use of Trade Credits is very similar to the Creation of Wealth formula developed 50 years ago in the real estate business and used perhaps a thousand years ago in some form in the barter business.

Consider as you read this that perhaps your future might lie within these pages; that just maybe a new door might open. The barter business is so huge it is almost incomprehensible. You can practice it from anywhere in the world, and with the Internet and your computer as partners, you are connected to potential entrepreneurial opportunities, investments, brokers and products with the click of the mouse.

Let's take a look now under the hem of what is in the Barter World. I hope the following pages will open some avenues of practical interest for you.

Thanks and good luck,
Robert W. Steele

Ron Moser

Foreward

Wherever we look, whatever we hear today, all over America and beyond, we are inundated with four letter words and we all know how nasty four letter words can be. However, when it comes to bartering and exchanging, my first thoughts go to something we were told by Bob Steele years ago.

"C A S H " is a four letter word! Steele told us way back then, "for every offer you get for cash, there are most likely a HUNDRED offers available that aren't." And, yes, those words are today just as true as they were way back then. There are so many transactions waiting to happen all over America today that WON'T, simply because most people, professionals and non, cannot see or hear anything that doesn't contain that disgusting four letter word, CASH!

They'll say, "that won't work here!" But it will, and it will everywhere. In fact, I'm currently helping someone complete the sale of a home that's been sitting here waiting over three years for an offer for over $300,000 in our city not affected by the recession as deeply as the rest of the country, but can now be finalized with a transaction that includes a $150,000 note secured by ROCK, an acceptable four letter word. Decorative rocks sell in the landscaping business here for $3,500 and up.

How can that be done? By learning through education provided right here, right now in this book! All you need is an open mind, no killer thoughts, brainstorming, with self and/or others, BENEFITS for all involved, and proper use of the tools Steele is sharing with you herein. Without these teachings I would not have become an SEC, and when I was told I was ready to become one, I knew I had learned that CASH was not the only way to do a deal, and so it came to be.

So, look at this book. Try it, you'll like it. LIKE is another acceptable kind of four letter word.

To paraphrase Chet Allen, like Bob another SEC Legend, I am deeply honored to write this forward.

Ron Moser 5/26/10

Is it CASH, or Kind, that bends thy ear,
be that the case, no romance doth near.
Forget not, that CASH is a 4 letter word,
but the Batmobile made Catwoman purr.

STRATEGY 276

Barter – The One-On-One Trade for Goods or Services

Barter has been ongoing since the beginning of time, but in the U.S. we often equate it to the days when the majority of our population lived in rural settings and we were predominately an agrarian society. As we moved across the country, from east to west, barter became fur trading for supplies and blankets, and cattle for guns and ammunition.

SITUATION	The farmer traded two mules for a horse. This later developed into the phrase, "horse trader." Back then in our family one of our family members would capture wild horses, break them and use them for trading. They traded chickens or eggs to the doctor or canned fruit & vegetables to the smithy in the forge. The school teacher received, in trade, her room and board as part of her salary at my grandfather's house. Gold and silver were the coin of the realm. It always retained its value and was the only monetary exchange vehicle, everything else was barter. Indians and mountain men trapped the beaver and traded their furs for supplies and settlers traded everything they had to move west and homestead. Homesteading was a tough life and many of them traded their homesteads, after they had proven them up and owned the title, for cattle from ranchers who accumulated the homestead and put together large cattle ranches. Barter morphed into exchange as we know it today, but barter has not and probably never will go away. It is a marvelous tool that our citizenry has forgotten how to use. Those who remember and keep the art alive will always prosper because they do not have to go to fiat currency to live.
NOTES	Horse trading connotes someone who is perhaps just a little fast or always looking for an advantage. In barter you want to realize that there are two sides to the trade: One, what you are leaving and two, what you are receiving. Motivation can be on either side of the barter. If you are trading fruit off your trees that is getting over-ripe and ready to fall and be lost, your motivation is different than it is still early in the growing season. As long as you get what you want, don't be overly concerned if you "paid a little too much."

STRATEGY 277

The Birth of the Trade Credit

My mother, as a young girl on a farm in North Dakota, churned butter every week, which was traded to the store in town for a credit that could be spent at the store.

SITUATION

The general store became the barter capital of small towns. In the field, companies headed by men like John Jacob Astor, in the fur trading business, actually took the general store into the wilderness and set up trading posts in order to trade with the trappers.

Fortunes were made in barter then and now.

The trapper received a credit with which he could trade within the store.

The Indians started to trade their furs and then they started trading other things, be it corn or blankets. The fur traders then turned into trading post and later mercantile stores.

As we moved more into the cities the agrarian barter systems started to phase out and by the time of the industrial revolution we were working in factories and the majority were off the farms and people no longer had something with which to barter.

The trading post and general store gave birth to the entrepreneur that could still see the benefits of the barter system and small barter transactions.

Most of our citizenry knows little about barter. They are content to look for a job when barter is available for anyone to use at any time. Everyone has a day of labor they could trade, they simple don't realize it.

In the 1970s the government eliminated the gold backing to the currency, which became fiat, and they started printing money in huge quantities. Who needed barter when cash was on every corner? Barter almost disappeared from our national stage.

Trade credits are backed by the integrity of the person or company you are dealing with.

In the small town it was usually someone you dealt with repetitively.

In the field the trapper might make a pilgrimage once or twice a year for barter purposes but still they usually were dealing with the same company and a relationship was established.

This changes as we move into commercial Trade Credits.

STRATEGY 278

Trade Credits #2 – Basic Trade Club

Fiat Trade Credits - two steps above basic barter.

SITUATION	Abel has a service that he sells. This can be anything: Doctor, lawyer, book-keeper, secretarial, laborer, photographer, etc. Baker sells something. This also can be anything: Shoes, cars, hats, airplanes, food in a restaurant, etc. Charley produces something. This also can be anything: Plastic, pencils, dresses, etc. Don owns a motel and sells rooms. Charley would like to trade his pencils for the food in Baker's restaurant but Charley doesn't want the pencils.
POSSIBLE SOLUTION	Enter the Barter Club Entrepreneur. He forms a club where members can use the club's Trade Credits to complete what amounts to three-way trades. The club facilitates the trade and acts as a fiat storehouse of value. A fee is charged by the entrepreneur, e.g., 10% in cash on each transaction. Charley joins the Barter Club. Now other club members who are in the club and have credits in their accounts can buy pencils from Charley using credits in their accounts. When Charley has credits in his account, he can then go to other trade club members and buy their goods and services, e.g., food in Baker's restaurant, with the credits.
CONCLUSION	Charley eats in Baker's restaurant. A three-way delayed exchange is made.
NOTE	Risk: Barter Club Trade Credits are fiat. You should acknowledge this risk or don't play. How do fiat Trade Credits come into being? The same way U.S. dollars or any other fiat currency arrives, from thin air.

STRATEGY 279

Three Options: Direct Barter, Direct Trade Credit, or Trade Club Trade Credits

There are three ways to approach barter: Through direct barter, creating your own Trade Credits, or using the barter club Trade Credits. There are no reasons why you cannot use them all.

SITUATION	Sally has a photography business. She does portraits and weddings as her basic business. She would like to increase her business.	Remember when you are entering the barter arena that what you want to do is to increase your business. You do not want to change existing cash paying customers to barter customers as you still want the cash business. When you are trading photography work it is a low expense/high margin asset and lends itself to barter. Pete's business in automobiles is different. It is high expense, low margin. That is why we offered cash to go with the Trade Credits.
POSSIBLE SOLUTIONS	**Direct Barter:** She knows that Jan, her CPA/accountant, is getting married. She offers to barter $1,000 worth of wedding pictures for prepaid accounting services. Jan agrees and the barter is made. Each party maintains its own records and signs an agreement, or often it is just an informal agreement. **Direct Trade Credits**: She likes the idea of expanding her photography through the use of direct barter Trade Credits. She creates her own Trade Credits in $500 and $1,000 increments. She advertises to trade these and she also offers them into the marketplace in various trades. For example, she wants to buy a used van for $15,000 from Pete at the auto dealership. She offers Pete $10,000 cash and $5,000 in pre-paid Trade Credits for photography work. Pete agrees and later uses the pre-paid photography credits as bonuses for his salespeople and for wedding pictures for his granddaughter. Pete had never used her services before so she created a new client as well as expanding her immediate business. **Barter Club Trade Credits:** She joined a major Barter Club and immediately started to do Trade Credit business with club members she had never done business with before. Google Barter Clubs: you will find hundreds of Barter Clubs to use.	

STRATEGY 280

Crop Futures Strategy

If the commodities brokers can use futures so can the real estate brokers or principals. There is literally no end to how far this particular strategy can go. It is truly open-ended.

<table>
<tr>
<td>COMMODITIES MARKET</td>
<td>Futures can be used by those wanting to protect a buying or selling price for some time in the future. The farmer growing corn can pre-sell his crops at a price now to insure the price in the future, if she thinks the market may go down. In this instance the futures are a hedge.</td>
<td rowspan="3">Building value $2,000,000.

$2,000,000 in tomatoes delivered at $400,000 worth per year. In this transaction the building was at a fixed price and the tomato price floated with the market. It can be designed both ways, either fixed or floating on either side.

This futures formula is a derivative of the Creation of Wealth formula, see Volume 1, plus it also moves into the stock market or commodities market, see Volume 11.</td>
</tr>
<tr>
<td>COMBINING WITH</td>
<td>It can also be structured so it guarantees a delivery some time in the future even though the price may change to a new market price but the delivery of product is guaranteed.</td>
</tr>
<tr>
<td>REAL ESTATE MARKET</td>
<td>Actual example from our files: Client exchanged tomatoes from a farm in California for a Big Box Building (old White Front Store) in Oregon that was leased. It was for a floating quantity of tomatoes delivered to the crop buyer, selected by the farmer, at the rate of 20% of the building's value per year for the first year plus the next four years. The building price was delivered at a fixed price but the tomatoes were delivered at market value at the time that their delivery was made direct to the wholesaler on behalf of the building owner.

Building owner gets fixed price on building. If price of tomatoes goes up during the coming four years, the tomato farmer makes additional profit because he delivers fewer tomatoes. He would lose if the price drops because he would have to deliver more. Tomato farmer had no interest to pay on loan by negotiations. There was actually a small $200,000 loan on the building which was paid off out of the first delivery of tomatoes.</td>
</tr>
</table>

STRATEGY 281

Trade Credit for Hotels

Specific hotel/motel design for long term guests so part of the cash requirement is met.

SITUATION	1. Abel owns a 200-unit hotel and is running 50% vacant (100 rooms). Rooms average $300 per night. 2. He estimates his transient tax and maid service costs at about $15% or approximately $50 per night. 3. There is a very soft rental market 4. These certain cash costs must be met for each guest in order for the hotel to be viable.	Price:	$ 300 ea
POSSIBLE SOLUTION	1. Discuss the problem with a Trade Credit broker. 2. It is decided that the Trade Credit broker will design 50 Trade Credits, one each on 50 different rooms, based on a price of $250 per night each or $90,000 for a three year period. These will be aimed at corporate users or individuals who would like to live in the hotel full time for the three year period. Must comply with zoning. User of each T/C will have to add $50 per night or $1,500 per month. 3. Exchange the Trade Credits.	Price: Nights: Each Year: 3 years 50 T/C	$ 250 ea 360 yr $ 90,000 $270,000 $ 13,500,000
CONCLUSION	1. $90,000 in Trade Credits are now exchanged into any asset agreeable to owner of hotel or motel complex: Examples, corporate lettered stock, land, advertising or, ? 2. Trade Credits are good for three years.	Users:	Pay $1,500/ mo in cash & $7,500/mo in trade
NOTES	1. Users get hotel living at a price they can afford 2. Hotel gets vacant space occupied. 3. Trade credit broker charges for design of credits and trading them.		

STRATEGY 282

Trade Credit for Assisted Living

Specific design for Assisted Living complex so part of cash requirement is met.

SITUATION	Abel owns a 200-unit assisted living complex and has 50 vacant units. One reason he feels locked to his price is a fear that if he lowered prices for new tenants, he would have to lower his existing prices for units already rented at $6,000 per month. There is a very soft rental market.There are cash costs that must be met for each tenant.	Price:	$6,000 ea
POSSIBLE SOLUTION	Discuss the problem with an Trade Credit broker. It is decided that the Trade Credit broker will design 25 Trade Credits, one each on 25 different rooms, based on a price of $5,000 each for a three year period. User of Trade Credits will have to add $1,000 cash per month. Broker charges $4,500 (1%) for design of credits. Exchange Trade Credits.	Price/mo: Months: Each TC: 25 TCs:	$5,000 36 $180,000 $4,500,000
CONCLUSION	T/C user trades $180,000 in any asset agreeable to owner of assisted living complex from land to personal notes. It could be a percentage of ownership interest in user's home, an assignment of insurance, etc. Trade Credits are good for three years.	Users:	Pay $1,000 per month cash and $5,000 per month in trade
NOTES	User gets assisted living at a price they can afford. Assisted Living facility gets vacant space occupied. Trade credit broker charges 10% fee for making trades. (See also Strategy #238 in Volume 10 for personal note tied to insurance policy.)		

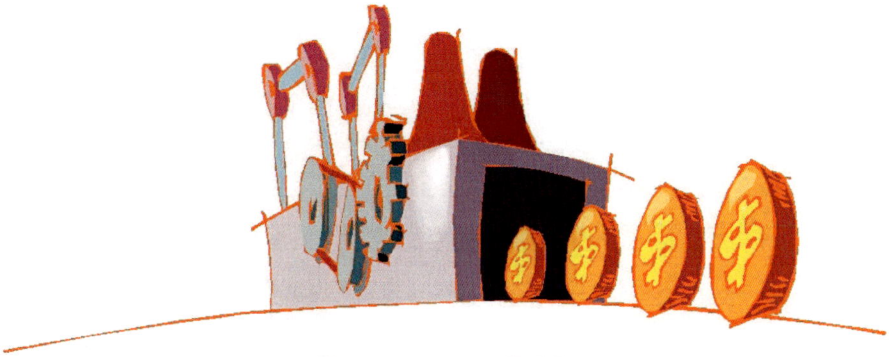

STRATEGY 283

Printing Your Own Money #1

Legally and Ethically Designing Your Trade Credits

Contracting to: You will deliver	Products: Services Labor Futures Vacancy Range: 2 for 1 Dinners $1 M In prepaid atty's fees $10 M Vacant Hotel Rooms	Price: At what price Straight trade Cash to be added for taxes or other items	Total Value: Increments Shipping Charges Delivery or pick up
Time Frame	Start Time Exceptions (maybe holidays)	Does time change price? Outlaw 1 to 20+ yrs	Outlaw Date and/or Extension on time for charge?
Be Aware	Accounting Control Holder in due course Assignments	Chrg for Assignment? Chrg. For Inflation?	Counterfeiting
Romance	Tell your sales story	Assign value to Assignee	Graphics
Breakage	Be aware of this: Like companies plan on over-selling airplane seats	Estimate 0 to ?	Extension on time for charge? Can they extend the time limit for a fee?
Fees	2% to 50%	Cash, or can be paid in kind	Design before you start
Charge for Design	$100 to $5,000	Design both in examples	How paid
Marketing	Local	National	International
Languages	English	Spanish	Mandarin Chinese

If this is in a seminar setting, design live Trade Credits and exchange same in actual situations and a live marketing session. This an extremely exciting way to show the value and usage of Trade Credits. Have each class member design his own Trade Credits without help, just using the above as a guide. Then to have a small marketing session in whch they exchange trade credits with each other. You will be amazed at the business that is done.

STRATEGY 284

$250 Trade Credit©

G.S. Consultancy

We specializing in helping companies and individuals protect themselves from the effects of the Falling Dollar.

"Projection: Over 30% of the people will lose the majority of their assets in the coming recession!"

Wake up! Stop listening to the spin. Protect yourself. Our company is one possible solution for you. Please phone for consulting service. "Inflation is under control," Right?

Food prices up 44% last year.

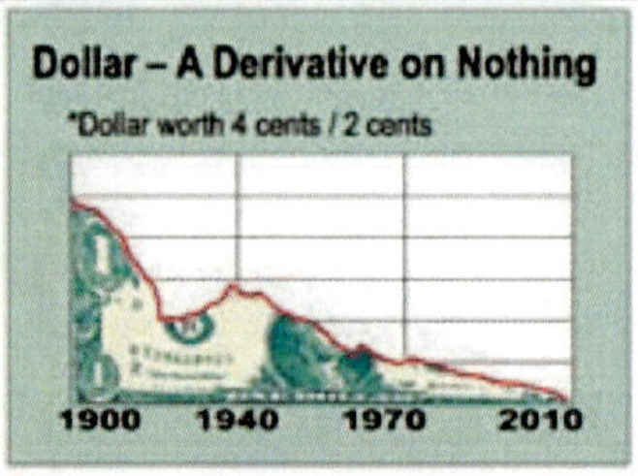

If you have your wealth in fixed dollar denominated assets, e.g. cash, CDs, bonds, etc., you are 100% at risk. A one hour consultation might save you one year learning curve and time is your enemy.

	Past Price	Price Now	% increase to date	Projected Price
USA				
Gasoline, per gallon	.09 cents	$3.00	Increase 3,333 %	$50.00 / gal.
Bread, per loaf	.10 cents	$2.00	Increase 2,000 %	$50.00 / loaf
Dinner for two	$1.50	$60.00	Increase 4,000 %	$500.00 dinner for two
EUROPE (in dollars)				
Fare on London Tube	1.5 cents	$7.80	Increase 52,000 %	$150,00 / fare
One Dinner, Rathskeller	.40 cents	$25.00	Increase 6,250 %	$250.00 / dinner
Pantheon Hotel, Paris	$3.00 / night	$219.00	Increase 7,300 %	$3,000.00 / night
Admission to Acropolis	.30 cents	$15.60	Increase 5,000 %	$200.00 / admission

SAMPLE TRADE CREDIT

Number _______ Date Activated _______ Expiration Date _______

This Trade Credit, when properly authorized and exercised, entitles bearer to $250.00 worth of telephone consulting service by G.S. Consultancy subject to terms and conditions and by appointment.

TERMS AND CONDITIONS:

1. Expiration date means that this Trade Credit (T/C) expires on this date and can no longer be used.
2. Any change of ownership via assignment in this T/C is to be processed through G.S. Consultancy (GS).
3. There is a 5% transfer and/or processing fee when T/C is exercised by bearer or is transferred via assignment to others.
4. All cash expenses incurred by GS in providing this consulting service, if any, shall be paid by bearer of T/C.
5. The consulting service hourly rate shall be the standard rate charged by G.S. at the time this T/C is exercised by bearer.
6. This T/C is activated when signed and dated by authorized personnel of G.S.
7. Consult your attorney and tax consultant about the ramifications of using Trade Credits.

Authorized	Bearer Check: Exercising ☐ Assigning ☐	Transfer and/or Assign Trade Credit to:
Date Activated: / Expiration:	Name:	Name:
	Address:	Address:
G.S. Consultancy		
By:		
Signature:	Phone:	Phone:
Address, Email, & Phone:	Email:	Email:
	Date:	Date:
	Signature:	Signature:

STRATEGY 285

Printing Your Own Money #2

Legally and Ethically Designing Your Trade Credits

Front and back side of a sample Trade Credit, 2 per page.
Put 2 fronts on one side and 2 backs on the other side.

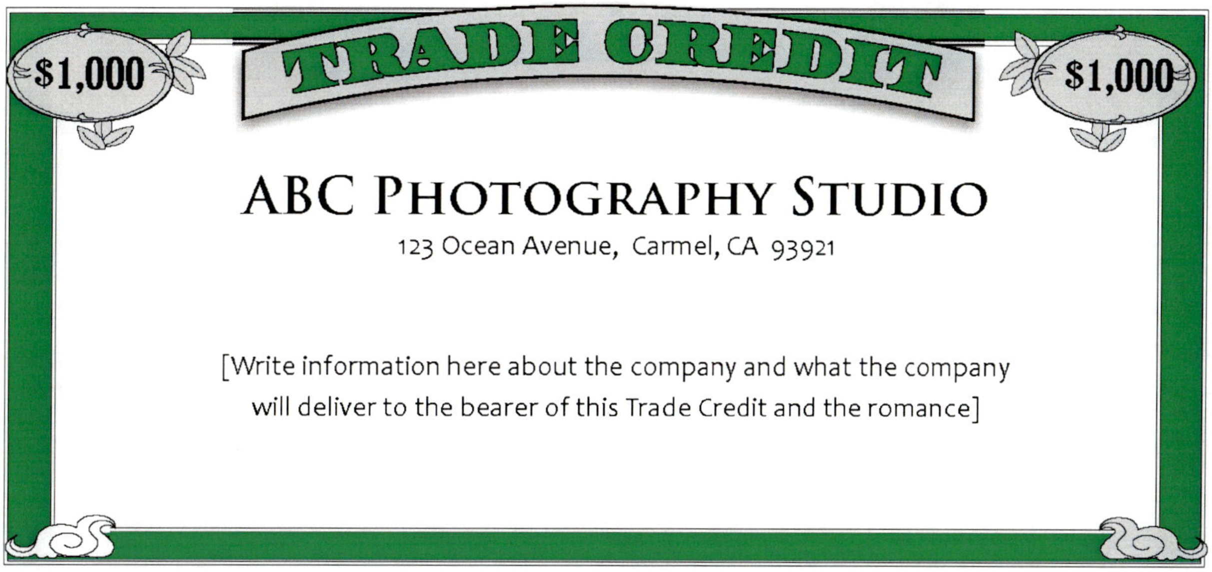
$1,000 TRADE CREDIT $1,000

ABC PHOTOGRAPHY STUDIO

123 Ocean Avenue, Carmel, CA 93921

[Write information here about the company and what the company will deliver to the bearer of this Trade Credit and the romance]

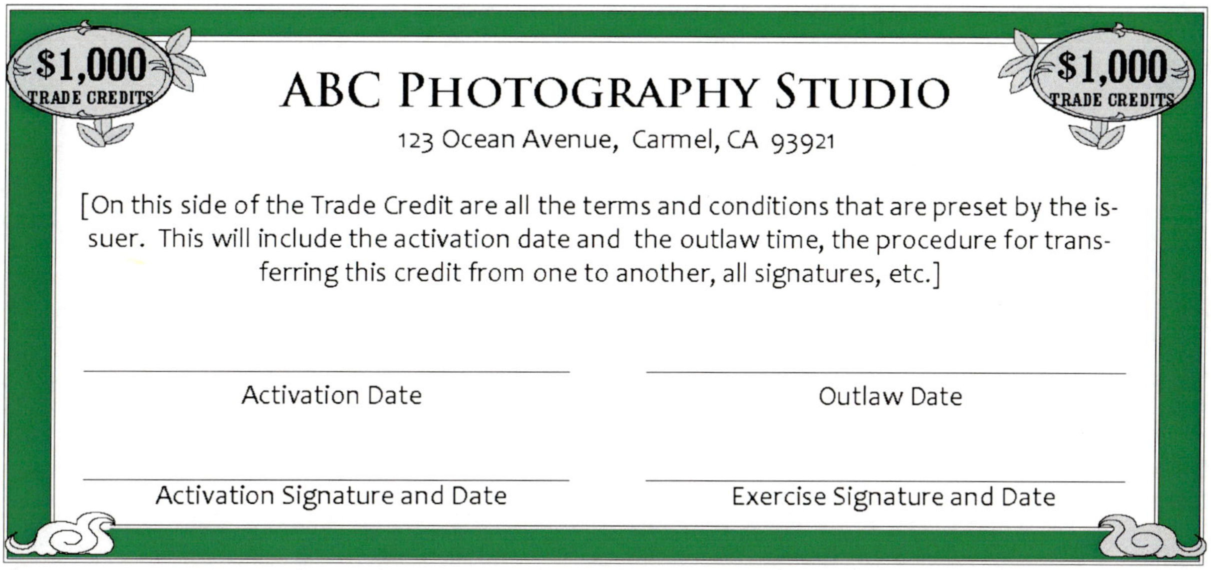
$1,000 TRADE CREDITS

ABC PHOTOGRAPHY STUDIO

$1,000 TRADE CREDITS

123 Ocean Avenue, Carmel, CA 93921

[On this side of the Trade Credit are all the terms and conditions that are preset by the issuer. This will include the activation date and the outlaw time, the procedure for transferring this credit from one to another, all signatures, etc.]

Activation Date | Outlaw Date

Activation Signature and Date | Exercise Signature and Date

STRATEGY 286

Printing Your Own Money #3

Legally and Ethically Designing Your Trade Credits

Design an outline herewith for a Trade Credit that you will deliver on. Use your imagination but make all the contractual portions exactly right. Design one on a page or two on a page.

Trillions of dollars in assets are wasted. Can you capture and use some of these via the use of Trade Credits or Direct Barter? Chet Allen's observation from Volume 10, *Half the World is Vacancy*: "About 40% of the world's hotel rooms remain empty every night. Airlines are running about 65% full. There are millions of square feet of vacant industrial, office and retail space. And then we can add in unbilled hours for attorneys, architects, engineers, doctors, dentists and other professionals. Thousands of freight cars, trucks and cargo ships are deadheading every day. Newspapers, magazines, radio and TV stations have capacities far beyond what they are using—all can in some way be bartered and/or turned into Trade Credits for exchange."

See the author's Strategy #169 *Reversal Brainstorm* in Volume 7, *The Art and Science of Brainstorming*. Design a Trade Credit for yourself or a client. Design it backwards, herewith, the first time. Set your own parameters, e.g., "I would like to add $1,000,000 worth of additional business to my operation via the use of Trade Credits." Now what can you design that will accomplish that target?

Write ten ideas in the space below:

STRATEGY 287

International Trade Clubs

There are several trade clubs that are international in scope. Some are very sophisticated and ingenious in their answer to the Central Banks of the world and their overuse of their privilege of printing money. Again, we need to note that all fiat currency and Trade Credits have a risk ratio.

SITUATION	It is often difficult to exchange items internationally, as there are many forms of trade barriers. By converting an asset to Trade Credits and trading the credits for things in another country, some of these barriers may be circumvented. A Swiss company that is about seven years old has designed a different model and is doing well internationally. It makes Trade Credit loans on vacant lands.	As there are trillions in assets that are unused then not only direct barter but Trade Credits can have a major play.
POSSIBLE SOLUTIONS	In general, it will make a Trade Credit loan up to 50% on the land. They leave the land in the company, so indirectly the Trade Credits that are issued do have some backing. The owners of the Trade Credits can now exchange them anywhere in the world where they can find acceptance. International Trade Clubs are free to join and there are no annual dues. Members are only charged when they do something. They enroll real estate brokers into their system and they are very careful who they allow to join. According to their pronouncements, they completed $7 billion in barter and trade transactions in 2008. They originated their program by purchasing a bank and the bank handles all the accounting, which adds a modicum of stability to their company. In our opinion, the International Trade Credit business has just barely been touched. There is a huge opportunity in this arena.	Countries use their central banks to print fiat currency whereas many countries have minerals and natural resources that could be backing for direct Trade Credits. It is like freeing up the sculpture that is already within the marble.

STRATEGY 288

Starting & Running a Trade Club

A friend of mine is a professional mini-storage person with many mini-units. He told me recently that when he first started building minis in Dallas, he thought there would be a market for perhaps 15 mini-warehouse units. He said there were hundred of units there now, and the market still had room. It is the same way with Trade Credits. There are so many assets that vanish or are idle that there is really no end to the opportunity for the use of Trade Credits. Everyone reading this book can offer some sort of a direct trade.

SITUATION	It is surprising to me that, whereas so many cities are suffering from a short fall in revenue, they have not looked into the area of barter and Trade Credits.	If you get involved in owning or running a Trade Credit company, be sure you get good tax and legal advice. There is also a national association of Trade Credit companies complete with a lobbyist in Washington.
POSSIBLE SOLUTIONS	Every major company could have a Trade Credit division. It makes you wonder why Boeing Airplane Company (and the like) don't have barter purchasing agents. Even small companies can design products aimed at the barter market. They should be a low cost of manufacturing and higher margin. Take, for instance, the book you are reading. It is one a series of 12 Volumes which took about a year to write. The set of E-books via download will be a good barter item. Once written (manufactured) the cost of adding pages and strategies to E-books is minimal. A set of books makes a good barter item. I have found an excellent way to grow a small barter or Trade Credit company: I used to hold a barter meeting every Saturday morning at a local hotel. The participants could use only our club's Trade Credits. These meetings grew from 10 people to 75 and up and products and services traded ran from Aunt Minnie's dish set to house painting and putting in swimming pools, as well as houses that builders were stuck with.	

STRATEGY 289

Breakage in Trade Credits

I don't think anyone can say for certain how much the breakage will amount to in any one Trade Credit issuing. It will vary. I have heard numbers like 30% and 40%, and I am sure, at least to some extent, it depends on the nature and value of the credits.

SITUATION	The dictionary denotation of the word Breakage is: **break • age** n. 1. The act of breaking. 2. A quantity broken. 3. Loss or damage as a result of breaking. 4. A commercial allowance for loss or damage. It is definition #4 that we are discussing when discussing Trade Credit breakage. A certain percentage of Trade Credits are simply lost. They go out into the world and just disappear. From the standpoint of the creator of the Trade Credits, this results in a front-end profit in that one side of the contract is left unfilled. The Trade Credits outlaw before they are used or collected.	In the case of hotel rooms the breakage results in a small savings of the cost of cleaning the rooms, etc. It also means that you can oversell in the creation of some Trade Credits just like the airlines over-book seats on a flight, as they are calculating that a certain number of people will not show up. Therefore, in order to take advantage of your knowledge, you should create $1,300,000 in Trade Credits and expect that only $1,000,000 will be collected.
POSSIBLE SOLUTIONS	This is telling us that if we created and traded $1,000,000 worth of Trade Credits on rooms in a hotel we owned, and that if these credits were good for a period of three years, that by the time the three years rolled by, perhaps only $700,000 of the Trade Credits had been submitted at the check-in counter. $300,000 credits then would have expired without being used. Our breakage then would be then 30% in that instance. You can use a breakage calculation in almost every direct Trade Credit creation. Some portion of the credits will not be used.	

STRATEGY 290

Outlaw Dates on Trade Credits

The Outlaw Date on a Trade Credit is the date after which the benefits of the Trade Credit cannot be collected. The date is set by the creator of the Trade Credit and is acknowledged by the recipient with acceptance of the credit.

SITUATION	Once the Trade Credit is issued it becomes a liability of the maker.
POSSIBLE SOLUTION	In the instance where hotel room Trade Credits are issued that have an Outlaw date of three years, that is a liability against the hotel for that period of time. If the hotel should be sold during that time, the new owner would have the liability of those Trade Credits against the hotel so some allowance or negotiation would have to be a part of the selling package. If there is no Outlaw Date established, then it is a forever liability against the hotel until the credits are used. If you issued Trade Credits for seats in a football stadium they might be good for one year. They might not be good for any play-off games, etc. You can make the Outlaw Date as short as you wish or as exclusive as you wish. You will try to set it so it has good value for a user, as you want to trade for things that are meaningful to you. If they are too restrictive you will not be able to exchange them. You can also Outlaw anyone using them except the party they are issued too, e.g., in the instance of an attorney, you would want the right to approve the client and the application.

STRATEGY 291

Holder in Due Course of Trade Credits

Trade Credits are often assigned to new beneficiaries. Depending on the nature of these transfers they can be informal or formal, requiring that the old credit be sent in and a new one issued to the new beneficiary, registered, etc.

SITUATION	Often Trade Credits are issued in an over-trade exchange. By this I mean that the issuer is often interested in getting a quantity of Trade Credits into the market and the one receiving the Trade Credits cannot make use of all that is received.
POSSIBLE SOLUTION	For example, a hotel owner exchanges $1,000,000 in hotels rooms (in $1,000 Trade Credits) to a radio station for advertising over a one year period. The radio station cannot use $1,000,000 in hotel rooms within, say, a three year outlaw date. It is the intent of the radio company to advertise these hotel rooms through their associate station in another city for 50 cents on the dollar. As they are sold, these Trade Credits are assigned to the new beneficiaries via endorsements. The new owners of the Trade Credits are the ultimate users. However, the radio station might be negotiating for the purchase of some new equipment and offer $250,000 in the hotel credits as part of their offer to purchase. The new equipment owners might, in turn, transfer some of the credits to employees as bonuses or Christmas presents. They are all holders in due course. The $1,000,000 might be offered in exchange for some vacant lots or used as a down payment into a $4,000,000 building. There is no end to the offers that can be made or to the motivations of others in accepting the credits. If you put them in the exchange market, you will get offers and usually in an over-trade position.

STRATEGY 292

Trade Credits Can Represent a Delayed Multiple Exchange

Google says it has 28,600,000 web sites about Trade Credits. If you are into exchanging or creative business of any form, is there just maybe something in this Trade Credit thing that you should know about?

SITUATION #1	On a single piece of paper you write, "The bearer of this instrument is entitled to one eight-hour day of physical labor from the undersigned." And you sign it. This is a Trade Credit. You trade this document to me for a sack of flour. I have your Trade Credit. I trade it to Jane for painting a room in my house. Jane now has your Trade Credit. Jane wants some yard work done. She calls you and you work a day in her yard and she gives you back the Trade Credit, marked paid.	Trade credits can be very simple or they can move right on up the line to being very complex. While a one page labor Trade Credit is sufficient it might take a 10 page Trade Credit to establish a one year credit for the use of a hotel room in a 5 star facility. Can you perform on $1,000,000 in Trade Credits or 100 times that amount? They are the epitome of the Creation of Wealth formula.
SITUATION #2	You are an attorney and you charge $500 per hour or $4,000 per day. You make up 10 Trade Credits, each for one day of your time (total 10 x $4,000 = $40,000) and you trade it to me for the down payment into a little $200,000 rental house. I trade your Trade Credit on for a used car, vacation time in Hawaii and a vacant lot, plus I use a day of your time (one Trade Credit) to get my affairs in order.	
SITUATION #3	You are a farmer growing corn. You issue five Trade Credits, each good for $100,000 worth of corn at market value. The first Trade Credit is due in one year, the second one in two years, etc. You have a total of $500,000 in Trade Credits to trade and you trade them for a yacht. The Trade Credit due in five yeas might be multiple traded a half dozen times before it is time to collect.	
SOLUTION	Is there any end to this wealth creation? No. Is there risk? Yes. Anyone can die at any time. Accept the risk or don't play. NOTE: See Volume our special book on Barter & Trade Credits.	

STRATEGY 293

International Trade Credits #2

$100,000 to $1,000,000 minimum sizes

In a marketplace where things are really backed up, as we are experiencing in 2010, and because there are a myriad of reasons why it is so congested, it is a good time to assess your position and the options open to you.

By the time you read this the correction may have already happened, but someplace in the world humans have caused some other catastrophic problem(s). Unwinding problems can result in nice profits.

We are showing the face design of this Trade Credit to emphasize the flexibility of using credits. This one was designed for a specific purpose and was used for assets exceeding $100,000. There is usually no end to the creative ways these Trade Credits may be structured. For instance, you could create a $1,000,000 Trade Credit that allows the holder to create sub-Trade Credits for smaller denominations off of it and so forth.

Trade Credits are also an excellent way to cross borders as they soften, not circumvent, the various currency issues.

A little creativity can open up tremendous opportunities.

STRATEGY 294

Trade Credits to Help Fill Shopping Center Vacancies

It takes a little ingenuity but it may pay off with a full shopping center.

SITUATION	1. We are currently in a situation where the economic forecasts become gloomier, and the potential recovery date predictions go farther into the future and the need for interim solutions intensifies. 2. Dozens of our best known retailers are going under, leaving hundreds of thousands of mall square footage dark. 3. Will this result in hundreds of shopping centers going under? Very possibly.	Remember, you do not have to spend the Trade Credits just on the shopping centers or office buildings. There are all kinds of other things that can be acquired from dental services to resort vacations. At one time in history, barter and exchanging made up a part of everyone's daily life. It is conceivable that those times might be returning. Being receptive to this change could prove beneficial.
POSSIBLE SOLUTION	1. One of our associates owns shopping centers and office buildings, and has managed to use "Trade Credits" for services or other opportunities. 2. The Trade Credit tenants may make the difference between holding on to an asset, or losing it in hard times. He keeps them afloat in hard times by accepting Trade Credits in lieu of cash rents, then spending the credits for services. His shopping centers probably would be 50% vacant without the Trade Credit tenants, and although he can't pay the property taxes with Trade Credits, he is able to keep the parking lot clean, lawns cut, and plumbing fixed by using contractors willing to take Trade Credits 3. Many times you can trade direct for services yourself, but sometimes it is better to employ the services of Trade Credit companies.	

STRATEGY 295

Barter & Trade Credits on the Internet

Companies abound to do business with in the field of barter and Trade Credits.

the barter company *barter is smarter.*™
www.thebartercompany.com

BizXchange®
Improving Business with Trade

ITEX
CONNECT • TRADE • SAVE

PARTNERS
ADP Small Business Services
MasterCard
Sysco iCare

Mister Sparky
Electrical Work on FULL BARTER!
301.449.9440
Montgomery County, P.G. County, Washington DC

BarterNews
The Official Journal of the Reciprocal Trade Industry
Our purpose at BarterNews is
to provide our readers with a storehouse
of information, ideas & contacts.

IRTA
Serving the Modern
Trade and Barter Industry

STRATEGY 296

Becoming a Trade Credit & Barter Broker

Whereas it has been estimated that well over 50% of the real estate brokers will fail out of the business during this economic depression, it might be wise to look at some of the other avenues available by becoming a specialist in the barter arena.

SITUATION	Almost every business can use make use of barter talent.	My guess is a Barter Broker could list $1,000,000 per day in Trade Credits wanting to be exchanged. Even though there are thousands of web sites relating to barter, the surface is barely scratched. And there never will be a substitute for the "Starbucks Effect." People like to associate with people. A Barter Broker will be met with open doors.
POSSIBLE SOLUTION	Many people who deliver a professional service, such as attorneys and CPAs, have unbilled hours. Just a 200-unit motel with rooms at $100 per night, and averaging the U.S. standard of 40% vacancy, has over $9,000,000 in vacancy loss in a three year period. A loss that never shoes up on its P/L. How can they not have a Barter Broker in the mix when this is a vanishing asset? At a chamber of commerce meeting, every person in attendance represents an opportunity for a Barter Broker to be of assistance. Google resorts in the South Pacific and everyone has an opportunity for a person who understands the ins and outs of barter. Dead head railroad cars, ships, boats and planes all have need for the person who knows barter and can fill their unused vacancy. Designing direct Trade Credits is an art that can be learned and utilized to open up all kinds of economic opportunities for a Barter Broker had his clients.	

STRATEGY 297

Trade Credit Trade

This is a very good method of getting your personal or direct Trade Credits into the market milieu.

SITUATION	You have a photography studio and you have developed your direct Trade Credits in the denomination of $1,000.	As you spread these out you are contacting people who have not used your services before, and will perhaps be generating new clients.
POSSIBLE SOLUTION	Either on a personal basis or under the auspices of a Barter Broker, you make contact with 10 other entrepreneurs who have direct Trade Credits for their businesses. These include a dentist, an electrician, a plumber, a florist, two motels, an artist, a private school, an attorney and an accountant. This "team" agrees to trade $10,000 in Trade Credits to each person in the team. This can be done on a one-on-one basis, but using ten makes the point very clear. You issue $100,000 of your photography Trade Credits and $10,000 is delivered to each member on your team. They in turn each issue $10,000 in their Trade Credits to you. You now have $100,000 in other Trade Credits from 10 separate sources. When you are negotiating now to obtain something you might want (e.g., a car, a vacation, etc.), you have not only your own photography Trade Credits to offer, but 10 others as well. Your chances of obtaining what you want just went up.	It is like a form of advertising but you are not really paying for it as you are receiving something in return.

STRATEGY 298

Multiple Barter Trades

This is a very good method of getting your personal or direct Trade Credits into the market milieu.

SITUATION	The basic technique is to start with one barter item and a client who is looking to move that item into something else.	International barter is easier than international real estate.
POSSIBLE SOLUTION	For instance, he might start with $10,000,000 in used commercial airliners that are sitting on the sidelines as the market has changed. ***The In-Lieu-Of Formula*** He located a trade for the planes with $10,000,000 in Teak Timber in Costa Rica. ***The In-Lieu-Of Formula*** The teak did not satisfy the owner of the airplanes so the teak is exchanged for $10,000,000 surplus white chocolate on the Ivory Coast of Africa. ***The In-Lieu-Of Formula*** Again the white chocolate is exchange for $10,000,000 in real estate in the State of Washington and this is acceptable to the original owner of the airplanes. Transaction closed.	Every country has a myriad of laws concerning real estate, and there can be rather steep learning curves sometimes in these transactions. Barter on the other hand flows between countries much easier.
NOTE	See: www.worldassetexcahnge.com for a group of Barter Brokers.	

STRATEGY 299
Bartering Education

There are many ways to barter education. It is easier to work with private schools or free enterprise, but there are some ways that barter will work with public or quasi-public education institutions.

SITUATION	One common technique is to enter into an agreement for a donation of assets to a school. Depending on the laws at the time, there are some definite tax advantages.	Thousands of classrooms are vacant, and many teachers are unemployed. At least part of this might be solved via barter. Could a year's tuition be put on a Trade Credit, and exchanged for equipment a school could use? A barter purchasing agent at a private school could exchange millions in education.
POSSIBLE SOLUTION	The schools will call these endowments. They are also referred to as charitable annuity trusts. The form can be a living trust, and in some instances the donor may retain the cash flow from a donated parcel of real estate for his lifetime, and on down to another generation. In the private sector all kinds of opportunities are available. Private schools have a great deal of latitude with which to work and barter. Private seminar companies often have barter programs. Book companies often have hundreds of books that could be bartered if they knew how to get them distributed.	

STRATEGY 300

300 Trade Credits for 12-Volume E-Book Set

$300 VALUE

TRADE CREDIT

"eBooks"

300 Strategies for Making Real Estate and Business Deals

from **Robert W. Steele**

$300 VALUE

These 12 amazing books—from the creative genius of Robert W. Steele and packed with contributions from many of today's leading real estate, financial and trade/barter experts—present the most concise and complete collection of strategies and formulas for today's challenging marketplace.

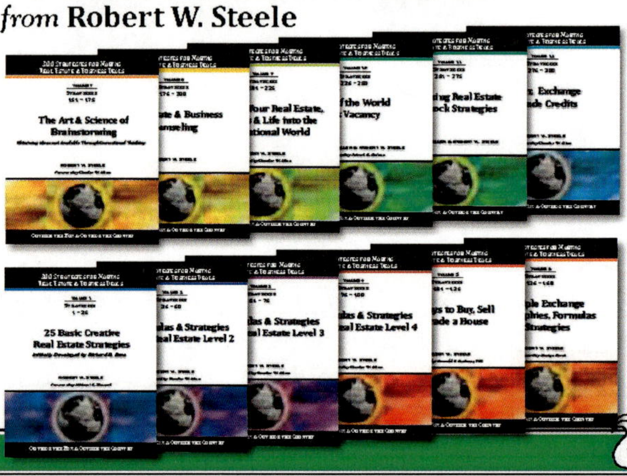

$300 VALUE

$300 VALUE

Number ______ Date Activated ______ Expiration Date ______

This Trade Credit, when properly authorized and exercised, entitles bearer to $250.00 worth of telephone consulting service by G.S. Consultancy subject to terms and conditions and by appointment.

TERMS AND CONDITIONS:

1. Expiration date means that this Trade Credit (T/C) expires on this date and can no longer be used.
2. Any change of ownership via assignment in this T/C is to be processed through G.S. Consultancy (GS).
3. There is a 5% transfer and/or processing fee when T/C is exercised by bearer or is transferred via assignment to others.
4. All cash expenses incurred by GS in providing this consulting service, if any, shall be paid by bearer of T/C.
5. The consulting service hourly rate shall be the standard rate charged by G.S. at the time this T/C is exercised by bearer.
6. This T/C is activated when signed and dated by authorized personnel of G.S.
7. Consult your attorney and tax consultant about the ramifications of using Trade Credits.

Authorized		Bearer Check: Exercising ☐ Assigning ☐	Transfer and/or Assign Trade Credit
Date Activated:	Expiration:	Name:	Name:
		Address:	Address:
G.S. Consultancy			
By:			
Signature:		Phone:	Phone:
Address, Email, & Phone:		Email:	Email:
		Date:	Date:
		Signature:	Signature:

NOTES

MASTER 12-Volume Index – Research & Study Guide

VOLUME 1
25 BASIC CREATIVE REAL ESTATE STRATEGIES
(Initially developed by Richard Reno)

#	TITLE
1	Unpriced
2	Creation of Wealth #1
3	Creation of Wealth #2
4	Creation of Wealth #3
5	Exchange & Buy Back
6	Missouri Waltz
7	REO-Real Estate Owned
8	The Don't Wanter
9	Multiple Exchanges
10	Un-Built Building
11	Share the Wealth
12	How to Play in a Falling Market
13	Brainstorming
14	People in Hell Want Ice water
15	In-Lieu-Of
16	Charlie the Thief
17	Share the Loss
18	Weasel Clause
19	Front Porch
20	Head 'em West 'til Their Hat Floats
21	Broker Cooperation
22	Verbal Exchange Offers Don't Work
23	Counseling & Control
24	Be Flexible
25	Un-priced Exchange Meeting

VOLUME 2
25 FORMULAS & STRATEGIES: CREATIVE REAL ESTATE LEVEL 2

26	Assess Yourself vs.The Deal
27	Are All the Legs in the Room?
28	Blanket Mortgage
29	Consulting Time
30	Front Side, Back Side
31	Front Gate, #1, 2 and 3
32	Tail Gate
33	Pencil Paralysis
34	Zeckendorf – Technique 1
35	Zeckendorf – Technique 2
36	Zeckendorf-Dornbush (SEC) 3
37	Is the Date Right?
38	The Truth is Only Momentary
39	We Create from the Inside Out
40	Who or What is the Most Important in an Exchange?
41	How To Operate at an Exchange Meeting
42	Haw To Write an Exchange Offer
43	Negotiating an Exchange Offer
44	Benefits that Grow
45	Kick 'em in the Kidneys
46	The Extra Value of a User
47	I'll Make You Quit in Negotiations
48	A Zero Means Nothing
49	Monday Morning Escrow Check
50	Trading Sardines & Currency Land

VOLUME 3
25 FORMULAS & STRATEGIES: CREATIVE REAL ESTATE LEVEL 3

51	Trade Percentage of Ownership
52	Funding with Sale of Notes Plus Courage
53	Idea Tracking
54	Taker Tracker Form
55	Baseball Formula
56	Keep the Income in a Trade
57	I'll Pay More Than You Are Asking, If...
58	Move from Defense to Offense
59	Gold & Silver Retirement Plan
60	Stutter Mortgage
61	A Bag, B Bag
62	Definance
63	Personal Notes to Balance Equity
64	Creating a Leasehold
65	Creating a Leasehold in an Exchange or Sale
66	Present the Correct Package for the Market You are In
67	Over-Trade
68	Specialty Clients (Like Users) & Partners
69	The Buyer is a Potential Lender
70	The Tenant Solution
71	Two Plus Three Equals Two
72	Creativity—We Are Going to Need It
73	Liquidate and Diversify
74	The Easiest 3-Way Exchange There Is
75	Prediction Heard: "Only 27% of the Real Estate Fraternity Will Weather the Storm"

VOLUME 4
25 FORMULAS & STRATEGIES: CREATIVE REAL ESTATE LEVEL 4

76 Crop Futures Strategy
77 A Bunt May Be Exactly The Right Play
78 The Performance Mortgage: A Wonderful Tool
79 Performance TD and Note
80 Performance TD and Note #2
81 Sample Performance TD Package
82 Great Formula for Growing a Corporation
83 Inflation
84 Superstar Strategy
85 The Un-Built Company Formula
86 Broker-Brokers & Finders
87 Bag of Silver Strategy & New Variation
88 Gold and Silver Mortgage Insurance
89 Note Payable in Silver (or Gold)
90 Learn to Spend Real Money
91 Linear vs. Spatial Idea Tracking
92 Performance Land Lease
93 Attorney's Strategy—Sit in the Office
94 Burn Bridges Formula—There is No Way Back
95 Turn Vacancies into Wellness Units
96 Counter Trade
97 Multiple Notes in Quantity
98 Derivative #1
99 Derivative #2
100-A Liquifing Mining Assets
100-B U.S. Dollar: A Derivative + Hyper-inflation Tactic

VOLUME 5
25 WAYS TO BUY, SELL OR TRADE A HOUSE

101 Buying or Selling a House for Cash
102 Owner Carry-Back Financing
103 List Below Market In a Buyer's Market
104 "Talk Story" About Buying Houses
105 Don't Drop Your Price If ...
106 Over-Trade a Viable Technique for Moving Equity in a House
107 Strategic Withdrawal (Default) on SFR Loans Not Uncommon
108 Short Sale in SFRs
109 Use Performance Mortages When You Can in Buying SFRs
110 Don't Buy Houses in Your Own Name
111 Use Gold & Silver to Offset (and Eventually Pay Off) Your Loan on an SFR
112 Refinance and Buy Gold & Silver
113 Buy 1,2, 3 or more SFRs to Form an Assisted Living Business
114 Sell, Trade or Donate a Percentage of Interest in Some SFRs
115 Diversify SFRs to Maximize Returns
116 Educate Yourself About Owning SFRs
117 Retirement Ploy Using SFRs
118 You Have 1000 Things (OPS) to Use As Down Payment into SFRs
119 Stretch Geographically to Acquire SFRs
120 SFR Wellness Rentals
121 Become a Teacher/Speaker on SFR Acquisitions
122 Motivation Is A Motivator
123 Sell Out Reverse Cash Flow in Rental SFR
124 Hitting Singles with SFRs
125 Foreign SFRs
125-A When to Buy Real Estate Again

VOLUME 6
MUTLIPLE EXCHANGE PHILOSOPHIES, FOR-MULAS & STRATEGIES

126 Using Multiple Exchange to Facilitate Breaking Up a Partnership
127 When to Formalize Multiple Exchange
128 The Logic of Multiple Exchanges
129 Idea Tracking
130 Selecting First Leg of Multiple Exchanges
131 Multi Exchanges Spawned by Smaller Groups
132 Taker Tracker Form
133 Easiest 3-Way Exchange There Is
134 The In-Lieu-Of Formula
135 Double In-Lieu-Of
136 Trading Into a Performance Mortgage
137 Multiple Exchange on One Property
138 Multiple Exchange Going Up - Zeckendorf
139 Multiple Exchange with Broker Buy Out
140 Missouri Waltz #1
141 Missouri Waltz #2
142 Definance Via a Multiple Exchange
143 Escrow Clockwise - Deeds Counterclockwise
143 A Middle Corp
144 Cowboy Auction — Recreation
145 Cowboy Auction — Professional
146 Credits Represent Delayed Multiple Exchanges
147 BLM Multiple Exchanges — Gov't Exchange
148 Continuous Multiple Exchange
149 Multiple Sale and/or Exchange of Business
150 International Multiple Exchange the Easy Way

VOLUME 7
THE ART & SCIENCE OF BRAINSTORMING

151 The Five Steps to Brainstorming
152 Assessing the Situation
153 Defining the Problem
154 Brainstorming the Problem
155 Use of the Subconscious
156 Using Judgment
157 Signs Following
158 Idea Tracking
159 Killer Thoughts
160 Forced Relationship Technique
161 Best Ideas Come Last
162 Quantity Breeds Quality
163 No Limitation to Creativity
164 Deferment of Judgment
165 Group vs. Individual Ideation
166 The Gordon Technique
167 Don't Drive With Your Brakes On
168 Hitchhiking and More
169 Reversal Brainstorm
170 Set a Deadline When Brainstorming
171 Association of Ideas
172 Dr. Osborn's Rules for Brainstorming
173 The Moveable Brainstorm
174 Diversification in Brainstorming
175 Brainstorming as a Way of Life

VOLUME 8
REAL ESTATE & BUSINESS CONSULTING

176 Consulting and Exchange: History and Evolution
177 Becoming a Counselor Takes Time
178 Information to Obtain Through Counseling
179 The Client Needs to Be Eyeball to Eyeball; Property Can Be Anywhere
180 Other Counseling Techniques
181 Pre-counseling Techniques
182 Counseling Time
183 Counseling and Control
184 Assess Yourself vs. the Deal
185 Setting Fees as a Consultant or Broker
186 Are All Legs Under the Table?
187 The Don't Wanter is a Key to Many Transactions
188 Counseled Clients Tell You *Their* Truth
189 Value, What is It? Is It in the Eye of the Beholder?
190 Value of an Asset in an Exchange
191 Would-Ya-Takes
192 Counseling Is an Individual Thing
193 People in Hell Want Ice Water
194 Head 'em West 'til Their Hat Floats
195 DFTP—Don't Fight The Problem
196 Miscellaneous Counseling
197 Counseling May Unearth a Good User
198 When You Have Exhausted All Possibilities, Remember This: *You Haven't*
199 Entitlement Syndrome: Call a Spade a Spade
200 Counseling for Escrow

VOLUME 9
BLENDING YOUR REAL ESTATE, BUSINESS & LIFE INTO THE INTERNATIONAL WORLD

201 Think International
202 St. Kitts & the Chinese Market
203 Gibraltar & the Spain Market
204 Zimbabwe
205 Vote with Your Feet
206 Falling Dollar
207 Virgin Vacancy Ploy
208 Butterfly Effect
209 Japanese Carry Trade
210 Liquefying Mineral Assets
211 Derivatives #1
212 Derivatives #2
213 Inflation
214 Hyper-inflation #1
215 Hyper-inflation #2
216 You Can't Play Baseball in a Hurricane
217 DMI International Wheel
218 Soft T.D. Exchange
219 Panama Trader Traces
220 International Trading Opportunities
221 Friday Is International Day
222 Wholesale Trade Credits
223 International Cold Calling
224 Reasons to Do International Business
225 Where Did This Dirt Come From?
BONUS The Time is Now for the International Exchange & Business Marketplace

VOLUME 10
HALF THE WORLD IS VACANCY

226 Turn Vacancies into Wellness Units
227 Virgin's Vacancy Ploy
228 The Un-Built Building
229 Vacant Air Rights & Mineral Rights
230 Use of Consignments Fills Commercial Vacancy
231 Personal Notes in Vacancy Exchange
232 Subdivide the Vacancy
233 Give Away Vacant Building
234 Trade Credits to Eliminate Vacancy
235 Apartment House with Many Vacancies
236 Trade Credit for Special Hotel Vacancy
237 Create Your Own Credit Card to Fill Vacancy
238 Assisted Living Note Tied to Insurance Policy
239 Assisted Living Tied to Reverse Mortgage
240 Combining These Two Strategies
241 Trading Vacant Lots for Corporate Stock
242 Trade Credits to Help Fill Shopping Center Vacancy
243 Create Low Percentage Land Lease and Exchange for Higher Yielding Asset
244 Create Low Percentage Land Lease on Vacant Land (or under Building) and Exchange for Trade Credits
245 Resort Hotel/Motel Vacancy Problems & Seminars
246 Vacancy Equals Equity #1
247 Vacancy Equals Equity #2
248 Trade Vacancy for Equity in Business
249 Give Vacancy to Charity
250 Use Vacancy as Investment
250A Extra - Telemarketing to Fill Vacancies
250B Extra- Hotel Vacancy for Semi-Retired
250C Extra - Trees for Vacancies, Etc.
250D Extra - A Vacancy in Your Mind Can Be Good
250E Extra - Sandwich Vacancies for Profit

VOLUME 11
COMBINING REAL ESTATE & STOCK STRATEGIES

251 PUT #1 (option) Using Real Estate
252 PUT #2 (pption) Using Real Estate
253 Stock Traded for Real Estate but Not Income
254 Covered Call #1 (Option) in Stock Vernacular
255 Covered Call #2 (option)
256 The Double or Nothing Contract
257 Variable Purchase Price Based on Performance
258 Disappearing Trust Deed
259 Real Estate Owner Keeps the Eat
260 Stock for Installment Sale
261 Stock for Geographical Trade
262 Mitigating the Down Side
263 Growing a Corporation with Real Estate
264 REIT – Real Estate Investment Trust
265 Crop Futures Strategy
266 Stock Exchange with Option to Buy Back
267 Corporate Internal Exchange Department
268 Major Trader Obtains a Seat on Board
269 Public Company Trades Stock for Expenses
270 Derivatives of Real Estate
271 Trading Stock for Space
272 Upsiding Currency Land
273 Charitable Trust Alternative
274 Funding Corporations with Real Estate
275 Stock for Troubled Paper

VOLUME 12
BARTER, EXCHANGE & TRADE CREDITS

276 Barter: one on One Trade for Goods/Services
277 The Birth of the Trade Credit
278 Trade Credit #2 — Basic Trade Club
279 Three Options: Direct, Trade Credit or Club
280 Crop Futures Strategy
281 Trade Credits for Hotels
282 Trade Credits for Assisted Living
283 Printing Your Own Money #1
284 $250 Trade Credit® Sample
285 Printing Your Own Money #2
286 Printing Your Own Money #3
287 International Trade Clubs
288 Starting & Running a Trade Club
289 Breakage in Trade Credits
290 Outlaw Dates on Trade Credits
291 Holder in Due Course of Trade Credits
292 Trade Credits Can Represent Delayed Multiple Exchange
293 International Trade Credits #2
294 Trade Credits to Help Fill Shopping Center
295 Barter & Trade Credits on the Internet
296 Becomming a Trade Credit & Barter Broker
297 Trade Credit Trade
298 Multiple Barter Trades
299 Bartering Education
300 300 Trade Credits for 12 Volumes E-Book Set

Robert W. Steele

Robert (Bob) W. Steele, S.E.C., has won numerous local and national awards, including the national Society of Exchange Counselors' *Counselor of the Year* award. He was awarded Lifetime Membership, the Society's highest honor, in 2001, and in 2008 he was selected as one of six people as a legend of the Society. Bob was also inducted into the Real Estate Exchangor's Hall of Fame. His practice today involves primarily working with major clients, individual and corporate, with serious real estate problems.

Bob has lived in places many of us only dream of or read about in National Geographic Magazine: Oaxaca, Mexico; Costa del Sol, Spain; London and Marlow, England. Bob has personally taught over 100 seminars, on the subject of real estate exchanging and related fields, throughout the United States and other countries for his own seminar company, as well as for the Reno and the Chatham Educational Foundations. He has written books and educated in this field for over 40 years, and he firmly believes that "with a knowledgeable and counseled client any problem can be resolved."

Two magazines were started by Bob; The Real Estate News Observer (in concert with Richard Reno and Cliff Weaver) which is now Creative Real Estate; and Global Wealth, published from Spain. With partners Reno and Weaver, Bob originated and ran Real Estate Expo, the largest private enterprise real estate exchange convention in the United States. The Real Estate Expo convention, held annually in Las Vegas grew to approximately 3,000 attendees in size.

Mr. Steele has authored seven books including the classic, 100 Ways to Make Real Estate Deals without Using Cash. For every person or company with one million in cash to invest, Bob can show you 100 that have a million dollars in equity wanting a reinvestment.

He has recentlyl published a series of twelve books, a total of 300 strategies, for making real estate and business deals. This book is Volume 12 of that series.

300 Series Books

by Robert W. Steele

Volume 1 Strategies 1 - 25	25 *Basic Creative Real Estate Strategies* (Initially developed by Richard R. Reno) by Robert W. Steele, Forward by Michael E. Stewart
Volume 2 Strategies 26 - 50	*25 Formulas & Strategies: Creative Real Estate Level 2* by Robert W. Steele, Forward by Chester W. Allen
Volume 3 Strategies 51 - 75	*25 Formulas & Strategies: Creative Real Estate Level 3* by Robert W. Steele, Forward by Chester W. Allen
Volume 4 Strategies 76 - 100	*25 Formulas & Strategies: Creative Real Estate Level 4* by Robert W. Steele, Forward by Chester W. Allen
Volume 5 Strategies 101 - 125	*25 Ways to Buy, Sell or Trade a House* by Robert W. Steele, Forward by Don DeBeau
Volume 6 Strategies 126 - 150	*Multiple Exchange Philosophies, Formulas and Strategies* by Robert W. Steele, Forward by Madge Davis
Volume 7 Strategies 151 - 175	*The Art and Science of Brainstorming: Obtaining Ideas not Available Through Conventional Thinking* by Robert W. Steele, Forward by Chester W. Allen
Volume 8 Strategies 176 - 200	*Real Estate and Business Counseling* by Robert W. Steele, Forward by Steven L. Cropper
Volume 9 Strategies 201 - 225	*Blending Your Real Estate, Business & Life into the International World* by Robert W. Steele, Forward by Chester W. Allen
Volume 10 Strategies 226 - 250	*Half the World is Vacancy* by Chester W. Allen & Robert W. Steele, Forward by Robert E. Baines
Volume 11 Strategies 251 - 275	*Combining Real Estate and Stock Strategies* by Robert W. Steele, Forward by Clifford L. Strand, SEC, EMS
Volume 12 Strategies 276 - 300	*Barter & Exchange Credits* by Robert W. Steele, Forward by Ron Moser

Other Books by Robert W. Steele

Creative Real Estate

Creative Real Estate Forms

50 Ways To Acquire Real Estate

An Extra House As An Investment

15 Ways To Buy Real Estate Without Using Cash

The Real Estate Exchange Market And How It Operates
(in cooperation with Doug Warren)

Investing In Trust Deeds, Mortgages & Contracts Through the National Network Of Private Money Mortgage Companies
(in cooperation with Tom O'Bryon)

Leasehold Document Kit

Order Online!

GO

www.steele300.com
Tel: 760 522-5362
Email: Robert@steele300.com